BUILDERS OF THE BAY COLONY

JOHN WINTHROP, JR.

BUILDERS OF THE BAY COLONY

BY

SAMUEL ELIOT MORISON

With a Foreword by
Edmund S. Morgan

Illustrated

Quamquam ridentem dicere verum
Quid vetat?

HORACE, *Satires,* i, 24

A Classics Edition
NORTHEASTERN UNIVERSITY PRESS
Boston 1981

FIRST NORTHEASTERN EDITION, 1981
© Copyright, 1930, by Samuel Eliot Morison
© Copyright renewed, 1958, by Samuel Eliot Morison
Reprinted by arrangement with Houghton Mifflin Company

Library of Congress Cataloging in Publication Data

Morison, Samuel Eliot, 1887-1976.
    Builders of the Bay colony.

    Reprint. Originally published: Boston:
Houghton Mifflin, 1930.
    Bibliography: p.
    Includes index.
    1. Massachusetts—History—Colonial period,
ca. 1600-1775. 2. Massachusetts—Biography.
3. Puritans—Massachusetts—Biography. I. Title.
[F67.M86 1981]   974.4'02'0922   [B]   81-9649
ISBN 0-930350-23-5   AACR2
ISBN 0-930350-22-7 (pbk.)

PRINTED IN THE UNITED STATES
OF AMERICA

FOREWORD

THE *New England Puritans were an embarrassment to nineteenth and early twentieth century
Americans. The filiopietistic historians of the
nineteenth century did their best to convert the Puritans
into pioneers of freedom by casting them as refugees
from Old-World tyranny, but that made it all the more
difficult to explain their intolerance in the New World
toward anyone who disagreed with them. In the twentieth century it seemed easier simply to denounce them,
as Brooks Adams (Henry's brother) did in 1886 in* The
Emancipation of Massachusetts *(emancipation from the
Puritans!). By the 1920s they were the whipping boys
for everything that was wrong in American life. And
when James Truslow Adams published his popular*
Founding of New England *in 1921 he "debunked" them
in the fashion of the times by arguing that they were
really a small minority of the first settlers, who imposed
their benighted views on the rest. The sensible majority,
he contended, had come to the New World for sound
economic reasons and were not Puritans at all.*

*At the approach of 1930, the three hundredth an-
niversary of the founding of Massachusetts, it was
predictable that there would be some new effusions of
the old filial piety. Although the Puritans were still an
embarrassment, anniversary festivities have seldom
been troubled by attention to the actualities of what
they commemorate. But something more than filial
piety was brewing in Boston. In 1930 Samuel Eliot
Morison had been studying the history of Massachusetts
for some time. Nine years earlier he had produced his*

classic study of the days of sail, The Maritime History of Massachusetts, 1783-1860. *The New Englanders he celebrated in that volume were post-Puritan (and sailors were never much good at Puritanism anyhow). But in preparation for 1930 Morison had set his sights on the unpopular early New Englanders, who, he had satisfied himself, were indeed moved by the religious beliefs which Adams had discounted and others despised.*

Morison had an eye for commemorations. They were a propitious time for historians to reach people who might otherwise be unwilling to listen; and he was bent on reaching such people. He scorned historians who wrote only for each other. Builders of the Bay Colony, *with which he greeted the tercentenary of Massachusetts, exhibits all the qualities that make him the most effective American historical writer of this century. It is a work of high scholarship; it helped to change the whole direction of professional historical studies of early New England. But it is not addressed to scholars. Without sacrificing historical accuracy, without slighting the most meticulous research in original sources, Morison recognized that the historian's task is to explain the past to the present, to simplify without oversimplifying, and to bring to life men and women who can speak across the centuries to their human kin. In* Builders of the Bay Colony *he takes the early New Englanders out of the drab clothes, drab houses, downcast faces, and overcast skies where convention had placed them and brings them into the clear light of day, laughing, drinking, working, and worshipping their almighty God. They are puritans—he declined the initial capital—but they are also flesh and blood like the rest of us.*

Morison always wrote about people. He never forgot that whatever the trends or forces or isms he might observe in the past, including puritanism, they did not exist except in people. And he never forgot that he was writing for people too. Assuming a relaxed, conversational tone, he treated his readers with the same familiarity he used toward the men and women he found on the shores of Massachusetts Bay. And yet he did not condescend either to his readers or to his materials. He took his puritans seriously. He did not spare their weaknesses; but by the time he has done with them we know that their weaknesses were not altogether unlike our own. In the process we have learned as much about ourselves as about them. And that is what makes history worth reading.

Since 1930 a host of scholars have told us much more about the Puritans, more even than they themselves could have told us, about the statistics of their births and their marriages, their deaths and their taxes, about their conscious ideas and their unconscious desires. For anyone seeking to master what is known (not to say imagined) today about our seventeenth-century forbears, the Puritans present an embarrassment only of riches, in the multitude of studies that pursue the details of everything they said or did. But for anyone who wants to recapture a sense of what it was like to be alive in early New England, Builders of the Bay Colony *remains indispensable, as lively and arresting today as it was in 1930 and is likely to be in 2030.*

YALE UNIVERSITY   EDMUND S. MORGAN

PREFACE

MOST *of the people described in this book would have led obscure lives but for a dynamic force called puritanism which drove them to start life anew in a wilderness. The commonwealth which they helped to create was not a large one in their time. In a fair day's sail one could view all the seaport towns and villages of the Bay jurisdiction. Two days' march took one to the outermost house on her settled frontier, about forty miles from tidewater. The total population was something between fourteen and sixteen thousand persons in 1640, and about twice that thirty years later. Search the modern world, where will you find another community of like extent and age, containing so many outstanding, pungent individuals as those described herein?*

Other and more eminent 'builders' might have been substituted. Eminence and importance did not, however, dictate my choice—a choice originally made for ten lectures on the Founders of Massachusetts Bay before the Lowell Institute. I have written about those characters of the first generation who appealed to me most, and who represent the various aspects of life—adventurous and artistic, political and economic, literary and scientific, legal, educational, and evangelical—which appear in the first fifty years of this colony.

Even by enlarging the scope of biography beyond the conventional lines of piety and politics, it is not easy to describe these people truthfully, yet with meaning to moderns. For the men of learning and women of gentle nurture who led a few thousand plain folk to plant a new England on ungrateful soil were moved by purposes utterly foreign to the present America. Their object was not to establish prosperity or prohibition, liberty or democracy, or indeed anything of currently recognized value. Their ideals were comprehended vaguely in the term puritanism, which nowadays has acquired various secondary and degenerate meanings. These ideals, real and imaginary, of early Massachusetts, were attacked by historians of Massachusetts long before 'debunking' became an accepted biographical mode; for it is always easier to condemn an alien way of life than to understand it. My attitude toward seventeenth-century puritanism has passed through scorn and boredom to a warm interest and respect. The ways of the puritans are not my ways, and their faith is not my faith; nevertheless they appear to me a courageous, humane, brave, and significant people.

If these sketches of a few individuals can convey some hint of the sincerity and the beauty in the lives of those who came out of Old England to begin the New, my purpose will have been fulfilled.

S. E. MORISON

HARVARD UNIVERSITY
March, 1930

To this new edition I have added a sketch of William Pynchon, Frontier Magistrate and Fur Trader. Originally delivered at Amherst College in 1930, this was printed, with full annotations, in the *Proceedings of the Massachusetts Historical Society*, Vol. LXIV (1932), pp. 67-111.

S. E. MORISON

NORTHEAST HARBOR, MAINE
August, 1962

ACKNOWLEDGMENTS

I WISH to acknowledge valuable assistance, advice, and various courtesies and facilities, from the persons and institutions already mentioned in the list of illustrations and the bibliography; from Messrs. Wm. Sumner Appleton, Charles E. Banks, Frank W. Bayley, Clarence S. Brigham, Michael J. Canavan, W. H. B. Court, George Francis Dow, Frank W. Grinnell, Kenneth B. Murdock, Theodore F. T. Plucknett, George W. Robinson, Wilfrid Wheeler, George Parker Winship, Lawrence C. Wroth; from the Master of Emmanuel College; from several librarians and other officers of the Massachusetts Historical Society over a period of some thirty-five years; from Miss Ann N. Hansen; from my research assistants, Clifford K. Shipton, William G. Land, and Waldo Palmer; and from my secretaries, Florence Berlin and Diana Hadgis.

CONTENTS

ILLUSTRATIONS

BUILDERS OF THE BAY COLONY

CHAPTER I

PROMOTERS AND PRECURSORS
RICHARD HAKLUYT, CAPTAIN JOHN SMITH,
AND MORTON OF MERRYMOUNT

NEW ENGLAND was founded consciously, and in no fit of absence of mind. Patriots seeking the glory of England first called the attention of their countrymen to these shores. Commercial enterprise made the first attempts at settlement. Puritanism overlaid these feeble beginnings by a proud self-governing commonwealth, dedicated to the glory of God and the happiness of a peculiar people. These three main streams in the life of old England, the patriotic, the commercial, and the religious, mingled their waters on every slope. Sea dogs turned from fighting to looting, and from looting to prayer, with no thought of inconsistency. Merchants turned soldiers of necessity, and praised God daily. Puritan parsons organized the fishing industry, and blessed the sword that cut down the heathen in his pride.

England was the last of the great colonizing nations of modern times, except Germany, to enter the game. Spain created a colonial empire in America a century before England had a foothold there. Until near the close of Elizabeth's reign only a handful of Englishmen kept alive the spark of colonial ambition kindled by John Cabot. The first efforts of England overseas were not to colonize America, but to get around it or plunder it; to tap the wealth of Cathay, or loot the treasure fleets of Spain. If Drake dreamed of an American colony, it was only to defend the Northwest Passage that he never found; and the seventeenth century was old before Englishmen gave up hope that around the next bend of the Kennebec, the Delaware, or the Potomac they would find the Great South Sea, and a water route to the golden East.

More important in the founding of Virginia and of New England than the voyages of Drake, Frobisher, and Gilbert, outweighing the discouraging fate of Raleigh's first colony at the Roanoke, was a literary event. In 1589 appeared a black-letter folio called 'The Principall Navigations, Voiages, Traffiques and Discoveries of the English Nation, made by Sea or Overland to the Remote and Farthest Distant Quarters of the Earth, at any time within the Compasse of these 1500 yeares, by Richard Hakluyt, Master of Artes, and sometime Student of Christ-Church in Oxford.'

Richard Hakluyt was born about 1552, son of a merchant, grandson of a country gentleman. In the 'Epistle Dedicatorie' to the first edition he tells the reader how his interest in discovery was aroused:

I do remember that being a youth, and one of her Majesties scholars at Westminster that fruitfull nurserie, it was my happe to visit the chamber of Mr. Richard Hakluyt my cosin, a Gentleman of the Middle Temple... at a time when I found lying open upon his boord certeine bookes of Cosmographie, with an universall Mappe: he seeing me somewhat curious in the view therof, began to instruct my ignorance.... From the Mappe he brought me to the Bible, and turning to the 107 Psalme, directed mee to the 23 & 24 verses, where I read, that they which go downe to the sea in ships, and occupy by the great waters, they see the works of the Lord, and his woonders in the deepe, &c. Which words of the Prophet together with my cousins discourse (things of high and rare delight to my yong nature) tooke in me so deepe an impression, that I constantly resolved, if ever I were preferred to the University... I would by Gods assistance prosecute that knowledge and kinde of literature.

At Oxford, Hakluyt fulfilled his promise. Having become a senior student of Christ Church, and taken holy orders, he gave the first lectures in that University on the post-Columbian geography. At once he set himself to collect all that could be obtained in the way of original narratives of discovery in the new world. His 'Divers Voyages,' a modest compilation, earned him a minor diplomatic post in France, where he was fired to still greater efforts by hearing 'other nations miraculously extolled for ther discoveries and notable enterprises at sea, but the English of all others for their sluggish security, and continuall neglect of the like attempts … either ignominiously reported, or exceedingly condemned.' On his return he brought out the first edition of the Principall Navigations, Voiages, Traffiques and Discoveries. The book fell on favorable ground, at the right moment. A number of Englishmen, to be sure, were already interested in colonial enterprise; but the public had not yet been aroused. Hakluyt's Voyages caught the imagination of the English people. A small inward-looking nation, nursing the thwarted ambitions of the Hundred Years' War, backward in civilization and unenterprising in business, turned a corner toward unity, colonial empire, world power; and, if she and her mighty daughter can agree, world peace.

In addition to this collection of voyages, many of them taken down word for word from the lips of seamen, or written by gentlemen adventurers whom the world had forgotten, Hakluyt wrote a persuasive tract for colonization — the 'Discourse on Western Planting.' To the English people Hakluyt pointed out colonization — planting, as they called it in those days — as the path that destiny intended them to follow. American colonies would afford an outlet for population, employment for the merchant marine, sources of supply for naval stores and raw materials, a market for English wares; precious metals too, perhaps, and a short route to the Indies. Besides these material arguments, he preached the duty of carrying the gospel to the Indians, and of establishing a seat of Protestant Christianity in the New World, lest

France and Spain divide North America between them. In twenty years' time this propaganda bore fruit, in the forming of the Virginia Company, of which Hakluyt was a prominent member, named in the royal charter.

Let no New-Englander forget that the Old Dominion antedates Massachusetts Bay by thirteen years, and that representative government was established on the banks of the James the year before the Mayflower Compact was signed. But it was a long, uphill work inducing Englishmen to finance or prosecute colonization, where no immediate return was forthcoming; for the average Englishman three hundred years ago was a stay-at-home. As Master John White wrote, 'We are knowne too well to the worlde to love the smoake of our owne chimneyes so well, that hopes of great advantages are not likely to draw many of us from home.' There were times when only a handful of brave men at Jamestown, and a few confident investors in England, stood between Virginia and extinction.

This same set of considerations turned the attention of public-spirited Englishmen to the coast of Norumbega, or Northern Virginia. Captain John Smith, sometime President of the Council in Virginia, named this region New England, and for long was the principal promoter of her settlement. Many voyages there had been to that coast before his time: mostly of fishermen who left no record except a fierce resentment in the breast of some wronged savage. Richard Hakluyt was partly responsible for the first English book describing a part of the Massachusetts coast: Brierton's 'Briefe and True Relation of the Discoverie of the North Part of Virginia,' the story of Bartholomew Gosnold's voyage of 1602. Gosnold spent a few weeks on Cuttyhunk, outermost of the rope of island jewels that trails from the shoulder of Cape Cod. That name, and the Elizabeth Islands, were coined by him. He brought thence so valuable a cargo of sassafras (then accounted a potent drug and a sovereign remedy) that Hakluyt found it easy to induce the merchants of Bristol to finance another voyage to our coasts the next year: the merchants seeking sassafras, and the reverend promoter, information. Captain Martin Pring, of the *Discoverer* of Bristol, was the first Englishman on record who 'bare into that great Gulfe which Captaine Gosnold overshot': the Massachusetts Bay. He spent six weeks hunting and fishing and cutting sassafras at the site of Plymouth, amusing the Indians when they were good with the 'homely musicke' of a 'Zitterne,' and terrifying them when they were bad with his fierce mastiff dogs Foole and Gallant.

The same year George Weymouth set up his cross off the mouth of St. George's River; Samuel de Champlain made the first accurate survey of the New England coast, but preferred the St. Lawrence with its wealth of peltry; Henry Hudson coasted along looking for the passage to the Great South Sea; and in 1607 the Northern Virginia Company attempted to colonize the Kennebec: a frigid and short-lived counterpart to Jamestown. Beside these explorers whose stories have come down to us, countless fishermen of several nations visited the waters of Massachusetts Bay and the Gulf of Maine, either to avoid the crowded Grand Banks of Newfoundland, or to truck with the natives for fur after a summer's toil. Yet, despite all these voyages, traffiques and discoveries, the colonization of our shores seemed no nearer accomplishment than in the time of the Cabots, until Captain John Smith turned his attention to the region that he named New England.

This John Smith was the son of a prosperous farmer in Lincolnshire, the English county to which so many New-Englanders trace their ancestry. Willoughby, his birthplace, is near the sea, and about sixty-five miles as the crow flies from the home of Bradford and Brewster, the Pilgrim fathers. Born in 1579, John Smith was nine years older than Governor Winthrop. He was educated in the free grammar schools which were common in that part of England, and at seventeen or eighteen became a soldier of fortune on the Continent. At this point his surprising adventures begin.

Historians have never been able to agree about the veracity of Captain John Smith. Some would have us believe every word he wrote, others denounce him as a mere lying braggart. The Pocahontas episode, by which he is known to every one in the English-speaking world, may well be true; but very little of his 'True Travells' could possibly have happened. The 'siege of Regall,' in which Smith distinguished himself by slaying successively three Turkish champions 'to delight the ladies,' is otherwise unknown to fame. The three Turks' heads, his patent of arms from Prince Sigismund, is a palpable forgery. Nor does authentic history know aught of the bloody field of Rottenton, whence our Captain was led away into Turkish captivity. Of his general the 'Earle of Meldritch, Salmaria and Peldoia,' a tithe of whose exploits as related by Smith would have made him the Roumanian national hero, no vestige can be discovered. Yet one puts down the 'True Travells' with the feeling that our Captain had seen plenty of fighting in Transylvania, although he imagined a good deal more than he actually performed; and that after matching stories on long sea voyages and telling tales around Virginia camp-fires, he became unable to distinguish the true from the false. The line between fact and fiction was less sharply drawn in Elizabethan days than in our own, and stretching the long bow was an old English custom which only lately became of ill repute.

John Smith was a liar, if you will; but a thoroughly cheerful and generally harmless liar, and a valiant Christian gentleman withal. A practical adventurer, with a touch of austerity:

> I never knew a Warryer yet, but thee,
> From wine, Tobacco, debts, dice, oaths, so free,

writes one of his old soldiers, in a poetical effusion. A business man with a touch of Don Quixote, common sense and exalted imagination, Christian humility and exaggerated ego. His style, which seemed 'barbarous and uncouth' to the fastidious Thomas Jefferson, is peculiarly irritating to those who like a good plain tale without trimmings; and whatever subject he touches leads back very shortly to Captain John Smith, his trials, hairbreadth escapes, bad breaks, and unappreciated virtues. His inclusion among the builders of Massachusetts Bay will probably cause some raising of eyebrows both there and in Virginia. Yet Smith was in Virginia only two years and a half, and left it forever in 1609, at the age of twenty-nine. The remaining twenty-one years of his life were largely devoted to promoting the colonization of New England.

In 1614 Smith's work on behalf of New England began with a voyage thither. Sir Ferdinando Gorges, one of the prominent members of the Northern Virginia Company, then appointed Smith 'to have the managing their authoritye in those parts.' On a second voyage in the Company's behalf, in 1615, he was captured by a French pirate. In order to keep his mind employed while tossing at sea, he wrote a tract with the significant title 'A Description of New England.' Captain Smith himself coined the name, suggested by Drake's Nova Albion on the Pacific Coast. This 'Description' first made the resources of the region favorably known to the English public; for as the writer declared, despite divers mariners who 'long before... have ranged those parts, within a kenning sometimes of the shore... the Coast is yet still but even as a Coast unknowne and undiscovered.'

On his first voyage Smith had made the island of Monhegan a base, leaving most of his men there to cure fish. In the meantime he sailed to the westward in a small boat with a crew of eight, trading trifles for valuable furs, gathering data for his Description of New England and the map that was printed with it.

Previous voyagers had been more attracted by the rugged

coast of Maine, with its spruce-clad islands, deep sheltered bays and noble rivers, than by the region to the westward. Captain Smith, however, found Maine 'a Countrie rather to affright, than delight one,' though 'the Sea there is the strangest fishpond I ever saw; and those barren Iles so furnished with good woods, springs, fruits, fish, and foule, that it makes mee thinke... the interior parts may well (notwithstanding) be very fertile' — a shrewd guess. At Angoam (Agawam, the future Ipswich), he reported 'many rising hilles; and on their tops and descents, many corne fields and delightful groves'; a prospect unchanged to-day, save for the country seats that cluster about the Myopia Hunt Club. Then came the fair headland which he named Cape Tragabigzanda after his imaginary Turkish lady love, but which Prince Charles, to our subsequent relief, renamed Cape Ann, after his mother. 'And then the Countrie of the Massachusets, which is the Paradise of all those parts. For, heere are many Iles all planted with corne; groves, mulberries, salvage gardens, and good harbours; the Coast is for the most part, high clayie sandie cliffs. The Sea Coast as you passe, shewes you all along large corne fields, and great troupes of well proportioned people.'

This was the first appearance in print, or in recorded literature, of the name of our Commonwealth. Although the name Massachusetts has passed through a variety of forms and spellings, John Smith's version, with an additional *t*, became the official one. The word means 'at the Great Hill' — the Great Blue Hill of Milton. Until after the colony was founded it was applied only to the region of Boston Bay, between Nahant and Scituate, and a few miles inland.

Then follows a brief relation of a brush with the Indians at Cohasset harbor, a description of Cape Cod: 'high hils of sand overgrowne with shrubbie pines, hurts [1] and such trash,

[1] Huckleberries.

but an excellent harbor for all weather'; of the shoals to the southward, and of Martha's Vineyard; of the extraordinary plenty of fish, fruit and fowl, and of the healthy, invigorating climate. And then an eloquent plea for the colonization of this pleasant, fruitful region, for the glory of God and the enlargement of the English nation. Why live at home idly and softly, letting England degenerate like Byzance, when you may live well and nobly in New England, helping to build a new commonwealth? If you seek pleasure, 'what pleasure can be more than (being tired with any occasion ashore)... to recreate themselves before their owne doores, in their owne boates upon the Sea, where man, woman and childe, with a small hooke and line, by angling, may take divers sorts of excellent fish, at their pleasures? And is it not pretty sport, to pull up two pence, six pence, and twelve pence, as fast as you can haule and veare a line?'

With the Description was published Captain Smith's engraved map of New England, embellished by ships and sea-monsters, birds and beasts, and a portrait of himself. It was not the best map of New England that had been made, but by far the most accurate that had yet been published, and made available. The nomenclature was unfortunately muddled because the Prince of Wales, at the Captain's request, altered the 'barbarous' Indian place names for English ones: consequently we find Ipswich where Saco belongs, Boston at Agamenticus (York), and the like; but three of the Prince's names: Cape Ann, the River Charles, and Plymouth, persist to-day. Further, as the Captain says, this 'Virgin's sister' was officially called New England at his 'humble suit, by our most gracious Prince Charles.'

The Description of New England appeared in 1616. In the same year Richard Hakluyt died, a wealthy man from the sale of his books and from the many ecclesiastical benefices that were bestowed on him by Queen Elizabeth and King James. Captain Smith's writings never afforded him more than a bare living, and the empty title of Admiral of New England. The Description did not immediately turn men's attention to New England; although it had great publicity value in the end. Virginia was beginning to prosper with the planting of tobacco, and thither went such Englishmen as could part with the 'smoake of their owne chimneyes,' and such moneys as business men cared to adventure overseas. Captain Smith was provided with three fishing vessels in 1617, but was held windbound at Plymouth for three months, and so sent them on the shorter voyage to Newfoundland. Two went in 1618, and again two the next year, and made good profit; but this was not colonization.

'I am not so simple to think,' wrote Captain Smith in his Description of New England, 'that ever any other motive than wealth, will ever erect there a Commonweale; or draw companie from their ease and humours at home, to stay in New England.' In this, he was mistaken. Religion was the motive that did erect not one, but five commonwealths in New England. The permanent settlement of New England began with the voyage of the *Mayflower* in 1620.

By rights I should devote a chapter on the Pilgrim Fathers, who form an indispensable link in the chain of circumstance that led to the founding of Massachusetts Bay. But the Pilgrims had their tercentenary ten years ago; and their story has become so familiar as to need no repetition here. 'It is the story of a small and feeble enterprise, glorified by faith and hope and charity, but necessarily and always limited by the slender resources of the poor and humble men who originated it. The founding of the Bay Colony, on the other hand, was less a colonial enterprise than a great puritan emigration. It was organized by men of substance and standing, supported by wealth of a great and prosperous body of the English nation, and consciously directed toward the high end of founding in America a great puritan state.'[1] It was in Massachusetts Bay, not Plymouth, that were worked out those characteristic forms of state, church, and school, which have set off New England as a province apart.

Captain John Smith offered his personal services to the Pilgrims, which they declined, 'to save charges,' he says, 'saying my books and maps were much better cheape to teach them, than myselfe.' Therein the Pilgrims showed their good sense. Captain Smith might have saved them some of their costly errors in pioneering; but New Plymouth was too small to hold such as he, especially in a subordinate position. Miles Standish played well the rôle which might have been Captain Smith's.

It was fortunate for the Pilgrims that a pestilence among the Indians of Massachusetts Bay — a special dispensation of Providence in the opinion of Captain John Smith and Thomas Morton — had decimated the tribes along our coast in 1617–18. From Maine to Cape Cod, and westward to the country of the Narragansett and the Nipmuc, there was only a pitiful handful of natives to dispute the white man. Their 'corne fields and salvage gardens' were ready for him to plant, without the usual pioneer efforts. The few Indians who had any spirit left had it knocked out of them by Miles Standish and his army of eight. This advantage became all the more palpable when in 1622 an uprising of the Indians in Virginia set that colony back a decade.

The Pilgrims' modest success helped the 'sales talk' of Captain Smith, who incorporated their earliest narratives in the second edition of his 'New England Trials' (1622) and his 'Generall Historie of Virginia, New England, and the Summer Isles' (1624). He was now Admiral of New England,

[1] J. Franklin Jameson, *Historical Writing in America*, p. 21. In view of the number of *Mayflower* descendants to-day, this may seem an understatement; but the Pilgrims only attained their present multitude of proud progeny by intermarrying with the hordes of puritans who came to Massachusetts Bay in the great emigration.

by order of the Council for New England, a reorganization of the old Northern Virginia Company. Under grants from this Council for New England — a colonizing company that never had the money to colonize — there began scattered, haphazard settlement of the coast. Within ten years, Massachusetts Bay was dotted with petty fishing and trading stations. There was William Blaxton, who set up bachelor quarters on the eminence later known as Beacon Hill; Thomas Walford, the pioneer of Charlestown; Samuel Maverick, at Winnesimmet (now Chelsea); David Thompson, a Scots gentleman who settled the island in Boston harbor that still bears his name; and William Morrell, a clergyman who wrote, in Latin and English, a descriptive poem on New England, the opening lines of which are quoted before this chapter.

One of these small trading groups deserves more than passing notice, since it provided the first strange interlude played in the neighborhood of Quincy. Thomas Morton, a gay gentleman with an eye for trade, author of the most entertaining book on early Massachusetts, gathered a knot of boon companions on Mount Wollaston, which he renamed, in conscious punning, Ma-re Mount; and well he lived up to its usual pronunciation. Morton was quick to improve the sporting possibilities of the neighborhood, which Captain Smith had observed. When not engaged in dickering with Indians whom he had previously well primed with lusty liquor, or playing 'mine host of Ma-re Mount' with 'claret sparklinge neate,' he roamed the forest with dog and gun, or sailed about the bay, fishing and shooting water-fowl. White men and Indians alike found good cheer at Merrymount. Young squaws were particularly welcome, and young Pilgrims probably found an occasional surreptitious visit to Merrymount as stimulating, and ultimately as exhausting, as their descendants do a trip to New York. In the spring of 1627, Morton and his friends 'set up a May-pole,' says

Governor Bradford of the Pilgrim colony, 'drinking and dancing aboute it many days togeather, inviting the Indean women for their consorts, dancing and frisking togither, (like so many fairies, or furies rather), and worse practises.' Which no doubt was true, as May Day in the Merry England of King Charles was by no means the chaste school festival of to-day; indeed Morton admits it was not. 'A goodly pine tree of 80 foote longe,' he writes, 'was reared up, with a peare of buckshorns nayled on somewhat neare unto the top of it: where it stood, as a faire sea marke for directions how to find out the way to mine Hoste of Ma-re Mount.' A mock-classical poem, whose mythological and somewhat phallic allusions puzzled the Pilgrims 'most pitifully to expound,' was nailed to the pole; and 'there was likewise a merry song made, which (to make their Revells more fashionable) was sung with a Corus, every man bearing his part; which they performed in a daunce, hand in hand about the Maypole, whiles one of the Company sung and filled out the good Liquor, like Gammedes and Jupiter.'

THE SONGE

Drinke and be merry, merry, merry, boyes;
Let all your delight be in the Hymen's joyes;
Io! to Hymen, now the day is come,
About the merry Maypole take a Roome.
Make greene garlons, bring bottles out
And fill sweet Nectar freely about,
Uncover thy head and feare no harme,
For here's good liquor to keepe it warme;
 Then drinke and be merry, &c.

Nectar is a thing assign'd
By the Deities owne minde
To cure the hart opprest with greife,
And of good liquors is the cheife.
 Then drinke and be merry, &c.

Give to the Mellancolly man
A cup or two of 't now and than;

This physick will soone revive his bloud,
And make him be of a merrier moode.
Then drinke and be merry, &c.

Give to the Nymphe that's free from scorne
No Irish stuff nor Scotch over worne.[1]
Lasses in beaver coats come away,
Yee shall be welcome to us night and day.
To drinke and be merry, &c.

Morton might have been let alone if he had not endangered
the safety and threatened the trade of his neighbors by purchasing peltry with firearms, and teaching the Indians how
to use them. We have so often been told how Morton's down-
fall was due to the Pilgrims' hatred of mirth and jollity, that
it is worth noting the facts. All the coast settlements between
Maine and Nantasket, none of them puritan, joined in re-
questing Plymouth to suppress Morton. The Pilgrim Fathers
first tried friendly admonishment. Morton declared he 'would
trade peeces with the Indeans in despite of all.' Plymouth
remonstrated a second time: 'the countrie could not beare
the injure he did; it was against their commone safetie.'
Morton 'answered in high terms as before.' Finally, in June,
1628, Plymouth was given the mandate to arrest him. Fiery
little Miles Standish, whom Morton calls 'Captaine Shrimpe,
a quondam drummer,' marched to Boston Bay, and ordered
mine host of Merrymount to surrender in the King's name.
At this point we will let Governor Bradford tell the story:

But they found him to stand stifly in his defence, having made
fast his dors, armed his consorts, set diverse dishes of powder and
bullets ready on the table; and if they had not been over armed with
drinke, more hurt might have been done. They sommaned him to
yeeld, but he kept his house, and they could gett nothing but scofes
and scornes from him; but at length, fearing they would doe some

[1] It is probably necessary to explain to the younger generation that the 'Irish
stuff' and 'Scotch' were clothing, not whiskey. The English of that time were beer
and wine drinkers, and although they appreciated an occasional shot of 'hot
waters' such as aqua vitæ or brandy, whiskey and rum were almost unknown to
them.

violence to the house, he and some of his crue came out, but not to
yeeld, but to shoote; but they were so steeld with drinke as their
peeces were too heavie for them; him selfe with a carbine (over
charged and allmost halfe fild with powder and shote, as was after
found) had thought to have shot Captaine Standish; but he stept
to him, and put by his peece, and tooke him. Neither was ther any
hurte done to any of either side, save that one was so drunke that he
rane his own nose upon the pointe of a sword that one held before
him as he entred the house; but he lost but a little of his hott blood.
Morton they brought away to Plimoth.

From Plymouth he was shipped to England; but this was
by no means the last of Thomas Morton. Before long he was
back at Merrymount with more liquor, and in the same
jovial, defiant temper. By this time the Massachusetts Bay
Colony had been founded. Governor Endecott, disliking the
Maypole as a rallying point for disorderly youth and runaway
servants, cut it down. Nevertheless he offered to take Morton
into the official fur-trading monopoly. Mine host of Merrymount preferred to play a lone hand; for he was making six or
seven hundred per cent profit. Again he was arrested, put
into the bilboes, and deported, his house on Mount Wollaston
burned before his eyes. In England, Morton very naturally
played in with the enemies of the Massachusetts Colony,
posed before Bishop Laud's committee of the Privy Council
as an Anglican martyr to puritan spite, and 'was comforted
by their lordships with the cropping of Mr. Winthrop's ears,'
an item which interested that gentleman when he read it in
an intercepted letter of Morton. Also at this time Morton
wrote his book, 'New English Canaan, or New Canaan.
Containing an Abstract of New England... by Thomas
Morton of Cliffords Inne gent.' He had high hopes of returning to New England in the company of Church and King men,
to destroy the Bible Commonwealth, and assume the government of Massachusetts in the King's name. When he finally
did drift back, ten years later, all hope of neat vengeance had
been swallowed up in civil war. Morton spent a winter at

Plymouth, where a Pilgrim father recorded his amazement that the sometime host of Merrymount was 'content to drink water.' Later, he ventured into the Bay jurisdiction, where the authorities were neither forgetful nor forgiving. For no good reason he was imprisoned, 'laid in Irons to the decaying of his Limbs' as he complained in a humble petition to the General Court. After being mulcted of his property under color of a heavy fine, Morton was released, made his way to York in Maine, and there died, a broken-spirited, half-crazed old man.

One would wish that the authorities had not struck an enemy when he was down; but that was the way things were done in the seventeenth century, by puritans and Anglicans at home or abroad. We are heavily in debt to Morton for the jolliest contemporary account of early New England. If he did not love our people, he at least loved our land. As the verses *in laudem authoris* of the 'New English Canaan' declare:

> To modell out a Land of so much worth
> As untill now noe traveller setteth forth;
> Faire Canaans second selfe, second to none,
> Nature's rich Magazine till now unknowne.
> Then here survey what nature hath in store,
> And graunt him love for this. He craves no more.
>   .   .   .   .

One might easily fill several chapters, as others have filled the pages of pleasant books, with the story of these fishing and trading stations along the New England coast. But with one exception — the Dorchester Colony at Cape Ann — these were isolated efforts, lacking any element of permanency, or germ of community life. Judged by what had been accomplished by these non-puritan settlers before 1630, and by what Gorges did in Maine, Massachusetts Bay was by way of becoming just such a colony as New Sweden on the Delaware: a chain of feeble trading stations, lacking the basis for economic success, the prey to the first strong and determined neighbor. Captain Smith writes the proper epitaph of these small efforts in the passage where he adverts to those 'who undertaking in small handfuls to make many plantations, and to bee severall Lords and Kings of themselves, most vanished to nothing to the great disparagement of the generall businesse.'

Yet if these trading stations began nothing for which Massachusetts and New England have been famous, they were the progenitors of a distinct way of life that has persisted along the New England coast to our own day: a scattered settlement along the shore, a predilection for fishing and other maritime pursuits, repugnance from agriculture or steady work on land, and indifference to school, church, politics, and other characteristic New England institutions. This coastal way of living has prevailed along the eastern part of Maine; Marblehead was an outpost of it on the Bay; Cape Cod was not untouched by the influence. Those of us who spend our summers in the less frequented portions of the New England coast have probably met more spiritual descendants of Thomas Morton than of John Winthrop.

Here we may take our leave of Captain John Smith. His last years were passed in London, where (says Fuller in his 'Worthies of England') 'having a prince's mind imprisoned in a poor man's purse, rendered him to the contempt of such who were not ingenuous.' His faith never wavered that God in his good time would bring the English to New England; his literary efforts to that end never slackened. Indeed his last work was a little pamphlet, 'Advertisements for the unexperienced Planters of New-England, or anywhere' (1631), dedicated to the Archbishops of Canterbury and York, but adverting in most friendly terms to 'those noble Gentlemen' the leaders of the Bay Colony, who had at length undertaken the work which he had projected seventeen years before when coasting the shores of Massachusetts Bay. In the preface to this tract is a touching poem by the author, 'The Sea Marke' in which he compares himself to a vessel foundered on a reef, a warning to those that come after:

> Aloofe, aloofe; and come no neare,
> the dangers doe appeare;
> Which if my ruine had not beene
> you had not seene:
> I onely lie upon this shelfe
> to be a marke to all
> which on the same might fall,
> That none may perish but my selfe.
>
> If in or outward you be bound,
> doe not forget to sound;
> Neglect of that was cause of this
> to steare amisse.
> The Seas were calme, the wind was faire.
> that made me so secure,
> that now I must indure
> All weathers be they foule or faire.
>
> The Winters cold, the Summers heat
> alternatively beat
> Upon my bruised sides, that rue
> because too true
> That no releefe can ever come.
> But why should I despaire
> being promised so faire
> That there shall be a day of Dome.

Our valiant Captain died in London on June 21, 1631, at the house of his friend Sir Samuel Saltonstall, a former free-man of the Virginia Company and cousin to Sir Richard Saltonstall of the Massachusetts Bay Company. With him, too, died the first conscious purpose that led to the founding of Massachusetts-Bay: that of enlarging the King's Domin-ions. Others than he carried out his work to a successful conclusion, and for other motives: but few of her founders gave to New England so much, and got so little, as Captain John Smith.

CHAPTER II

MASTER JOHN WHITE, OF DORCHESTER

THE colony of Massachusetts Bay was a corporate enterprise, in which the efforts and sacrifices of some hundreds of men and women, most of them unknown to us even by name, played an essential part. It was not founded by one man, as Maryland was by Lord Baltimore, or Pennsylvania by William Penn, or Rhode Island by Roger Williams. Yet, as from any group, certain individuals stand out as leaders, and of these the first, in point of time, was Master [1] John White of Dorchester. John Winthrop and Thomas Dudley both paid tribute to the priority and the high importance of his labors in behalf of Massachusetts Bay; and William Hubbard, the first historian of the colony, who graduated from Harvard when the fathers were still ruling, called John White 'under God one of the chief founders of the Massachusetts Colony in New England.'

Why, then, I fancy your asking, have we never heard of John White? Why is his name never coupled in our histories with those of Winthrop and Dudley, Johnson and Saltonstall? For the simple reason that John White never emigrated. His essential labors for the colony were over in 1631. No descendants of his came to this country, no town can claim him as a father, and there has been no family or corporate interest to perpetuate his name among us. A modest and self-effacing man, he labored much but published little over his own name. His papers were scattered to the four winds during the Civil War. Yet, if his services are considered

[1] The title Reverend was seldom if ever used for clergymen in England or New England before the close of the seventeenth century. Instead they were called Master (abbreviated Mr.) because almost invariably they had taken the degree of Master of Arts.

in the light of what we know to-day, they fully confirm the truth of what Hubbard wrote two centuries and a half ago: that John White was one of the chief founders of the Massachusetts Colony.

A few miles east of Oxford, nestling in the gentle hills that give a hint of the near-by Chilterns, is the village of Stanton St. John. The neighborhood teems with historical association. A Roman road runs hard by, crossing Shotover Hill at right angles to the old post road from London to Oxford and Gloucester. Between the two, and a short walk from Stanton St. John is the village of Forest Hill, its name reminiscent of the ancient royal forest that stretched from Shotover north into the Midlands. Forest Hill was the scene of John Milton's first courtship and marriage; Milton's father for a time lived at Stanton. A landmark to the northeast is the gray old town of Brill, clamped to its hill-top since Saxon times. The thirteenth century parish church of Stanton St. John, in whose registry you may read the baptismal record of John White, stands on the steep main street of the village; and across the street is the stone house of the manor farm where he was born in 1575.

This manor then belonged (and still belongs) to New College, Oxford. The Warden of New College from 1553 to 1573 was Thomas White, who had the reputation of being something of a nepotist. No doubt it was through his influence that John White's father became lessee of the Manor Farm at Stanton St. John. The boy was well educated. From Winchester, he proceeded with a fellowship to New College, where he resided eleven years, during the latter part of Elizabeth's reign and the first years of her successor: a stimulating period, when there was freedom of discussion on the great problems of theology and church polity that had been shaking men's minds since the reformation broke out in England. John White took holy orders, and according to the normal practice, retained his fellowship until he could get a living. In 1606 he was installed rector of the Church of the Holy Trinity at Dorchester.

Dorchester, in Wessex, is familiar to all readers of Thomas Hardy as Casterbridge, and was the poet-novelist's residence during the last forty-three years of his life. Elizabeth Jane's remark, in Hardy's 'Mayor of Casterbridge,' that Dorchester was 'huddled all together and shut in,' was even more true in John White's day, when the old Roman walls still enclosed the town. The young parson could have found little time to carry on his studies, for the town presented a social problem that interested his humane and charitable mind much more than the speculations of theologians. It was the shire town and metropolis of Dorset, but the houses for the most part were mere hovels of wood and plaster with thatched roofs, and the greater part of the people were miserably poor. England was going through a painful period of economic adjustment. The enclosing of arable land for the raising of sheep drove thousands of peasants from the soil. Even in the Mayor of Casterbridge's time, Dorchester had its Mixen Lane, 'the Adullam of all the surrounding villages, the hiding place of those who were in distress and in debt and trouble of every kind.' In White's day conditions were much worse. The unemployed crowded into the town, where the closed corporations of handicraftsmen would have none of them; the market for common labor became glutted, and in consequence the roads and lanes of England were full of sturdy beggars. Men such as Hakluyt and John Smith turned this condition into an argument for colonization as the only remedy for apparent overpopulation. John White eventually came to the same conclusion, although he succeeded in bettering the local situation.

John White was just such a shepherd of his flock, and a leader of his people, foremost in every civic and charitable enterprise, as the early ministers of New England. Casterbridge needed no mayor when John White was rector of

Trinity Church. 'He absolutely commanded his own passions, and the purses of his parishioners,' says Thomas Fuller, in 'The Worthies of England.' He induced the town authorities to erect a free primary school, such as his emigrating parishioners set up at Dorchester, Massachusetts. When a fire wiped out most of the town in 1613, John White was foremost in getting subscriptions to rebuild promptly, thus affording labor to the people while the means of their livelihood were being restored. All able poor were set on work, writes Fuller, and the impotent maintained by the profit of a public brewhouse; thus 'knowledge causing piety, piety breeding industry, and industry procuring plenty unto it. A beggar was not then to be seen in the town.' But there were still beggars abroad, and John White thought of them.

Dorchester lies in a valley between the North and the South Downs, on an old Roman cross-roads which leads three ways to the sea. Eastward the road takes you through Wareham ('Anglebury' in the Wessex novels) to Swanage 'lying snug within two headlands as between a finger and thumb,' and to Poole, famous for pirates and smugglers; beyond lies Southampton. Westward the road leads to Bridport, where the cordage was made for the West Country ships, and to Lyme Regis; beyond lie the fishing ports of South Devon. Southward from Dorchester it is only eight miles over a gap in the South Downs to Weymouth, the Budmouth of Thomas Hardy: Weymouth, which furnished Queen Bess with six ships to meet the Spanish Armada, and which sent a fleet of fishermen to American waters every spring. Of Dorchester as a corn market in the eighteenth century, Thomas Hardy has told us much. Of Dorchester as a clearing point for the dried fish (cod, ling, and poor-john) which the neighboring fishermen brought from Newfoundland every autumn, Hardy never wrote. I like to imagine that the rich, pungent odor from a wagon-load of salt fish, assaulting the nostrils of the rector of Holy Trinity while he was pondering unemployment, started the train of thought that led to the founding of the Massachusetts Bay Company.

The train of thought thus started may well have been carried farther by a pamphlet of Captain John Smith. In the 'Description of New England' and in both editions of 'New England's Trials,' Captain Smith eloquently pled the national advantage of fishing, and scornfully compared English fishing enterprise with that of the Hollanders, French, and Portuguese. More than once he pointed out that the way to improve codfishing was to plant a base colony in New England, and that the way to colonize New England was through the cod. 'Nothing is here to be had which fishing doth hinder, but further us to obtain,' was his favorite epigram, and a successful prophecy: for the 'sacred cod' was the key to the prosperity of maritime Massachusetts for almost two centuries.

The trouble with the fishing industry as then conducted from the West of England, was the large 'overhead.'[1] The season lasted from eight to ten months, but a large part of this was taken up in the voyage out and home, including a call at France or Spain for a market. During this voyage out and home the fishermen of course were idle. All the salt and other supplies had to be brought out from England. During the fishing season the ship lay 'dead on the harbour' while the fishermen hand-lined from small boats. Other men had to be brought over to 'make' or cure the fish. A fishing stage — the same sort of spindly fish wharf that we see on the Eastern coast of Maine to-day — had to be built in order to handle

[1] The West Country fishing was organized by a system that had come down from the Middle Ages, and which lasted to our own days in New England. One group of capitalists, the 'adventurers,' provided the vessel; a second, the 'undertakers' or 'victualers' furnished the supplies; the master and men contributed their time and labor. Profits were divided equally between these three groups, the men's third into shares or 'lays,' with three or four shares to the master. Consequently, if the voyage was a failure, the men had no money coming to them at its end; if successful, they shared the profits. Captain Smith wrote that one West Country ship earned £17 a share on her fish alone in 1621, exclusive of profits on furs.

the catch, and flakes (wooden frames or hurdles for drying), kenches (salting boxes) and other gear, had to be provided. All this meant considerable outlay, which had to be renewed annually, as long as there was neither law nor government in New England. If you left the small boats behind and built elaborate stages and flakes, another fisherman would probably get there first next spring and appropriate the works.

It was partly in order to cure this condition of affairs that a group of West Country merchants in 1623, with John White as an active partner, planned a permanent colony in New England. If they could count on an all-the-year-round base, with a permanent population, the vessels would need carry but men enough to work the ship. The colonists would do a large part of the fishing, 'serve a stage, carry a barrow, and turne Poor John' on the flakes, as Smith wrote; make salt from sea water, keep the gear in repair, and raise 'fresh victuall,' so that there would be nothing left for the big ship but her proper business of freighting. The saving in overhead would soon repay the cost of planting, and English unemployed would get a new start in life. A further advantage, from the clerical point of view, was the hope that the colony might attract a clergyman to administer to the spiritual welfare of the fishermen, who otherwise were left without it nine months of the year. A clergyman might also evangelize the Indians, and plant outposts of Protestantism against the Jesuits in Canada. Combining as it did piety, patriotism, and profit, 'this proposition of theirs tooke so well,' wrote the reverend promoter, 'that it drew on divers persons to join with them.'

About one hundred and twenty persons of substance, including merchants, clergymen, members of Parliament, and country gentry, formed the Dorchester Company of Adventurers. One member was that strong minded and vigorous Mistress Elizabeth Poole of Taunton, Somerset, who later founded Taunton, Massachusetts. The treasurer was

John Humfry, who became a Magistrate of the Bay. 'Compassion toward the Fishermen and partly some expectation of gaine, prevailed so farre that for the planting of a Colony in New England there was raised a Stocke of more than three thousand pounds,' wrote White. The whole West Country was talking about the enterprise. The Bishop of Bath and Wells, a fellow student with John White at Winchester and New College, even declared that he would have gone himself as the colony's chaplain, but for his advanced years.

It was this joint-stock company, the Dorchester Adventurers, which begat the Governor and Company of the Massachusetts Bay in New England. Historians have been apt to hold it a small local affair, since the immediate results were meagre. On the contrary, it was a company of much wealth, prestige and dignity, whose General Court, meeting at Dorchester, was called 'The New England Planters' Parliament.'

What, if anything, did puritanism have to do with the Dorchester enterprise? Those members of whom we have any information, were identified with the puritan party in church and state. For the most part they were 'conformable puritans' of a type more common in the west than in the east of England; not greatly discontented with the ecclesiastical settlement made by Archbishop Bancroft, willing to use the Book of Common Prayer so long as good preaching were provided, and obnoxious 'popish' ceremonies unenforced. Many would be driven out of this position by the reforms of Laud, which were so little anticipated in 1623 that no clerical member of the Dorchester Company would leave his English parish in order to minister to the New England fishermen. John White was a conforming puritan of this sort: a clergyman who took life seriously but not sadly, a stickler for good morals and good conversation 'who would willingly contribute his shot of facetiousness on any just occasion.' A great preacher and expounder of the Bible, but a faithful minister according to the canons of the Church; a respecter of just authority, but an upholder of English liberty who regarded the imprisonment of the five members in the Tower as an infamous act of tyranny, and so influenced public opinion in Dorchester that when the Civil War broke out it was solidly for Parliament. So we may call the Dorchester Adventurers a company of puritans, but not a puritanic company, in the same sense that we apply that term to the Massachusetts Bay corporation; for there is no evidence that its promoters intended to establish a puritan refuge in New England. We may infer that they did not, since there was no need of such a refuge, in 1623. And their avowed motive of evangelizing the natives was equally prominent in the inception of the Virginia Company, and the writings of John Smith and William Morrell. The Dorchester Adventurers appear to have been a group of public-spirited men who wished to do something for their country, a little for the Indians, somewhat for the fishermen, and a good deal for themselves.

During the summer of 1623 the Dorchester Company sent out a company of fishermen and planters, in the *Fellowship* of Weymouth. They landed on Cape Ann, and erected a fishing stage and house at a rocky point a little south of Gloucester Harbor, still called Stage Fort Point. Presumably a patent to this territory had been obtained from the Council for New England. About fourteen men were left there that winter, and the Adventurers sent the *Fellowship* out with another vessel and more men in 1624 and 1625.

In spite of the fine prospects in theory and on paper, the Dorchester enterprise at Cape Ann was a dismal failure. Fishermen are among the most conservative people in the world. The idea of spending the winter in this bleak and lonely spot, instead of returning to spend Christmas in jolly Devon, did not appeal to them; and the few who were induced to remain convinced Master White of two principles that all New England history has confirmed: 'First, that no sure fishing place in the Land is fit for planting,' nor is the fishing good where farming is. 'And secondly, rarely any Fisher-men will worke at Land, neither are Husband-men fit for Fisher-men but with long use and experience.' The people 'fell into many disorders and did the Company little service.' No clergyman was secured until 1625, when a weak vessel expelled from Plymouth was thus employed. Neither fresh victual nor salt were produced. The Company's ships, too, were ill-managed and unlucky; either going to the wrong market, or arriving too late at the right one. So in 1626 the Dorchester Company dissolved, having lost all they had put in, and as much more. Yet something more than failure was to come out of the Cape Ann venture. In the words of John White, 'As in building houses the first stones of the foundation are buried under ground, and are not seene, so in planting Colonies, the first stockes employed that way are consumed, although they serve for a foundation to the worke.'

During the last year of the settlement at Cape Ann, it was placed in charge of an able and prudent man of thirty-four named Roger Conant. He was the youngest of eight children of Richard Conant, a prosperous farmer of East Budleigh in Devon, the home of Walter Raleigh. The family was typical of the class that furnished New England with its best blood; typical, too, of what good New England families would be. Roger Conant had brothers in farming, in business, in the Church, and at the University. He followed an elder brother to London, served apprenticeship as a salter, and in 1623 emigrated to Plymouth Colony, which he left shortly out of dislike of their rigid Separatism. His brother John, a member of the Adventurers, called the attention of the Company to Roger, when they made him manager of their plantation at Cape Ann. He was appointed just in time to prevent bloodshed. The Pilgrims, having bought a worthless title to a part of Cape Ann, erected a fishing stage, which one of the West Country ships appropriated in the spring of 1625. Miles Standish and his company were sent by Governor Bradford to get it back; the West Countryman barricaded himself on the stage, and invited Miles to come and take it. 'The dispute grew to be very hot, and high words passed'; there would undoubtedly have been a battle for the stage had not Roger Conant interposed, and settled the dispute by inducing the West Countrymen to help the Pilgrims build another stage.

The winter after this successful arbitration, the Dorchester Company broke up, tired of throwing good money after bad; and the disorderly and discontented fishermen returned to England. Apparently one more colonizing experiment on the New England coast, beginning with the fairest prospects, had gone down to defeat.

It was only the darkness before the dawn. Conant remained, for Conant had caught the vision of the new day. Secretly hoping (so he told the historian Hubbard in his old age) that New England might prove a religious refuge, he sent intimation thereof to his friends in the old country. 'Wherefore that reverend person Master White (under God one of the chief founders of the Massachusetts Colony in New England), being grieved in his spirit that so good a work should be suffered to fall to the ground by the Adventurers thus abruptly breaking off, did write to Master Conant not so to desert the business,' promising that if he and three others would stay, he would procure for them a new land grant, and fresh support. In the meantime, Conant had determined on a more suitable site for the plantation. During the autumn of 1626 he and the remnant of the Cape Ann settlers, twenty or thirty persons at most, made their way by Indian trail along the North Shore to a place called by the Indians Naumkeag. John White believed that the name indicated 'some commerce with the Jewes in times past,' since Nahum Keike in Hebrew signifies 'The bosome of consolation.' However that may be, the place was well chosen, since Naumkeag under the more familiar name of Salem, became one of the most prosperous seaports in the Commonwealth.

One is tempted, then, to give Conant the credit for first grasping the 'big idea' of the Bay Colony, of a Canaan where English puritans might pursue their way of life without hindrance. But it is a delicate matter in history to trace ideas to their source; and especially in this case. Roger Conant, reminiscing fifty years after the event, would naturally have read later events into his purpose of remaining in 1626. John White, to be sure, does not mention the Bible Commonwealth idea in his 'Planters Plea'; but that tract was written with the express idea of disclaiming any exclusive puritan purpose for the Bay Colony. It is purely a matter of inference whether the idea originated with White in 1623, with Conant in 1626, with the Lincolnshire puritans in 1627, or whether it simply grew out of circumstances in which the English puritans as a whole found themselves in 1629.

Whatever the motive, it is a fact that Roger Conant and his followers built a few thatched cottages on the peninsula which is now the city of Salem, in the autumn of 1626.[1] How they fared during their first winter at Naumkeag we do not know; probably not well, since there was talk in 1627 of abandoning the place for Virginia; but Conant persuaded the most of them 'to wait the providence of God in that place where now they were.' After a second winter, Providence vouchsafed itself in what must have seemed to the Old Planters a questionable dispensation: the transfer of their property to a new company, which placed them under the stern rule of John Endecott.

This new enterprise, 'The New England Company for a Plantation in Massachusetts Bay' as it was called in the only known document that refers to it by name, owed its existence to the continued zeal of John White; although his name did not appear, as he had no money to contribute. Sir Henry

[1] The exact site of this 'old planters' settlement was the triangle between the North River and the Boston and Maine Railroad, just before it enters upon the bridge leading to Beverly.

Rosewell the high sheriff of Devon, Sir John Yonge his predecessor, John Humfry the treasurer of the old Adventurers, two Dorchester merchants, and John Endecott (of whom more anon), obtained from the Council for New England on March 19, 1628, a patent to 'all that parte of Newe England in America' lying between parallels three miles north of 'a greate river there, commonlie called Monomack, alias Merriemack,' and three miles south of 'a certen other river there, called Charles river, being in the bottome of a certayne bay there, commonlie called Massachusetts, alias Mattachusetts, alias Massatusetts Bay... from the Atlantick and westerne sea and ocean on the east parte, to the South sea on the west parte.'

Why were so twisty a river as the Merrimac and such a modern Meander as the Charles, selected as boundaries? Because no Englishman in London had as yet seen more than their mouths; and on Captain Smith's map (no doubt the only map available) the Charles and the Merrimac fade out a few miles from the sea. It was therefore assumed that both rivers flowed due east, that they would make good boundaries, and that just over their watershed — somewhere near the Berkshires — would be found the rivers that flowed westerly to the South Sea, or Pacific.

The probable purpose of the Dorchester Adventurers, as we have seen, was to establish a fishing and trading colony, with a minister. In spite of their failure to attain this limited objective, White and Humfry seem to have broadened their purpose when obtaining this patent to a generous slice of New England. Their motive had become broadly colonial: they proposed to plant a northern counterpart to Virginia. Whether or not the idea of a puritan refuge was already in their minds it is impossible to say with any certainty. My own opinion is that it was, for their instructions to Endecott the second year have a strongly puritanic flavor. Each head of a family should have morning and evening prayers. 'Ill weeds' must be 'nipt before they take too great a head,' lest the plantation government be 'esteemed as a scar crowe.' 'Our desire is to use lenitie all that may bee, but in case of necessitie not to neglect the other, knowing that correccion is ordained for the Fooles back.'   And, above all, 'keepe youth from falling into many enormities, which by nature wee are all too much enclyned unto.' This prophecy respecting the probable course of the younger generation in Massachusetts proved entirely correct.

For a year, the position of White and his associates was precarious. Their land patent not only cut the heart out of New England; it overlapped several grants by the Council for New England to Mason, Gorges, and others. Sir Ferdinando Gorges declared that the patent had been obtained surreptitiously from this Council during his absence in the war with France, through the influence of the puritan Earl of Warwick; and he was probably right. The New England Company, before they could feel sure that their territory would not be taken away by the same authority that gave it, wanted a guaranteed title; and the only way that they could get it, was by a royal charter.

Further, money was wanted to finance sending over a colony to Massachusetts Bay, and money was what the gentry of the West Country were short of. Their purses had been emptied by the Dorchester adventure. Accordingly, in the year 1628, there was much going to and fro between Dorchester and London. White and Humfry were trying to interest some of the big men of the metropolis, precisely as an inventor to-day with a new gadget to launch will try to get capital in Boston or New York. It was our indefatigable clerical promoter who 'managed a treaty' or in modern parlance, arranged a deal, with an important group of London merchants. Matthew Cradock, who owned £2000 worth of East India Company stock; Sir Richard Saltonstall, nephew and heir of a Lord Mayor of London who was Master of the Worshipful Company of Skinners (what we should call the hide and leather men); John Venn, a wool merchant and sometime warden of the Merchant Taylors' Company, later a colonel in the new model army and signer of the death warrant of Charles I; Theophilus Eaton, deputy-governor of the Eastland Company that traded to the Baltic, later the founder of New Haven; Samuel and William Vassall, interested in the Guinea trade and sons of a Huguenot member of the Virginia Company who commanded a ship against the Spanish Armada; and, in addition, a group of East Anglia puritans: William Pynchon, squire of Springfield in Essex, Isaac Johnson, and Richard Bellingham, of whom more anon. These were men of standing and substance; they had money, and commanded more in the City of London. But it is not to be supposed that they used the sort of sales-patter that Edward Johnson puts in their mouths:

> For richest Jems and gainfull things most Merchants wisely venter:
> Deride not then New England men, this Corporation enter;
> Christ's call for Trade shall never fade, come Craddock, factors send:
> Let Mayhew go and others more, spare not thy coyne to spend;
> Such Trades advance did never chance, in all thy Trading yet:
> Though some deride thy losse, abide, here's gaine beyond mans wit!

Men of money generally get what they want, even though they belong to a party out of favor at court. It was Saltonstall, Cradock, and their friends, in association with White and the New England Company's patentees, who obtained for the same area from the Merrimac to the Charles, and the same avowed purpose of colonization and Indian conversion, a charter, under the name of the Governor and Company of the Massachusetts Bay in New England (March 4, 1629). This charter consolidated the position of the New England Company by making it a corporation; and this very document, transferred to the soil of New England in 1630, served for over fifty years as the constitution of the self-governing colony of Massachusetts Bay.

Even before it had obtained the royal charter, the New England Company sent out settlers to Naumkeag. By the end of June, 1628, the *Abigail* sailed from Weymouth with about fifty colonists, and a generous stock of supplies, including five tuns of beer, thirty hogsheads of malt and two of 'aquavity,' twelve runlets of 'strong waters' and two pipes of Madeira. Also six hogsheads of water were carried in case of emergency. Captain John Endecott, a stout soldier of Devon, accompanied the fleet as governor of the plantation. He and the colonists, most of whom were hired servants of the Company, were ordered by way of return to the investors to make fish, cure sturgeon, prepare beaver, timber, sassafras, sarsaparilla, 'as alsoe good store of shoomacke' and 'a tun waight at least of silke grasse.' In addition they were instructed, in their moments of leisure perhaps, to get a few Indian children 'to trayne up to readinge, and consequentlye to religion, whilst they are young.'

London's Plantation in the Massachusetts Bay, as the enlarged colony at Naumkeag was called, bore precisely the same relation to the Company in England that the Jamestown Colony had to the Virginia Company. Governor Endecott had a position similar to that of Captain John Smith, or any other early governor of Virginia, and like them had a council appointed by the Company, to assist him. Constitutionally, he was little more than the manager of a commercial plantation, and the boss of the company's hired servants.

Why was not Roger Conant appointed governor of the new plantation at Naumkeag? Faithful over a few, he might have made a good ruler over many. A moderate and kindly puritan, conciliatory and peaceful, he would have given to this prelude of the Bay a very different rhythm from the rough psalmody lined out by Governor Endecott. Yet the Company believed a military man like Captain Endecott a more suitable leader for their enlarged enterprise than one of Conant's stamp, and probably they were right; for the excellent Roger, though frequently in after years selectman or deputy, never obtained sufficient reputation among his fellows to be elected a magistrate and assistant. 'Strong valiant John' is described by his contemporary Edward Johnson as 'a fit instrument to begin this Wildernesse-worke, of courage bold undanted, yet sociable, and of a chearfull spirit, loving and austere, applying himselfe to either as occasion served.' During his long years of service to the Bay Colony, John Endecott left slight evidence of human charity, much of stout courage and sense of duty.

Although Governor Endecott was instructed by the Company to be tender of the 'Old Planters' (Conant's company), and to accord them equal rights with the new, almost his first act of authority was to remove the frame of their 'great house' from Cape Ann to Naumkeag for his own use, and to appropriate their garden lots and houses for the new settlers. So Conant had to make the best of a bad situation by giving them up, in exchange for an inferior location on Bass River. Thither removed the old planters, to establish a quiet village which in their lifetime grew into the township of Beverly — 'Beggerly,' as the Salemites called it, to Roger Conant's great grief.[1] They must have been good stuff, these Old Planters — Conant and Palfrey, Woodbury and Balch, Gray and Gardner; for no small group of New England settlers founded families more eminent in letters or enterprising in commerce.

In 1629, to commemorate some further adjustments between the new planters and the old 'after expectance of some dangerous jarre,' Naumkeag was renamed Salem, the Hebrew for 'peaceful.' It was anything but that.

In the spring of 1629, as we have seen, the New England Company obtained fresh blood, more money, and a royal charter as the Massachusetts Bay Company. The Massa-

[1] This Bass River settlement was on Beverly Creek just west of the main line of the railway. The Balch house is one of the oldest still standing in New England.

chusetts Bay Company at once began doing business on a
larger scale, although of the same sort. That same spring it
sent three hundred colonists to Salem in the *Talbot*, the *Lion's
Whelp*, and three other ships. The most interesting members
of this group were two ministers, Francis Higginson and
Samuel Skelton, who were chosen to organize the first
church in Salem, and in the Colony.

The engagement of these men shows that the Massachusetts Bay Company was rapidly getting in touch with the
heart of the puritan movement. Both were graduates of the
University of Cambridge. Higginson was a leading figure in
Leicester, and one of the best-known non-conformist ministers
in England. At a time when he was in hourly expectation of
being summoned to London to answer for his non-conformity
before the Court of High Commission, there came a handsome
offer from the Massachusetts Bay Company to go to Salem.
After preaching a farewell sermon on Luke xxi, 20, 21: 'And
when you see Jerusalem compassed with armies,... then let
them which are in Judæa flee to the Mountains,' he embarked at Gravesend on April 25, 1629, in the *Talbot*, with
about a hundred other passengers. 'And when they came to
the Land's End,' writes Cotton Mather, 'Mr. Higginson calling up his children and other passengers unto the stern of
the ship to take their last sight of England, he said "We will
not say as the Separatists were wont to say at their leaving
of England, Farewel *Babylon!* Farewel *Rome!* But we will
say, Farewel Dear *England!* Farewel the Church of God in
England, and all the Christian friends there! We do not go
to New-England as Separatists from the Church of England;
though we cannot but separate from the corruptions in it:
but we go to practise the positive part of church reformation,
and propagate the gospel in America." '

Separating from the corruptions of the Church, and practising the positive part of Church reformation meant, in puritan parlance, discarding the Book of Common Prayer, ig-

noring the canons of the Church, and putting worship on the basis of the primitive, apostolic Church. The Company should have known that they were in for this when engaging non-conformist ministers like Higginson and Skelton. Their instructions of April 17, 1629, to Endecott, left such matters to the two parsons, 'hooping they will make God's word the rule of their accions' — in effect a blank check. Yet the Company·was somewhat embarrassed by their organizing the First Church of Salem on the separatist or congregational model, within a month of their arrival.

In July and August there were three simple but important ceremonies that accomplished this practical break with the Church of England. We may imagine them as taking place in Endecott's 'great house,' or in the open air; for the Salem edifice which used to be shown to visitors as Higginson's meeting-house afterward proved to be a Quaker meeting-house of later date. About thirty heads of families, having formed a church covenant, spent the morning of July 20 in prayer and preaching, and in the afternoon elected Higginson and Skelton their teacher and pastor by ballot, the two ministers having admitted that they had no right to officiate as such without an 'outward calling' from the faithful. About a week later occurred an even more significant ceremony — ordination by laymen. 'Mr. Higginson with three or four of the gravest members of the church laid their hands on Mr. Skelton, using prayer therewith. This being done, ther was imposission of hands on Mr. Higginson also.' On Thursday, August 6, the elders and deacons were chosen and ordained. Governor Bradford and Elder Brewster of the Plymouth Colony, hindered by head winds, arrived just too late for the ceremony, but in time to give the 'right hand of fellowship' to the brethren, and, let us hope, to enjoy what was left of the beer, the aquavity, the strong waters, and the Madeira.

It has puzzled many to find that Higginson, after protest-

ing his loyalty and affection for mother church, should have
adopted the Congregational polity and joined fellowship with
the Plymouth separatists, however much he and his successors might protest that they had merely separated from the
'corruptions' of Episcopalianism. For he had accepted from
the Salem Saints a form of ordination that implicitly denied
the validity of holy orders in the Church of England, and
joined a covenant which excluded from the sacraments any
communicants of the Church of England who were not agreeable to the First Church of Christ in Salem.

It clears up matters somewhat to find that Samuel Fuller,
the Plymouth physician, summoned to Salem in order to
cure an outbreak of the scurvy, had applied propaganda with
his pills. His long talks with Endecott and others had convinced them, before Higginson arrived, that the Pilgrims'
way was the way of Christ: that Congregationalism was the
only church government authorized by Holy Writ. At least
so Governor Endecott stated in a letter to Governor Bradford. This was a good deal for Endecott to admit, for the
vast majority of English puritans, knowing little of Separatists except stories of their brawls and contentions in Holland,
regarded them as desperate radicals and fanatics. Such
Separatists as had not left England twenty years before had,
as it were, gone underground; and there were in 1629 not
more than half a dozen English Separatist Congregational
churches in existence. Still it would seem that something
more than the persuasive Pilgrim doctor would be required
to make men like Higginson and Skelton split altogether
from the liturgy and polity of the Church of England.

Robert Baillie, a hostile but well-informed Scots critic of
the New England church discipline, probably came as near
the truth as we shall ever get, when he wrote that the First
Church of Plymouth 'did incontinent leaven all the vicinity.'
The Salem settlers 'were ready to receive, without great
question, any pious form which might be presented by their

neighbours, whose mind served them to be active in such matters. Also that [Congregational] way of New-Plymouth, beside the more than ordinary shew of devotion, did hold out so much liberty and honour to the people, that made it very suitable and lovely to a multitude who had lately stepped out of the Episcopall thraldom in England, to the free aire of a new World.'

There, I think, we have the secret of why not only the Salem people, but all the early churches of Massachusetts-Bay, chose the Separatist form of worship and the Congregational polity. It was another case of what has occurred so often in social and political institutions: the 'free aire of a new world' liberating repressed desires and energies, rendering explicit in America what was implicit in England. One aspect of puritanism was the revolt of the laity from priestly control: desire for self-expression, to have a share in running the Church. In the old country, puritans had to compromise with the law, with tradition, with the terms of pious foundations, with their bishops, their pastors, and their neighbors. The touch of New England soil cast these shackles from them. Free now to do what they had always really wished to do, however unwilling they might have been to admit it; free now to think principles through into action, non-conformists became separatists in all but name, and Congregationalists in fact.[1] But if Salem meant peace and liberty to Endecott's and Higginson's way of thinking, it meant oppression for others.

The thirty members who signed the church covenant and elected Higginson and Skelton must have represented a

---

[1] Precisely the same thing had happened in Bermuda ten years before. Lewes Hughes, a Church of England minister, gave up using the Book of Common Prayer, and established a church government by minister and elders. Possibly the same thing would have happened in Virginia, if the Church of England had not been promptly established there by law, and conforming Anglican ministers sent over. 'It seemed indeed that as soon as Englishmen engaged in commerce left their native soil, their first thought was to throw away the Prayer-book.' S. R. Gardiner, *History of England*, vii, 314.

majority of the two hundred or so people then in Salem, for one hundred had already left to settle Charlestown. A minority clung to the ancient forms. John and Samuel Browne, the one a lawyer and the other a merchant, were two of the most important settlers, freemen of the Corporation, and as such appointed by the Company to Governor Endecott's council. They gathered a company of the discontented to read service out of the Book of Common Prayer. There was an open dispute, of the Governor's seeking, between them and the ministers; the Brownes asserting and they denying that the new church was separatist. Endecott ended the debate in characteristic fashion by informing the Brownes that 'New England was no place for such as they,' and shipping them home to England.

This high-handed action of Endecott was disturbing to the Company, and painful to John White. Not only had their endeavors to prevent Separatism been practically thwarted: but news of the fact, should the English authorities get wind of it, might deprive them of their precious charter. Fortunately the Brownes consented to keep quiet when compensated for their loss. The Company cautioned rather than rebuked Endecott against these rash 'innovacions,' which became cornerstones of the ecclesiastical state founded the next year by Winthrop.

During the preparations for the departure of the Winthrop fleet in 1630, John White organized an emigration from his own region, and wrote a tract called The Planters Plea, repeating the economic and social arguments for colonization with which he was only too familiar as minister of an overpopulated market town.

Many among us live without employment, either wholly, or in the greatest part... and that doe not onely such as delight in idlenesse: but even folke willing to labour... Warrantable and usefull callings are overcharged,... as Shoomakers, Taylors, nay Masons, Carpenters, and the like, many of whom with their families live in such a low condition as is little better then beggery.... Yea, of such as are imployed, a great part of their labour were needlesse, if their workes were faithfull and loyall.

The only remedy for this condition of affairs is emigration, and the best destination for such is New England. There the air is wholesome and 'The Land affords void ground enough to receive more people then this State can spare,' with fish and fur and tar and timber. John White then adopted the favorite parson's device of stating objections in order to have the pleasure of refuting them.

Objection 1: Ireland is a fitter place to colonize than New-England; being nearer, more fruitful, and 'Needing our helpe for their recovery out of blindnesse and superstition.' Answer: 'Ireland is well-nigh sufficiently peopled already,' and religion 'hath reasonable footing in Ireland already.' Objection 2: the New England climate, wild beasts and mosquitoes. Answer: 'The cold of Winter is tolerable,... and is remedied by the abundance of fuell.... As for the Serpents, it is true, there are some, and these larger then our Adders; but in ten yeares experience no man was ever indangered by them... The Muskitoes indeed infest the planters... but after one yeares acquaintance, men make light account of them; some sleight defence for the hands and face, smoake, and a close house may keepe them off.'

Those same 'muskitoes' were a sad cross to the early settlers of New England, and from that day to this have been the occasion of more profane cursing than anything else in the country. A 'close house' on a hot July night must have been a worse remedy than the disease. Governor Bradford wrote, 'they are too delicate and unfitte to begine new-plantations and collonies, that cannot enduer the biting of a muskeeto; we would wish shuch to keepe at home till at least they be muskeeto proofe.' A gentlewoman of the Bay Colony writes:

When I remember the high commendations some have given of the place, and find it inferior to the reports, I have thought the reason thereof to be this, that they wrote surely in strawberry time. When I have thought again of the mean reports, and find it far better than those reports, I have fancied the eyes of the writers were so fixed on their old English chimney tops, that the smoke put them out. The air of the country is sharp, the rocks many, the trees innumerable, the grass little, the winter cold, the summer hot, the gnats in summer biting, the wolves at midnight howling, &c. Look upon it, as it hath the means of grace, and, if you please, you may call it a Canaan.

There must have been many readers of The Planters Plea who thought that John White, too, wrote in strawberry time.

Most significant, however, is his answer to Objection 4, that New England offered at best only hard labor and a bare living, whereas the West Indies with their rich soil promised wealth and ease. This was a vital point for the Massachusetts enterprise, for the Earl of Warwick and John Pym were promoting a puritan colony in the island of Old Providence, and Barbados was in the first flush of prosperity.   White's answer showed great sagacity, and foretold exactly what would be the future of society in New England, in contrast with tropical islands of quick returns and swift decay:

If men desire to have a people degenerate speedily, and to corrupt their mindes and bodies too, and besides to tole-in theeves and spoilers from abroad; let them secke a rich soile, that brings in much with little labour; but if they desire that Piety and godlinesse should prosper; accompanied with sobriety, justice and love, let them choose a Countrey such as this is; even like France or England, which may yeeld sufficiency with hard labour and industry: the truth is, there is more cause to feare wealth then poverty in that soyle.

As for the human material of which the colony should be composed, White follows John Smith in strongly recommending that the immigrants be chosen from a variety of trades and professions, mainly the former, in order that the colony be a cross-section of the most industrious and wholesome part of English life. He had evidently been impressed by Smith's sarcastic account of the lapidaries, sword-polishers, and gentlemen of leisure which the Virginia Company had sent out in the early days.

Ill humours soone overthrow a weake body; and false stones in a foundation ruine the whole building: the persons therfore chosen out for this employment, ought to be willing, constant, industrious, obedient, frugall, lovers of the common good, or at least such as may be easily wroght to this temper; considering that workes of this nature try the undertakers with many difficulties, and easily discourage minds of base and weake temper. It cannot, I confesse, be hoped that all should be such; care must be had that the principalls be so inclined, and as many of the Vulgar as may bee, at least that they bee willing to submit to authority; mutinies, which many times are kindled by one person, are well nigh as dangerous in a Colony, as in an Armie.

If John White concluded that mutinies were as dangerous in a colony as in an army, he must have been reading John Smith's Generall Historie of Virginia, whose early history had been so full of faction. The founders of Massachusetts Bay were determined that whatever else they might have, they must have unity. A mere difference of opinion on a matter of doctrine, criticism of a law or protest against the act of a magistrate, too often seemed in their eyes mutiny and sedition, and was promptly suppressed as such.

And now we must anticipate a bit of the next chapter. Charles I had dismissed his last parliament. The ecclesiastical courts, stimulated by Bishop Laud, were coming down heavily on puritan clergymen. Reaction was in the saddle, and a return to the practices of Queen Mary's reign seemed imminent. At this juncture a group of East Anglia puritans, led by Isaac Johnson, obtain control of the Massachusetts Bay Company on the condition that charter and government would be transferred with them to Massachusetts Bay, making the colony independent of English control. Word gets about the city and the market towns and the countryside that at last a colony will be founded where puritans may be free from coercion by bishops and courts. Many families and even neighborhoods sell their property to meet the expense; funds are provided by the Company or by charitable persons for those of good stuff who cannot afford to go.

A contemporary ballad, satirical of the puritans but in a kindly way, tells us more of this folk-movement than pages of description:

> My Brethren all attend me,
>   And list to my relation:
> This is the day — marke what I say —
>   Tends to your renovation.
> Stay not amongst the wicked
>   Lest that with them you perish,
> But let us to New England goe
>   And the Pagan people cherishe.
>   *Then for the truth's sake come along,*
>   *Come alonge!*
>   *Leave the place of supersticion!*
>   *Were it not for we that Brethren be,*
>   *You'd sinke into perdicion!*
>
> There we may teach our hymnes
>   Without the lawe's controulment,
> We neede not feare the Bishops there,
>   Nor the spirituall courts inrolment;
> Nay, the sirplis shall not vexe us,
>   Nor supersticions blindnese,
> Nor scandall rise when we disguise,
>   For our sister's kissing kindnesse.
>   *Then for the truth's sake,* etc.
>
> Our Company we feare not —
>   There goes my Cosen Hanna —
> And Ruben doe perswade to goe,
>   His sister, faire Susanna;
> With Abigall and Lidia
>   And Ruth noe doubt comes after,
> And Sara kinde wil not stay behinde
>   My Cosen Constance after.
>   *Then for the truth's sake,* etc.
>
> Nay, Tom Tyler is prepared
>   And the smith as black as a Cole,
> And Raph Cobler too with us will goe,

For he regards his soule;
And the Weaver honest Symon,
  With Prudence, Jacob's daughter,
And Agatha and Barbara
  Professeth to come after.
    Then for the truth's sake, etc.

When we that are elected
  Arive in this faire Country,
Which by our faith, as the Brethren saith,
  We neede not feare our entry;
The Psalmes shalbe our Musicke
  And our tyme spent in expounding,
Which in our zeale we will reveale
  To the Brethrens Joyes abounding.
    Then for the truth's sake come along,
      Come alonge!
    Leave the place of supersticion!
    Were it not for we that Brethren be,
      You'd sinke into perdicion! [1]

The first contingent of the Great Emigration is assembling. One of the first to sail is the *Mary and John* from Plymouth, with one hundred and forty passengers from various parts of the West Country, recruited in part by John White. One of these, Roger Clap, wrote in his old age an account of this company, which founded the town of Dorchester, Massachusetts:

These godly people resolved to live together; and therefore, as they had made choice of those two reverend servants of God, Master John Warham and Master John Maverick, to be their ministers, so they kept a solemn day of fasting in the New Hospital in Plymouth, in England, spending it in preaching and praying; where that worthy man of God, Master John White of Dorchester in Dorset, was present, and preached unto us the word of God in the fore part of the day; and in the latter part of the day, as the people did solemnly make choice of and call those godly ministers to be their officers, so also the reverend Master Warham and Master Maverick did accept thereof, and expressed the same. So

[1] Bodleian Library, Ashmole MSS., xxvi, 37. Another version will be found in Masson's *Life of Milton*, ii, 547.

we came, by the good hand of the Lord, through the deeps comfortably, having preaching or expounding of the word of God every day for ten weeks together by our ministers.

Besides actively promoting the puritan emigration, Master White exerted himself to prevent the Bay Colony from adopting a separatist polity, as seemed likely from what had occurred at Salem. In order to commit the leaders of the Winthrop fleet against separatism he wrote, and induced them to sign, the remarkable tract called the 'Humble Request of His Majestie's loyall Subjects, the Governour and the Company late gone for New-England; To the rest of their Brethren, in and of the Church of England. For the obtaining of their Prayers, and the removall of suspitions, and misconstructions of their Intentions.' In this address, dated aboard the *Arbella* at Yarmouth in the Isle of Wight, on April 7, 1630, Winthrop and Saltonstall, Johnson and Dudley, describe themselves as men who esteem it an honor to call the Church of England their 'dear Mother,' acknowledging that such hope and part as they have obtained of salvation, they 'have received in her bosom, and sucked it from her breasts.' They will always 'rejoice in her good, and unfeignedly grieve for any sorrow that shall ever betide her.' They pray the ministers of that Church to pray 'for a Church springing out of your own bowels,' and compare themselves to the 'Church of Philippi (which was a Colonie from Rome),' and for which St. Paul prayed.

The language of this Humble Request probably represented a compromise between White and Winthrop; for like most compromises it lacked definiteness. If the emigrating puritans, as Cotton Mather declares, meant by the Church of England all English people who professed and called themselves Christians, the Humble Request committed them to nothing except a friendly attitude; and even that they did not observe. John White, however, believed that he had obtained a sort of treaty against separation; for in his

Planters' Plea he used the Humble Request as proof that
the emigrants had no intention, open or secret, of separating.
He even attempts with it to refute Objection No. 6: 'Yea
but if they doe not separate, yet they dislike our discipline
and ceremonies, and so they will prove themselves semi-
separatists at least, and that is their intention' — which is
precisely what did happen. Three out of four emigrants of
that year, White asserts, 'have lived in a constant course
of conformity'; Governor Winthrop has 'beene every way
regular and conformable' all his life; and though the ministers
who have gone with them are non-conformists, none other
could be induced to go: 'pardon them if they take such
Ministers as they may have, rather than none at all.' He
admits that some may expect 'greater libertie there than
here in the use of some orders and Ceremonies of our Church';
and that for their sake, even the strict conformists of the emigration may 'be wonne to consent to some variation from
the formes and customes of our Church' for the sake of
peace and unity. But that the leaders plan to make Massachusetts Bay a 'Nursery of *Schismatickes*' or a 'seminary of
faction and separation,' he indignantly denies. Yet that is
exactly what they did, from the high Anglican point of view.
In their own conception, the puritans were merely establishing the true Church according to the word of God; they were
separating from the corruptions of the Church of England,
not from the Church itself. They represented, as they believed, the great body of the Church of England: Brownists
and Baptists and High Churchmen were the 'schismatickes.'

Although the Planters' Plea might well prepare us for an
indignant repudiation by White of the religious polity
actually adopted by the puritans in New England, his affectionate interest in the Bay Colony continued long after the
transfer of the charter. For several years he intended to
come over himself, but never found means or opportunity.
He collected provisions for Massachusetts with such zeal

during the scarcity of 1631 that certain people in Dorchester accused him of diverting parish funds to that charitable purpose. Two letters of his to Governor Winthrop, for the years 1636 and 1637, have been preserved. In the one he rebukes the Bay merchants for profiteering, and lays down the same Christian principles of business that John Cotton endeavored to enforce.[1] In the other he inquires why the codfisheries are not pushed more briskly, and cautions the Governor against abusing his religious liberty by binding 'all men to the same tenets and practise in things which, when they are well examined, will be found indifferent' — an allusion to the suppression of Anne Hutchinson. 'But above all things lett me request you to avoyd that rocke of separation which if you once light on you will finde shake you in pieces.' Yet he has no fault to find with the Congregational principles which had been adopted in all the churches established in the Bay jurisdiction.

By this time, White's own views had evolved so far that he could not consistently have accused the Bay puritans of abandoning all connection with the Church. He refused to read the Book of Sports from his pulpit in 1633, as ordered by the Archbishop; an outspoken sermon brought him under suspicion of non-conformity; his study was searched for incriminating evidence, and later ravaged by Prince Maurice's cavalry. He became a prominent member of the Westminster Assembly of Divines, 'one of the most learned and moderate among them... a person of great gravity and presence,' says Anthony Wood. When Episcopacy seemed out of question, White rallied to Presbyterianism, against the Independents and the Sectaries.

Civil War and the dissolution of ancient bonds had done for White what the sea change did for Higginson, and brought him to accept a creed and a platform which in 1630 he would have regarded as heretical. Retiring to his old parish in

[1] See below, Chapter V.

Dorchester at the age of three score and ten, he expressed his ripe wisdom and knowledge in a little tract, 'The Way to the Tree of Life.' On July 21, 1648, the Patriarch of Dorchester, 'under God one of the chief founders of the Massachusetts Colony,' was gathered to his fathers, and buried with the simple rites of the puritans under the south porch of St. Peter's Church.

Such then, were the labors of John White in behalf of American colonization. Promoter of the Dorchester Adventurers who planted Cape Ann in 1623; saviour of the remnants of that colony when abandoned by the Company which sent it out; organizer of a new company to settle the country between the Merrimac and the Charles; the means of obtaining new blood, the interest of public-spirited men of wealth, and the Royal charter; author of two tracts which disarmed the suspicions of the English public, and enabled the Winthrop fleet to sail unmolested to our shores. All this in addition to his unremitting labors for his own parish, town, and church. He had started something too great for him to control. The modest ambition of the Dorchester Adventurers had been swallowed up in a great enterprise, the founding of a self-governing puritan commonwealth: — a seminary of separation indeed; separation from the Church of England, and in due time, separation from the Crown of England.

CHAPTER III

JOHN WINTHROP, ESQUIRE

1. The Puritan Squire

IN the early part of the reign of Henry VIII, a bright country lad named Adam Winthrop told his father that he was through with farming, and went up to London to seek his fortune. There, in a ten years' apprenticeship to a member of the Clothworkers' gild, he learned the secrets of that ancient trade and mystery of working up wool into cloth. After his indenture was up he became journeyman, then master clothier, and full-fledged member of the gild. At the age of forty-six, having acquired a fortune, and in a fair way to become Master of the Worshipful Company of Clothworkers, Adam did what Englishmen in his position have done time out of mind: purchased a country estate and joined the landed gentry. Such estates were easily come by in that day, for Henry VIII had laid violent hands on the vast possessions of the monasteries, and was finding new owners for them, with the double purpose of increasing his revenue, and enlarging his following. So Adam purchased, for £408 18s. 3d., the manor of Groton in Suffolk, formerly belonging to the Abbey of Bury St. Edmunds, with the manor house and all and singular its buildings, tenements, messuages, and hereditaments; with all rights of pasturage, fishing, and woodcutting; with its wardships, heriots, mercates, mills, and tolls; with the right and duty to hold court baron for the free tenants and court leet for the customary tenants, and the presentation of Groton Church. All this, with much additional land, was inherited by his son, the second Adam Winthrop, who practised law in London for a time, but during the greater part of his life found sufficient occupation in farming and governing Groton Manor. He acquired a coat of arms, and a settled position among the country gentry of Suffolk, where his son John was born in January of the Armada year, 1588.

Groton to-day is a tiny village on a hillside, overlooking the market town of Boxford. An ancient mulberry tree marks the site of Groton Hall, but the old parish church is still there, with the tombs of the early Winthrops. Suffolk is the most homely part of Old England, to a New Englander: a gently rolling country of quiet horizons, less wooded than most parts of New England to-day, but with the regular irregularity and even unevenness which Westerners find so charming (or exasperating) in Massachusetts. Stone walls enclosing meadow and tillage, mowing and pasture; narrow roads winding and dipping in unexpected ways; and always a smooth-crested hill to vary the skyline. The old houses, too, are of the style and proportion of our seventeenth-century New England dwellings, though covered with plaster and thatch instead of clapboard and cedar shingle; the same great central chimney, overhanging second story, high-pitched roof, and small casements with leaded diamond panes. Out in the country they stand, surrounded by farm buildings (barn doors opening on the side, in the old New England pattern), or generously spaced about a village green, like a New England town common.

Here is our very homeland. In an afternoon's drive of seventy or eighty miles, we may visit Framlingham, Ipswich, Dedham, Braintree, Boxford, Groton, Sudbury, and Haverhill, and spend the night at Cambridge. Suffolk is the heart of East Anglia, the section of England, which, according to Havelock Ellis' 'Study of British Genius,' has produced the greatest statesmen, scientists, ecclesiastics, scholars, and artists in English history, and which has always been distinguished for a profound love of liberty and independence. In East Anglia, the puritan movement bit deepest. From East Anglia came the heaviest contingent for the planting of

Massachusetts Bay; and Massachusetts as colony and commonwealth, by every known test of eminence, has produced more distinguished men and women in proportion to her population, than any other state of the Union.

The lordship of the Manor of Groton involved many duties and obligations. Adam Winthrop, like many a country gentleman of to-day, was a self-made business man; but we must not carry the analogy further by supposing that he had nothing to do but make over the mansion, join the local smart set, and pretend that his farm paid its expenses. To be a country gentleman in Elizabethan England meant to be an active member of the governing class: a justice of the peace, holding petty sessions and sitting on the bench with fellow magistrates at the quarter-sessions and grand assizes. The early magistrates of Massachusetts Bay were of this class. They had been local leaders and rulers over the same sort of people who came with them, a fact which explains both the deference that they obtained and the ability that they displayed. Yet the founders of New England made no attempt to transplant the manorial system or hereditary government to our soil. They were through with feudalism, as they were through with ritualism.

John Winthrop was Justice of the Peace at eighteen, and in a few years' time began to hold court leet for his father, and act as steward of the manor: excellent training in administration. In addition he had to direct the ordinary farming work of the demesne, and of outlying estates that he owned or leased. Adam the second's diary is full of entries that carry us back almost to his namesake, and forward to the other day in New England: sowing, reaping, and threshing wheat, rye, pease, and barley; calvings and foalings; dogs biting sheep and cows in the corn; riving logs and thatching roofs; drowning the meadow and casting the pond; clowns a-wooing maids, and getting them with child; together with a few items typical of the period, such as highway robberies, forced loans to the

Queen's Majesty, news of King James' progress from the North.

So John Winthrop grew up an English squire, governing and directing the common English rustic, and mingling socially with his peers. Besides, his family maintained contacts with the City and the University. Both Adam and John practised law in London, and kept up with the solid members of the city livery companies; Adam also served as auditor of Trinity College, Cambridge. Groton was about the same distance from that university town as Groton, Massachusetts, is from ours; so it was a pleasant recreation for Adam to ride up to Cambridge four times a year to go through the college books, to play bowls with the dons, eat the great audit dinner, and drink the heavy audit ale. He entered John at Trinity at the age of fourteen, only a little younger than the average freshman. The boy remained there less than two years. Few sons of the country gentry took university degrees in those days unless they were destined for the Church. We may infer from John's severe remarks on the dissoluteness of Cambridge undergraduates, and from sending his eldest son to Trinity College, Dublin, that further residence in college was regarded as a waste of time. For the Winthrops were puritans, and of all puritanic tenets, perhaps the most lasting in New England is the prohibition to waste your 'precious time.'

.   .   .   .

The time has come, the Walrus said, to talk of puritanism and the puritans. I had hoped to get through this book without that disagreeable task of definition; but it cannot be done. What then is meant by puritanism, and who were the puritans?

Puritanism was a way of life based on the belief that the Bible was the word of God, and the whole word of God. Puritans were the Englishmen who endeavored to live according to that light. Having been so round, I must shade off, for puritanism has had various meanings at different times. Originally a nickname (οἱ καθαροί, *puritani*) flung about on the theological controversies of the late Roman Empire, it was revived in Queen Elizabeth's reign to describe that party of English Protestants who wished to carry out the Reformation to its logical conclusion, and purge the Anglican Church of forms and ceremonies for which there was no warrant in the Bible; or, to use a phrase of Cartwright which became a watchword for one party and a jest for their opponents, to restore the Christian Church 'pure and unspotted.' At first it was applied only to persons within the Church of England; but by 1630, the term puritan had been stretched to include separatists like the Pilgrims who obtained purity outside the Anglican communion, and even the Scots Presbyterians, who had a different organization. Further, the Church of England puritans were divided into non-conformists, who disobeyed the law rather than compromise with conscience, and the conformable puritans like John White and John Winthrop who performed or attended the prescribed services according to the Book of Common Prayer, while hoping for better things.

Beside this purely religious meaning of puritanism, there was a moral aspect. Persons who read the Bible and sincerely believed in it, adopted or attempted a very exacting code of morals; and as they believed that this code was gospel ordinance, they endeavored to enforce it on others. Such persons were originally called precisians, and were not necessarily puritans in a religious sense. The most thoroughly puritanic diary I have ever read, full of moans and groans over the mildest peccadilloes of himself and others, is that of Samuel Ward, master of Sidney Sussex College, a stout Royalist and Anglican who was expelled by Cromwell. We mean this moral preciseness when we use the term puritanism to-day; yet moral puritanism is by no means confined to the Protestant or English-speaking churches. The Catholic counter-reformation of the sixteenth century was quite as puritanic in a moral sense as the Protestant reformation. Jansenism was a puritanical movement within the Gallican Church in France; and no sect within the last century has been more puritanical in a moral sense than the Catholic Church in Ireland. In England there was what we might call high church puritanism, of which the 'divine Herbert' was the highest example. King Charles and Bishop Laud were both persons of high moral standards. Laud's ecclesiastical courts were as zealous to punish immorality as to enforce conformity; and the reforms that he began in the University of Oxford were continued by its later puritan rulers. If Bishop and King had not attempted religious innovations in the direction of Rome, if they had respected the ritual and doctrine of the Church as Elizabeth or even Archbishop Bancroft had left them, the puritans might never have become associated with radicalism and democracy.

And what of the political side of puritanism? Charles Borgeaud, and other political scientists, have traced democracy to puritanism. I do not think that this theory will hold water, although there is something in it. The Englishman of 1630 was politically mature, compared with other Europeans. He was beginning to feel his way toward popular government, and during the Interregnum he went far on that road. As we have seen in the case of the Salem Church, the congregational polity which one branch of the puritans favored, made laymen the governing body of the church. But the connection between puritanism and political liberalism was fortuitous. English puritans in 1630 rallied to representative government and traditional English liberty because that was their only refuge against innovating Bishops and a high church King; but in New England where they had things their own way, their political spirit was conservative and their temper autocratic. If American democracy came out of puritan New England (and it may equally well be traced to Virginia), it came from the English and not the puritan in our ancestors, and from the newness not the puritanism of New England.

We would do well then to remember that puritanism in the seventeenth century had a purely religious connotation. I will not detain my readers here with a summary of their beliefs and practices; these will appear as the lives of those commonwealth builders, puritans all, unfold. Yet pardon me if I caution you against certain current delusions about the early puritans upon which historians have placed the stamp of authority. The one is that they were mainly preoccupied with hell and damnation. On the contrary, fire-and-brimstone sermons, and poems such as Wigglesworth's 'Day of Doom,' belong to a later generation or to the eighteenth century, when puritan pastors tried to frighten their backsliding congregations into good behavior. The second delusion is that puritanism is synonymous with Calvinism. Broadly speaking the English puritan theologians were Calvinist in their theology rather than Lutheran or Arminian; but being learned in the ancient tongues they derived their ideas mainly from the Bible and the Fathers. Calvin's 'Institutes' was never to them a sacred book, and I have found Calvin less frequently quoted in their writings than English theologians like Ames, Perkins, and Whitaker. A third delusion is that puritans were prohibitionists, responsible for banning alcoholic drinks. Their faith put more stress on the joys of the inner life than on those of the senses, but they made no attempt to proscribe one of God's good creatures, whose temperate use was sanctioned by the Bible, and by our Lord's example. Finally, readers of New England history must be cautioned against ascribing to puritanism alone a coarseness that was common to the age, and a bigotry that was common to all Christian sects, and still is far too common. We will not often find breadth of mind among the English puritans; but we will find a spiritual depth that belongs only to the great ages of religious experience.

John Winthrop was happy to have lived in the golden age of English puritanism, when some of its early fanaticism had been sloughed off, without losing the bloom of youth. It had not altogether broken with the stately and cadenced ritual of the Book of Common Prayer; it had grasped firm hold of the evangelistic principle, the 'tidings of great joy' that our Saviour brought to men. Whatever puritanism may have come to mean in later ages — and I will freely admit that its more recent manifestations have been negative, narrow, and altogether unlovely — it meant three hundred years ago, a high sincerity of purpose, an integrity of life, and an eager searching for the voice of God. The intellectual strength of the puritan was his knowledge of the Bible; the moral strength of the puritan was his direct approach to God. No puritan ever said, as did the children of Israel when they heard the thunder and the trumpet blasts on Mount Sinai, 'Let not God speak to us, lest we die.' His home, his study, his meeting-house, were filled with the reverberations of the awful and gracious voice for which he listened. If he rejected the intercession of the saints, it was because he would meet God face to face. If he despised the ancient pageantry of worship, it was because he would have no false and sensual symbols between him and his Redeemer. Often, like the ancient Hebrews, he misunderstood the voice of God. Often he mistook for it the echo of his own wants and passions. But the desire to hear it, the sense that life consisted in hearing and obeying it, never left him.

.   .   .   .

The Winthrops were puritans of that sort, as we may infer from the books they read, the friends they valued, and the preachers they liked to hear. One of John's uncles was a friend to John Fox, compiler of the Book of Martyrs. They were conforming puritans, for the presentation of the living at Groton was in their hands, so they would not choose a 'dumb minister' who could do nothing but read out of the Prayer-Book, but a 'godly, learned and painefull (pains-taking)' vicar who would neither bend the knee nor wear the surplice, and would hurry through morning prayer to preach a meaty sermon on Christian duty and doctrine. Their delight in sermons helps to make puritans incomprehensible to the present age, which values sermons inversely to their length. 'She hath in her time taken inttollerable paines to hear sermons,' wrote one of that day of his mother; although when a girl she could not imagine what ailed people 'to keep such a strirre in praying, reading, and running to sermons.' Among persons whose minds were filled with thoughts of God, and the desire to learn and do his will, a sermon by a learned and pious man was of absorbing interest and assistance. One of the 'common grevances groaninge for reformation' of which John Winthrop complains, is the punishment of laymen 'for goeing to another parrish to heare a sermon when there is none in there owne.'

We have a fairly full record of John Winthrop's religious experiences in a diary that he kept of his inner life. The family portraits show him, his father, and his son, to have been of the dark, sanguine, and passionate type of English-man; so we may believe John when he tells us that he was 'wild and dissolute' as a lad, and at all times tempted by the lusts of the flesh. He first drew near to God when lying ill at Trinity College. Backsliding followed, but shortly after his first marriage, at the age of seventeen, he came 'to some peace and comfort in God and in his wayes.' It was long, however, before he reached that serene conviction of divine favor which the puritans called conversion. Numerous *experienciae* of his riper years record constant wrestling with animal desires, long periods of prayer, stern self-abasement, and joy at recovering the pathway of life. His ideal was to devote every waking moment to God, when not engaged in his calling, or in reasonable recreation. It was a matter of self-congratulation that his horseback journeys to London could be employed in praying, singing, and meditation, instead of 'eyes runninge upon every object,' and 'thoughts varieing with everye occasion.' These soul-searching records were common among sincere puritans of that time. They gave rise to what is known as the New England conscience, which was nothing more nor less than the English puritan conscience, transplanted. They could easily be carried to a morbid excess, and often were. John Winthrop's *experiencia* is often tiresome, and even ludicrous in one instance, where he gives his reasons for giving up shooting birds out of season: (1) it is illegal; (2) it offends his neighbors; (3) 'it wastes great store of tyme'; (4) 'it toyles a man's bodye overmuche'; (5) it endangers his life; (6) it brings no profit; (7) the penalty, if caught, would be heavy; (8) 'it brings a man of worth and godlines into some contempt'; (9) after he has gone shooting with 'woundes of conscience,' he has missed most of the 'fowle' that came his way, and often returned with an empty bag! One may suspect that the last reason, which would suffice for most men, was really the first; and one may trace to this sort of thing that tendency toward self-deception, still strong to-day in those of puritanic antecedents, and apt to slop over into hypocrisy.

John Winthrop was a more pronounced puritan than his father. Adam's diaries deal with material things; John's only with religion, until he sets sail for America. Adam could be merry; John regarded mirth and jollity out of place in an earnest life. Adam was at ease among his fellows; John felt lonely among the jovial magistrates at quarter-sessions. 'O Lord, keepe me that I be not discouraged!' he confides to his diary. 'Thou tellest me, and all experience tells me, that in this way there is the least companie, and that those which

JOHN WINTHROP

SIR RICHARD SALTONSTALL

doe walke openly in this way shalbe despised, pointed at, hated of the world,... called puritans, nice fooles, hipocrites.' This entry in his diary reminds us that the term puritan was still one of opprobrium. If you had cried 'Puritan! Puritan!' at a stout fellow embarking for New England, he would have knocked you down. Doubtless he would have prayed God to be forgiven, but he would have knocked you down first. The puritans called themselves the People of God, or simply Christians, for they believed that their faith was what Christ and his apostles preached. It was not until the end of the century that they came to accept the term puritan for themselves, and to glory in it.

For all these soul-strivings one gathers from the Winthrop family papers the impression of a busy, wholesome, happy family life. There was plenty of quiet recreation, even after John decided it did not pay to go shooting: falconry, badger hunting with hounds, shooting with bows and arrows at a mark, good cheer at family gatherings. To his four successive wives, John was a tender husband. No woman could want more affectionate letters than those of John Winthrop to his 'sweet wife' Margaret, mingling gossip with kind messages and talk of God, ending 'many kisses of love I sende thee. Farewell. Thy faithful loving husband, John Winthrop.'

Yet there is much uneasiness in that quiet household at Groton, and grave forebodings for the future of the family, of the Church, and of England. As early as 1624 there is a hint that John Winthrop might follow his uncle's example and emigrate to Ireland, could he find opportunity. Manners and conditions were fast changing, much as they are now, and to the same dismay of quiet gentlemen with limited incomes. The rich were getting richer and the poor becoming poorer. It was becoming difficult to bring up children properly. The universities were full of riot and frivolity. Luxury was so rife among the landed gentry, that people like the Winthrops

could not keep up with them. Saddle horses and rustic
serving men no longer suffice for a gentleman; you must have
liveried servants, and the latest model coach. Manners are
corrupted. 'He that hath not for every word an oath... they
say hee is a puritan, a precise fool, not fit to hold a gentleman
company.' Wild parties become good form. It was Chief
Justice Popham, says John Aubrey, who 'was the greatest
howse-keeper in England; would have at Littlecote 4 or 5
more lords at a time. His wife (Harvey) was worth to him,
I thinke, £60,000, and she was as vaine as he,... and in her
husband's absence would have all the woemen of the countrey thither, and feast them, and make them drunke, as she
would be herselfe.'

These changes are brought home to us by a contemporary
ballad, a satire on the times:

> You talke of Newe England; I truly beleeve
> Oulde England's growne newe and doth us deceave.
> I'le aske you a question or two, by your leave:
> And is not ould England growne new?
>
> Wher are your ould souldiers with slashes and skarrs
> That never used drinkeinge in noe time of warrs,
> Nor sheddinge of blood in madd drunken Jarrs?
> And is not ould England growne new!
>
> And what is become of your Bills and your Bowes,
> Your Bucklers and Targetts that never feard blowes?
> They'r turnd to stillatoes and other vaine showes.
> And is not ould England growne new?
>
> New Captaines are come that never did Fight
> But with Potts in the daie and Puncks in the night —
> And all ther chieff caire is to keepe ther swords bright!
> And is not ould England growne new?
>
> Wher are your ould Courttiers that used to ryde
> With forty blewe coates and footmen beside?
> They'r turn'd to six horses, a coach with a guyde!
> And is not ould England growne new?

And what is become of your ould fashiond clothes,
Your longsided Dublett and your trunck hose?
They'r turn'd to new fashions — but what the Lord knowes!
    And is not ould England growne new?

Now your gallaint and his tayllor some halfe yeare together
To fitt a new sute to a new hatt and fether,
Of gould or of silver, silke, cloth stuff, or lether.
    And is not ould England growne new?

You have new fashon'd Beards and new fashon'd locks
And new fashon's hatts for new pated blocks,
And moor new diseases besides the French Pox!
    And is not ould England growne new?

New Fashons in houses, new Fashons at table,
The ould servants discharged, the new are moor able;
And every ould custome is but an ould fable!
    And is not ould England growne new?

New trickings, new goeings, new measurs, new paces,
New hedds for your men, for women new faces;
And twenty new tricks to mend ther bad cases!
    And is not ould England growne new?

New houses are built and the ould ones pull'd downe,
Untill the new houses sell all the ould ground,
And then the house stands like a horse in a pounde!
    And is not ould England growne new?

New tricks in the Law, new leases, new houlds,
New bodies they have — they look for new soules
When the mony is payde all for buildinge ould Powles!
    And is not ould England growne new?

Then talke you noe more of New England!
New England is wher ould England did stand,
Newe furnnishd, newe fashond, new woman'd, new man'd
    And is not ould England growne newe![1]

Political conditions were even worse than the social.
The horizon was darkly overcast with clouds of the counter-
reformation. Bishop Laud is the King's right-hand man.

[1] Bodleian Library, Ashmole MSS., xxxvi, 37.

Conformity is the order of the day. Preachers and lecturers are silenced, sermons forbidden, and all ministers who will not wear a surplice, genuflect, and make an altar of the communion table, are under suspicion. The Queen is a Catholic. Discreet Papal emissaries and sleek Catholic chaplains swarm at court. The King refuses to lift a finger to help his Protestant brother-in-law the Elector Palatine. Spanish infantry under Wallenstein overrun the Palatinate, Cardinal Richelieu destroys the power of the French Huguenots; yet the English government has not a word to say. Putting these things together, how could an English puritan doubt that his country had been caught in the backwash of the Catholic reaction, that the days of Queen Mary would return, and once more the flesh of Protestant martyrs would roast at Smithfield?

A crisis came in the spring of 1629: Parliament is always puritan; so King Charles shall govern without Parliament. March 2. The day of the three resolutions declaring every supporter of High Church and royal prerogative a capital enemy to this Kingdom and Commonwealth, resolutions passed with a tumult of ayes, the usher of the Black Rod thundering at the door, and speaker Finch held down in his chair, so he will not end the session. The Royal Guard breaks in, carries off the puritan leaders to the tower, and for eleven years King Charles governs without a parliament.

John Winthrop, as a known puritan, loses his attorneyship at the Court of Wards and Liveries, but that is the least of his troubles. 'My dear Wife,' he writes on May 15, 1629, 'I am verily persuaded, God will bringe some heavye Affliction upon this lande, and that speedylye; but be of good comfort... If the Lord seeth it wilbe good for us, he will provide a shelter & a hidinge place for us and others, as a Zoar for Lott, Sarephtah for his prophet; if not, yet he will not forsake us.'

2. THE TRANSFER OF THE CHARTER

For some time, several prominent puritans of Lincolnshire have been talking of emigrating to New England. The social center of this group is Tattershall, the seat of the Earl of Lincoln, near Sempringham and Boston. John Humfry, treasurer of the old Dorchester adventurers, is the person who, with Master John White of Dorchester, has aroused the interest of this nucleus, and in the course of his negotiations Humfry marries Lady Sarah Fiennes, the Earl's daughter. Other members of the group are Isaac Johnson, a wealthy landowner of Rutland, and husband to Lady Arbella Fiennes; Thomas Dudley of Northampton, former captain of English volunteers under Henry of Navarre, lately a devoted parishioner of John Cotton at Boston, and sometime steward to the Earl of Lincoln; his successor in that office, a young Cambridge graduate named Simon Bradstreet, who is about to marry Dudley's daughter Anne. Thomas Leverett, alderman of Boston, and Richard Bellingham, recorder of the borough, are probably also of their circle of friends. Several are members of the Governor and Company of the Massachusetts Bay. Why not transfer the charter and government of the Company to the soil of New England, and make it the framework of a puritan commonwealth?

Such a thing had never been done before, but why not now? The Massachusetts Bay Company was a joint-stock corporation, organized very much as business corporations are to-day. The stockholders or freemen chose the president and board of directors — there called Governor and Assistants — to manage the company's affairs. Freemen and officers met quarterly in a Great and General Court, to choose officers and keep track of the Company's business. The Company's offices are in London; the colony at Salem is subordinate to them, just as British India, for almost two hundred years, was subordinate to the General Court of the

East India Company in London. In the Massachusetts Bay charter, no mention was made of the place where the company must hold its meetings. Whether by accident, or by greasing the palm of some government clerk who drafted the document, this important proviso was left out. The puritan leaders must have read, in Captain John Smith's works if not elsewhere, how annoying it was for colonists to be subject to meddlesome orders and instructions from English business men who knew nothing about American conditions. And every one remembered that the Virginia charter had been confiscated in 1624, because it was in London where the Crown could lay hands on it.

Whoever conceived this idea of transferring the charter, it was not Winthrop. Either the London group of stockholders — Saltonstall, Eaton, and their friends — or the Lincolnshire group, was responsible. When they came to discuss the transfer, it appeared that Matthew Cradock, the Governor of the Company, could not or would not emigrate, although he would and did provide money generously. Nor would any Assistant take the governorship. The principal persons who wished to emigrate with the charter agreed that the one man for that position was John Winthrop, and that without him they would not go.

However justified this decision was, it is still a mystery why Winthrop should have been selected as the leader. He was not a member of the Massachusetts Bay Company, nor related to any member. In the affairs of his county he does not appear to have been more prominent than any other squire or magistrate. But as attorney at the Court of Wards and Liveries, with an extensive clientage among county families, his acquaintance was wide; and we may therefore infer that the 'chief Undertakers' of the transfer had been impressed by his character and ability.

It took Winthrop some time to make up his mind. Fortunately we can follow the arguments, pro and con as they presented themselves to him, and to others. One or more papers, with arguments for and against emigration, were circulated among leading puritans. John White had a copy, Winthrop a second, and Sir John Eliot a third, which John Hampden asked to borrow. Who besides Winthrop had a leading part in drafting these papers is uncertain; but the most detailed copy, containing 'Particular Considerations in the case of J: W:' [1] is found among Winthrop's papers, together with a letter from his friend and neighbor Robert Ryece, combating the idea of emigration. The gist of Ryece's arguments was that English puritans should stick together, and that Winthrop was too elderly (forty-one!) and gentle for the task. 'The Church and Common welthe heere... hathe more neede of your beste abyllytie in these dangerous tymes then any remote plantation.' 'Plantations ar for yonge men, that can enduer all paynes and hunger.' 'How harde wyll it bee for one browghte up amonge boockes and learned men to lyve in a barbarous place, where there is no learnynge and less cyvillytie.' And finally, he quoted John Smith's History of Virginia, to prove that good order was hard to maintain in a new settlement, and gospel order impossible.

Winthrop, like men in every age who felt the urge to pioneer, was not to be turned aside by timorous and prudent considerations. He felt an inward call to New England, which he was candid enough to admit came in part from personal ambition. For some years, one infers, Winthrop had felt a longing for some greater public service than his attorneyship and the local magistracy. He had drafted petitions to Parliament, and very likely had looked forward to becoming a member at the next election; but the King had decided to summon no more parliaments. 'If he should refuse this opportunitye' for New England, writes Winthrop of himself,

---

[1] Not John White, as the arguments used could not have been applied to his circumstances.

'that talent which God hath bestowed upon him for publike service, were like to be buried.' His means were straitened by losing his attorneyship, by half the family estate going to his boys; and keeping up with the Joneses of that day was repugnant to him, as we have seen. Mistress Winthrop and their three grown sons were keen to go. But beyond these personal considerations, Winthrop was deeply apprehensive of the future, in view of the recent fate of Protestant churches in Europe, and disgusted with social conditions at home. He longed to get away from the 'Ould England grown newe' of the ballad, from corruption in almost every phase of English life; to found a New England that would preserve the waning virtues of the old. This opportunity to lead a colony and shape it according to the word of God, was not one to be lost. He accepted the governorship.

The Massachusetts Bay Company, in the meantime, was holding its meetings in London, at the house of Governor Cradock or Deputy-Governor Goffe. At a General Court on July 28, 1629, 'Mr. Governour reade certain proposicions conceived by himselfe, that for the advancement of the plantacion, the inducing and encouraging persons of worth and qualitie to transplant themselves and famylyes thether, and for other weighty reasons therein contained, — to transferr the government of the plantacion to those that shall inhabite there, and not to continue the same in subordination to the Company heer, as now it is. This business occasioned some debate,' and the decision was postponed to the next General Court.

On the same day that this discussion was going on in London, John Winthrop and his brother-in-law Emmanuel Downing were riding north from Groton to visit the Lincoln family seat. His horse got into a soft spot in the fen country, and gave the future Governor a bad ducking; but fortunately he did not construe this accident as an omen of disaster. At Tattershall the whole question was threshed out with Johnson,

Humfry, and Dudley. These three accompanied Winthrop on his return journey. At Cambridge they met Increase Nowell and William Pynchon, stockholders who had been at the Company meeting, together with Saltonstall and William Vassall, who also were officers of the Company. I like to imagine that they met in some room of Emmanuel College, where Isaac Johnson had graduated and one of his brothers was still a student, together with Sir Richard Saltonstall's son and two sons of Thomas Dudley; and where John Harvard was just finishing his freshman year. On August 26, 1629, they signed and dated at Cambridge a compact, which with the Charter is the basis of the Commonwealth of Massachusetts:

It is fully and faithfully agreed amongst us, ... that ... we will be ready in our persons... to embarke for the said plantation by the first of March next, ... to the end to passe the seas (under God's protection) to inhabite and continue in New England. *Provided always*, that before the last of September next the whole government together with the patent for the said plantation be first by an order of court legally transferred and established to remain with us and others which shall inhabite upon the said plantation.

Six signers of this Cambridge Agreement reached London in time for the meeting of the General Court on August 29, summoned to decide upon the question of removal. After a long debate, say the records, Deputy-Governor Goffe put it to the question, as followeth: 'As many of you as desire to have the pattent and the government of the plantacion to be transferred to New England, soe as it may bee done legally, hold up your hands. So many as will not, hold upp *your* hands.' The ayes had it.

After this momentous decision events moved rapidly toward the founding of the Massachusetts colony. At a General Court on October 20, 1629, 'having received of extraordinary great commendacions of Mr. John Wynthrop, both for his integritie and sufficiencie, as being one every [way] well fitted and accomplished for the place of Governour,' he was so elected for the ensuing year.

Under Winthrop's lead in East Anglia, Saltonstall's in London, and White's in the West Country, preparations for the voyage moved so rapidly that the first ship sailed in February, 1630, and fourteen vessels of the fleet had cleared from England by June. In view of the long time it takes nowadays to prepare even a summit conference or a tercentennial, it seems almost incredible that in the slow-moving days of horse and sail, when even good roads were wanting, when the beef for a long voyage had to be bought on the hoof, and the corn on the stalk, only nine months were required to assemble sixteen vessels all found and sound, and a thousand colonists prepared in mind, body and estate for a fresh start in the New World. One would think that nine months would have been little enough, in that newspaperless age, even to make known the transfer proposition. It was, wrote one of these pioneers in his old age, 'as if a Royal Herald, through our Nation from Berwick to Cornwall had made Proclamation to summon and muster up volunteers to appear in New England for His Sacred Majesties Service, there to attend further orders.' Surely the proposed emigration had long been discussed in every puritan center; and, owing to the bad turn of events in church and state, thousands of puritans were 'r'aring to go.'

Almost the entire financial burden was shouldered by the actual colonists, so that the future planters would not suffer as the Pilgrim Fathers had, from servitude to English merchants. Members of the Company who did not wish to emigrate resigned whatever office in the Company they might hold; but Winthrop persuaded them not to withdraw their subscriptions from the joint stock, which was used for ships, supplies, and free passage for poor but desirable emigrants.

At this point I cannot refrain from quoting the English

historian, Arthur Percival Newton, who has made English colonization his lifelong study:

The Massachusetts migration was an event entirely without precedent in the modern world; Virginia, Newfoundland, and Guiana had attracted merely the adventurers and the needy; the Mayflower pilgrims, though later ages have glorified them, were too few in number, too humble in station, and too far removed from the main currents of English life to be of importance; but now sober, well-to-do men of middle age, to whom the spirit of adventure was entirely foreign, were contemplating a transfer of themselves, their families, and their goods to new homes across the seas, there to found not a colony, but a commonwealth.... Winthrop and White, guided as they felt by a Higher Power, were resolved upon a course that was new. The men of the future had their way and the great human stream was directed to the New England shore.

If the leaders of the Bay Colony were idealists, their handling of the practical details shows that they were no strangers to big business. The West Country emigrants embarked from Bristol and Plymouth; those from East Anglia, London, the Home Counties and the Midlands, from Southampton. Thus it was hoped to avoid the usual detention at the Downs, consuming stores and breeding sickness, while waiting for an easterly breeze. Master John Cotton, Vicar of St. Botolph's church at Boston, who accompanied the Lincolnshire group to Southampton, there preached the farewell sermon on the text of 2 Samuel VII, 10: 'Moreover I will appoint a place for my people Israel, and will plant them, that they may dwell in a place of their own, and move no more; neither shall the children of wickedness afflict them any more, as beforetime.'

A most interesting and significant sermon it was, striking the notes of faith, learning, conversion, public spirit, and righteousness, which make the puritan scale. Master Cotton must have made the hearts of his hearers swell with that radiant joy that comes to the devout of every faith, when they feel that God is with them. He rehearsed all the arguments for the New England colony, which we have already

heard. He begged the emigrants to take root in the ordinances of God, when the Lord would make them a fruitful
vineyard. 'Goe forth, every man that goeth, with a publick
spirit,' with that 'care of universall helpfulnesse' which was
so strong in the primitive church. 'Have a tender care... to
your children, that they doe not degenerate as the Israelites
did.' 'Offend not the poore Natives, but as you partake in
their land, so make them partakers of your precious faith.'
And forget not Old England: — 'Oh pray for the peace of
Jerusalem, they shall prosper that love her.... Forget not the
wombe that bore you and the breasts that gave you sucke.
Even ducklings hatched under an henne, though they take
the water, yet will still have recourse to the wing that hatched
them: how much more should chickens of the same feather,
and yolke?'

It is pleasant to record that the point pressed home with
this farmyard simile, has penetrated so deeply that the
people of Boston in New England have helped to restore the
stately church of St. Botolph, where John Cotton served as
Vicar until he, too, emigrated.

Cotton's sermon was of a nature to inspire these new children of Israel with the belief that they were the Lord's chosen
people; destined, if they kept the covenant with him, to people and fructify this new Canaan in the western wilderness.

What hee hath planted he will maintaine. Every plantation his
right hand hath not planted shalbe rooted up, but his owne plantation shall prosper and flourish. When he promiseth peace and
safety, what enemies shall be able to make the promise of God of
none effect? Neglect not walls and bulwarkes, and fortifications
for your owne defence; but ever let the Name of the Lord be your
strong Tower; and the word of his Promise, the Rocke of your
Refuge. His word that made heaven and earth will not faile, till
heaven and earth be no more.

In the course of the voyage, Governor Winthrop delivered
a sermon entitled 'A Modell of Christian Charity' in which he

struck with even greater emphasis the note of public spirit
already sounded by John Cotton; and called it by the deeper
and better name of Love. 'We are a company,' he said, 'pro-
fessing ourselves fellow members of Christ,' for which reason
though we come from many regions and divers classes, 'we
ought to account ourselves knitt together by this bond of
love.' Our immediate object is to seek out a new home 'under
a due forme of Government both civill and ecclesiasticall.'
Hence 'the care of the publique must oversway all private
respects.... The end is to improve our lives to do more service
to the Lord... that ourselves and posterity may be the better
preserved from the common corruptions of this evil world.'

How may this be effected? First and foremost by love.
'Wee must love brotherly without dissimulation; wee must
love one another with a pure hearte fervently. We must bear
one another's burdens.' For 'we are entered into a covenant'
with God 'for this worke. We have taken out a Commission;
the Lord hath given us leave to draw our own Articles... If
the Lord shall please to heare us, and bring us in peace to the
place wee desire, then hath hee ratified this Covenant and
sealed our Commissions, [and] will expect a strict perform-
ance of the Articles contained in it.' But if we fail him, 'the
Lord will surely breake out in wrathe against us.'

Now the onely way to avoyde this shipwracke, and to provide
for our posterity, is to followe the counsell of Micah, to doe justly,
to love mercy, to walke humbly with our God. For this end, wee
must be knitt together in this work as one man... Soe shall wee
keepe the unitie of the spirit in the bond of peace... Wee shall finde
that the God of Israell is among us, when tenn of us shall be able to
resist a thousand of our enemies; when hee shall make us a prayse
and glory that men shall say of succeeding plantations, 'the lord
make it like that of NEW ENGLAND.' For wee must Consider
that wee shall be as a Citty upon a hill. The eies of all people are
uppon Us, soe that if wee shall deale falsely with our god in this
worke wee have undertaken, and soe cause him to withdrawe his
present help from us, wee shall be made a story and a by-word

through the world... Therefore lett us choose life, that wee and our seede may live by obeyeing his voyce and cleaveing to him, for hee is our life and our prosperity.

Herein is the clearest statement we have of the principles that guided the leaders of the Bay Colony, and their conception of the sort of commonwealth they were to found. It explains much that followed, both good and bad, in the early history of Massachusetts. We need not expect men who believe that they have a commission directly from God, to be eager to share their responsibility or power with others. We should not look to them to be tolerant of other points of view, to suffer the foxes to spoil the vines which they have tenderly planted. The rights of the individual they will hold as nothing in the scales against the public interest, as they conceive it. King Charles I, too, believed in his divine commission. John Winthrop will serve his people according to his lights, and serve them well; but he will make some of the same mistakes as those of his sovereign.

From the high seriousness of this sermon, we may turn to the tender affection in John Winthrop's farewell letter to his wife, who remained behind to care for Groton Manor until it could be sold.

My faithful and dear wife, — It pleaseth God, that thou shouldst once againe heare from me before our departure, and I hope this shall come safe to thy hands, I know it wilbe a great refreshinge to thee. And blessed be his mercye, that I can write thee so gud newes, that we are all in verye gud health, and, havinge tryed our shipps entertainment now more then a weeke, we finde it agree very well with us, our boyes are well and cheerfull, and have no minde of home. They lye both with me, and sleepe as soundly in a rugge (for we use no sheets heer) as ever they did at Groton; and soe I doe my selfe, (I prayse God). the winde hath been against us this weeke and more; but this day it is come faire to the North, so as we are preparinge (by Gods assistance) to sett sayle in the morninge... And now (my sweet soule) I must once againe take my last farewell of thee in old England, It goeth verye neere to my heart to leave thee; but I know to whom I have committed thee, even to him who loves the much better that any husband can ... and (if it be for his glorye) will bringe us togither againe with peace and comfort. oh, how it refreseheth my heart, to thinke, that I shall yet againe see thy sweet face in the lande of the livinge — that lovely countenance, that I have so much delighted in, and beheld with so great contente! ... I hope, the course we have agreed upon wilbe some ease to us both. mundayes and frydayes, at 5: of the clocke at night, we shall meet in spiritt till we meet in person. yet, if all these hopes should faile, blessed be our God, that we are assured we shall meet one day, if not as husband and wife, yet in a better condition, let that staye and comfort thy heart. neither can the sea drowne thy husband, nor enemyes destroye, nor any adversity deprive thee of thy husband or children. therefore I will onley take thee now and my sweet children in mine armes, and kisse and embrace you all, and so leave you with my God. Farewell, farewell...

Thine wheresoever   JO: WINTHROP.

from Aboard the Arbella,
    rydinge at the Cowes march 28, 1630.

Winthrop's journal, the most precious chronicle of the Bay Colony, begins the next day with this entry: 'Easter Monday. Riding at the Cowes, near the Isle of Wight, in the *Arbella*, a ship of three hundred and fifty tons, whereof Capt. Peter Milbourne was master, being manned with fifty-two seamen, and twenty-eight pieces of ordnance.' She was a stout, well-found ship, larger than the average emigrant vessel, and as the *Eagle* had seen hard service as a privateer of Sir Kenelm Digby. She was the admiral or flagship of a fleet of four (the *Talbot*, *Ambrose*, and *Jewel*) which decided to set forth together, leaving the other seven to follow as soon as might be. The last Court of Assistants of the Company to be held in England, had a few days before assembled in the *Arbella's* cabin. Winds came westerly, and it was ten days more before they got clear of the Isle of Wight; as late as April 6 ex-Governor Cradock came aboard at Yarmouth for a farewell visit, and was given a parting salute from the ship's battery.

The next day, presumably, Master John White arrived to get his 'Humble Request' signed 'on the dotted line'; since that charming if somewhat deceptive farewell to the Reverend Brethren of the Church of England is dated 'from Yarmouth aboord the *Arbella*, April 7, 1630.' The Lady Arbella Johnson herself was on board, with the Squire her husband; as well as Master George Phillips, who became the first minister of Watertown, the Saltonstall, Dudley, and Bradstreet families, William Pynchon, with some score of humbler folk, and numerous horses and cattle. Even the family dogs were not forgotten, for we hear of a settler the next winter, swapping his pup with an Indian for a peck of corn. It is not likely that they brought much furniture other than a favorite chair or two; for there would have been no room for massive court cupboards or four-posters, and no economy in bringing tables and settles which could easily be made from New England pine. But there must have been many household utensils in pottery, pewter, iron, brass, and silver, irreplaceable in a new country.

We may suppose that the voyage was a 'pious and Christian-like passage' such as Higginson had enjoyed the year before on the *Talbot*, with morning and evening prayer, two sermons every Sabbath, and the watches changed 'with singing a psalm, and prayer that was *not* read out of a book.'

There was plenty of excitement as well, since war was still on with France. Many other vessels were sighted, and some were spoken. The *Arbella* was cleared for action when eight sail, supposed to be corsairs of Dunkirk, hove in sight. Cannon were well charged, women and children placed amidships, while each man ground his cutlass to a razor edge and prepared for rough work. On the return voyage three of the Winthrop fleet 'were set upon by Dunkirkers' in the English Channel, and badly mauled; but on this occasion the ships proved to be peaceable merchantmen. Later a small Frenchman scuttled off before the wind when the *Arbella* put forth her 'ancient' (ensign), and the *Jewel* and *Ambrose* almost picked a quarrel with a friendly Dutchman, thinking him French. Two ships were spoken bound for Quebec, which the English had taken the previous summer; and Captain Milbourne went aboard for a conference.

Transatlantic voyages were unpleasant at best, in the short-ended high-pooped vessels of that day: six to twelve weeks tossing at sea amid the effluvia of men and cattle in crowded quarters; but the voyage of the *Arbella*, by Winthrop's account, was better than the average. Three of the four ships were usually within sight and hail, so that boats passed back and forth in calm weather, dinners were exchanged, and on one important occasion the *Arbella* borrowed a midwife from the *Jewel*. There was plenty of fun aboard. After the first gale a line was stretched from the steerage to the mainmast, and the seasick who 'lay groaning in the cabins' were fetched out on deck and required to 'sway it up and down till they were warm, and by this means they soon grew well and merry.' Games and horse-play with the seamen kept the young people's minds off their stomachs, and they 'gave themselves to drink hot waters very immoderately.' A maid-servant took so much of this seasick cure that she passed out, and all but away. After passing Cape Sable they were becalmed in thirty fathoms, so the *Arbella* was hove to 'and took, in less than two hours, with a few hooks, sixty-seven codfish, most of them very great fish, some a yard and a half long, and a yard in compass.' Did the Governor consult his conscience as well as his yardstick before he handed down that yarn to posterity?

On June 8, just two months out, the *Arbella*, now alone, raised the bald summits of Mount Desert. It was one of those heaven-sent June days in the Gulf of Maine, with clear sunshine, light fleecy clouds, and an off-shore wind: 'so pleasant a sweet air as did much refresh us, and there came a smell off the shore like the smell of a garden.' The *Arbella* proceeded cautiously, picking up landmarks like the Camden Hills. On June 10, Cape Porpoise and Agamenticus were sighted, and Boon Island weathered. The next day she stood off and on between Cape Ann and the Isles of Shoals, waiting for a southwest gale to moderate. In the night Cape Ann was weathered, and at daybreak on June 12 Marblehead loomed up on the western horizon. The *Arbella* fired two guns, sent her fast rowing skiff ahead, and received a visit from Isaac Allerton, on his way down east in a fishing shallop. Then with colors streaming and sails bellying to a light easterly breeze, she fanned through the main ship channel between Baker's Island and Little Misery, a stately and beautiful sight. Having reached good shelter and holding ground off Mingo Beach or Plum Cove, she came to an anchor for the first time since leaving soundings in the channel of old England.

Governor Endecott came aboard in the early afternoon, to learn that he was no longer governor; and while the gentry were rowed three miles to Salem, to sup on 'a good Venison pasty and good beer' the rest of the passengers landed on the near-by Beverly shore to feast on delicious wild strawberries, a heaven-sent refreshment after eight weeks of ship diet. The next day Masconomo, sagamore of Agawam, came aboard to pay his respects and see what he could pick up; and on June 14 the *Arbella* was warped up Beverly Harbor to a final anchorage in the North River, then Salem's front door.

The *Lion* was already there, the *Mary and John* had dumped her passengers at Nantasket; and one by one the rest of the fleet straggled in — the *Talbot* taking three months, and losing fourteen passengers. By the end of the summer almost a thousand people and two hundred head of cattle had been landed. The Bay Colony was already thrice as populous as New Plymouth, founded ten years earlier.

A preliminary exploration convinced Winthrop and the Assistants of the Company that Boston Bay should be the center of population and government rather than Salem. Charlestown, where a settlement had been started under Endecott's order the year before, was selected as the temporary capital. In the old minute book of the Massachusetts Bay Company, following the record of the last Court of Assistants held in England on March 23, 1630, there comes, in Simon Bradstreet's hand, that of the first Court of Assistants held on the soil of Massachusetts, at Charlestown on August 23. Governor Winthrop, Deputy-Governor Dudley, Sir Richard Saltonstall, Roger Ludlow, Edward Rossiter, Increase Nowell, Thomas Sharpe, William Pynchon, and Simon Bradstreet, made up this first political assembly; and their first item of business was to provide house and maintenance for two ministers, George Phillips and John Wilson.

The transfer of the charter was completed; the trading company of the Massachusetts Bay was dead; the Commonwealth of Massachusetts was born.

3. GOVERNOR OF THE MASSACHUSETTS

To tell the story of the rest of John Winthrop's life would be to relate the history of the Bay Colony until his death in 1649. During nine of those nineteen years he was properly addressed as 'The Right Worshipful John Winthrop, Esquire, Governour of the Massachusetts'; and during the other ten years he served as Deputy-Governor or Assistant. At all times he was a most devoted public servant, neglecting his private affairs to the ruin of his estate, and during the critical first winter his faith, energy, and steadfastness kept the colony together.

Governor Winthrop intended to form a compact settlement protected by a fort, at Newtowne (Cambridge); but the multitude proved too great for him to shepherd into one fold. There were many pleasant places on the harbor, and along the winding valleys of the Charles and Mystic. Medford, Watertown, Roxbury, Dorchester, and Lynn were founded before the winter set in. Owing to lack of fresh water at Charles-town, several of the magnates accepted an invitation of William Blaxton of Beacon Hill, a solitary survivor of the Gorges colony, to move over to Shawmut or Trimountain; and the Court of Assistants 'ordered that Trimountaine shalbe called Boston' on September 7. The first General Court summoned since the transfer of the charter was held there the following month in order to reëlect the officers, whose terms had expired.

During the first winter there was much sickness and suffering. The people arrived too late to plant a crop, and the months that followed were critical indeed. Busy months for Winthrop, but sad, for his son Henry was drowned shortly after the arrival, and some of his nearest and dearest friends fell victims to disease and hardship. Endecott's plantation at Salem had been weakened from sickness, and had little provision to spare. The Indians' supplies were inadequate; and though Samuel Maverick, the Episcopalian proprietor of Winnesimmet, 'a man of very loving and curteous behaviour, very ready to entertaine strangers,' did what he could, there was a limit to the hospitality that he and the old planters could offer. So the people lived largely on the salt junk and hard-tack left over from the voyage. One hundred and eighty indented servants had to be turned loose to fend for themselves.

'It was not accounted a strange thing in those days to drink water, and to eat samp or hominy without butter or milk,' remembered Roger Clap. Smelt, clams, and mussels kept many from actual starvation; but the Englishman of that period considered himself starving without beef, bread and beer; and even to-day, if you will try a steady diet of shellfish and spring water for a week, you may feel some sympathy for these puritan colonists bereft of their stout British fare. Scurvy set in, and a contagious fever, probably typhus. Young Lady Arbella died, and her husband Isaac

Johnson, not yet thirty: 'a holy man and wise, and died in sweet peace, leaving some part of his substance to the colony.' He was buried in what is now the King's Chapel burying ground in Boston; and such love had he inspired among the people in the short months he had been with them, that for years after Bostonians would direct that their bodies might be laid as near his as might be. Biting cold set in Christmas Eve; and many of the people were yet inadequately housed, living and dying in bark wigwams or sailcloth tents, 'soe that almost in every family, lamentation, mourning and woe was heard, and no fresh food to be had to cherish them.'

We are fortunate to have the 'low-down' on the situation, in a letter from a Suffolk yeoman to his father.

Her is good stor of feishe ife we had botes to goo 8 or 10 leges to sea to feishein. her are good stor of weield foule but they ar hard to come bye. It is hardur to get a shoot then it is in ould eignland... The cuntrey is not so as we ded expecte it tharefor lovinge father I wolld intret you that you woolld send me a ferckeine of buttr & a hogseit of mault onground for we dreinck notheinge but walltre ...we do not know how longe we may subseiste for we can not live her witheought provisseyenes from ould eignland... beseides God hath tacken away the chefeiste stud in the land, Mr Johnson & the ladye arabella his wife wiche wase the cheiffeste man of estate in the land & on that woold a don moste good.

There was much discontent among the common sort, who found it more difficult to adjust themselves than the gentry, and were probably less moved by religious motives. The hired servants made trouble, as they always do in a new country. One such named Ratcliffe, for 'foul, scandalous invectives against our church and government,' was whipped, cropped, and was banished, *pour encourager les autres*. Similar punishment, together with branding and life imprisonment, was at the time being inflicted by Star Chamber for like utterances against Laud.

The month of February, 1631, just before this discouraging letter was written, was the worst time. According to the writer there was some bad profiteering: £5 for a pig and £3 for a goat, but there was charity as well. The Governor gave freely of what he had. His last batch of bread was in the oven, and his last handful of meal given away to a poor man, when a relief ship appeared. This was the *Lion*, which the Governor had prudently sent back to Bristol for provisions; and which had been well stocked by the devoted efforts of John White and other friends of the colony. Her arrival was the occasion for a February thanksgiving day. She brought a quantity of lemon juice which cured the scurvy, and her cargo of grain, peas and barrelled beef was distributed among the several towns, at the Company's charge. Another ship with corn from Virginia, and one or two from Ireland, with all kind of provision, ended the shortage by planting time, and a good crop was put in that spring. Many discouraged settlers returned in these ships, and of them 'many died by the way and after they were landed.'

Only a few hundred persons came to Massachusetts Bay in 1631 and 1632, but the following year the full tide of the Great Emigration set in; Boston harbor frequently contained ten or a dozen ships at a time bearing recruits for the puritan Canaan. For in 1633 William Laud, from a position of great influence, was promoted to one of great power as well — the Archbishopric of Canterbury. Ritualism was now forced on every parish, puritan tracts were suppressed, more puritan lecturers silenced, and the gentry forbidden to keep chaplains. Archbishop Laud was even more efficient than the Massachusetts authorities proved to be, in enforcing a superficial uniformity. He succeeded in stopping up every hole, save emigration, through which puritan feeling could find vent; so many puritans emigrated and others bided their time. By 1643 there were a score of towns and churches in the jurisdiction of Massachusetts Bay, with over sixteen thousand people, more than all the rest of English America put together.

Edward Johnson in his 'Wonder Working Providence of Sions Saviour in New England' computes the total cost of this Great Emigration as £192,000 — in purchasing power equivalent to something between ten and twenty million dollars to-day. The original stockholders of the Company contributed a small part of this sum, charitable persons gave much; but the most was paid out by the settlers themselves. 'Gentle Reader,' asks Johnson, 'where had this poore people this great sum of money? the mighty Princes of the Earth never opened their Coffers for them, and the generality of these men were meane and poore in the things of this life, but sure it is the work is done, let God have the glory, who hath now given them food to the full, and some to spare for other Churches.'

The transfer of the charter did not give the Bay Colony a completely workable government; only a bare framework, and practical independence. Fourteen years were required for the complete evolution of the government from that of trading corporation to commonwealth. The government thus established was not a democracy, and was not intended to be; but the puritan builders left out of their foundations two principles of government, the feudal and the hereditary, upon which democracy had always found it difficult to raise a house. They made no attempt to establish manors, as did the proprietors of Carolina, Maryland, and New York. Nor did they admit the least hereditary element into their government. In 1635 Lord Say and Sele, Lord Brook, and other persons of quality in the puritan party proposed, as the conditions of their removal, that the commonwealth of Massachusetts should consist of two ranks of men, gentlemen and freeholders, the former constituting an hereditary colonial House of Lords, and the latter electing a House of Commons. The Massachusetts magistrates wanted badly such men as these. Like other Englishmen they dearly loved a lord, especially when he combined social eminence with puritan orthodoxy. They instructed John Cotton to reply in the name of the government, that although it was the custom of the country — a country barely six years old! — to regard such men as the gentry, as well as 'others of meaner estate' who showed their worth; and although the Colony would be glad to elect to office any member of a 'noble or generous family with a spirit and gifts fit for government,' yet 'if God should not delight to furnish some of their posterity with gifts fit for magistracy' it would not be proper 'if we should call them forth, when God hath not, to public authority.' Their lordships took the hint, and did not emigrate.

However, the point of departure for this rejection of the heredity principle was not democracy, but godliness. As we have seen from Winthrop's shipboard sermon, the leaders of the emigration, already invested with authority as Assistants of the Company, conceived that they had a divine commission to govern the Colony according to gospel ordinance. They did not propose to share this authority any further than circumstances required. The charter, to be sure, established a definite form of government and definite days of election: the Governor, Deputy-Governor and eighteen Assistants must be annually elected by the General Court, consisting of all freemen or stockholders of the Corporation; and the freemen, in General Court, had the supreme legislative power. But what is a charter between friends? It so happened that no freeman of the Company who was not also an Assistant, crossed in the Winthrop fleet. Hence the first government assembly on the American side of the Atlantic was a Court of Assistants at Charlestown. This court took a very important step to enhance its power individually and collectively. It appointed six of its nine members to be magistrates or judges, 'in all things to have the like power that justices of the peace hath in England for reformacion of abuses and punishing of offenders,' and it soon became the practice to consider every Assistant, when elected, a magistrate *ex officio*.[1] At the next meeting of the Court of Assistants it assumed supreme judicial power, in sentencing Thomas Morton to deportation. At the first meeting of the General Court, consisting of exactly six Assistants beside the two chief magistrates, it was decided, in direct violation of charter terms, that the Governor and Deputy-Governor be elected out of the Assistants, by the Assistants. In other words, the first Board of Assistants, not one half of the legal number, arrogated to themselves complete legislative, executive, and judicial power. And for the first four years of the settlement they exercised it.

This governing oligarchy, with Winthrop at its head, showed a keen political sense in knowing when and how far to yield its power; and every concession had to be purchased at a heavy price. The first was in the matter of extending the body of freemen, who annually elected the Assistants. At the meeting of the General Court in October, 1630, over one hundred settlers, both old planters and new, demanded the franchise. Winthrop saw perfectly well that they could not be denied. Accordingly these and a few others were enfranchised the following May. But at the same time the Court declared that no one in future could be a freeman or voter, unless a church member. And a church member, as understood by the polity already established in Salem, meant not merely a church goer, or member of a parish, but a communicant, admitted only after he had satisfied the brethren that he was one of the 'visible saints.' Thus the electors were limited to God's elect: a logical restriction for the Bible Commonwealth that Winthrop intended to found. 'Do ye not know that the Saints shall judge the world? (1. Cor. vi, 2),' as John Cotton observed to Lord Say and

---

[1] For this reason I shall follow the seventeenth-century practice of using the terms Assistant and Magistrate interchangeably.

Sele, 'and Solomon maketh it the joy of a commonwealth, when the righteous are in authority.'

This ghostly qualification for the franchise lasted until 1664, though it did not apply to local government after 1647, or to the portions of Maine and New Hampshire annexed to Massachusetts Bay between 1639 and 1658. Church-member suffrage was the rock on which the Bible Common-wealth was built; and the only movement to widen the franchise, the remonstrance of Robert Child, was promptly suppressed. In a sense, however, this sort of franchise was democratic, for it made no account of social standing or estate. Many poor men, who needed charity to live, became freemen because they fulfilled the religious qualification; while rich men who could not get a church to take them in, were left without the vote. Narrow as the franchise was, it cut through the community vertically, not horizontally.

The first body of Visible Saints thus honored with the vote were not content merely to elect the Assistants. At the annual election in 1632, the latter were forced to allow them to elect the Governor and Deputy-Governor as well; and in 1635 they extorted the right to use secret paper ballots. Grains of Indian corn for the *ayes* and beans for the *noes* were substituted in 1644 for paper ballots, and the freemen were encouraged to vote at home in their respective towns; but they much preferred to vote in person at Boston on the 'last Wednesday in Easter terme' (the day before Ascension) as the charter prescribed; and Election Day became a sort of spring holiday for the Colony. The freemen assembled at the town house (on the site of the Old State House), listened to an election sermon, dropped their corn or beans or papers in the ballot box, and delivered the sealed-up ballots from the towns to be counted. As the maximum vote cast by this very select electorate was never more than a few hundred, the result was soon announced. The Governor, Deputy-Governor and Assistants for the ensuing year were sworn in, and the Great and General Court opened its session. Spring became so firmly associated with elections in the New England mind, that the date was not essentially changed in Massachusetts until 1831. Even now there is a survival of the old spring election in the anniversary week of the Congregational clergy, and in the annual drumhead election of a commander for the Ancient and Honorable Artillery Company, on Boston Common.

It must not be supposed that this annual election was agreeable to John Winthrop and the Magistrates. It was simply a necessity which the plain terms of the charter, and the wishes of the freemen imposed upon them. John Cotton, who came over in 1633, strongly supported their idea of government as a sacred stewardship, and preached an election sermon to the effect that magistrates once elected should never be defeated save for just cause. The freemen promptly repudiated this doctrine by electing Thomas Dudley governor for the ensuing year. Winthrop put a good face on it, and invited the new governor and assistants to the banquet which had been prepared at his house [1] for a different administration. Magnanimity toward opponents was one of Winthrop's most attractive traits. Roger Williams he attempted to shield, and his friendship retained. In his Journal much evil is recorded in sadness, but nothing in malice. Sir Harry Vane, the figurehead of the Antinomian controversy, 'showed himself a true friend to New England, and a man of noble and generous mind.' Thomas Dudley was 'a very wise and just man, and one that would not be trodden under foot by any man.'

Dudley had the privilege of presiding over the first Massachusetts legislature that contained elected representatives of the freemen, and not merely assistants. This was a serious breach in the exclusive power of the magistracy. Watertown,

[1] A few doors down State Street from the Old State House, on the site of the Exchange Building. Later he built a house on the site of the Old South meeting-house, Washington Street.

which seems to have contained more upstanding lovers of liberty than any other of the first settlements, objected to a tax levy made by assistants alone. Master George Phillips, the minister, and elder Richard Browne assembled the people and declared 'that it was not safe to pay moneys after that sort, for fear of bringing themselves and posterity into bondage.' So soon had the echoes of Runnymede reached the New England forest. In consequence they were haled before Winthrop, admonished and silenced, but not convinced. The Governor and his colleagues, as a gracious concession, then invited each town to appoint members of an advisory committee on taxation. The freemen, not to be put off with such chaff, chose deputies just before the spring election of 1634, and respectfully requested the Governor to give them a look at the Charter, which hitherto had been carried about on state occasions in its large leather-covered case, to impress the populace. (It did not impress Morton of Merrymount, who declared that the vulgar sort of people took it for a musical instrument, and guessed that the Governor had been a fiddler in his youth!) Winthrop yielded. One can imagine the deputies poring over the parchment, wading heavily through its redundant phraseology, and finally with a shout of triumph finding just what they expected to find:

... Greate and Generall Courts of the saide Company: In all and every, or any of which saide Greate and Generall Courts soe assembled, Wee doe for Us, our heires and successors, give and graunte to the said Governor and Company and their successors ... to make lawes and ordinances for the good and welfare of the saide Company, and for the government and ordering of the saide landes and plantation, and the people inhabiting and to inhabite the same, as to them from tyme to tyme shalbe thought meete. soe as such lawes and ordinances be not contrarie or repugnant to the lawes and statutes of this our realme of England.

That little visit to the Governor's house punctured the legislative power of the oligarchy. The deputies of the freemen took their seats in the General Court, sitting as one house with the Assistants, and pushed through three important resolutions, which may be said to have founded representative government in Massachusetts Bay:

That none but the Generall Court hath power to chuse and admitt Freemen.

That none but the Generall Court hath power to make and establishe lawes, nor to elect and appoynct officers...

That none but the Generall Court hath power to rayse moneyes and taxes and to dispose of lands....

In the meantime, trouble had begun within the Board of Assistants. It was due to a practice which the puritans believed to be enjoined by the Epistles of St. Paul, of calling each other to account for their faults, and speaking their minds without the tact and reticence usual in personal intercourse among gentlemen. Deputy-Governor Dudley, an energetic old soldier some ten years Winthrop's senior, early became obsessed with the idea that the Governor was too soft, evasive, and lenient. Early in 1632 he offered to resign his position, 'because he must needs discharge his conscience in speaking freely; and he saw that bred disturbance.' The Assistants denied his right to resign, and Winthrop, with amazing tactlessness, proceeded to call his colleague to account for selling seven and a half bushels of corn to poor men, in return for ten to be paid at the next harvest; and for building at Newtowne what he regarded as a luxurious house. 'There arose hot words about it.' Dudley justified himself and called the Governor weak, speeches which (says Winthrop) he bore 'with more patience than... upon a like occasion, at another time.'

The storm subsided at dinner, but arose again when Winthrop announced that the time had come to let the freemen choose Governor and Deputy-Governor and not merely the Assistants. At that Roger Ludlow, one of the West Countrymen of Dorchester 'grew into passion, and said that then we should have no government,'—he would return to England if they allowed such a thing. Then another squabble, about the men of Watertown being compelled to watch and ward at Newtowne. 'Thus the day was spent and no good done, which was the more uncomfortable to most of them, because they had commended this meeting to God in more earnest manner than ordinarily at other meetings.' What a New England small-town flavor the whole session has, even as Winthrop tells it!

Seven days later Dudley consented to withdraw his resignation, 'and the governor and he being reconciled the day before, all things were carried very lovingly amongst all.' But the love did not last long. A little meeting was arranged between the three chief officers, the secretary of the Colony (Increase Nowell), and four ministers. First, the matter of the Governor's removing the frame of his house from Newtowne to Boston, was threshed out. Then Dudley brought in a series of charges to the effect that Winthrop had of his own authority, without vote of the Court of Assistants, lent twenty-eight pounds of powder to Plymouth, had allowed Watertown to erect a fish weir, had allowed the crop-eared and banished Ratcliffe to stay until spring (when a winter departure would have probably lost him his life); and a few similar acts of tyranny. Hot words passed again, counter-charges, and the ministers apparently had some difficulty to restrain these pillars of the state from coming to blows. The best that could be done for the present was to agree to disagree. In the end, however, the two became reconciled over the marriage of their children, and sealed it in a manner that reveals the vein of tenderness in the Puritan heart:

The governor and deputy went to Concord to view some land for farm, and, going down the river about four miles, they made choice of a place for one thousand acres for each of them... The governor yielded him the choice. So, at the place where the Deputy's land was to begin, there were two great stones, which they called the Two Brothers, in remembrance that they were brothers by their children's marriage, and did so brotherly agree, and for that a little creek near those stones was to part their lands.

Canoeists on the placid Concord may still see, on the Bedford side, the two boulders which mark the reconciliation of these founders of the Commonwealth.

If the Assistants' assumed duty to be their brothers' keepers produced unedifying scenes in their worshipful Court, they were as a unit when their collective power was called into question. A very tender point was their assumption of magisterial powers. An incident which Winthrop does not mention in his journal, no doubt because he realized it did him small credit, is in a letter of Israel Stoughton, deputy from Dorchester. When the first deputies were admitted to the General Court, in 1634, the Assistants, by a rather doubtful construction of the Charter, claimed a 'negative voice' or veto on the deputies' decisions, as if an upper house; while the deputies naturally wished to make their superior numbers felt in a unicameral assembly — like the *tiers état* at the opening of the French Revolution. A pro-magisterial sermon by John Cotton bore them down for a time, and the matter rested. Israel Stoughton then drew up a brief against the 'negative voice.' It was passed around among the ministers, and by Cotton sent to Winthrop, then Deputy-Governor. At the next General Court Winthrop, to Stoughton's astonishment, denounced him as a 'worme,' a 'troubler of Israel,' 'an underminder of the state'; and accused him of having declared that the Assistants were ministers with no discretional authority, not magistrates.

Stoughton demanded that his brief be read to disprove the charge. He observed that the meaning had been perverted for want of a comma. Stoughton then read it aloud himself, and brought out what he really had said, that the Assistants' authority was both ministerial and magisterial, but not arbitrary. Nothing would satisfy the Assistants, however, but to have the brief burned. 'Let the booke be burnt if that pleases them,' said Stoughton, and burnt it was. Still the Assistants were not satisfied, Ludlow and Winthrop returning to the charge, and insisted that Stoughton, for sedition, be disqualified for office for three years. The deputies, still somewhat surprised at their own audacity in getting into the General Court, weakly submitted, and Stoughton was disqualified. But general feeling was that both Ludlow and Winthrop had 'too much forgott and over shott' themselves; and in the election of 1636 John Haynes was chosen governor, Ludlow defeated as assistant, and Winthrop chosen to the board by a much reduced vote. 'He is indeed a man of men,' concludes Stoughton. 'But he is but a man; and some say they have idolized him, and do now confesse their error. My opinion is... that he is a godly man, and a worthy Magistrate notwithstanding some few passages at which some have stumbled.'

The matter of the negative voice came to a head a few years later, over the *cause célèbre* of Goody Sherman and her stray sow. This poor widow accused Robert Keayne, a wealthy and grasping merchant, of having impounded her errant swine, and sued him for recovery of lost property. Acquitted in the Court of Assistants, she appealed to the General Court (the supreme judicial as well as the supreme legislative assembly), which voted to reverse the judgment. The Assistants then claimed a negative on the appeal against themselves. The reverend clergy were called into consultation, the whole colony was in an uproar, and a forcible denial of negative voice was only prevented by the eloquence of Winthrop, on the ground that a unicameral legislature would be democratic. 'If we should change from a mixt aristocratie to a mere Democratie, first we should have no warrant in scripture for it: there was no such government in Israel... a Democratie is, amongst most civil nations, accounted the meanest and worst of all forms of government.' That

Massachusetts was not yet ripe for democracy may be conceded; but it must have been a sad outlook for the average Englishman in the Bay Colony to learn that no forms of government which were unknown to the ancient Hebrews would be permitted. However, Winthrop's speech had its effect; the negative voice was admitted; and the General Court separated into a House of Deputies and a House of Assistants. If, as is claimed, this was the first full-fledged bicameral legislature in the English colonies, a monument on Beacon Hill to Goody Sherman's sow, as the mother of Senates, would seem to be in order.

Throughout this controversy, two of the magistrates, Richard Saltonstall and Richard Bellingham, stood with the deputies against their own class. This occasioned much grief to Winthrop, and doubtless inflicted on them sundry repetitions of his shipboard sermon. Yet he took pains to record in his journal his belief that 'these gentlemen were such as feared God, and endeavoured to walk by the rule of his word' and 'in all those differences and agitations they continued in brotherly love' with their fellow magistrates, 'and in the exercise of all friendly offices to each other.'

By 1644, then, the transition of the Massachusetts Bay government from trading company to commonwealth was complete. The officers, originally intended to serve as president and board of directors of a joint-stock corporation, were now governor and executive council and upper house and superior court of justice of a colony. They were elected annually by the freemen, who were originally the stockholders of the company, and now the holders of a franchise determined by sanctity. A new representative body, the House of Deputies, had been created in order to obviate the necessity of personal attendance by the freemen to exercise their legislative rights. It was a typically English political compromise, satisfying nobody, expressing no logical system or consistent theory, yet working because it was composed of politically

minded Englishmen, ready to compromise their dearest con-
victions if only government might go on. This government
proved powerful enough to preserve Massachusetts independent of all outside control, to defend it from domestic and
foreign enemies, to regulate the economic life of the community, and to maintain law and order on the edge of the
wilderness.

In the development of American institutions, this re-
vamped trading company of the Massachusetts Bay was
momentous. For the transferred and transformed charter
proved so workable a constitution that other colonies, even
beyond New England, used it as a model; and in the American
revolution most of the thirteen colonies adopted state con-
stitutions on the same principle. The particular features
of this government which proved successful and enduring
were the election of all officials at stated intervals, and the use
of the ballot. It did not much matter that the Massachusetts
electorate was confined to members of the puritan churches;
that could be and was remedied later. The important thing
was that representatives, assistants, and the governor himself, had to go before the voters on a fixed day every year. In
contrast to the English or parliamentary system, this corporate mode of election put an almost continuous check on the
government. It became an essential principle of every state
constitution and of the federal constitution; and the ballot
enabled the freemen to exercise their rights without undue
publicity.

Despite these concessions in a democratic direction, the
Assistants, with their combined power as upper chamber,
court of appeals, and executive council, remained the most
powerful part of the Massachusetts government; and the
civil list of Assistants reads like the chronicle of Israel before
the flood. Although ten to fifteen were annually elected,
only thirty-five new names appear in forty-eight years.
John Winthrop was governor or assistant for nineteen years,

when he died. John Endecott was assistant or governor for twenty-three years, and governor for ten years more, when he died. Simon Bradstreet earned a promotion to the governorship by fifty years' faithful service on the Board of Assistants. He was nine times reëlected governor, but forced into premature retirement at the age of eighty-nine by the arrival of a new charter. It has often been wondered why the freemen, whose deputies often quarrelled with the Assistants, did not elect a new board. The probable answer lies in a complaint of the General Court in 1652, of the scarcity of persons 'fit for magistracie.' Men with the qualities, the education and the training for so many-sided an office were rare in a colony; and if the freemen of the Bay had set their faces toward democracy, they still wished to be governed by their best, not their average men.

Winthrop, who thought much on political science, submitted to popular participation in legislation, but always protested against 'referring matter of counsel or judicature to the body of the people, *quia* the best part is always the least, and of that best part the wiser part is always the lesser. The old law was, Choose ye out judges, etc., and thou shalt bring the matter to the judge, etc.' In the more democratic Connecticut, where men of little learning or judgment were elected to high office, Winthrop observed that the state business was actually done by the parsons, 'who, though they were men of singular wisdom and godliness, yet stepping out of their course, their actions wanted that blessing which otherwise might have been expected.' In his own 'Government of the Massachusetts' he was satisfied that there was a proper balance between the rights of the freemen and the authority of the magistrates; 'a mixt Aristocratie, and no wayes Arbitrary.'

Governor Winthrop was an intense patriot, and his country was New England. Massachusetts, a word uncouth to English ears, was not a word to conjure with in the seventeenth century. The people called themselves New Englanders, and their jurisdiction, the Bay. It was doubtless Winthrop's intention that the Bay take in all New England. He was bitterly disappointed that Haynes and Hooker set up a separate government for their river towns, when they emigrated to the Connecticut in 1635; but Hooker and Haynes found the polity of Massachusetts too oligarchical for their taste. When the Eaton and Davenport company came to Boston, the Court offered them practically any township or tract they might choose, in order to keep them in the Bay Colony; but Eaton and Davenport thought the government of Massachusetts too lax, and its trade too crowded; so they founded a theocracy and commercial center at New Haven.

Relations between 'the River' and 'the Bay' were not very pleasant for a number of years, William Pynchon's colony at Springfield being one of several bones of contention. Governor Winthrop received an angry epistle from Hooker accusing the Bay authorities of malice and hatred toward them in cramping the River Colony; of instructing innkeepers to 'entertain their guests with invectives against Connecticut,' of even sending out boats to immigrant ships in Boston harbor to tell the passengers what a terrible place Connecticut was. Winthrop replied in the most humorous letter we have from his pen. The picture of himself peddling anti-River propaganda through barroom and waterside gossip, evidently tickled his fancy. 'Your large and lovinge lettre... makes me a little merrye,' says he; but our Hartford friends, having opened the back door on the frontier, and invited all and sundry to that 'most fatt and pleasant country' must not take it amiss if the head of the Bay house endeavor to keep his family together, and prevent the lad who took the coat from getting the cloak too. 'We are brethren,' he continues in a more serious vein. 'One in consotiation, in the same worke of God, in the same community of perill'; then for God's sake, let us 'labor in peace and love.'

A solution of these ill-boding disputes was provided by the New England Confederation, the league of Bible commonwealths of which Winthrop was an architect. It is pleasant to record that after the first meeting at Boston to organize the Confederation, Thomas Hooker wrote 'to his much Honoured freind John Wyntropp [1] Esquier, Governor of the plantations on the Matcheshusets Bay,' a glowing expression of gratitude for his 'candid and cordiall cariage in a matter of so great consequence,' and his 'speciall prudence to settle a foundation of safety and prosperity in succeeding ages.' Herein we may discern the gift of prophecy descending on the doubting Thomas, for, if the New England Confederation did not survive the century, the federal principle did: and it is not the least of Winthrop's glories that he helped to bring into practice a principle of immeasurable benefit to these States, and of wide promise to the world.

In relations with the mother country, Winthrop would not brook the slightest interference with the charter, or the self-government of the Bay. As we shall see when we come to the remonstrance of Robert Child, Massachusetts Bay acted as a free state. When King Charles sent for the charter in 1634, and gave Gorges and Mason a commission to govern New England, Governor Winthrop mounted ordnance at the Castle, put the militia in a state of preparedness, and had the beacon constructed on Beacon Hill to arouse the country in case of invasion. During the English Civil War he maintained the neutrality of the Bay, and promptly punished the captain of a parliamentary privateer which fired on a royalist vessel in Boston Harbor. When certain members of Parliament offered to confer favors on Massachusetts, Winthrop persuaded the General Court to decline, lest by admitting Parliamentary jurisdiction over the colony an inconvenient precedent be established.

[1] This appears to have been the contemporary pronunciation of Winthrop. My late friend Henry H. Edes, a great stickler for traditional Boston pronunciation, always said Governor Wint'rop, John Hahv'd, John Eli't, and Funnel Hall.

He was particularly disturbed by the persistent efforts of the
Earl of Warwick and his associates to attract settlers from
the Bay to the Caribbean; and John Humfry, who lent himself to these schemes, was one toward whom Winthrop found
it most difficult to exercise Christian charity. Humfry was a
curious character. Though an original Dorchester Adventurer, active in promoting the emigration of 1630 and in sending relief ships, he soon began talking of removing the Massachusetts Bay colony further South. He was elected an Assistant even before emigrating, and received a good land grant
at Lynn, and belonged to the church; but was unsuccessful
and discontented, finally accepting the governorship of Warwick's island in the West Indies. Winthrop records in his
journal, that when the ship in which Humfry was returning
neared the English coast, several passengers spoke reproach-
fully of New England. Gales and tempests promptly arose,
and tossed them about, until, in imminent peril, they prayed
the Lord to pardon them for speaking ill of New England.
The prayers of Master George Phillips, who had wisely re-
frained from these revilings, saved them from being dashed
on the rocks, and brought them to the haven where they
would be. 'Yet the Lord followed them on shore,' says Winthrop. Some were forsaken by friends, one lost two children
by the plague, one of Humfry's daughters went mad, and two
others, both under ten years of age, were found to have been
'often abused by divers lewd persons, and filthiness in his
family.'

That is the kind of statement which flies up in your face
when you are beginning to think that the puritans were
pretty good fellows. It shows us what a chasm separates the
thoughts of even the best men of that time and persuasion,
from ourselves. Shall we laugh, or should we weep at the God
of John Winthrop, whose interest in New England prosperity is such that he raises a gale to drown the 'knockers,' de-
cides to save them because a good 'booster' is on board, and

then visits his wrath on their innocent children with the most revolting of crimes?

The puritans, taking literally some of the ill-tempered outbursts of the Hebrew prophets, and the parables and oriental imagery that Our Lord employed in his teaching, believed that every occurrence, however trivial or loathsome, was God's will. At the same time they conceived God as infinitely just. They craved to know God's will toward them and their commonwealth, and his opinion of the manner in which they were keeping the covenant. This case of the Humfry children caused the colony great scandal and shame. There were long conferences with the elders as to whether or not the criminals should suffer death by Mosaic law. Among others, Charles Chauncy, first scholar of his time at Cambridge, and a former fellow of Trinity, applied his mind to the problem. God must have permitted the crime; yet God was just. What could be the explanation? *For I the Lord, thy God, am a jealous God, visiting the sins of the fathers upon the children unto the third and fourth generation of them that hate me....*

Yet that conclusion was not inevitable for a sincere puritan. Governor Bradford of the Plymouth Colony, musing over this and other sexual outbreaks in New England, deduced three reasons for them: (1) the Devil was working hard to shame them; (2) ' — as it is with waters when their streames are stopped or dammed up, when they gett passage they flow with more violence... then when they are suffered to rune quietly in their owne chanels'; (3) ' — hear (as I am verily perswaded) is not more evills in this kind, nor nothing nere so many by proportion as in other places; but they are more discovered and seen and made publick by due serch, inquisition, and due punishment.' These common-sense conclusions, one must admit, stamp the self-educated Pilgrim as a man of greater breadth than the eminent Governor of the Bay. One feels the force in the remark of Thomas Hutchinson, a century later, that Winthrop 'was of a more catholic spirit than some of his brethren before he left England, but afterwards he grew more contracted.'

Undoubtedly Bradford's second reason was the correct one. The puritan standard of sexual morality was too high for the meaner sort of people. Early marriage and frequent child-bearing was a healthy outlet for the independent yeomen and gentry; but the indented servants, who caused almost all the trouble, were recruited from the brutish elements of a coarse age. Forbidden marriage while serving their time, and forced to heavy labor in the fields, they found an outlet where they could. Precisely the same sort of trouble occurred with the indented servants in Virginia, and for the same reason.

At this point I wish to take issue with Mr. James Truslow Adams' pronouncement that the puritans took a 'morbid interest in the most indecent sexual matters.' [1] If Winthrop and Bradford had passed over these events, leaving them to be discovered in the court records, our modern puritan-baiters would have enjoyed accusing them of concealment, hypocrisy, and 'ignoring the facts of life.' It seems hard that their frank human interest in such facts should be considered morbid. There was something more to it, however, than curiosity. The puritan chroniclers classed sexual outbreaks, monstrous births, and the like, with earthquakes and cyclones: regrettable phenomena to be reported along with the contrary evidence of God's favor. Puritan housewives do not sweep the dirt under the bed. Winthrop is not morbid and obscene, but simply natural and coarse like Shakespere, when he writes of a certain man: 'He was ripped out of his mother's belly, and never sucked, nor saw father nor mother, nor they him.'

Winthrop's superstition has also attracted the scorn of

---

[1] *Founding of New England*, p. 265, note. This was *à propos* stripping suspects for examination for marks of witchcraft, a part of the regular procedure against witches in all countries in the seventeenth century.

superior minds in later times. His stories of the snake which crept into the elders' seat at the Cambridge synod, and of the mice eating his son's Prayer-Book but respecting the Psalms and Greek Testament, have often been quoted to show what a petty and barbarous community Massachusetts must have been, when the mind of its chief magistrate worked that way. Superstition, like persecution and coarse language, was part and parcel of the age in which Winthrop lived, and he was no better nor worse than the average educated Englishman of the time. The University of Cambridge was all stirred up in 1626 by the discovery of a small book called 'A Preparation to the Cross' in the maw of a codfish. Samuel Ward, master of Sidney Sussex, thought 'it may be a special admonition to us at Cambridge,' and even Archbishop Ussher wrote, 'The incident is not lightly to be passed over.'

In his private affairs Governor Winthrop was not what New Englanders would call a good manager. He consistently neglected them for the public business. For many years he refused a salary, spending the proceeds of the sale of Groton Manor in public concerns, when there was no money in the colony treasury. He gave generous hospitality as befitted the station of chief magistrate, although so temperate in his own habits that his friends called his attention to Paul's precept to Timothy: 'drink no longer water, but use a little wine for thy stomach's sake.'

He was almost recklessly charitable, and died 'land poor.'

> What goods he had he did not spare;
>   The Church and Commonwealth
> Had of his Goods the greatest share,
>   Kept nothing for himself

declares Perciful Lowle with truth, in his 'Funeral Elegie on the Death of the Memorable and Truly Honourable John Winthrope Esq.'

A dishonest agent in England embezzled the Governor's property there; and a rascally steward of his Ten Hills estate on the Mystic, diverted to his own use the profits of the Governor's crops and cattle. Winthrop did not mind these losses at Ten Hills so much as the discovery, after the steward was sacked, that the neighbors had taken advantage of the man's unfaithfulness to make some very questionable bargains, which some of them insisted on carrying out to the letter. To Ezekiel Rogers, the minister of Rowley, he wrote on this subject, 'I suppose you intended me a Courtesye in offeringe to accept a heifer for your 2 Calves and 4 *l.*, and accordingly I desired Mr. Carlton to choose one for you; and I think if you value your Calves... of a weeke old at 5 *l.* or 6 *l.* (which is the most they can be worth) and my heifer (as I sould her fellowes before winter) at 13 *l.* you will find yourselfe mystaken, but that is a small matter between yourselfe and me.' One could hardly tell a parson more tactfully that he was a close bargainer.

Winthrop never appeared to better advantage than in one of those tempests in the colonial teapot, the Hingham militia affair. The town of Hingham, under the lead of the minister Peter Hobart and his three stout brothers, mutinied against an unpopular militia officer imposed on them by the Court. Winthrop was accused of exceeding his powers in dealing with the mutineers. Hingham petitioned the General Court against him, and a process equivalent to impeachment took place. As in the famous impeachments of history, the motives were political. Saltonstall, Bellingham, and a bare majority of the deputies, conceiving 'that the magistrates exercised two much power, and that the people's liberty was thereby in danger,' baffled by their defeat in the matter of the negative voice and in their efforts to get a definite law code adopted, were resolved to make an example of Winthrop. The rest, feeling that authority was too much slighted, that the existence of the colony was at stake, defended him. Winthrop left the bench, placed himself in the position of one on trial, and insisted that the whole thing be thrashed out, and a clean-cut decision be reached. He got it, because the Magistrates threatened to appeal to a clerical board of arbitration, and the deputies knew from past experience that the clergy would always uphold the magistrates, right or wrong.

So Winthrop was acquitted, and the chief petitioners and rioters fined. It must have been an impressive scene when Governor Dudley read the sentence in the crowded Boston meetinghouse, and Winthrop resumed his seat among his colleagues, and delivered himself of this 'little speech' on liberty:

I entreat you to consider, that when you choose magistrates, you take them from among yourselves, men subject to like passions as you are. Therefore when you see infirmities in us, you should reflect upon your own, and that would make you bear the more with us, and not be severe censurers of the failings of your magistrates, when you have continual experience of the like infirmities in yourselves and others... When you agree with a workman to build you a ship or house, he undertakes as well for his skill as for his faithfulness, for it is his profession, and you pay him for both. But when you call one to be a magistrate, he doth not profess nor undertake to have sufficient skill for that office, nor can you furnish him with gifts, therefore you must run the hazard of his skill and ability...

Concerning liberty, I observe a great mistake in the country about that. There is a twofold liberty, natural (I mean as our nature is now corrupt) and civil or federal. The first is common to man with beasts and other creatures. By this, man, as he stands in relation to man simply, hath liberty to do what he lists; it is a liberty to evil as well as to good. This liberty is incompatible and inconsistent with authority, and cannot endure the least restraint of the most just authority. The exercise and maintaining of this liberty makes men grow more evil, and in time to be worse than brute beasts: ... The other kind of liberty I call civil or federal... This liberty is the proper end and object of authority, and cannot subsist without it; and it is a liberty to that only which is good, just and honest. This liberty you are to stand for, with the hazard (not only of your goods, but) of your lives, if need be. Whatsoever crosseth this, is not authority, but a distemper thereof. This liberty is maintained and exercised in a way of subjection to authority; it is of the same kind of liberty wherewith Christ hath made us free...

Other events and controversies in which Winthrop took a leading part might be related, and some have been postponed to later chapters; but I have told enough for you to judge what manner of man he was. Keeping in mind the basis and principle by which he governed, that he and his fellow magistrates were God's vicegerents divinely commissioned to maintain gospel ordinance in a new colony, Winthrop justified those 'extraordinary great commendacions' of him. Without that basis, he would not have been Winthrop. From his fellows of the ruling class, strong and able men, he stands out as a superior man of noble character, with a single eye to the common weal. One may regret that he did not more often insist on that comparative mildness and mercy in administration which was natural to him. One welcomes the tradition that upon his deathbed, when Dudley pressed him to sign an order for banishing a dissenter, he refused, saying 'he had done too much of that work already.' Yet Winthrop's capacity to take advice and yield to the majority, was part of his equipment for leadership.

There is no better summary of the Governor's life than that of William Hubbard, the earliest historian of Massachusetts: 'A worthy gentleman, who had done good in Israel, having spent not only his whole estate... but his bodily strength and life, in the service of the country; not sparing, but always as the burning torch, spending...'

CHAPTER IV
MASTER THOMAS SHEPARD

IN forming the New England character and in setting the rhythm of New England life, the clergy must take first place. In old England, broadly speaking, the Anglican clergy were socially despised; in New England the puritan clergy had more influence than any other class or profession. They enjoyed almost universal esteem and reverence, and belonged by right to the upper class in society, although many were of humble birth, and most were poor in estate. The puritan mother prayed that her favorite son might be a scholar and a minister, just as the pious Catholic mother in Ireland or New England to-day prays that her 'white-headed boy' may become a priest of the Church.

We have often been told of late years that the clergy owed this position to legal privilege, and to the exciting of superstitious terror. The explanation is too neat. Compared with the authority in which an Anglican or a Catholic priest was clothed, the New England parson was naked. Wielding no authority derived from bishop or vicar of God, he was merely the elected of God's elect: *servus servorum Dei* in the original and literal sense of the phrase. Once called by a local church to be pastor or teacher, he had to stand on his own feet, and make his own place in the community. No celibate set apart and above the common chance, he had hungry mouths to feed, and must be a thrifty farmer to supplement his meager salary. He claimed no apostolic succession and administered only two of the seven sacraments; the keys of heaven were not his to grant or withhold. Any member of the congregation could question the soundness of his doctrines. A lay ruling elder shared his authority in the church, and a lay messenger accompanied him to council or synod. The lay dea-

cons managed the church finances. Church members, not
the minister, had the right to censure, discipline, admit, ex-
pel and excommunicate; and these church members, as John
Norton said, were 'a royal priesthood, all of them prophets,
and taught of God's spirit.' No wonder that a few of the
parsons like Peter Hobart of Hingham, had secret yearnings
for Presbyterianism, which kept laymen in place!

Under such conditions, how can we explain the powerful
influence that the clergy exerted over an exacting, unsub-
missive race of Bible readers? Are we not forced to the conclusion that they were men of unusual character and ability?
Or that, lacking these gifts, they drew upon a power outside
themselves, on the very fountain of life itself? I venture to
declare that the secret of the clergy's power was their character, and the love that they bore to their people and their God.
For the clerical function as the puritans conceived it, was not
so much priestly as educational; and the secret of all good
teaching is love of the pupil and love of the subject. John
Wilson, pastor of the Boston Church, was once viewing a
muster of the Suffolk militia, when a bystander said to him:
'Here's a mighty body of people, and there is not seven of
them all, but what loves Master Wilson.' To which he replied: 'And there is not so much as one of them all, but
Master Wilson loves him.'

Of the clerical founders of Massachusetts, the one who
most exemplifies this principle, is Thomas Shepard, first
pastor of the First Church of Cambridge. His was not the
greatest intellect in New England, but he was one of the best
loved men. John Cotton, Thomas Hooker and John Davenport of New Haven enjoyed a greater reputation in their day
as theologians, but their fame did not outlast the century.
In Shepard's writings there is a vital force that earned for
them a collected edition in the nineteenth century; and they
are still read in Scotland. Alexander Whyte, one of the most
beloved and learned of Scots divines of the last generation,

was forever quoting Shepard in his sermons; and only twenty years ago he published a little biography of the Cambridge pastor, in order to spread to a wider circle of readers 'Shepard's matchlessly pungent lessons in spiritual and experimental religion.' John Cotton was a fine, ruddy, upstanding man, the idol of the Boston women of his time; Wilson came to us the smooth product of a Windsor deanery, of Eton and of King's. From Hooker, eloquence flowed as easily as water from a jug. Shepard had none of these advantages. A 'poor, weak, pale-complectioned man' of humble birth, timid by nature, no great scholar, sweating out every sermon with moans and groans at his own vileness and inadequacy; 'his naturall parts were weake,' says Edward Johnson, 'but spent to the full.'

All that we know of Shepard's early life is contained in his autobiography. He was born in Northamptonshire on the gunpowder treason day, the fifth of November, 1605, the son of a grocer's apprentice and a grocer's daughter. He grew up a jolly little boy in what he calls a 'blind town' (what we should call a gay town), singing and dancing at Whitsun' ales. A local schoolmaster-preacher took an interest in Tom when left orphan at ten, prepared him for the University, and introduced him to a fellow of Emmanuel, who got him admitted as a pensioner or poor scholar, in 1620.

Emmanuel College was only a generation old when Tom first entered its gates. It was expressly designed by Sir Walter Mildmay, Chancellor of the Exchecquer, to provide the Church of England with able and learned preachers. 'So, Sir Walter, you have erected a puritan foundation?' said Queen Elizabeth to the founder; to which he replied, 'No, madam, far be it from me to countenance anything contrary to your established laws; but I have set an acorn which, when it becomes an oak, God alone knows what will be the fruit thereof.' Harvard College was one of the first fruits; and, through Harvard, the universities of the United States. One quarter of the one hundred and thirty-four university alumni who are known to have emigrated to New England before 1650, had their education at Emmanuel; and the fact that it was the largest college in the University of Cambridge when Shepard went there, indicates the strength of the puritan movement in England. Thomas Hooker, 'the light of the Western churches'; Simon Bradstreet, sixty years a magistrate of the Bay; William Blaxton, the hermit of Beacon Hill; Daniel Denison, the soldier of Essex; Nathaniel Ward, the 'simple cobler'; Richard Saltonstall, the younger; Ezekiel Cheever, the great schoolmaster; all were Emmanuel men.

This college was no theological seminary. Her children took the same general course of philosophy and classics as those in other colleges, and among them was a due proportion of frivolous young men; for the puritans believed that exposure to the world was wholesome for those who were to be preachers to ordinary men and women. Emmanuel provided a tennis court, a bowling green, and a swimming pool, as outlets for youthful energy; but we also find in the old book of discipline sundry cases of haunting ale-houses, coming over the walls after the gates were locked, riding the neighbors' horses, going abroad to hunt with greyhounds, quarrelling and fighting, 'and other loose and idle behaviour.' According to Shepard, these were the sort of amusements in which he indulged during his first two years. 'And I dranke so much one day that I was dead drunke, and that upon a Saturday night.' Waking up Sunday morning in a strange college with a bad head, 'in shame and confusion I went out into the fealds and there spent that Sabbath lyinge hid in the corne feelds, where the Lord who might justly have cut me off in the midst of my sin, did meet me with much sadness of hart and troubled my soule.' A sermon from the Master of Emmanuel on Romans XII, 2, 'Be ye transformed by the renewing of your mind,' set him in the way to meditation, hard study, wrestling with his sins, and salvation. Finally, to cut a long story short, 'the Lord made me see that so many as receive him, he gives power to be the sons of God (John I, I2), and I saw the Lord gave me a hart to receive Christ... and so the Lord gave me peace.'

For six months before taking his M.A. Shepard lived with Master Thomas Welde, the future minister of Roxbury, and enjoyed the preaching of the great Thomas Hooker, who had been a fellow of Emmanuel before Shepard came up.

During the early seventeenth century, the English Puritans provided for the sort of preaching they liked by endowing town lectureships, the incumbent of which preached twice or thrice a week, in the parish church if the parson permitted, otherwise in any place he could obtain. Having compromised with his conscience by receiving ordination from the Bishop of Peterborough, Shepard obtained such a lectureship at Earles Colne in Essex, where dwelt his college friends Richard and Roger Harlakenden. There he preached the gospel of redemption through Christ, to such good purpose that Bishop Laud summoned him to London to answer for nonconformity. There is a vivid scene in one of Shepard's manuscripts describing how tremblingly he confronted the great Bishop:

As soon as I came in the morning, about eight of the clock, falling into a fit of rage, he asked me what degree I had taken in the University. I answered him I was a Master of Arts. He asked me of what College? I answered, of Emmanuel. He asked me how long I had lived in his diocese. I answered, three years and upwards. He asked who maintained me all this while, charging me to deal plainly with him, adding withal that he had been more cheated and equivocated with by some of my malignant faction, than ever was man by Jesuit. At the speaking of which words he looked as though blood would have gushed out of his face, and did shake as if he had been haunted with an ague fit, to my apprehension, by reason of his extreme malice and secret venome. I desired him to excuse me. He fell then to threaten me, and withal to bitter railing, calling me all to nought — saying, 'You prating coxcomb, do you think all the learning is in your brain?' He pronounced his sentence thus — 'I charge you that you neither preach, read, marry, bury, or exercise any ministerial function in any part of my diocese; for if you do, and I hear of it, I'll be upon your back, and follow you wherever you go in any part of this kingdom, and so everlastingly disenable you.' I besought him not to deal so in regard of a poor town —here he stopped me in what I was going on to say, 'A poor town! You have made a company of seditious factious bedlams. And what do you prate to me of a poor town!' I prayed him to suffer me to catechize in the Sabbath days in the afternoon. He replied — 'Spare your breath — I'll have no such fellows prate in my diocese. Get you gone! And now make your complaints to whom you will!' So away I went. And blessed be *God* that I may go to *him*.

Shepard was now a 'silenced minister.' For half a year he remained at Earles Colne, as guest of the Harlakendens. A pursuivant of the Bishop was sent to apprehend him, and Thomas Welde; but 'away we rid as fast as we could; and so the Lord delivered me out of the hand of that Lyon.' Ezekiel Rogers of Rowley got him a position as chaplain or tutor in a knight's household in Yorkshire. Like Sir Roger, the chaplain in Beaumont and Fletcher's Scornful Lady, he married a waiting gentlewoman of the household and the knight's kindred. Other friends then obtained for him a parish in Northumberland, but it proved a rude, unresponsive community for an educated and spiritual puritan. By 1633 the long arm of Laud reached him even there, and he 'preached up and down in the country,' and again in a private house. 'And so seeing I had bin tossed from the South to the North of England and now could goe no farther, I then began to listen to a call to New-England.'

Like Winthrop, Shepard tells us the arguments that overcame his natural timidity at so radical a change of life. If called away suddenly, he would rather leave his dear ones in New England 'amid God's people' than unprovided for in old England. The compromises he was found to assent to by remaining within the Church smote his conscience; he desired the 'fruition of all God's ordinances, which I could not enjoy in Old England.' There was no reason why he should 'stay and suffer for Christ... now the Lord had opened a doore of escape'; and if he tarried too long, the seaports might be watched and stopped — as indeed they were for a time, when Laud was informed of the emigration. In short, he honestly admits, 'though my ends were mixt and I looked much to my own quiet, yet the Lord let me see the glory of those Liberties in New England.' A miraculous deliverance from shipwreck at Yarmouth caused him to doubt the call to emigrate, and he delayed a year; but on August 10, 1635, with his wife and infant son, and Roger Harlakenden his 'most dear friend,' he finally set sail in an ill-found ship, the *Defense*. After a rough voyage they reached Boston on October 3. Such were the persecutions that drove many a young minister to New England, and such were the difficulties of getting there; but, as Governor Bradford wrote, emigration to New England by that time was going to a bridal feast compared with the hardships of early Jamestown or Plymouth.

It was now five years since the Winthrop fleet had arrived. Massachusetts Bay was in the full tide of her first prosperity. Every month, during the summer and autumn, emigrant ships arrived; and the settlers were thriving by supplying the newcomers with corn and cattle. Boston was a prosperous little seaport. Shepard and his friends happened to arrive just at the moment when Hooker and Haynes and the Church of Newtowne were preparing their emigration to the Connecticut. They were eager to sell their houses and lands, and the newcomers were glad to purchase a settlement ready-made. So the Church of Christ at Newtowne set its face to the setting sun, and began the first stage in that long westward migration of the puritan way of life, which ended only at the Pacific.

'These people and Church of Christ being thus departed from New-towne,' writes Johnson, 'the godly people who came in their roomes, gathered the eleventh Church of

Christ, and called to the Office of a Pastor, that gratious sweet Heavenly minded, and soule-ravishing Minister, Master Thomas Shepheard, in whose soule the Lord shead abroad his love so abundantly, that thousands of souls have come to blesse God for him, even at this very day, who are the Seale of his Ministrey, and hee a man of a thousand, indued with abundance of true saving knowledge for himselfe and others... His natural parts were weake, but spent to the full.'

Having made arrangements to settle at Newtowne and purchase the houses and meeting-house of the emigrants on the instalment plan, the next thing to be done was to form the church. This church, like many others in early Massachusetts, began in friendship. Those whom Shepard calls his 'dear friends — most dear saints,' who came over in the same vessel and settled at Newtowne, formed the nucleus. Governor Winthrop describes the gathering of this church in much detail, as it was the first use of a method that later became orthodox and prescribed in New England. Salem and the earlier churches had gathered themselves with no outside help, and the members had both called and ordained the elders. But Shepard and his friends invited all the neighboring churches to send their elders and messengers to assist; and all did so except Watertown, where Master Phillips insisted that every church was competent to act alone.

The ceremony took place in the primitive meeting-house that had been built for Hooker's church on the southwest corner of Dunster and Mount Auburn Streets, Cambridge. 'Mr. Shepherd and two others (who were after to be chosen to office) sate together in the elder's seat. Then the elder of them began with prayer. After this, Mr. Shepherd prayed with deep confession of sin, etc., and exercised out of Ephesians v.' He then conferred with the visiting ministers as to 'what number were needful to make a church, and how they ought to proceed in this action. Whereupon some of the ancient ministers, conferring shortly together,' reported that seven seemed about right, and that the proper way to proceed was 'that such as were to join should make confession of their faith, and declare what work of grace the Lord had wrought in them; which accordingly they did,' Shepard leading off. Then the covenant was read:

> ... to forsake the Devill and all his workes, and the vanities of the sinfull world, and all their former lusts, and corruptions they have lived and walked in, and to cleave unto and obey the Lord Jesus Christ, as their onely King and Lawgiver their onely Priest and Prophet, and to walke together with that Church, in the unity of the faith, and brotherly love, and to submit themselves one unto another, in all the ordinances of Christ, to mutuall edification and comfort, to watch over and support one another.[1]

Master John Cotton, in the name of the other churches, then gave Shepard 'the right hand of fellowship,' with a short speech. Shepard exhorted his fellow members 'and commended them to the Lord in a most heavenly prayer.' Another member then declared that they intended to choose Shepard their pastor, and if anything against him were known, it should be made public before the day of ordination. No record of that final ceremony at Newtowne has survived, but presumably it was like others that followed. At least two neighboring churches sent their elders and messengers to ordain Shepard with prayer and the laying on of hands, as in the primitive church. Then followed the ordination feast.

At these functions the hosts always laid themselves out to impress the visitors. The long trestle tables fairly groaned with the contents of sundry iron kettles and brick ovens; the special brew of 'ordination beer' passed about freely in leather jacks, while the clergy and gentry put away choice Canary sack. Then a farewell was said to the guests, some of whom may have mounted their horses a bit unsteadily; and

---

[1] The actual Cambridge covenant is lost. This is one of another church reproduced by Thomas Lechford in his *Plain Dealing*, p. 17.

the minister and his wife went home to a house-warming. The nature of this may be inferred from a clerical diary of a slightly later date. 'Goodman Tucker brought some currant wine and cakes and a loaf of bread. Goodman Crane sent a cheese, and apple pie, some turnips, and bread. Young Daniels sent a quart of wine; Master Holman a quarter of mutton and some tobacco. Master Swift a joint of roast mutton for supper, and some beer... Old Goodman Vose... a barrel of cider and some honey.'

Thus, with only minor variation have all the Congregational churches of and derived from New England been organized, and thus their successive ministers have been ordained. We have taken the puritan church so much for granted in New England history, that we do not sufficiently recognize how remarkable is this unanimity in the Congregational way. Endecott and Higginson, you will remember, had been reproved by the Massachusetts Bay Company in England for their 'innovacions.' John White had done all in his power to restrain the emigrants in Winthrop's company from falling into a like error. Three out of four persons of that emigration had, he tells us, been conformable puritans. Winthrop, Dudley, Johnson, Saltonstall, and Phillips, in White's 'Humble Request,' attested their affection for the Church of England. There was nothing whatever to prevent them if they chose from setting up Church of England parishes as in Virginia, with vestry and church-wardens, honoring the Anglican orders, and worshipping according to the Book of Common Prayer. Yet when the First Church of Boston (first of the Winthrop migration) was formed, it was on the same congregational model as Salem. John Wilson was elected 'teacher,' Increase Nowell, ruling elder. 'We used imposition of hands,' writes Winthrop, 'but with this protestation by all, that it was only as a sign of election and confirmation, not of any intent that Master Wilson should renounce his ministry he received in England.' And George

Phillips told Dr. Fuller of Plymouth in private, that he would not accept the ministry of Watertown by virtue of his holy orders, but only after Congregational ordination. These facts are significant. They very strongly suggest that neither Winthrop nor Saltonstall liked these Congregational goings on, but that the nonconformist ministers felt very strongly on the subject, and the laymen submitted with good grace.

Every other church formed in the Bay or in Connecticut was on the same model. John Cotton of St. Botolph's, who felt so strongly on the subject of Anglican orders that he refused on the voyage over to baptize his seaborn son, on the ground that without a church there could be no minister, soon added the weight of his theological learning to the views of Wilson and Phillips, and began the process of molding the early churches to uniformity. But, so far as we know, each church was organized substantially on the Congregational model, by local groups of settlers, without coercion or dictation from outside. There was no law on the subject until 1636. No attempt was made to enforce an orthodox doctrine or prescribe the form of public worship until 1637, and the determinations of the synod of that year did not become the law of the land for ten years.

Under conditions of complete liberty, then, eleven separate churches organized on the same lines. There was substantial agreement among the leaders of the emigrating puritans, who in their own view represented no mere sect, but were trustees for the principles of the Protestant Reformation. As such, they were particularly keen to preserve this unity, and to prevent sectarianism, the bane of the Protestant movement. Thomas Shepard had not long been settled over the church at Newtowne when he and the civil authorities were faced with the issue of religious toleration, against which Shepard took a very decided and emphatic stand.

It appears to me that if ever a case could be made out for religious persecution it was in early Massachusetts Bay.

The Colony had not been founded with a view to establishing religious liberty. The phrase 'liberty of conscience' which the puritans frequently used, did not mean to them what it means to-day. Their consciences had been hampered in England by the necessity to subscribe to religious tests and oaths, by conformity, by the difficulty of living the good life in a corrupt atmosphere: they sought a refuge where they would have liberty to live according to their own consciences. For the consciences of Anglicans and sectaries they were not concerned. Toleration had never been offered or promised to the immigrants. 'The design of our first Planters,' wrote Cotton, 'was not Toleration; but were professed Enemies of it... their business was to settle, and (as much as in them lay) secure Religion to Posterity, according to that way which they believed was of God.' An invitation to all sects to take refuge in New England might attract 'so many as would sinke our small vessel; whereas in that greater ship of England, there is no such danger of those multitudes to founder the same.' So, to-day in our state colleges and greater universities dedicated to the service of truth, we expect liberty of instruction and freedom of discussion; but no reasonable person would criticize a Catholic college for dismissing a member who attacked the Roman hierarchy, especially if the college were a new one, struggling for existence, and if there were plenty of others which dissenting students might attend. Some writers on the history of Massachusetts appear to have forgotten that there was still a good deal of room left in America north of the Merrimac and south of the Charles.

Magistrates of the Bay like Winthrop and Dudley, ministers of the Bay like Shepard and Wilson, were on the lookout for heresy. They knew perfectly well that one consequence of removing the authority of the Church was the breeding of 'the dissidence of dissent.' They knew that English churches in Holland, the only puritan bodies established overseas be-

fore those of New England, had been a by-word and a jest
for their brawls and contentions. That is why White in his
Planters Plea, and Winthrop in his Modell of Christian
Charity, placed such emphasis on unity. It was a period
when new sects were beginning to swarm in England. There
was too much brooding over salvation, too much searching of
the Scriptures by unbalanced and whimsical minds. Earnest
fanatics everywhere were discovering some little bit of truth
in the Bible and organizing a church or a fierce little sect
around it. The same thing had happened in Germany the
previous century; the same thing could happen in the future,
in the United States. Winthrop and Dudley had promised,
John White and John Smith had proclaimed, that the
Massachusetts colony would not be a nest of sectaries,
schismatics, and 'factious humorists.'

For five years the colony was untroubled by anything of
the sort. The ministers, solidly grounded in the Church
Fathers, agreeing substantially on the Augustinian interpretation of the Scriptures, dealt individually by argument and
admonition, with their more opinionated parishioners. If
any minister showed a tendency to become unorthodox, his
fellows 'ironed it out in conference,' as the modern business
man would say. For instance, the minister of Lynn, from
pondering over Acts II, 44, 'and all that believed were together, and had all things common,' began to preach communism; so Thomas Shepard and the President of Harvard
College went down there and talked him out of it. Master
George Phillips and Elder Browne of Watertown announced
the shocking doctrine that the Roman Catholic Churches
were true churches; so Winthrop and Dudley and Nowell,
with some of the Boston church, went over to Watertown
and held a forum on the question. The vote at the end found
Phillips and Browne in a minority of three.

In 1635, the very summer that Shepard came over, the
Roger Williams case gave signs that trouble was brewing. At

the same time a stiffening-up policy was initiated by two other recent arrivals from England who later became leading figures of the English Civil War: Sir Henry Vane and Hugh Peter. Sir Harry had been sent to New England by his father, an important official at the court of King Charles, in the hope of curing him of puritanism; Hugh Peter, an energetic busybody, came to New England by way of Rotterdam, where he had been pastor over a highly factious English church. Shortly after their arrival, Peter saw reason to fear lest the difficulties between Winthrop and Dudley, the one favoring a comparatively tolerant and the other a more strict policy, would grow into political factions and endanger the state. He therefore called a conference between the six most eminent magistrates and the ministers, at which Vane, who never lacked assurance, took the chair and called upon the rival fathers in Israel for a 'show-down.' Winthrop, not relishing this interference by newcomers, declared 'it was very strange to him'; and Dudley proclaimed his complete agreement with Winthrop. Apparently there was nothing to do but call it a love-feast and go home; when John Haynes, who had just succeeded Dudley as Governor, observed that Winthrop as a magistrate had 'dealt too remissly in point of justice.' Winthrop answered 'that it was his judgment, that in the infancy of plantation, justice should be administered with more lenity than in a settled state, because people were then more apt to transgress, partly of ignorance of new laws and orders, partly through oppression of business and other straits'; but he was open to conviction that his policy had been mistaken. The ministers were invited to confer over night and report, which they did, to the effect 'that there should be more strictness used in civil government and military discipline.' All agreed to do just that, and to 'ripen their consultations beforehand' in order to appear unanimous to the public.

It is a remarkable scene, when you come to think of it: Vane and Peter undertaking to set things right, and Winthrop

GOVERNOR SIR HENRY VANE

allowing his natural feelings of mercy and humanity to be overruled by Haynes and Hooker, who had already decided to vacate Massachusetts and set up a colony of their own. The first result of the new 'hard-boiled' policy was an attempt to seize Roger Williams and deport him; but Roger betook himself instead to the site which he named Providence.

Sir Harry Vane, partly as a tribute to his personal qualities, and partly out of deference to his father's position, was elected Governor in the spring of 1636. Shortly after, there broke out the Antinomian controversy, the first and the worst internal conflict in the history of the colony.

The story is well known, how Mistress Anne Hutchinson, the vital, vivid consort to a Bostonian 'of very mild temper and weak parts,' attracted people to her house by her wit and personality in order to discuss sermons; how from discussion she fell to prophesying, and to spreading the doctrine that an immediate revelation from God was the only evidence of salvation. 'As all errour is fruitfull,' writes Shepard, 'so this opinion did gender above a hundred monstrous opinions in the countrey.'

This 'covenant of grace' doctrine was sufficiently alarming to the authorities, since it had led in Germany to the Antinomian heresy of John Agricola, who taught that the man assured of his justification by immediate revelation, could do anything he liked without sin. Shepard thought it more resembled Familism; but all agreed that it stank. Still more alarming were the immediate consequences. Anne Hutchinson proposed to discredit Master John Wilson on the ground that he was preaching the erroneous 'covenant of works,' and replace him in the Boston pulpit by her brother-in-law Master John Wheelwright, whom Shepard calls 'a man of bold and stiff conceit in his own woorth and light.' Her parlor meetings, more popular than public worship, undermined the regular clergy and fed the belief, dear to religious fanatics in all ages, that God was more likely to reveal his truth to an ignorant than to an educated person. 'Come along with me,' said one of her proselytes to Captain Johnson. 'I'le bring you to a Woman that Preaches better Gospell than any of your black-coates that have been at the Ninneversity, a Woman of another kinde of spirit, who hath had many Revelations of things to come, and for my part, saith hee, I had rather hear such a one that speakes from the meere motion of the spirit, without any study at all, then any of your learned Scollers, although they may be fuller of Scripture.'

Massachusetts was still so small that a religious faction soon became a political party. 'It began to be as common here,' wrote Winthrop, 'to distinguish between men, by being under a covenant of grace or a covenant of works, as in other countries between Protestants and Papists.' The Magistrates and most of the ministers stood out against Mistress Hutchinson, but Boston town and church were nearly unanimous for her; and she had the powerful support of John Cotton and Sir Henry Vane.

Sir Harry has been called the noblest figure that ever trod the streets of Boston, and Milton has immortalized his services for English liberty in verse. But he was still young in years, and in sage counsel young; a man 'tossed about by new opinions,' as Winthrop once remarked. Earlier in the year, Vane had signed up to the 'hard-boiled' policy, which emerged from the conference that he had called. Now, he lost his temper at the ministers for calling a meeting to discuss what they should do about Anne Hutchinson. Hugh Peter rebuked Sir Harry, reminded him of his youth and short experience, and that before he came the churches were in peace. 'The Governor answered, that the light of the gospel brings a sword, and the children of the bondwoman would persecute those of the freewoman.'[1] I can well imagine Hugh reporting this speech to the other magistrates: Win-

[1] Galatians IV, 23–40.

throp looking grave, Dudley taking up his belt a hole, Ende-cott clapping hand to sword, and rasping out that if there were to be any persecuting, Sir Harry would run with the hare, not hunt with the hounds.

Naturally the governing class, feeling their authority challenged, did what governing classes have always done under such circumstances. They struck back, and hard. Their first blow was to convict Master John Wheelwright of sedition, for a sermon in which there was talk of bringing not peace, but a sword. This brought a protest from Boston against interference with the right of free speech, reminding the magistrates that 'Paul was counted a pestilent fellow, as a moover of sedition, and a ringleader of a sect.' When election day arrived, in May, 1637, the whole colony was seething with excitement. Vane was candidate of the 'blue coats' for reëlection; the 'white coats,' as the conservatives were called, put up Winthrop. 'There was great danger of a tumult that day for those of that side grew into fierce speeches, and some laid hands on others...' The magistrates cannily transferred the place of election to Cambridge, in order to prevent a full attendance of schismatic Bostonians; and the ruse succeeded. Boston had her revenge by refusing to provide the governor-elect with his usual armed escort, so the worshipful Master Winthrop reëntered the capital forlornly attended by two of his own servants, armed with borrowed halberds. Vane returned to England in disgust.

A few days after this signal defeat of the enemy in their midst, the two puritan colonies of the River and the Bay declared war on the Pequot Indians. The struggle was short, bloody, and decisive. Most of the Pequot nation, men and women, young and old, were slaughtered—a 'divine slaughter,' Shepard called it; the remnant was sold into slavery. Woe to all such who dared oppose God's elect in New England! It would have been well for the Antinomians if they had been silent for a season until the aftermath of war were gathered in the barns. Master Cotton did at this time begin to hedge and prepare for retreat; but Wheelwright and Mistress Hutchinson, made of stouter stuff, stood their ground. In the August heats, as the warriors returned to Boston bearing grisly trophies of Mystic fight, the fighting chaplains converged on Cambridge, where a synod had been called in the hope of restoring peace to the New England churches.

Thomas Shepard was the presiding officer of this first church council in New England. It condemned some eighty 'erroneous opinions, which were spread in the country,' together with sundry 'unwholesome expressions'; upon which 'some of Boston departed from the assembly, and came no more.' But it did also attempt to find common ground on which the Boston and the country churches could agree; and succeeded in finding a formula to which Cotton, but not Wheelwright, would subscribe. Resolutions were passed against disorderly meetings of female church members, and against heckling parsons from the meeting-house floor. Wheelwright and Mistress Hutchinson had another opportunity to be silent and submit, but this they proudly rejected; the one continued his preaching and the other her prophesying as before, daring and defiant.

The Great and General Court then took the matter in hand. The suspended sentence over Wheelwright for sedition was put in execution. He was disenfranchised and banished; and two of his prominent supporters, William Aspinwall and John Coggeshall, the representatives of Boston in the General Court, were unseated, disenfranchised, and banished. All members of the party in Boston were disarmed. Anne Hutchinson remained to be dealt with.

The lady with the gift of tongues was tried in November, 1637, by the General Court, presided over by Governor Winthrop, and sitting in the Cambridge meeting-house. The magistrates, who acted both as accusers and (with the deputies) as judges, had not prepared their case well. Up to a certain point her self defence was admirable. With dignity and ready wit she parried the charge of bringing godly ministers into contempt; and when the trial turned on her actual words in a certain conference with the ministers, John Cotton gallantly denied all that had been alleged against her. Just at the point when the prosecution appeared to have broken down completely, Anne's unruly member completely gave her away. She arose to speak her mind, and declared, even boasted of her revelations from the Almighty. This was to confess the worst. For direct revelation was of all things the most offensive to these conservative English puritans. They agreed with Anglicans and Catholics in this, that God's last revelation was the last chapter of the Apocalypse; all claim to the contrary was blasphemy. God might speak directly to the heart of any believer, but not on matters of doctrine. Convicted out of her own mouth, Anne Hutchinson was sentenced to banishment for 'the troublesomeness of her spirit' and 'the danger of her course amongst us.'

Thomas Shepard had shown the proper way to deal with her, in the free trade of truth. She made no converts from his Cambridge flock, although many must have gone to Boston to hear her. There is a striking evidence of Shepard's evangelistic power in Edward Johnson's personal narrative, incorporated in his 'Wonder-Working Providence.' Returning to New England in 1636, Johnson was utterly unwrought by the Boston pythoness. Wandering in the woods in his distress, by an Indian trail that led westward from his house in Charlestown, he 'came to a large plaine' — of which the Harvard Yard is a part — and 'hearing the sound of a Drum he was directed toward it by a broade beaten way.'

Following this rode he demands of the next man he met what the signall of the Drum ment, the reply was made they had as yet no Bell to call men to meeting; and therefore made use of a Drum. 'Who is it,' quoth hee, 'Lectures at this Towne.' The other replies, 'I see you are a stranger, new come over, seeing you know not the man, it is one Mr. Shepheard.' — 'Verily,' quoth the other, 'you hit the right, I am new come over indeed, and have been told since I came most of your Ministers are legall Preachers, onely if I mistake not they told me this man preached a finer covenant of workes than the other, but however I shall make what haste I can to heare him; fare you well.' Then hasting thither hee croudeth through the thickets, where having stayed while the glasse was turned up twice,[1] the man was metamorphosed, and was fain to hang down his head often, lest his watry eyes should blab abroad the secret conjunction of his af-fections, his heart crying loud... to the blessed Spirit that causeth the speech of a poore weake pale complectioned man to take such im-pression... clearing his soule from all those false Doctrines, which the erronious party had affrighted him withall. And now he resolves (the Lord Willing) to live and die with the Ministers of New England.

Of all the elders of the Bay, wrote John Cotton, Mistress Hutchinson 'esteemed best of Mr. Shepeard'; but in the contemporary record of the trial I can find no ground for her biographer's singling him out as the one minister who showed her charity and forgiveness. It was Shepard who declared that he was not satisfied with her disavowal of certain 'gross and fundamental errors' with which she was accused. 'I fear it doth not stand with true repentance; I confes I am wholy unsatisfied in her expressions, to some of the errors. Any heretick may bring a slye interpritation upon any of thease errors, and yet hould them to thear death, therefor I am unsatisfied. I should be glad to see any re-pentance in her that might give me satisfaction.' The use of the term heretic is a little startling considering Shepard's late interview with Bishop Laud; but it is merely another sign that the puritans were certain of their grasp on God's truth.

Shepard concurred in the banishment of Anne Hutchinson,

[1] A sermon over two hours long. The puritans timed their sermons by an hour-glass in the pulpit.

and gloried in the resultant peace. 'The Churches here are
in peace,' he wrote in 1644. 'The Common wealth in peace;
the Ministry in most sweet peace; the Magistrates (I should
have named first) in peace; All our families in peace; We can
sleep in the woods in peace, without fear of the Indians, our
feare is fallen upon them.' The title of this tract is 'New
England's Lamentation for Old England's Present Errours.'
Old England's chief error was toleration of the multitude of
sects that had broken forth. To his old friend Hugh Peter,
who had experienced a change of heart on returning to England, he wrote: 'You seeme to thinke a letter I writ... to be
too sharpe, and that honest men who are for Christ should be
suffred tho' they run out into opinions. I desire to shew the
utmost forbearance to godly men if for a time deluded; but
otherwise I see no more reason to beare with good men in
their opinions then in their morall transgressions, for they
commonly are coupled together. You have had experience
of the gangreene in New England, and have seen it spread in
a little time, and how God hath borne witness agaynst that
generation... There is but one truth, you know.'
     That was just what Master Peter was beginning to doubt.
If more in early Massachusetts Bay had shared his doubts,
life would there have been more pleasant and civil. It might
have been a good thing for the clergy if some one had reminded them every day, as did Sir Richard Saltonstall in a
memorable letter: 'Doe not assume to yourselves infallibili-
tie of judgment, when the most learned of the apostles con-
fesseth he knew but in part and saw but darkely as through
a glass, for God is light, and no farther than he doth illumine
us can we see, be our parts and learning never so great.' Yet
the historian may be permitted to doubt the value of doubt
in all times and places. It is at least arguable that the suppression of the gifted lady was necessary to preserve all that
the puritans had to give, or bequeath. The special circumstances of a new colony yet in the gristle, the danger from the

very quality and temper of Anne Hutchinson's creed (an illuminism but one step removed from Fifth Monarchy and Ranters, placing the reasoned creed of scholars on perpetual defense against any fanatic who could gain an ignorant following): give strength to the Devil's advocate for intolerance.

There is more ground to say that the Bay Colony had better never been, than that it had better taken Anne to its bosom. The later persecutions of Baptists and Quakers were no necessary consequence of silencing her; they would have been persecuted under the 'covenant of grace' as well as under the 'covenant of works.' Intolerance was stamped on the very face of the Bay Colony by the conscious purpose of its founders to walk by the ordinances of God, as interpreted by themselves.

Whether the honorable roll of rebels and intellectual pioneers of nineteenth century Massachusetts came as a reaction against puritanism, or (as Emerson thought) by way of natural development from it, the puritans built better than they knew. The price that all communities must pay for intolerance was soon paid by the loss of such men as Dunster, Child, and Pynchon, and in keeping away other free spirits, of whom we know nothing. The reward came two hundred years later, when the sturdy, sufficient tree of puritanism, well rooted in New England soil by the jealous gardeners of the first generation, burst into flower with such as Channing, Emerson, Hawthorne, and Thoreau.

On Shepard at least the Hutchinson controversy did not have the souring influence that it had on Wilson. He continued 'heavenly, soul-ravishing' as before, in his proper business of the cure of souls. Although dubbed a 'legal preacher' by the Antinomians he was primarily an evangelist. 'It is a wretched stumbling block to some,' say his first London editors, in 1652, 'that his Sermons are somewhat strict, and (as they terme it) legal: — some souls can relish none but meal-mouth'd Preachers, who come with soft and

smooth, and toothles words, *byssina verba byssinis viris:*
But these times need humbling Ministries, and blessed be
God that there are any; for where there are no Law-Sermons,
there will be few Gospel-lives, and were there more Law-
preaching in England by the men of gifts, there would be
more Gospel-walking both by themselves and the People.'

Shepard's sermons were moving but not sensational, delivered in a low voice that had a strangely penetrating and com-
pelling quality. Violent gestures and shouting were as abhor-
rent to the puritans as 'toothles words.' Religious enthusiasm,
they believed, engendered what Shepard called 'Gospel
Wantons' and 'Spiritual Drunkeness.' His own method was
to quote a text, make a short commentary, and then drive it
home to his congregation with a simile, aphorism, or pithy
exhortation. 'Take heed you chop not at your comfort too
soon.' 'Men can tub it out with a quietness of spirit, when
some of their money loose in their pockets is lost.' 'This is
the nature of love, where it cannot go, it will creep.' 'There
be temptations enough to make men fill and pester God's
house with swine.'

Even his modern Scots admirer admits that Shepard's
English was atrocious. It was no wonder, for the published
sermons were not written out by the author. Disciples and
admirers expanded his brief notes, or notes taken by a member of the congregation; and after his friends in Cambridge
and the local printer and his friends in England and the
London printer had all had a whack at it, the English became
rough as a chopping-block. Shepard knew this himself. His
'Sincere Convert,' which Master Giles Firmin called 'a Book
very solid, quick, and searching; it cuts very sharply,' the
author called his 'ragged child.' Yet as you read his sermons
in the old leather-bound volumes with the Boston or London
imprints, the pages worn at the edges and soiled with the
loving hands that in other days turned them seeking light
and truth; and when you think of Shepard preaching them in

the primitive meeting-house at Cambridge, of his high sincerity and his intense rapport with his congregation; you begin to feel the extraordinary power in this little, weak, pale-complectioned man. And occasionally you will find growing in the rough-cast prose, a poetic flower of rare beauty. For example this, on the love of Christ:

As 'tis with Woman when the fulnesse of the Husband's love is seen, it knits the heart invincibly to him, and makes her do any thing for him; so here. And as we say of Trees, if the Tree begins to wither and dye, the only way is...water the root. Love is the next root of all Grace. Love Christ, and you will never be weary of doing for Christ; love him, and he will love you. Now what kindles love so much as this comprehending knowledge of the Lord Jesus, and his love; this will make a man a burning Beacon of love; make a man melt into love which is as strong as death — much water cannot quench it. Faith is our feet whereby we come to Christ, Love is our hand whereby we work for Christ....

The doctrine that Shepard preached was that any might be saved, if only they would open their hearts to God. Occasionally he preached a hell-and-damnation sermon, but it gives a distorted impression of him to quote that alone, as Moses Coit Tyler does. Love and Grace are the words and thoughts endlessly repeated in his printed sermons. Shepard quotes Calvin less often than he does the great Jesuit theologian, Bellarmine.[1] Shepard preaches a gospel of love, of infinite compassion. He admits that most of the stubborn world is going to hell, but he gives the First Church of Cambridge every encouragement to join the minority. 'I pray God such a race [who look not for Christ's coming and company] come not hither, where God looks you should get a higher pitch; put off your wildernesse-shoes, get those sins

[1] E.g., *The Sincere Convert* (London, 1650), p. 187. It must not be supposed that the New England clergy were afraid of Catholic books. In the inventories in the first volume of Salem Probate records, I find one copy of Aquinas's *Summa*, and only one of Calvin's *Institutes*. John Harvard had more volumes by the 'angelic doctor' in his library than he had volumes by Calvin. Hugh Peter bespeaks the late Archbishop Laud's library for Harvard in 1645 (*Amer. Hist. Rev.*, v, 106).

removed that provoked God there... Oh are you born to so great hopes, and are they not worth the looking after?'

That sentence reveals the practical weakness of the puritan creed. It required a higher pitch of religious feeling and conduct than poor human nature in New England was capable of. The second generation, who had not known the trials of God's people in England, began to slip away; and the relative number of sincere converts declined. Yet somehow this high-pitched fervor, this intense desire to hear and obey God, left a substratum of faith that still remains in the New England mind, though expressed in other forms, even in what Barrett Wendell aptly called a reverent unbelief. After three hundred years it no longer seems so important what sort of religious faith the puritans had, as that they had faith.

Shepard's sermons were not 'high-brow.' They are full of hints as to contemporary life. In his *Theses Sabbaticae* he lays down the rules for a New England Sabbath — it should begin at sundown, and in it you must do no manner of work, unless of necessity; you may rub ears of corn and dress meat for comfortable nourishment, just as you must water your horse on the Sabbath; you should keep the home fires burning. But you must do nothing on the Sabbath that you can as well do on the day before or after, such as buying and selling, washing clothes, and setting sail. These are much broader rules than those observed in the average New England household a century later, where cooking on the Sabbath was supposed unlawful. But the flock must still keep their high pitch all the Sabbath day. No telling of tales and jests or idle gossip, or sleeping at sermons or foolish pastimes.

From a characteristic passage we gather that the church members were already getting a bit exclusive in their attitude toward more recent immigrants:

Many complain that *New England* hath so little love, Non-members not visited, not regarded (though many times unjustly). Oh, they thought to see so much love, and care, and pity; but here they may live and never be spoken to, never visited; Oh take heed of this; Nothing beautifies a Christian in the eyes of others more than much love, (hypocrisie is naught) Oh excel here; visit poor families, sit one half hour and speak to discouraged hearts, shew kindness to strangers; such you were.

If the Cambridge church members were none too cordial to the parish at large, they were a mutual benevolent society among themselves. A legacy of £20 left to the church by Roger Harlakenden, Shepard's most dear friend, was expended on a young cow, whose milk was given to a poor widow and an impecunious brother. The church paid half the debts of one of its members when the creditor agreed to forgive the other half. The following items are preserved from the church accounts in Shepard's times:

Given my brother Towne toward his expenses in a sicknesse	£1–0– 0
Lent Brother Towne	5–0– 0
Given to our brother Hall toward the rearing of his house that was blown down	1–0– 0
Payd our brother Briggam for something for clothinge for his sone	0–7– 6
Given sister Grizzell in a hard time	0–5– 0
To our sister Albone 1 pk of malt	0–1– 6
Sent our sister Albone 7 lb. venison	0–1– 2
Sent our sister Albone 1 bottell sack	0–0–11

[Two more sisters and three brethren came in for a similar benefaction in the course of the year. Brother Sill even got a 'dividend' as follows:]

For the refreshing my brother Sill in time of fayntness sent him 4 pints of sack	0–2– 4

Refreshing indeed it is to record those comfortable offices of the New England church towards its members; a pleasant balance to the censorious activities of which we have been told so much.

Preaching twice on the Sabbath and a Thursday lecture was only part of a New England minister's duties. His relation to his flock was the true pastoral one. There was a continual round of visits to catechize the children, and chat pleasantly with their elders. It was the minister's function to compose family and neighborhood quarrels before they got into the courts, to encourage the more scholarly boys to attend Grammar School, and even take up subscriptions to send them to college. Many practised medicine for want of a settled physician in their town: Thomas Thacher, minister of the Old South, wrote the first medical treatise that was printed in the Colonies; and in a later generation Cotton Mather led the fight for inoculation. Whenever the frame of a house, barn, or mill was raised, the parson was expected to be present, and to ask God to bless it to the use of his servants. The raising of a new meeting-house was an important affair in which the whole community took part, and the people of neighboring towns came to help. Beer, cider, and even hard liquor were provided at town expense to attract unpaid helpers, and to provide the necessary courage to walk out on a stringer or ridge-pole; and if no one fell through over-confidence, and the minister was not called upon to set broken bones, it was considered a very special dispensation of providence. In a frontier town the minister often took a leading part in measures of defense against the Indians. For we find these graduates of Oxford and Cambridge, and later those of Harvard and Yale, at the remotest outposts on the wilderness. There could be little of a material nature in a pioneer colony to compensate such men for the placid amenities of a college fellowship, or the well ordered duties of an English country parish. And once settled over a church, the seventeenth-century pastor was settled for life; there could be no promotion for him to a vacant Boston parish. Like the true gentlemen they were, these pioneer pastors accepted hardship and privation without complaint, happy to devote their gifts to bringing up their people in the way of truth. To them, more than to any other class New England owes what she has been, and what she is.

There were occasional unfaithful shepherds, of course. Thomas Gilbert, one of the few New England ministers of the century who was not a university graduate, was in continual trouble with his congregation at Topsfield. Goodwife Gould testified in court that he left very little wine in the chalice for communicants. One day he was overcome by it, sank down in his chair, forgot to give thanks, and sang a psalm with very lisping and unintelligible utterance. At the afternoon service he arrived so late that many went away. He went to prayer, and as another testified, 'I perceived that he was distempered in his head, for he did repeat many things many tymes over, in his prayer he lisps and when he had don to prayer, he went to singing and read the Psalm so as it could not be well understood, and when he had done singing he went to prayer again, and when he had done he was going to sing again, but being desired to forbear used these expressions: "I bless God I find a great deal of comfort in it," and came out of the pulpit. He said to the people "I give you notis I will preach among you no more."' Mistress Gilbert loyally testified that his conduct was due to a distemper that came upon him sometimes when fasting and in rainy weather, and the court took this charitable view of her husband's infirmity. But he was soon in trouble again, and the ministerial relation had to be severed by court action.

Compared with his brethren on the frontier, the lot of Thomas Shepard was cast in pleasant places. Harvard College was established at his door; Boston could be visited in the course of a day; John Eliot at Roxbury and John Harvard at Charlestown were neighbors. His first wife died of consumption in 1636, but a daughter of Thomas Hooker consented to become his second. Yet life never came easy to Shepard, so exalted was the standard that he set for himself. Although reputed the most successful pastor of his day in leading lost souls to God, he was never satisfied. His meditations are filled with the most distressing groans at his own shortcomings. He was too tender-hearted always to reprove sin sharply when he observed it. He could never get his

sermons prepared in time, but would meditate and procras-
tinate until there was left only the fag-end of Saturday night
and early Sunday morning. He was too fearful of lack of
success in his previous sermon, too apprehensive of the next,
too sensitive to outward things, such as extremes of heat
and cold. In the breathless, oppressive dog-days, when the
meeting-house was a damp oven, Shepard could not catch
the divine spark. His feeble vitality was congealed in late
winter, after the cold had got into every plank and nail of
the building, when snow sifted through cracks in the clapboards, the congregation shivered in their thickest woolens,
and the sacramental bread froze so hard that it 'rattled
sadly' when broken into the paten.

Shepard spent too much time in his study, to the neglect of
his family. He could not bring himself to speak of religion in
time or aright to his children and servants; family prayers
never seemed to hit the mark; and there were times when he
felt that the Romans had the right idea, and Christ's ministers should be celibate. Yet he was blessed in seeing three
sons fairly on the way toward the ministry, and his namesake
was the choice young man of his generation at Harvard.
'Natural dulness and cloudiness of spirit,' he complained of;
yet one Harvard student recorded that the preaching of
Master Shepard made the four years of college seem like
four years of heaven. Want of power to deliver Christ's
message was his constant infirmity, so Shepard imagined;
'Yet so searching was his preaching,' said one of his flock,
'and so great a power attending, as a hypocrite could not
easily bear it, and it seemed almost irresistible.' There were
times when nothing could console Shepard but the reflection
that if he were insufficient, God was all-sufficient, both to
make him a fit instrument of the divine purpose on earth, and
to perfect him in heaven.

This was not a healthy state of mind for a shepherd of men.
Far better to forget each page in the ledger of life as it is

turned, and face the new day serene and unafraid. Shepard had an extreme case of the New England conscience. Yet we must not cavil at the ways of saints: they are rare enough at all times. We can only regret that serenity and peace were denied to the man who wrote: 'Faith is our feet whereby we come to Christ, Love is our hand whereby we work for Christ.'

Death came earlier to Shepard than to most of his fellow ministers. Never robust and often ailing, he was only forty-three when in the summer of 1649 he caught a sore throat riding home from a church council at Rowley. There came on a fever 'which suddenly stopped a silver trumpet, from whence the people of God had often heard the joyful sound.'

Yet Thomas Shepard lived long enough in the land to feel that whatever his own shortcoming, the work of settling the gospel in New England had been singularly blessed. In a reminiscent passage he reminded the rising generation that the first comers 'were not rash, weak-spirited, inconsiderate of what they left behind, or of what it was to go into a wilderness.' He recalled with wonder how not only the stout-hearted, but the weak and tender, reluctant to leave their native country, expecting want and privation, and fearful of the dangers and difficulties of the sea, yet persisted in leaving friends, comforts and country for liberty of conscience in New England. 'The singular providence of God bringing so many shiploads of his people through so many dangers as upon eagles' wings,' the 'cheerfulness and contentment' of God's people in their wilderness Commonwealth, moved his gratitude and caused him to exclaim, 'Who is a God like our God, that pardons iniquities, and passes by the transgressions of the remnant of his heritage, even because he delighteth in mercy!'

CHAPTER V

JOHN HULL OF BOSTON, GOLDSMITH

1. THE ARTIST

ALTHOUGH religion was the dynamic force which gave the Bay colony character and consistency, it was not an all-absorbing interest. Even puritans did not live by faith alone, nor did puritanism blight the creative and expansive side of human nature. Man's urge to build and create, his age-long yearning for comfort and security, his sense of form and beauty, found outlet in early New England, as in few other settlements of like age. He who best combined these aspects of life with the religious was John Hull, captain of militia and owner of ships; business man and magistrate, master of the mint, and deacon of the church, first in a long line of master goldsmiths who enriched the churches and homes of New England with beautiful examples of their art.

The men and women whose acquaintance we are making, moved in a colorful scene, 'incomparably more picturesque than at present,' as Hawthorne wrote. Yet Hawthorne, more than any man, was responsible for the somber picture of early New England dear to popular illustrators, and already embalmed in tradition. A brooding sense of gloom; a village of log houses, pierced only by a few square-paned windows; a stalwart puritan dressed in black except for a broad white collar; on his arm a woman in mouse-colored gray, wearing a white coif. As a matter of fact, the puritans normally dressed in bright colors, they never built a log house, and the moral and Sabbatarian atmosphere, which doubtless would prove depressing to us, was what they came to America to enjoy.

Log cabins were introduced to America by the Swedes and Finns on the Delaware, and did not appear on the New England frontier until the eighteenth century. The first temporary shelters in Massachusetts were conical huts of branches and turf, such as the charcoal-burners used in England, or wattle-and-daub cottages with thatched roofs. These were soon replaced by houses of hewn and sawn timber. A frame of stout oak (post and sill, plate and beam, neatly mortised and fastened with wooden trunnels), was erected around a central chimney of brick,[1] a filling of clay, straw, and rubble placed between the joists, the outside sheathed with riven clapboard, and the inside plastered or sheathed with wide upright pine boards. Window-openings were sometimes single and sometimes grouped, but always hung with leaded casements and glazed with diamond panes. Roofs were steep-pitched as if for thatch, which the first-comers used, and were slow to abandon for cedar shingles. Salem and Boston in John Hull's day resembled more a town of mediæval Europe, than anything that exists in America to-day. It is not until 1680 that we find a building in Massachusetts (the Province House) which owed anything to Palladio or Inigo Jones. The puritan housewright followed the mediæval tradition, and his detail was gothic. His frame was planned for use, and his house was built to the frame, instead of with a view to effect and proportion, as in the architecture of the Renaissance. Similarly the cabinet makers, iron-workers and silversmiths brought over the best traditions of mediæval craftsmanship. Their art was dynamic, not academic.

Far from condemning the beautiful, the generation which planned the New England villages, divided the fields, and built the first houses, seemed incapable of making anything ugly. If their laying out of homestead, village common, stone wall, road, and meeting-house was unconscious, the more to the credit of their instinct; for it was done in harmony with the lay of the land, the contours of valley and slope, the curve of stream and shore. Cambridge, on a level plain like a

---

[1] Originally the chimneys, even of such important people as the Downings, were 'catted'; i.e., built of wood and daubed with clay.

bowling green was laid out square; across the river the paths and lanes of Boston followed a scalloped sea-front and looped around three mamelons. At first the New England village was crude and raw with mud and stump-studded fields. Given time for flowers to bloom in dooryards and wine-glass elms to rise about the comely houses, it grew into the sort of unconscious beauty that comes of ordered simplicity.

John Hull lived in a large, rambling house on the Great (now Washington) Street in Boston, near the south corner of what is now Summer Street, with garden and grounds running well back. It was begun by his father, but added to by the son, the two families living under the same roof until the father's death in 1666. In John's childhood it contained only the hall on the ground floor, with the chimney at one end; but John built an addition to the house, bringing the chimney to a central position so that it served the 'old hall,' the new 'little hall,' and a kitchen in the rear, covered by a lean-to extension of the roof. There all the cooking was done over an open wood fire, on a hearth at least eight feet long. On the fourth side of the chimney was the staircase, facing the front door. The second story overhung the first,[1] and probably the lower ends of the second-story posts were carved into pendants or drops.

This house was somewhat remote from the business center about Dock Square, and Hull himself wrote an English correspondent, 'my Habitation is greatly disadvantaged for trade; yet because I alwayes desired a quiet life and not two much business, it was alwayes best for mee.' Probably his stores and silversmith's shop were in a separate building. We have several intimate glimpses of domestic life in the Hull house through Samuel Sewall. Hannah Hull, John's only child, set her cap at young Sam when delivering his master's

---

[1] One still meets the silly 'tradition,' vouched for by Weeden, that these overhanging upper stories were for defense against the Indians. It was simply a mediæval architectural device brought over from England.

oration at Harvard Commencement, 'though I knew nothing of it till after our Marriage,' records that writer of a prodigious diary. You have surely read Hawthorne's pleasant story of John Hull dowering his plump daughter by setting her on one side of the mint-house scales, while the servants heaped the other with pine-tree shillings until her weight was balanced. The fact is that Hannah's endowment was paid by the installment plan; but the amount, £500, would just about balance a middling-sized maiden with pine-tree shillings.[1]

Whatever the financial arrangements may have been, the wedding took place in John Hull's house within eighteen months. 'Governor Bradstreet married us in that which we now call the Old Hall,' records Sam Sewall; ''twas then all in one, a very large Room.' And there the young couple set up housekeeping with the old, using the 'little hall' as their living-room. The old man found the younger prudent and judicious, but there was at least one tiff which made Sewall feel so badly that he recorded it in Latin. John Hull, then treasurer of the Colony, came home *pene fervidus*, almost glowing with passion, because a delinquent tax-payer had dumped a load of oats on him in lieu of money. While he was fulminating about it, Sam heaved a larger log on the fire than his father-in-law thought necessary or meet. The older man berated the younger for his foolishness, and declared he could put no trust in such a fellow, with *ventosam mentem* — a mind unstable as the wind. Poor Sam slunk off to bed, and resorted to the thirty-seventh psalm for consolation.

Another domestic scene is given by Sam's description of the birth of his son and heir.

[1] Dowries were the rule rather than the exception among the New England puritans, and were often arranged by the parents. To his friend John Richards, who married Sarah Gibbons, Hull writes: 'Your mother desired me also to enforme you that Mr. Gibbons of Hartford was prety earnest with her about you know what; and told her that iff she would give one hundred, he would make her worth three hundred. If your heart have had any recoylinge aboute it, since your departure, you may againe revolve it in your thoughts, and se whether Providence may not speake some thinge.' — 4 *Coll. Mass. Hist. Soc.*, VII, 535.

Feb. 16. Brewed my Wives Groaning Beer.

.   .   .   .

April 1. About two of the Clock at night I waked and perceived
my wife ill: asked her to call Mother. She said I should goe to
prayer, then she would tell me. Then I rose, lighted a Candle at
Father's fire, that had been raked up from Saturday night, kindled
a Fire in the chamber, and after 5 when our folks up, went and gave
Mother warning. She came and had me call the midwife, Goodwife
Weeden, which I did. But my wives pains went away in great
measure after she was up: toward night came on again, and about a
quarter of an hour after ten at night, April 2, Father and I sitting in
the great Hall, heard the child cry, whereas we were afraid 'twould
have been 12 before she would have been brought to bed. Went
home with the midwife about 2 o'clock, carrying her stool, whose
parts were included in a bagg. Met with the watch at Mr. Rocks
brew house, who bad us stand, enquired what we were. I told the
woman's occupation, so they bad God bless our labours, and let us
pass.

None of the early houses like John Hull's still exist in their
original state. When fuel became scarce and comfort was
more regarded, the size of fireplaces was reduced, the great
chamfered beams and adze-marked manteltrees were con-
cealed beneath moulded panelling and wainscoting, and
square-paned sash windows were substituted for the leaded
casements. The house frames, however, were too solid to be
scrapped. Judicious architects of to-day may strip off the
later screening to reveal the good brown beams, and restore
the casement windows from examples found in garrets and
outhouses. Several of these restored houses and rooms are
shown in the illustrations to this volume, with the stout oak,
pine, and ash furniture of the period; as well as others in the
state that the next century left them.

The Massachusetts puritans disliked extravagance; but
they appreciated comeliness, whether in a ship, a house, or a
woman; and they loved bright-colored paint on ships and
houses — but not on women. An example in point is Captain
John Endecott, so rigid an iconoclast that he defaced the

cross on the English ensign as an emblem of idolatry and superstition. Yet Captain Endecott tricked out the trim of his great house at Salem with scarlet paint, hung carved bargeboards under the eaves, and lived there well and generously. Puritan costume was distinguished from court costume by comparative plainness, and absence of lace and spangle, rather than by color. Only the ministers followed the ancient sacerdotal tradition in wearing black. 'Sad colored' clothes there were, of russett, gray, green and dark blue, and for working clothes men wore leather and undyed homespun woolens; but on great occasions your puritan might be gaudy. Governor Bradford left a red waistcoat with silver buttons, a colored hat, a violet cloak, and a Turkey-red grogram suit. Governor Bellingham wears a scarlet cloak in his portrait, painted in 1641. A snatch of inventories in the Essex County probate records, for 1636–44, yields a purple cloth suit, doublet, and hose; a green doublet, a long blue coat with silver buttons; blue, black, red, and green waistcoats; purple and russett gowns; aprons of green and tawny; blue and red petticoats; plain and embroidered women's caps of various bright colors. As for headwear, the puritan did wear on occasion the broad-brimmed, high-crowned, black felt hat dear to modern illustrators, but not exclusively. Each servant of the Massachusetts Bay Company in 1629 was provided with one, doubtless for Sabbath wear; but he also drew a Monmouth cap (a sort of close-fitting cloth beret), and five red knitted caps. 'Portugal caps' are mentioned in John Hull's orders; skull caps were worn in the house by ministers and magistrates. Thirty years later, John Hull is importing from England hats of various shapes and colors, blue duffels and red penistones, red and yellow flannels, red galant cloth and blue ditto: red and blue worsted stockings. 'Sad colours' are wanted only in the kersies and serges; black taffetas he found impossible to sell.

As to interior decorations and furnishings; here is an inventory to make the collector envious, from the household of the first President of Harvard College. In a lawsuit over the estate, an ancient domestic thus testified about the contents of the President's house:

Eleven feather beds or Downe, all well furnished ... having philip and cheny[1] curtains ingrain with a Deep silk Fringe on the Vallance and a smaller on the Curtain, and a coverlet ... made of Red Kersey and laced with a green lace round the sides and two down the middle. Also there apertained to that bed an outlandish quilt, also to another a blew serge suit, very rich and costly, curtains and valances laced and fringe, and a blew rug to the bed. Also a Greene suit in the same manner, also another Red wrought suite with a sheet and all things complete. Also a Canopy bed with curtains, a chest of Drawers, of part of this Chest was filled with rich linen, a Damask Suite, several Diaper Suites, a fine hollen suit with a stech: with abundance of Flaxen Linnen for common use. In another part of the Chest of Drawers tape tafety for Chaire and stooles. A pair of Greate brasse andirons, and a pair of small andirons of brass: of brasse Cetle of all sorts a great brasse pot, much brasse of all sorts useful for a family, much Latten wear of several sorts: and also abundance of pewter of all sorts great and small: ... 29 silver spoons, A very fair salt with 3 full knobs on the top of it[2], 3 other silver salts of lesser sorts, A great silver trunk with 4 knobs to stand on the table and with sugar: 6 porrengers, 1 small one: 3 bere bouls, 4 wine cups, a silver grate with a Cover on it: 6 silver trencher plates: also blankets and Coverletts and Rugs.

This was the inventory of a well-to-do family. The poorer sort lived in two-room cottages often with a thatched roof and an outside oven, and no cellar; but so far as we can learn from the inventories they never put up long with an earth floor, which satisfies even the better peasants in Brittany. For £21 in 1640 a Boston weaver builds a house 14 by 16 feet, framed, sheathed and finished, with a 'chamber floare' and a 'cellar floare.' They slept under coarse woolen rugs

---

[1] An odd name for a kind of cloth.

[2] This is the 'great salt' which was given to Harvard College by Mrs. Dunster's brother Harris, and which is still owned by the College and shown in the Fogg Museum. It will be noted that there are no forks in the inventory. Governor Winthrop brought over one in a case, doubtless regarded as a great curiosity.

on flockbeds, and the furniture was made by the goodman with his axe and lathe. An iron kettle or two, a skillet, a frying pan and wooden spoons and trenchers made up the kitchen equipment. It is striking evidence of the standards which even the common people had reached, that we seldom hear of women working in the fields, although they took full charge of the dairy. Perhaps puritan standards of house-wifery were too exacting to permit of field labor, and the household spinning and weaving consumed all the 'precious time' not devoted to preparing food and drink. Nor is there evidence that the poorer people housed animals under the same roof with themselves, as the peasants in parts of Europe do to this day.

At this point I hear some one remark, 'That's all very true perhaps, but these housewrights, artisans, and silversmiths were not stark puritans but hearty Englishmen, held in terror and subjection to the bigoted, cruel, superstitious, beauty-hating puritan governing class.' Referring the curious to an appendix wherein I discuss this interesting theory, I must get on with John Hull, whose ardent and consistent puritanism appears on every page of his diaries. The first page of one of them (for he kept two) opens in this wise:

The state of England our dear Native Countrey being by the usurpation of the Bishops under great declinings both civill and chiefly ecclesiasticall; god's faithfull ministers silenced, sentenced also to Imprisonment and banishment, if they would not conform to read the kings and Bishops edicts granting liberty for profanation of the Lords day, etc.; and also imposing upon the ministry many pop-ish Injunctions, which proved a snare unto some honest minds and a burden unsuportable to many others both ministers and people whose harts God stirred up rather to endure a voluntary Exile from their native soyl and to hazard the loss of all their sweet outward comforts and relations, than to defile their Consciences and ensnare themselves by holding their rich revenues. God therefore moved the hearts of many to transport themselves far off beyond the seas into this our New England and brought year after year such as might be fitt matterialls for a Common wealth in all respects and

Among others some of the choycest use both for Ministry and magistracy. Millitary men, sea men Tradesmen etc. and of larg Estates and free spirits to spend and be spent....

John was born at Market Harborough, Leicestershire, in December, 1624, a good generation later than the builders whose acquaintance we have already made. At the age of ten he was taken from school to emigrate with his father, a blacksmith of some little property and standing in the community. Their ship, the *George*, struck on the edge of Sable Island, and the panic-stricken seamen tried to hoist out the longboat and get away; but she caught on a fluke of the anchor, and the ship floated free. After a little more schooling John became his father's helper in the fields. At eighteen or nineteen, he writes, 'I fell to learning (by the help of my brother) and to practising the trade of a goldsmith,[1] and through God's help obtained that ability in it, as I was able to get my living by it.'

A puritan goldsmith in glacial Boston! And not alone in that pursuit. Boston supported a dozen goldsmiths before she was able to find employment for a single lawyer — so uncivilized were the early puritans.

John Hull must have been launched in his trade when the colony was pulling out of the economic crisis of 1641–42. For ten years the people had been living by selling cattle and labor to immigrants who came well stocked with money and goods. When these stopped coming, agricultural produce was unsalable, and the bottom dropped out of the cattle market. Many returned to England to take part in the Civil War, others emigrated to the West Indies, debts could not be collected, and even the steadfast Winthrop confided to his diary

[1] Hull and the contemporary records use the craft name 'goldsmith,' which at that time covered those who worked in both precious metals; but as I have found no evidence that any of the New England goldsmiths of the seventeenth century actually worked in gold, I have rather fallen into the modern term silversmith. Hull's half-brother, Richard Storer, was apprenticed to James Fearne, goldsmith of London, in 1629 (Records of Goldsmiths Company, communicated by E. Alfred Jones, Esq.).

that if all these events could have been foreseen, he would not have left England. The crisis brought the first real test of Yankee inventiveness and energy. 'These straits set our people on work to provide fish, clapboards, planks, etc.... and to look to the West Indies for a trade,' wrote the Governor. From stark necessity, maritime and industrial Massachusetts came into being. Men built ships and sailed them laden with the products of farm, forest, and fisheries to the West Indies and the Mediterranean; they penetrated further inland, in search of richer land and more abundant peltry; household industries and ironworks were established.

The ministers of the colony were of two minds about this returning wave of prosperity. They bewailed the outlet opened by the merchant marine for hot-blooded youth and the luxuries that it brought in; yet were not these showers of manna a singular instance of God's watchful care for his chosen people, and a blessing in their wilderness work? So at least believed Master Samuel Danforth, minister, mathematician and poet. His allegorical poem of 1648 on the tree (New England) and its fruit, refers to the first fall in the Boston stock market, and the consequent rise of foreign commerce:

> Few think, who only hear, but doe not see,
> That Plenty groweth much upon this tree.
> That since the mighty Cow her crown hath lost,
> In every place shee's made to rule the rost:
> That heaps of wheat, pork, bisket, beef and beer,
> Masts, pipestaves, fish, should store both farre and neer.
> Which fetch in wines, cloth, sweets, and good tobacc —
> O be contented then, you cannot lack.

Quite a different view of these 'fabulous forties' is presented by Benjamin Tompson, master of the grammar school at Charlestown. Tompson, who graduated from Harvard in 1662, had doubtless heard the older generation talk much of the 'good old times' before his birth. The prologue to his 'New-Englands Crisis' (1676) opens thus:

The times wherein old Pompion [1] was a Saint,
When men far'd hardly yet without complaint
On vilest Cates; the dainty Indian Maize
Was eat with Clamp-shells out of wooden Trayes
Under thatcht Hutts without the cry of Rent,
And the best Sawce to every Dish, Content.

. . . .

These golden times (too fortunate to hold)
Were quickly sin'd away for love of gold.

. . . .

Twas ere the Islands sent their Presents in,
Which but to use was counted next to sin.
Twas ere a Barge had made so rich a fraight
As Chocholatte, dust-gold and bitts of eight.
Ere wines from France and *Moscovadoe* too
Without the which the drink will scarsly doe,
From western Isles; ere fruits and dilicacies,
Did rot maids teeth and spoil their hansome faces.

Young John Hull, we may be sure, found the new prosperity good; for many of the chinking 'bitts of eight' brought home by traders from the wealthy Islands came his way. Into the crucible they went, to emerge under his skilful hands as the beautiful articles of church and household silver that are the pride of our ancient parishes and of the collectors and museums so fortunate to possess them. The vessels that he made expressly for the communion service of a church were in the traditional form of the chalice and paten. A few such, like the cup of which Governor Winthrop presented to the First Church of Boston, had been brought over from England. Presumably John used those as models, but attempted little in the way of ornamentation. His work is distinguished for dignity and beauty of proportion, rather than for richness of detail.[2]

In addition to the orders for churches, the burghers of

[1] Pumpkin. The Forefathers' Ballad, handed down from early days in the Plymouth Colony, says:
> We have Pompion at morning and Pompion at noon.
> If it was not for Pompion we should be undone.

[2] The beakers in the illustration are among the few surviving pieces that show the work of John Hull without that of his later partner, Robert Sanderson.

Boston waxing rich ordered silver cans, salts, tankards, beakers, tumblers, bowls, candlesticks, caudle cups, platters, porringers, and wine tasters, for their family use. Many of the drinking vessels and round plates in course of time found their way by will or gift into the possession of the churches, and so were saved for us. For in the eighteenth and nineteenth centuries there was a deplorable practice of melting down ancient pieces of family plate to have them reworked in the latest style.

At twenty-three John Hull had got on in the world so well as to take to himself a wife: Judith, the daughter of Edmund Quincy. Governor Winthrop tied the knot. John had been brought up under the ministry of Cotton and Wilson, but it was not until the year after his marriage that they managed, as he expresses it, 'to beget me to God, and in some measure to increase and build me up in holy fellowship with him, through his abundant grace, he gave me roome in the hearts of his people, soe that I was accepted to fellowship with his church, about the 15th of October, 1648. And He made me allso (according to the talent he betrusted me with,) in some small measure serviceable to his people and also gave mee aceptance and favour in their eyes, and (as a fruit thereof) advancement (I must needs say) above my deserts.'

What was this undeserved advancement which John mentions in the same breath with church membership? The franchise? Election to the General Court, or to the Board of Selectmen? No, none of these — 'I was chosen and acepted A Corporall under the command of my honored Major Gibons.' Smile if you will, but many of my readers will remember how they felt themselves when first adorned with a pair of chevrons.

It was an excellent militia system in which John Hull then obtained his first distinction. The puritans resuscitated the mediæval assize-at-arms and the principle of universal military training, long obsolete in England itself. Every lad when he reached the age of sixteen, unless a student at the college, had to provide himself with a musket 'not under three foote nine inches in length, nor... above fower foote three inches,' together with 'a priming wyer, worme, and scourer fitted to the bore of his musket'; or if a pikeman, with a six-foot pike and 'a sufficient corslet, buffe coate, or quilted coate.' In England the trained bands were called out hardly once in five years, and few of their members before the Civil Wars even knew how to load a musket; but the Massachusetts militia had monthly company drills under arms, and an annual muster of the regiment from each of the four counties (Suffolk, Middlesex, Essex, and Norfolk). In addition the men at arms had to perform their turn at nightly watching and warding, and they were subject to draft for the military expeditions in the Indian wars.

John Hull's regimental commander, Edward Gibbons, called by Edward Johnson, 'the crown of the military affairs in this Commonwealth,' was an interesting character: a former member of Thomas Morton's gay company at Merrymount who repented (it seems) and joined the church of Salem, but is suspected to have retained a hankering for illicit trade. A little pinnace of his registering but thirty tons, returned from a voyage to the West Indies with a suspiciously rich freight, an 'aligarto' for the Governor, and a cock-and-bull story which Winthrop records with an innocent air, as though it were no business of his to bring out the obvious fact that Gibbons had been receiving stolen goods from the buccaneers of Hispaniola. One did not like to look too closely into the Major's private business, for there was no doubt of his superior military ability. Captain Edward Johnson describes him as 'a man of a resolute spirit, bold as a Lion, being wholly tutor'd up in New England Discipline, very generous and forward to promote all military matters; his Forts are well contrived, and batteries strong and in good repair, his great Artillery well mounted and cleanly kept, half-cannon, culverins and sakers as also field-pieces of brass very ready for service; his own company led by Lieutenant Savage, are very compleat in their arms, and many of them disciplin'd in the military garden beside their ordinary trainings.'

This was the company to which John Hull belonged. Lieutenant Thomas Savage, Anne Hutchinson's son-in-law and defender, returned to Boston in a repentant mood after six months in Rhode Island and was treated as the prodigal son. The most interesting of the early portraits painted in Massachusetts shows Thomas Savage in his old age serving one of many terms as Captain of the Ancient and Honorable Artillery Company. This was an élite organization outside the militia, an offshoot from the Artillery Company of London, still in existence and much in evidence on Boston Common in early June with its antique uniforms and ancient ceremonial. John Hull, always a good 'joiner,' followed his lieutenant into the Ancients and Honorables, and in due time rose to the command, when we may picture him like Savage in russet coat, white lace collar, and scarlet sword-sash, drilling the valiant defenders of the city in the artillery garden on Boston Common. No office in the colony short of the magistracy was held in such esteem; and to the magistracy John Hull eventually attained.

Whatever it may have been on the Sabbath, the ordinary week-day scene in Boston of the sixteen-fifties was active and colorful enough to suit a Dutch painter. 'Holland, France, Spain and Portugal coming hither for trade, shipping going on gallantly,' taverns doing a roaring trade with foreign sailors and native citizens; 'boys and girls sporting up and down' the streets, between houses gay with the fresh color of new wood and the red-painted trim; the high tide lapping into almost every back-yard and garden; and Beacon Hill towering over all. Seamen were coming home with money to spend, merchants prospered, and there was much call for the work of John Hull.

CAPTAIN THOMAS SAVAGE
Troops, Beacon Hill, and Boston Harbor in the background

Let the episode of Captain Cromwell stand for much that occurred outside politics and religion. Ten years after he had left the Bay as a common seaman, this stout fellow returned as a privateer captain in charge of three Spanish prizes, having 'abord his vessels about 80 lustie men (but very unruly) who, after they came ashore, did so distemper them selves with drinke as they became like madd-men.' This was at Plymouth, 'Divine providence' (in the shape of a stiff northwest wind) forcing the fleet in there 'for the comfort and help of that town, which was now almost deserted,' says Governor Winthrop. Governor Bradford thought it a very doubtful decree of divine providence. The seamen 'spente and scattered a great deal of money among the people, and yet more sine (I fear) than mony, notwithstanding all the care and watchfullness that was used towards them, to prevent what might be.' One 'desperate drunken fellow' of the company, running at his commander with a rapier, had it snatched from him, and his head broken in with a blow from the hilt. Captain Cromwell was tried for murder by a court martial of militia officers, and promptly acquitted. The Plymouth militia, each man provided with an ell of black taffeta from the pirated cargo, accompanied the seaman's body to the grave; and a pleasant time was had by all. From Plymouth, the fleet proceeded to Boston, and proved that they had plenty left in money, plate, and jewels. Captain Cromwell was offered a furnished mansion, but 'took up his lodging in a poor thatched house' whose owner had entertained him as a common sailor when the better taverns would not let him in. He presented Governor Winthrop with a splendid sedan-chair, destined by the Viceroy of Mexico to his lady sister, but captured on the way. The Governor did not like the idea of being carried around the streets of Boston in a sedan de luxe; but he was glad to have it on hand when something was wanted to placate the D'Aulnays of Acadia, claiming £8000 damages for the unneutral aid given to La Tour.[1] After considerable haggling the sumptuous sedan was tendered by way of settlement, and accepted with thanks; though what D'Aulnay could have done with it in Nova Scotia passes comprehension. A guard of musketeers escorted the sedan and the French commissioners to their boat at Long Wharf, a barrel of sack was rolled aboard, and amid the crashing of salutes from Major Gibbons's artillery, the delighted Frenchmen dropped down Boston Harbor.

This increase of wealth and influx of silver doubtless gave John Hull business, but did not help the currency problem, a difficulty here as in all new countries. Pirates and honest traders alike were bringing in specie in every conceivable form: golden Spanish doubloons and silver dollars; Portuguese johannes and moidores, French crowns; Dutch ducats and rix-dollars; silver bars, sows, and pigs from the mines of Peru. Yet there was no proper currency to be had. For want of a staple the balance of trade with England was so adverse that whatever sterling money came with the immigrants went back for remittances; the foreign coin was confusing, and much of it proved counterfeit or clipped. Most of the business in the colony was done by barter, taxes paid in kind, and small change made by 'muskett bulletts of a full boare' at a farthing apiece ('provided that noe man be compelled to take above xii d. att a tyme in them'); white wampum at four a penny and blue at two a penny, the rate being lowered from time to time. So in 1652 the General Court, in pursuance of its steadfast policy of building up a prosperous, self-sufficient commonwealth, decided to exercise the sovereign prerogative of coining money. By coining shillings that weighed only three-quarters of the sterling standard, they hoped both to supply the want of currency, and (perhaps from some dim perception of Gresham's law) to keep it at home. Accordingly, the Colony provided a mint-house sixteen foot square and ten foot stud, with tools, implements

[1] See below, Chapter VII.

for melting, refining, and coining of silver. John Hull was appointed Master of the Mint, and directed to coin 'bullion, plate, or Spanish coine' into shillings, sixpences and three-penny bits 'flatt and square on the sides and stamped on the one side with N E and on the other with the figure XII^d VI^d and III^d,' taking a suitable seigniorage for his pains.

John Hull called into partnership his friend Robert Sanderson, another godly goldsmith who had learned his trade in England, and removed to Boston after a temporary sojourn at Hampton, New Hampshire, and Watertown. Together they took an oath to coin all moneys by 'the just allay of the English coine,' and to give true weight. That they kept their promise faithfully is shown by the fact that some sample coins were assayed by the royal mint in 1684, and found to be of 'allay equal to his Majesty's silver Coyns of England' and of proper weight according to the New England standard.

The simple and irregularly shaped coins made under this act (examples of which are shown on the top line of the illustration) lent themselves so readily to clipping and washing that the act was changed the same year, providing an inscription and a tree design, within two concentric rings. Under this law Hull and Sanderson began the coinage of what are generally known as the pine-tree shillings, and fractions thereof. The act, however, said nothing about the tree being a pine, and the earliest coins, bearing the closest resemblance to the official design, show a tree which is anything but a pine. In fact there are three different types of Massachusetts shillings, known to collectors as the willow-tree, the oak-tree, and the pine-tree coins. Each of the three denominations in the willow- and oak-tree types shows from three to six different dies, and there are no less than twenty-seven varieties of the pine-tree type.

Examples of all three types, with three varieties of the oak and four of the pine, are shown in the illustration. A steady improvement in design and execution will be noticed, those in the last pine-tree shillings being not inferior to the coinage of the poorer European states in the seventeenth century, and certainly equal to much of the state coinage during the American Revolution. The pine-tree pattern did not appear until after 1662, and it was undoubtedly oak-tree money that Sir Thomas Temple produced in his famous interview with Charles II.

After the Restoration, attention of the English government was called to the fact that Massachusetts Bay had usurped an unchallenged royal prerogative by coining money. Sir Thomas Temple was deputed by the General Court to placate offended Majesty. He began the interview apologetically. The colonists did not know they were doing wrong; they needed currency and had to make it themselves, since His Majesty, to their great grief, had been in no position to supply them. A shilling was produced and showed to the King. Charles inquired what tree that was? Sir Thomas had the wit to declare it to be the royal oak, which the good people of the Bay had placed on their coins as token of loyalty, daring not to incur the usurper's displeasure by using the royal name! The King was greatly pleased, called the New Englanders 'a parcel of honest dogs,' and allowed the Boston mint to continue operations.

Joseph Jencks, an inventive Welshman formerly employed at the Lynn ironworks, is credited, on not very good authority, with having made some of the dies. John Hull's brother Edward writes to him from London in 1654, offering to send over a German die-cutter who would be useful; but we have no record of his coming. Judging by the other work of Hull and Sanderson, they were capable of cutting dies themselves. But it is strange that with at least thirty-five different dies for the shilling alone, the original date of 1652 was never altered. Actually the coins were being struck every year as late as 1683, when John Hull died. Neither is it clear why the spelling 'Masathusets' was employed, since the modern

MASSACHUSETTS COINAGE BY HULL AND SANDERSON

Upper line: 'N E' shilling and sixpence
Second and third lines: 'Willow-tree' sixpence and shilling
Fourth and fifth lines: Pine-tree shillings

From the cabinet of the Massachusetts Historical Society

SILVER MADE IN BOSTON IN THE SEVENTEENTH CENTURY

Above: Chalices by Hull and Sanderson, and beakers by Hull
Below: Salver by Timothy Dwight, and tankards by Henry Hurst

spelling was used in the act of 1652. Although the dies differ considerably in diameter, all the coins of the same denomination contain the same amount of silver.

The reduced value of the Bay coinage as compared with the English did not altogether prevent its being shipped out of the country, and severe laws were passed to keep it at home. Nor could the mint supply all the currency required for trade, since it was more profitable to export bullion and foreign money than to have it coined with the loss of seigniorage. Consequently Spanish dollars were made legal tender in 1672, if tried and weighted by the mint-master, and stamped 'N. E.' The ratio of dollar to Massachusetts shilling was fixed at six to one. As no money was coined in Massachusetts from 1686 to 1775, the pine-tree shillings circulated to some extent until the Revolution, and the pound of twenty pine-tree shillings or $3.33⅓ remained the 'lawful money' of New England. Long after the federal decimal coinage was established, New Englanders continued to reckon in pounds of $3.33⅓ and shillings of $0.16⅔. The editor of Hull's diaries, writing in 1857, says 'almost all prices in retail trade are stated in the terms of that currency to this day'; and I can remember an instance forty years after that. An old countryman selling Christmas greens at Faneuil Hall market said, 'I guess I'll hev t' cha'ge ye a shillin' each.' My grandfather understood perfectly, gave him a dollar bill, and told me to pick out six wreaths to carry home.

John Hull was reputed to have made a very good thing out of the mint. He should have, as the seigniorage and allowance for waste, amounting to 1s. 7d. in the £, was considerably more than was taken by any royal mint of Europe. Sanderson and he always refused to reduce it, although frequently requested to do so by the General Court; but they found it politic to make an annual 'free gift' to the colony treasury. Naturally the populace believed that their gains were enormous; Governor Hutchinson's statement that Hannah Hull was endowed with £30,000 must have been gathered from the old wives' tales of his childhood in Boston.

Whatever the profits of the mint may have been, it required a very small portion of the time of Hull and Sanderson. Their partnership extended to the goldsmith's business as well; on almost all the surviving pieces Robert Sanderson's mark will be found beside that of John Hull. From the seigniorage they obtained silver to make up articles for sale, instead of merely executing the orders of customers who brought their own bullion. We may imagine that the visitor to their shop found a brave array of all manner of domestic vessels, with tankards predominating, to choose from. It is disappointing to find no reference in John Hull's letter-book to his work as a goldsmith, for that was a retail business if not wholly done on order; but a letter from Governor Sanford of Rhode Island to Elisha Hutchinson of Boston, 'Cozen, I pray send my wine Cupp from Mr Hull,' shows that he did work for people outside the colony. And John Hull's account with John Winthrop, Jr., presented March 1, 1661, is an interesting study in comparative prices. Since 1656 Winthrop had owed him 3s. for a thimble, 10s. 6d. for a bodkin and a pair of buttons, £2 6s. for 'one silver tunn' delivered in 1659, and £3 10s. for 'one silver Beker' delivered the following year. Hull credits him with 18 bushels of wheat at 4s. 3d., and with £1 2s. 4d. for two beaver skins. At this rate, our ancestors would have done well by their descendants had they converted more fur and wheat than they did into the work of John Hull and Robert Sanderson!

As for the quality of their work, Mr. E. Alfred Jones, an international authority on the goldsmiths' art, has kindly allowed me to quote him as follows:

Hull and Sanderson were most efficient craftsmen, and their silver, within its limits, is quite equal in technical achievement and in downright honest work with contemporary English silver. Unfortunately, their larger and heavier vessels have long since been consigned to the melting pot, having been regarded as mere bullion. Were these treasures now in existence, they would doubtless be found to compare very favorably with the silver wrought by London craftsmen.

Hull and Sanderson were the teachers of a race of Boston-born goldsmiths. Sanderson's three sons followed their father's business. John Hull received into his house in 1659 two Boston boys, Jeremiah Dummer and Samuel Paddy, to serve as apprentices for eight years. Although Sam was the son of 'blessed William Paddy' he turned out a bad boy, went to London to seek his fortune, and did not prosper. His old master wrote him in 1681, 'Had you abode here and followed your Calling you might have bene worth many hundred pounds of cleare estate and you might have enjoyed many more helpes for your sole. Mr. Dummer lives in good fashion hath a wife and three children and a good Estate is a member of the church and like to be very useful in his Generation.' So he was. Jeremy set up for himself shortly after his time was up, and worthily carried on the artistic and secular traditions of his master's house. He was an officer of the artillery company, judge under the provincial government, member of the Council of Safety after the Revolution of 1689, and deacon of the First Church, for which he made the two beautiful chalices shown in one of our illustrations. As a goldsmith, Dummer executed many graceful and refined things, both in domestic and church silver, which must have gladdened the heart of his master, as they delight us. He died in 1718, at the age of seventy-three.

Nine years junior to Jeremy Dummer was Timothy Dwight, son and namesake of a citizen of Dedham who founded the distinguished New England family of that name. Timothy became John Hull's apprentice, as successor to Jeremy Dummer.[1] He died in 1691 at the age of thirty-seven,

---

[1] I infer this from the fact that Dwight witnesses an agreement made at John Hull's house in 1672, when he was eighteen years old, and that the other witness, Daniel Quincy, is known to have been Hull's apprentice.

yet some excellent domestic and ecclesiastical pieces survive, stamped with his mark. Dwight was partial to the ornate style of Charles II's reign; a winged tankard of his shows the embossed acanthus and palm leaves then so much favored. The salver shown in our illustration is an amusing piece, since Dwight, perhaps thinking of the charger on which John the Baptist's head was served up, engraved the edge with figures which he believed to be animals of the orient. There is a strange beast half dromedary and half wild ass, probably meant for a camelopard; and an elephant with a castle on his back. The flowers appear to be conventional carnations. Eleven years younger than Dwight was Henry Hurst, whose substantial tankards are shown on either side of Dwight's salver. The tankards of that generation were so solid and heavy, that the ladies of the late eighteenth century generally persuaded their husbands to have them melted down and turned into tea-sets.

John Coney, born in Boston in 1655, is the next on the honorable roll of Boston goldsmiths. We have no knowledge of his artistic education, but as he and Jeremy Dummer married sisters, it is likely that Dummer or Hull was his master. Coney was a member of the Second Church, but not so active in public affairs as his fellow silversmiths. He engraved the plates for the first Massachusetts paper money in 1690, setting the style for paper currency that continued through the next century. Coney lived into a period when social life in Massachusetts was becoming more stately and elaborate. The chocolate pot shown in our illustration was made by him in 1701, out of a legacy of £20 from Lieutenant-Governor William Stoughton, the witch-hanging judge, to his niece. The two silver candlesticks might have graced the same table as the chocolate pot; in the braziers, spirits were burned to keep dishes warm. Eighteen or twenty years later Coney made a remarkable silver punch bowl with a scalloped edge for James Alexander of New York, the father of General Lord

Stirling. It was in the shop of John Coney that Apollos
Rivoire, a clever immigrant from the Channel Islands, served
an apprenticeship. His son and namesake, anglicized to Paul
Revere, was the patriot-silversmith of the Revolution.

After Dwight and Coney comes a new generation of silversmiths, men such as Henry Hurst (1665–1717), Edward Winslow (1669–1753), David Jesse (1670–1705), all born at Boston
in the late seventeenth century, but doing much of their work
in the eighteenth; and John Dixwell (1680–1735) a son of the
regicide judge, who probably came to Boston in 1700. In all,
there are records of no less than thirty-two goldsmiths in
Boston, as against thirteen outside New England, who were
at least twenty-one years old at the end of the seventeenth
century. Their work, as a whole, shows an artistic and technical quality of which any town in the British Empire, short
of London, might well have been proud; and I doubt whether
the work of Winslow and Dixwell has ever been surpassed in
America. That the artists themselves were appreciated by
their puritan neighbors is shown by the numerous offices,
political, military and ecclesiastical to which they were
chosen. That they were proud of their profession is shown
by the fact that Hull to the end of his days, even after he had
become a merchant and colony treasurer, always signed himself in legal documents 'John Hull of Boston, goldsmith.'

In the art of painting, there is nothing to boast about. The
earliest portrait painting in the colonies was done by limners,
who painted taverns and shop signs, coats of arms for hatch-
ments, or for the panels of carriages. A Boston limner once
offered to paint the portrait of the venerable Master John
Wilson, but met with a flat refusal; for some of the stricter
puritans regarded portraits as vanities. Although there have
survived twelve or fourteen Boston portraits of the period
1666–1686, very few can be assigned to a definite artist.
Evert Duyckinck, a Dutch limner of New York, is known to
have painted the excellent 'Athenæum' portrait of Chief-

Justice Stoughton at Dorchester in 1685; but it is only a guess to assign the portrait of Governor Bellingham painted in 1641 and signed 'W. R.' to a local map-maker named William Read. There are in existence several alleged portraits of New England worthies with inscriptions assigning them to Bostonians, and some authorities on colonial portraiture accept these as genuine. When one reflects that it takes only a neat inscription to lift an anonymous portrait out of a London junk-shop to an 'early American' worth something in four figures, one will be cautious in accepting such 'discoveries' unless they have a well-attested pedigree. There is not known to be in existence a single landscape or genre painting or even drawing of a New England subject until well on in the eighteenth century.

Here is no stick to beat the puritans, however. Pioneering is not conducive to artistry. The age of colonization was the greatest age of Spanish art; yet the two Americas provided hardly a subject for a Spanish brush; and of the thousands of Dutch interiors of the seventeenth century, not one is of New Netherland. Even Magna Graecia could show little achievement in the arts to compare with Athens; and in modern times, whether in New Spain, New France, or the overseas dependencies of England, at least a century and a half had to elapse before the colony could produce anything in creative art comparable with that of the mother country.

The only medium for sculpture in New England was the gravestone; and it was improved to the full. The first generation was content with a simple inscription and a crude death's head; the second and third generations showed excellent taste in conventional borders of foliage and fruit, in the lettering, and in the composition of the hour-glass, scythe, skull, angel's wings, and other emblems of mortality and resurrection. In the examples here reproduced we find the beginning of a true folk art, which followed a consistent development through the next century as the puritan creed softened, replacing the skull and crossbones by a winged cherub, and finally attempting a portrait. Few names of gravestone-cutters of the seventeenth century have been preserved, but the nature of the stones proves that the work must have been done locally.

What, then, becomes of the favorite notion of 'stark' puritanism, with its cult of ugliness, and inveterate hostility to the arts? Only this: that puritanism was not a way of life favorable to the development of the highest art, since it forbade the use of symbolism in religion (with the fortunate exception of the Lord's Supper), and discouraged extravagance and display. By rejecting religious music, religious sculpture, and religious painting, as misleading symbols diverting man from direct communion with God, the puritan deliberately closed some of the principal outlets for the æsthetic sense. Yet the men of the Bay Colony, magistrates and ministers, deacons and church members, have left sufficient evidence that they appreciated beauty in the things of daily use, and were capable of producing it themselves. The evidence is so concrete and conclusive as to preclude chance; nor is it chance that so many of the best architects, sculptors, painters, musicians, poets, and prose writers of America, have been descendants of Bay Colony puritans. The puritans of that day had no grudge against civilization, only against its corruptions; and he who dedicates his life to the beauty of holiness, is not far from the sight of all beauty.

2. THE BUSINESS MAN

If John Hull was first of the colonial artists, he was also high in the ranks of the colonial business men. He owned vessels and freighted them with his own ventures coastwise and abroad, imported English goods and exported peltry, employed men cutting timber on the Piscataqua, owned farms in various parts of the Bay Colony, bred horses in Rhode Island. He dealt in mortgages, lent money at interest, and as treasurer of the Colony during a great Indian war, sustained the public credit by his own.

This phase of John Hull's career reminds me that I have said nothing as yet about the relation of puritanism to business. Max Weber, a German economist of the last century, propounded the interesting theory that Calvinism released the business man from the clutches of the priest, and sprinkled holy water on economic success. According to him, John Calvin defended the taking of interest on loans, which the mediæval church had condemned under the name of usury. Since God would not justify reprobates by prosperity, so the argument goes, the successful business man was probably one of God's elect; hence the puritan sought success as evidence of his election to eternal bliss.

Whatever may be thought of this theory in relation to what Calvin actually taught and wrote, it will not hold water here. Never have I found the slightest suggestion in New England puritan writings of a mind working that way. In none of the scores of funeral sermons which I have read, is it hinted 'Our departed friend was successful, so he must be in Heaven.' On the contrary, the economic ideas of the New England puritans were mediæval; and so far as their church had political power, it regulated rather than stimulated business enterprise.

The classic instance of this, related in Governor Winthrop's journal, was the case of Robert Keayne, a wealthy merchant of high social standing in early Boston. He was a church member, yet had been frequently admonished for 'oppression' (profiteering). At the General Court in 1639, he was convicted on several counts of taking from fifty to a hundred per cent profit on his goods, and a dispute arose between the deputies whether he should be fined £100 or £200. Keayne was an unpopular man — as we have seen in the case of Goody Sherman's sow — and the deputies wished to make an example of him. The magistrates stood out for the lower fine because there was no express law against profiteering, because every one had been doing it that could, and 'because it is the common practice in all countries, for men to make use of advantages for raising the prices of their commodities.' If any of the deputies present had come over in the *Arbella*, they might have replied out of Governor Winthrop's shipboard sermon, in which he expressly condemned usury, oppression, and extortion. Keayne got off with the lower fine, and a censure from the Boston church, which made him 'with tears acknowledge and bewail his covetous and corrupt heart.' Master Cotton took the occasion to deliver a sermon on business ethics, and to announce the following principles which the godly should follow in trade.

The rules for trading were these (records Winthrop):

1. A man may not sell above the current price, i.e., such a price as is usual in the time and place, and as another (who knows the worth of the commodity) would give for it, if he had occasion to use it...

2. When a man loseth in his commodity for want of skill, etc., he must look at it as his own fault or cross, and therefore must not lay it upon another.

3. Where a man loseth by casualty of sea... it is a loss cast upon himself by providence, and he may not ease himself of it by casting it upon another...

4. A man may not ask any more for his commodity than his selling price, as Ephron to Abraham, the land is worth thus much.

It is clear from this statement that John Cotton accepted the mediæval doctrine of the just price. On economics he saw eye-to-eye with the greatest of mediæval schoolmen, St. Thomas Aquinas.[1] If Massachusetts ever came to an attitude of fawning on the wealthy and successful, it would

[1] Compare Aquinas' *Summa Theologia*, Part II, second number, question lxxvii (English translation of 1918, pp. 317–28). The *Summa* was well known to English puritans. It was one of the recommended books at Emmanuel College. Governor Winthrop quotes from it extensively in his discourse on arbitrary government, and Ezekiel Rogers willed his copy to the library of Harvard College.

not be the fault of her parsons. Grouped together at the Day of Doom, says Master Michael Wigglesworth:

> Adulterers and Whoremongers
>   were there, with all unchast:
> There Covetous, and Ravenous,
>   that Riches got too fast:
> Who us'd vile ways themselves to raise
>   t'estates and wordly wealth,
> Oppression by, or Knavery,
>   by Force, or fraud, or stealth.

The puritan clergy were no respecters of persons, and the spectacle of Robert Keayne, Boston's richest business man, blubbing and begging pardon from his Church, is one to delight Mr. Cram or Mr. Chesterton.

The idea of *laissez faire*, that each person should be free to buy cheap and sell dear, to follow what calling he pleased and choose between work and idleness, was utterly strange to the early New England puritan. He brought with him from England the contrary ideal of regulation, of social and economic life carefully ordered in the interest of the common good. The founders of Massachusetts Bay brought no gospel of economic freedom; on the contrary, they attempted to preserve in New England both the class distinctions and economic restrictions of Old England. A class of gentry was legally recognized by exemption from the punishment of whipping, and by the titles Master and Mistress — the ordinary respectable people being known as Goodman and Goodwife, or Goody. In order to keep the lower classes from aping their betters, sumptuary legislation was passed, providing that no women should wear silk hoods and scarves unless their husbands were worth £200; and later this was amended to include those decayed gentry who had formerly been worth £200. These regulations were enforced. At the Ipswich Quarterly Court in September, 1653, eleven women were presented for wearing silk hoods or scarves illegally — but only two were fined. Four got off by proving their husbands 'better worth than two hundred pounds.' Another presented a long letter from her husband, declaring that although he was not worth £200, there were four good reasons why his wife should wear a silk scarf and hood:

(1) She was brought up to it; (2) 'I am bound by conshens and love to mainetaine my wives honnour and that good education that shee was brought up in but neither conshens nor love doth yet teach me to maintaine her worss then I found her'; (3) 'When she doth weare a scarfe it is not becaus she would be in the fashon or that she would be as fine as another; but (4) for the necessity and presserving of health, and this appears to me thus becaus she ordinarily weares a scarfe but two seasons, the first is in winter when it is very colde, the other Season is when it is very wett weather. More, I conceive if she did weare her scarfe for prid she would be as proud in summer as she is in winter and in dry weather as in wett. She have a disspossison contrary to most women.'

This sort of thing hurt business, of course. Yet John Hull, the puritan merchant, approved of such restrictions, and complains in his diary of the introduction of new and extravagant fashions.

A second class of restrictive legislation in Massachusetts Bay was that on choice of occupation. The puritans approved of the mediæval gild. Workers skilled in some particular trade and mystery, which they had attained by a long apprenticeship, had a right to protection from those not so well trained, and the public had a right to protection from inferior work. A shoemakers' gild and a coopers' gild with full powers of regulation and admission, were established on the English model by the General Court in 1648, but only for the space of three years.[1] These privileges were not renewed.

Probably the process was already under way which turned a one-occupation English peasant or artisan into a Yankee

[1] The organizer of the coopers' gild was an interesting character named Thomas Venner, who arrived in the colony too late to take part in the Hutchinson affair, but after his return to England became preacher at a conventicle of Fifth-Monarchy men in London. He was executed in 1661 after leading a bloody and desperate attack by his disciples on the monarchy of Charles II.

Jack-of-all-trades and master of most. The goldsmiths never attempted to organize; the length of time it took to learn their art and mystery was sufficient protection to them, and their own sense of honor protected the public from inferior ware.

What with the raising of cattle, and the need of leather for clothing, shoes, and saddlery, the hide industry early became one of great importance. An assize of leather was adopted to check 'the several deceits and abuses which in other places are commonly practiced by the Tanners, Curriers and workers of leather, as also the abuses and inconveniences which acrue to the severall members of this Common-wealth, by leather not sufficiently tanned and wrought.' Butchers, curriers, shoemakers are forbidden to 'use or exercise the feat or mysterie of a Tanner,' or to bargain, buy, or bespeak raw hides. 'Warm woozes' and other short-cuts in tanning are forbidden under heavy fines; and every town where tanning is, shall appoint Sealers and Searchers of Leather to destroy what is bad, and put the town mark on the good. The export of hides was forbidden, in order that they be kept in the colony and worked up there; just as England forbade the export of wool, in the interest of her wool industry. Massachusetts, too, forbade the export of wool, after the West-Riding men had established the textile industry at Rowley. The importation of hides was not forbidden, however, and John Hull brought in many from the West Indies.

In 1655 the General Court passed a protective tariff high enough to please the insurgent farmers of the present wheat belt:

The Court, taking into theire serious consideracion the great necessitie of upholding the staple comodities of this countrie for the supply and support of the inhabitants thereof, and finding by experience that the bringing in of maulte, wheate, barly, bisket, beife, meale and flower, which are the princippall comodities of this countrie, from faraigne parts, to be exceeding prejudiciall to the

Subsistance of this place and people here, have therefore ordered that no person whatsoever either inhabitant or straunger shall... import into this jurisdiccion from any part of Europe any of the aforesaid provissions under poenalty of confiscation of the same.

Thus, mercantilist and protectionist ideas were not only brought over from England, but applied against England, in order to build up colonial industry. No wonder that when English economists of the mercantilist school came to examine the economy of New England, they should consider it prejudicial to the mother country.

Standard weights and measures were provided by the Colony, and each town required to keep a set, in comparison with which those used in trade were to be 'sized and sealed,' and the rest destroyed. Bakers were brought under the English assize of bread, a sliding scale giving the prescribed weight of the penny white loaf for each probable price of wheat. The amount of malt in beer was similarly regulated, and licensed ale-houses were compelled to furnish 'ordinaries' — regular meals, at a fixed price. Freighting profits in the coasting trade, in which John Hull engaged, were restricted to $3d.$ in the shilling; but on the whole John Hull kept out of those forms of business which were closely regulated. He took the principle of regulation for granted, so far as it was applied by his own government; but the English Acts of Trade he regarded as unreasonable and unjust, and paid no attention to them.

Other regulations by the General Court were designed to maintain the reputation abroad of New England products such as dried fish and pipe-staves, of which the oversize wine hogsheads of the day were made. 'Whereas information hath come to this Court from divers forrein parts of the insufficiencie of our Pipe-staves in regard especially of worm holes, whereby the commoditie is like to be prohibited in those parts, to the great damage of the Countrie'; every town whence the commodity is shipped shall appoint Viewers of Pipe-staves, who shall cull and reject from proposed exports to Spain and Portugal, all pipe-staves that are wormy, unsound, or falling short of a prescribed measure.

There was a third group of economic regulation, the laws against idleness, which we may connect with puritan doctrine. Idleness has never been regarded as a virtue by any governing class. It has always been a belief common to menfolk and the rich that it is the business of womenfolk and the poor to be industrious:

> All vice she doth refuse,
> And hateth Idleness

sings the Elizabethan poet of his mistress. But few communities have legislated so frequently and minutely against idleness as the New England colonies, beginning with the first church covenant of Salem, whose signers promised to 'shun idleness as the bane of any state.' To the puritans, time was a gift of God which must be improved to his service by pursuing some legitimate calling. 'Seasonable recreation' they did not deny; but to sit chatting idly or merely relaxing, was a sinful 'waste of precious time,' God's time. It is only countries in the Calvinist or puritan tradition that regard time as precious. The mediæval Church allowed its members to spend their time in any lawful way, provided they supported their families properly and performed their religious duties. A Frenchman will save peapods, pins, and bits of paper, but he will not save time; and to us the banking and business methods of all Latin nations seem designed to waste as much time as possible. Americans in recent years have been taught the duty of wasting goods in order to keep prosperity revolving. But your typical Yankee still uses his leisure to think up some labor or time-saving device, so that he will have more time to think up other labor and time-saving devices. Although the chapter on Idleness in the Lawes and Libertyes of 1648 is no longer in force, the basic idea is still part of New England folkways:

It is ordered by this Court and the Authoritie thereof, that no person, Housholder or other, shall spend his time idlely or unprofitably under pain of such punishment as the Court of Assistants or County Court shall think meet to inflict. And for this end it is ordered that the Constable of everie place shall use speciall care and diligence to take knowledge of offenders in this kinde, especially of common coasters, unproffitable fowlers, and tobacco takers.

The last clause is significant as well as amusing. Common coasters meant 'longshore loafers, who picked up a living by desultory and occasional fowling, fishing and clamming. *Unprofitable* fowlers who, like the youthful John Winthrop, were bad shots, must not waste their precious time in pursuit of wild fowl; but if any good gunner chose to shoot duck and partridge for a living, and keep the community supplied with game, that was a legitimate and profitable calling. Similarly, the puritans frowned upon gambling, holiday-making, and other social diversions of Merry England, not as sins *per se*, but because they led to sin, and entailed waste of precious time. So with tobacco. The General Court forbade it to be smoked in barns or by thatched roofs and hay-stacks, because that was dangerous; or in taverns, because that would tempt men to lounge about. But tobacco-taking was not forbidden in private houses, or at Harvard College; and the practice soon spread to both sexes and all classes.

Mistress Rowlandson of Lancaster, in the account of her Indian captivity, tells us that she rejected a pipe of tobacco tendered by her royal captor, King Philip, not because it was wicked or unladylike, or because her reverend husband objected (for he sent her a pound or so to console her captivity), but because tobacco 'seems to be a Bait, the Devil layes to make men loose their precious time. I remember with shame, how formerly, when I had taken two or three pipes, I was presently ready for another, such a bewitching thing it is: But I thank God, he has now given me power over it; surely there are many who may be better employed than to ly sucking a stinking Tobacoo-pipe!'

The 'precious time' motive also comes into the early legislation of Massachusetts Bay fixing maximum wages, a natural course to take for men who had been doing the same thing in England, as justices of the peace. At the first Court of Assistants held on the American side, the Governor and Company fixed wages of carpenters, joyners, bricklayers, sawyers and thatchers at 2s. per day. Common labor was fixed at 18d. in 1633, 'in regard of... the greate disorder which grewe hereupon by vaine and idle waste of much precious tyme,' and the same year the Court began the regulation of prices in order to protect the workmen from 'oppression.' The maximum wage scale proved so difficult to enforce that in 1641 the wage-fixing function was delegated to the towns; but even with public opinion and 'persuasion of the elders' enforcing local regulations, they 'held not long,' wrote Winthrop.

Moral and police regulations proved much easier to enforce in New England than in the old country; then why was it impossible to keep wages down? The Governor answered his own question. If a worker did not like the maximum wage, he fell back on the land for a living, and 'would not be hired at all.'

Broadly speaking, immigrants to New England were just as eager to be farmers as the average American now is anxious to be anything but a farmer. So the skilled artisans who in large numbers emigrated to Massachusetts Bay, tended to get absorbed in the land, and to be replaced by other skilled artisans from England, such as the father of ·Benjamin Franklin and the ancestor of Nathaniel Bowditch, both late arrivals in the seventeenth century. For farm labor, household drudgery, and labor in big business, the New England was dependent largely on indented servants, people who bound themselves to serve seven years in return for their passage, and who had to work for wages when their indenture was up, before they could procure a farm.

Such were the economic ideas which the founders of Massachusetts Bay brought over, and the framework of economic legislation which they adopted. It was not as square and even a frame as one would wish. Puritanism was an enemy to big profits at other people's expense, and it did nothing toward enlarging the needle's eye to accommodate the camel; but, on the other side, it brought idleness into disgrace, and regarded activity as an end in itself. As Fuller wrote of John White's work at Dorchester: 'knowledge caused piety, and piety bred industry.' Inherited economic ideas damped individual enterprise, but wise regulation gave New England a reputation for 'quality products.' Nature, too, was both favorable and unfavorable. If she denied to the puritan planters a rich staple such as the tobacco of Virginia and the peltry of Canada, she gave the sea, England's new pathway to wealth, and timber for the framing and masting of vessels. On the whole the climate was favorable for enterprise; the summers, not too hot to enervate, were sufficient to ripen corn, the long-lying snow gave cheap inland transport, and the long winters invited household industry by the kitchen fireside. Only wanting for economic success were the right sort of men. The great emigration brought in plenty such, but for the most part their accounts and documents have disappeared. Fortunately there has been preserved a letter-book of John Hull which gives us a picture of the activities of a God-fearing merchant.

Our mint-master was a member of John Cotton's church, and had been converted through the ministry of him whose loss, so he wrote in his diary at Cotton's death, 'seemes unparaleled with respect to the living, and noe less gain to the dead.' I infer from the favor he enjoyed among the clergy, that he endeavored to follow the Cotton principles of fair trade, instead of the Keayne principles of passing on losses to your customers. So, too, from an entry in his diary from 1659: 'The Lord made up my lost goods in the two vessells last year by his own secret Blessing, though I know not which way.' We may assume that John assisted the Lord somewhat by his own prudence, but it is significant that his name is not to be found in the court records as party to a suit, although he was a prominent merchant doing business by credit. With the mature wisdom of fifty years, he writes: 'I have ever bene averse to strive att the law never haveing sued any man nor been sued and I observe the law to bee very much like a lottery — greate charge little Benefitt.' Methodical himself, he insisted on promptness and punctuality in others. The procrastination of Master William Hubbard, minister of Ipswich and historian of the colony, to whom he had lent £300 at five per cent, caused him to write: 'I have binn very slow hither to to seu you at the law becaus of that dishonor that will thereby come to god by your failure, but if you make noe great matter of it I shall take myself bound to make use of that help which god and the Country have provided for my just indemnity.' He never carried out the threat—in commiseration perhaps of the heavy charges and prolonged labors involved in writing history. It was left for his administrators to collect, and they never got it.

John Hull's letters reveal him a cautious business man, undertaking no rash speculation, refusing to enter new lines of trade to the Canaries and Africa, punctual in his dealings and requiring punctuality in others. They, too, are a mirror of the puritan mind. Religion and business were not in separate compartments of John's brain. His faith penetrates his every transaction, and crops out in the most prosaic business letters; while piety seeks to bring the mysterious purposes of Providence to the credit side of the ledger. For instance, in a letter to his 'Loving Cozens' Thomas Buckham and Daniel Allen of London, he tells how he had followed their orders in laying out a large sum in sugars and logwood at once. No sooner was the logwood bought than war was declared in Holland, the price tumbled, and shipping was not to be had.

It ware better iff you left mee at liberty at least sometimes but indeed it is hard to foresee what will bee and therfore it is best willing to submit to the great governing hand of the great Governor of all the greater and lesser revolutions that wee the poore sons of men are involved in   by the invoyce you see the whole amounteth to £405:16:3   so much mony I have indeed payed down for them and have frely given the storehouse roome of the sugers it being my constant custom in all my unkles buisness   I never had any thinge for ware house roome though sometimes it hath cost me thirty poundes in a yeare... in truth had I not been urged unto speed I should not have shiped youre goodes home till phrait had been cheaper or wee more asured of peasable times but sure tis man's infirmity wee know not wheather wee move tow fast or to slow or wheather it bee better to sit still or goe... forced to throw away your padlocks unsold the cand[le]sticks and other bringumes [1] — cannot sell them togather for what thay cost   your callicoes have sold about on third part... the french hatts I could never get in any quantity any advance neither will thay sell for mony at all but becaus of the Remembrans of my deare unkle and willingnesse to serve you my dear cozens I will either sell them as I can for you or take them to my owne account as thay cost... the bill of ladeing and invoyce is heare inclosed   recommending mee to youre good wifes I ad noe farther at Present.

These 'french hatts' were a sore point. Apparently not only the late departed 'unkle,' but his son, John's 'loveing cozen' Edward Hull, 'Haberdasher of Hatts at the Hatt-in-Hand within Aldegate in London' were in the habit of sending to Boston all the imported headwear they could not sell. 'Have yet by mee severall hundred poundes of hatts' writes John, 'that are out of fasion, and I have sent them up and downe [the] Country and have them returned home to mee againe but as [I said] formerly what I did ingage through the helpe of [God] I will pay though I shall never sell them.'

John Hull owned, first and last, quite a fleet of vessels:

[1] Brummagem goods, i.e. hardware made in Birmingham. In his orders to a captain, Hull writes 'if you goe to liverpool I suppose [you will load] course manchesters and tapes etc. Bremogem Knives etc. Red Cotton duffals, such things as are made att or neere the place but may be bought cheape.'

the *Friendship, Society, Dove, Sea-flower, Hopewell,* and *Try-all* are mentioned in his letters over a space of three years. All these were ketches, small decked vessels probably about forty to fifty feet long, square-rigged on the mainmast and carrying a lateen sail on the mizzen. Ketches were the seventeenth-century ancestors of coasting schooners. John Hull's vessels were of local construction, as Massachusetts Bay had already become a great shipbuilding center by 1650.

A good sample of John Hull's orders to his shipmasters is the following to John Alden (son of why-don't-you-speak-for-yourself John), master of his ketch *Friendship,* dated September 18, 1671. As a portion of the right edge has been torn, I have had to guess at the missing words, in square brackets:

Mr Jno. Alden you one the first faire wind to set saile [in the] Keth frendeship and to goe to some part of Virginia make [what speed] you can to put off what you carry for good tobacco and so speed [thence to] Ireland what part you think most likely for A markett If you [should] meet with a Good oppertunyty to sell the Keth in Virginia [I grant you] liberty to make A trip home with youre tobacco or ship them [to England or] otherwise, I know not but it may be as good as the other way [of selling it] in Ireland but iff in Ireland remitt the whole by exchange for England and then Invest it into Good mixt serges and prest serges with some lead and shott unless you meet with any such things in Ireland as you know will be better heer and therefore seing you may spey many Advantages that I heer cannot foresee I leave it to you from first to last in every thinge to doe with vessele and cargo what ever may conduce in youre best Judgment for my reale benifitt and advantage. leave noe debts behind you whereever you goe, I know you willbe carefull to see to the worship of God every day on the vessell and to the sanctification of the lords day and suppression of all prophaines that the lord may delight to be with you and his blessing upon you which is the hearty prayer of your frend and owner

John hull

John Alden had read the last sentence before, and he was to read it again; for John Hull invariably concluded his orders to his shipmasters thus, even when he sent his sloop *Endeavor* to salvage sunken treasure from a 'wrack' in the West Indies. He warned Captain Roots that if there were Sabbath-breaking and swearing on board, and 'man-stealing' of Indians, the Lord would certainly execute vengeance and frustrate the design. We do not know how these pious injunctions were observed on the *Endeavor*; but we do know that William Phips, who impressed Indian divers, and whose crew of cutthroats indulged in every known form of vice, located the 'wrack' and salvaged the treasure. In spite of Hull's horror at man-stealing, he once sent two negro slaves from Boston to Madeira for sale, the returns to be made in 'red Madera wine.'

Not many voyages were made by Hull's vessels to Virginia and Ireland, like the one enjoined on Captain Alden. The usual route for his cautious trade was the famous triangular one, Boston–West Indies–England–Boston, which was the key to the prosperity of maritime Massachusetts until the Revolution opened up new routes to the Far East. Just three weeks before Captain Alden was ordered to take the first fair wind to Virginia, the ketch *Society*, Josiah Roots master, was sent to Jamaica with orders to bring home a good freight for England, or to proceed to the Bay of Campeachy at his discretion for logwood — the valuable dye wood which the English persisted in cutting on the coast of Mexico and Honduras. It was one of the principal commodities that Hull handled, but he had a good deal of trouble with it first and last. One of his English correspondents became unpleasant when 'some of the loggwood proved plumtree.' Hull said it was not his fault. Mr. Dummer had bought the lot for him, and only experts could tell the difference; but somewhat reluctantly he made restitution. This unfortunate transaction cost him much peace of mind. Jealous of his reputation for honesty, Hull wrote in a strain of righteous indignation to his cousin Thomas Buckham who had been calling him 'a very knave' amongst company: 'I can through the grace of God bid defiance to you and all men to challenge any one action in my whole life in all my dealeings amongst men since I attained the yeares of a man, I thank God I have dealt honestly not in Craftyness nor in Guile but in the feare of God.' A prompt apology is called for, 'else I shall desire I may have no more to doe with you in this world, for the sin of Backbiteing and slandering is to be hated by all good men.'

As Captain Smith and John White had predicted, salt fish proved the principal staple for New England export; and the best market for the better sort, as in John Smith's day, was Spain. In return the Boston ships brought Cadiz salt, Bilboa iron, and wine of Xeres and the Western Islands. John Hull did a certain amount of business with Spain, freighting his consignments on the ships of John Usher, the Boston bookseller and merchant. In the midst of one of his letters to a Spanish correspondent, on matters of pork, wine, and salt fish, Hull writes: 'I thanke you for your two birds you sent mee I rec'd them in safty though noe letter but thay are both dead the Country is too cold for them pretty creatures it is a pitty thay should bee sent to dye for they cannot live heare in the winter nor have any Joy...'

The Barbary pirates made the Straits of Gibraltar dangerous waters for New England ships. Twice John Hull sends to an English correspondent money to redeem Massachusetts seamen from Algerine slavery: £50 for one, collected by his mother (and that did not prove enough) and £53 15s. 6d. for another, 'contributed from the love and compassion of the people' of his home town.

Salt cod and mackerel, barrels of flour, salt beef and pork, casks of biscuit, firkins of butter make up the commodities which Hull sent to Barbados and Jamaica, Nevis and 'Antego' stowed away in his little ketches. The market that the tropical islands afforded for these homely commodities was the mainstay of New England's prosperity. In John Hull's time few farms in Massachusetts were more than twenty miles from tidewater or navigable rivers, and all felt the ebb and flow of seaborne commerce. In another generation the ancient feud between town and country would be revived, but in that day the farmer loved the shipping merchant as the man who found vent for his corn and cattle. As John was elected deputy to the General Court from four inland towns in succession: Wenham, Westfield, Concord, and Salisbury, he must have enjoyed a reputation among the farmers for fair dealing. We have an amusing letter from him about a country correspondent's fat oxen which he kept in his own pasture pending their sale to a butcher. The oxen became so agitated when the Boston cows passed them by, going to and from the Common, and 'did soe tread my grass and in the wett ground make soe many holes with there feete that I had better have given twenty shillings they had never come there, but I will have nothing because your loss is great.'

At the West Indies Hull's captains sold these products of New England farms and fisheries to some island merchant such as Cesar Carter, Peter Lorphelm, or Solomon Delyon, who is referred to as 'Solomon the Jew' when he does not pay up promptly. From the same merchants the little ketches laid in a cargo of logwood, hides, indigo, cocoa, sugars, Spanish iron, pieces of eight and bullion, according to their masters' best judgment; but never in any instance molasses, as the famous rum industry had hardly begun. Once they tried a consignment of cotton wool, which the country people used to spin and weave, but it proved to be 'much fowle' with seed, and Hull's country correspondents threw it back on his hands. This round voyage to the West Indies consumed the winter season. By the early spring the 'wooden birds' (as Sam Danforth called them in his almanac verse) were back in Boston, and John Hull assembled his cargoes for England.

The same ketches were occasionally sent to Virginia for

tobacco which they sold in Ireland, Liverpool, or Bristol; but it took them too long to negotiate the English channel and the Downs. For consignments to London, Hull depended on 'constant traders,' such as the ship *Blessing*, William Greenough master. These vessels left England in the autumn with assorted cargoes of English and European goods, arriving in Boston between late October and early December, and in severe winters were apt to be frozen up in Boston harbor before getting away. In such cases, or if they had no space for his 'phraite,' Hull used the mast ships which sailed from the Piscataqua, and of which the *King Solomon* is frequently mentioned in his correspondence. She charged £5 a ton freight on logwood.

His returns to London are partly in specie, logwood, 'Brazeleto wood' and other Caribbean products; partly in beaver by the hogshead and truss, and moose skins by the hundred. Beaver came from the interior of New England; and the fact that Hull was elected a deputy by the pioneer town of Westfield, suggests that he handled the products of that lively center of the peltry trade. Westfield, founded in 1669, was an offshoot from Springfield, which William Pynchon had planted as early as 1636, in order to tap the fur-bearing region drained by the Connecticut River; and for several years the Pynchon family made heavier exports of beaver than the Hudson's Bay Company during its first decade. Moose skins probably came from Nova Scotia. In January, 1673, Hull sends to London over two hundred of them, weighing 3239 pounds. One surprising consignment to Bristol in his own ketch *Dove*, is 'six barrells of pottotess.' Potatoes are unheard of in New England before the next century, except as occasional imports from Bermuda; one would suppose that Bristol could have had them cheaper from Ireland.

Hull's imports from England are mainly textiles: bales of dowlass, duffells, cambric, and say; bright-colored galant cloth and penistones, sad-colored serges and kerseys. Small wares are also called for, and on one occasion, coral whistles for children. His 'loveing unkle Pariss' of London is mildly reproved for sending by Master Greenough 'a piece of white damask and a chyna sute which I doubt are like to be long house keepers neither are they good for the Countrey but onely to nourish Pride.' One would like to know whether the set of china did sell, or did the conservative Bostonians declare that old-fashioned pewter was good enough to serve their hearty meals? There could have been no call as yet for china cups, as tea and coffee had not been introduced.

One of the correspondents, Mistress Hooker of London, consigned to Hull's care her daughter Mary, to go into domestic service and perhaps pick up a husband. But Mary proved a stubborn wench, changing her place three or four times a year, and so ill-favored that no Yankee rustic would have her. Hull writes to her mother: 'I have been willing to hope that she [may] grow elder and wiser but when that time will come I know [not and] it renders mee a little the more doubtfull becauss when I sp[eak] with her shee thinkes shee doth all things well and hath felt no faults in her selfe and indeade I would have kept her in [mine] owne house to have seene wheather I could have prevailed [over] her but my wife is not willing thereunto.' Next winter Mary has to be seen through a fever, writes Hull. She 'desireth me to Present her duty to you and doth intreate you of your motherly affection to send for her home, and indeed Mrs. Hooker I doubt some part of the Cause of her sickness or slow mending might be her affection to you and her long absence from you.' Mistress Hooker does not act promptly on this kindly hint, even when repeated three months later; and finally Master Hull ships Mary home on the ship *Seaflower*, assuring the Captain that her mother would pay her passage at the other end, and urging him 'to give her some fresh broth now and then when he had any.'

John Hull also did a certain amount of coastwise business. In 1673 he sells £60 worth of textiles to merchants in New York. Two years later he sends his ketch *Seaflower* with a cargo of miscellaneous goods to Long Island, to load whale-oil and bone for London. He is part owner of a sawmill on the Piscataqua, and has a good deal of trouble with his agent there, who is neglectful in delivering logs and plank, and not alone in that, judging from one of Hull's letters: 'I am informed that you doe not dayly seeke god in your famyly nor attend your father's famyly worshipe and what but blastinge insteade of blessing can bee expected from such nedglects... Do not imploye drunken sottes nor tipplinge fellowes who will bringe nothing but disapointment in the end.'

Of the various farms and tracts of land that John Hull owned in different parts of New England, the most interesting was Point Judith in Rhode Island, so named after his wife. Hull was one of six associates who purchased from the Narragansett Indians in 1657 the Pettaquamscut Purchase, embracing the western shore of Narragansett Bay up to the latitude of Newport. Few persons could be induced to settle there until the warlike Indians of the regions had been disposed of in King Philip's War, but the climate and soil proved ideal for stock-raising. There and on Block Island off Point Judith, Hull kept his cattle, sheep, and swine, in charge of a man named Thomas Terry. In 1672 he shipped a load of salt to this man, with orders to 'kill so many as all the salt will save' and the following precise instructions for packing:

Let none of the best peices bee keep out but put into each barril, and put in none of the heades or no shankes bones and let them be exceeding well salted and filled else thay will not hold here when thay com to bee repacked. Alsoe if you have any good fatt hogges you may slay and salt them up heads and all only cutting off the foot and snoughts youre hides drye them and fold them smooth and handsome and send them soe. And the tallow melt up into great Caskes...you must not heat it too hot in melting that it may bee very white. Alsoe you may send what fat weathers or barren ewes you have...Your actions are so strangly slow and uncouth that I am sometimes ready to doubt whether your Intentions bee right honest...I hope you will do as you ought for him who is youre loving friend. If thare be more salt then you have fatt meet to save sell the remainder to my best advantage and send mee the retourne.

At the same time John Hull owned a herd of horses 'most of them marked with a slit in top of near ear and some branded with B on near shoulder,' which took their pleasure 'running in the willderness called Wequoiett' on Cape Cod. Stephen Skip of Sandwich, who occasionally rounded up the herd, is asked 'If at any time he could bring any to the saddle or to the hand to send me now and then one down'; and 'if he knew any good Amblers or could change any away for a good fair Ambling beast or a couple of fair Trotters that was much of a hight color and likeness,' to 'send them down to me at any tyme.' After King Philip's war was over, John Hull wrote to Governor Benedict Arnold of Rhode Island, one of his associates in the Pettaquamscut Purchase, suggesting that they 'procure a verry good breed of large and fair mares and stallions' for Point Judith, and fence off the neck 'with good stone wall at the north end thereof... that noe mungrell breed might come amonge them... We might have a verry choice breed for coach horses, for the saddle some, and for the draught others, and in a few yeares might draw off considerable numbers and ship them for Barbadoes, Nevis, or such parts of the Indies where they would vend.' Ordinary 'naggs' bred on Massachusetts farms had been exported in large numbers to the West Indies for many years, for use as horse-power in the sugar mills; but with increased wealth there had come a demand both there and at home for well-gaited saddle horses and coach horses. Hull suggested that the partners might fit up a vessel especially for horses. It is certain that a part at least of this scheme was carried through, from a sarcastic letter that Hull wrote to a resident of the Narragansett country:

I am informed that you are so shameless that you offered to sell some of my horses. I doe hereby warne you to take heed of doeing any such thinge least I cause you to bee arested as a Felon and alsoe least I have noe longer patience with you for my greate Debt that I have soe longe forborne you... but doe you bringe mee in some good securyty for my money that is justeley oweing and I shall bee willing to give you some horses that you shall not need to offer to steal any.

It is a likely inference that from Hull's experiment developed the Narragansett pacers for which that region became famous in the next century, and which were bred on fenced-off promontories like Point Judith. Unfortunately Hull's letter-book affords no solution to the question long debated by horsemen, whether the pacers owed their remarkable gait and staying qualities to an Andalusian sire, or to the famous hobbies of Connemara; but we may infer that the dams at least were culled from Hull's 'amblers' on Cape Cod.

When King Philip's War broke out, John Hull was in his fifty-first year, and was probably considered too old for active service at the head of his company. In the spring of 1676, before the war was over, he accepted the important post of Treasurer of the Colony. It may safely be said that no state treasurer, not even those of the Revolution, had so vexatious a term of office as John Hull. In the absence of fluid capital, the Colony financed a most devastating and desperate war by successive tax-levies on the towns, no less than fourteen in a single year. Many towns were unable to meet these demands, and such as did, paid in commodities which the Treasurer had to sell; and he had to look sharp to see that the town constables did not work off on him all their mouldy corn and spoiled fish. John Hull had continually to draw on his own credit and property to pay for supplies and the soldiers' wages. He left the treasury in 1680, the country's creditor for £1500 for war disbursements alone.

Shortly after the war came an opportunity for Massachusetts to purchase Maine from the Gorges heirs for £1250. For that purpose Hull took up £700 from the 'merchants and gentlemen' of Boston, secured by his personal bond, and borrowed the balance in London on his own credit; yet in 1681 neither his bond had been discharged nor himself repaid. His petition to that effect concludes thus:

> I do account it my duty to Spend and to be Spent for the Publique welfaire yet I think it (with all humility) also your duty Honored Gentlemen not to suffer me to loose more then needeth.
> I leave my selfe with God and you and am,
> > Gentlemen, your Humble Servant
> > > John Hull

The war debts were not settled during his lifetime, and remained a burden on his estate. As Samuel Sewall wrote in November, 1683, Hull 'laboured under the weight of this accompt with his own hand, untill weakenesse of body and the bulke thereof necessitated him to take in Captain Daniel Henchman to his assistance... and besides his own paines, one of his Relations and two of his Apprentices did labour much in this service for all which he hath not charged one penny.' The total amount then owing him by the colony was in the neighborhood of £2125; and his total estate, including debts, was appraised at less than three times that sum.

During the summer of 1683 John Hull began to fail, and could no longer perform his duty as Assistant. On August 14 he stood his last turn at watching and warding. On the eighteenth he wrote his last letter, about a loan to a stranded Virginia seaman, Thomas Lee of the *Golden Faulcon*; and on the first of October he died. Samuel Willard, pastor of the Old South Church (of which John Hull was a charter member) preached the funeral sermon, praising him as one of a 'sweet and affable disposition and even temper' who had proved an honorable member of the Church, a worthy captain of militia, a kind master to his household, a liberal friend to the poor, and a saint upon earth. Elijah Corlet, the venerable master of the Cambridge Latin School, added to the printed sermon an elegiac poem in Latin hexameters. New England's flower-crowned springtime has fled, summer time with fruits and flowers has passed away, now comes cruel autumn when God gathers to his barns our prophets, saints, and leaders of renown. Sad winter soon will bind the land with chains of frost and snow.

'If the Tree be known by its Fruits, his works shall praise him in the Gates,' said Master Willard, meaning of course the charitable works of Master Hull. But neither Master Willard nor Master Corlet thought it worth while to mention those more concrete works of John Hull of Boston, goldsmith, which long will praise him in those pleasant places where things of beauty are a joy forever.

CHAPTER VI

HENRY DUNSTER, PRESIDENT OF HARVARD

LEARNING was one of the by-products of English puritanism that came over in the Winthrop fleet; a by-product which we have come in time to value more than the leading article. New England was founded at a time when England was better provided with schools and colleges in relation to her needs than at any period of her history before the present century. Of all classes and elements in the English population, the puritans placed the highest value on learning, and paid the greatest attention to education. High-church Anglicans were not indifferent to learning, but popular education they viewed with some apprehension. The sects which sprang up during the Civil War were hostile to learning, and threatened to scrap the schools and colleges which had been painfully built up through centuries of devotion. But the puritans desired that the poorest church should have a minister disciplined and informed by learning, in order rightly to interpret the sacred scriptures; and they insisted on giving the people sufficient education to receive the Word, and understand the minister. Learning they valued more highly than any element in their English heritage. Undaunted by the difficulty of preserving a culture while wrestling with a wilderness, they strove to place learning on such solid foundations as to defeat 'that old deluder Satan,' as well as the levelling influence of the frontier.

Of that body of New Englanders engaged in bringing up a new generation in the way it should go, the most eminent and the most loveable was Henry Dunster, the first President of Harvard College. He found the college almost extinct two years after it had been opened, its handful of students 'dispersed in the town and miserably distracted,' the college building not half finished, and John Harvard's legacy almost exhausted. He left Harvard fourteen years later, still a small college and slenderly endowed, but provided with sufficient buildings, well conducted by young and enthusiastic teachers, corporate independence secured by a charter, discipline regulated by college statutes, degrees recognized by the universities of Oxford and Cambridge as equivalent to theirs; graduates occupying positions of trust and honor on both sides of the Atlantic. Yet the manner of Dunster's separation from the Harvard presidency was tragic.

The leaven of learning was already present, and the basis for a college established, when Dunster began his labors. In 1640 there were about 113 university men in New England, 71 of them in Massachusetts Bay; or about one to every forty families. This was a much larger proportion of educated men to the population than could be found in any part of England at the time. In the history of modern colonization, it is unprecedented. Graduates of the English grammar schools, which took boys as soon as they had learned their letters and carried them through Latin grammar to the University, must have been even more numerous.

It is one of the curious phenomena of education that men complain about their own schooling and then insist on giving the next generation the nearest equivalent that they can find. No doubt the small boys who came to New England in the great emigration expected to play Indian the rest of their lives. If so they were soon deceived. Their fathers promptly engaged an ex-schoolmaster among the emigrants, and set the wretched youngsters learning their *amo, amas, amat.* The most noted of these early wielders of the birch were Ezekiel Cheever, a contemporary of John Harvard at Emmanuel, and Elijah Corlet, who was educated both at Oxford and at Cambridge.

> Tis CORLET'S pains and CHEEVER'S, we must own,
> That thou, New England, are not Scythia grown,

declares Cotton Mather. Corlet is the first recorded master of the Cambridge Grammar (or Latin) School; Cheever taught thirty-eight years at Boston after twelve years at New Haven, eleven at Ipswich, and nine at Charlestown. Both lived to a prodigious age, 'and to vast age no illness knew.' Cheever, like a great schoolmaster of the Renaissance, established a tradition of learning to which the Boston Latin School is ever faithful. Cotton Mather, speaking as one of his old pupils, tells us

> His work he lov'd: Oh! had we done the same!
> Our Play-dayes still to him ungrateful came.
> And yet so well our Work adjusted lay,
> We came to Work, as if we came to Play.

'Cheever's Accidence,' the Beginning-Latin book that he wrote, held its place in school curricula for almost two centuries, and was last reprinted in 1838. Cotton Mather preached his funeral sermon and wrote an elegy, in which he imagined 'blessed Cheever' posthumously recommending the methods that made him respected, feared, and loved by New England lads over a space of seventy years:

> TUTORS be strict; but yet be gentle too:
> Don't by fierce cruelties fair hopes undo.
> Dream not that they who are to Learning slow,
> Will mend by arguments *in ferio*.
> Who keeps the Golden Fleece, Oh let him not
> A Dragon be, tho' he *three tongues* have got.
> Why can you not to Learning find the way,
> But thro' the Province of *Severia?*
> 'Twas Moderatus who taught Origen,
> A youth which prov'd one of the best of men.
> The lads with honour first, and reason, rule;
> Blowes are but for the refractory fool.
> But oh! first teache them their great God to fear,
> That you like me with Joy may meet them here.

There is a good deal of competition among the learned antiquaries about Boston as to which town established the 'first public school.' At least three of them had grammar schools by 1640, but the exact date of their foundation is not known, and it is difficult to determine whether a given school was supported by private subscription, public taxation, or a combination of the two. All, however, were public in the English sense that they were open to anyone who could 'make the grade,' and in the American sense that no one was denied an education which he was fit to receive, for want of money. It was a matter of local circumstance how soon the effort to establish a town school would be made, and how it would be supported and managed. By 1647 it became evident that the newer towns needed a little prodding in this respect, so the famous Massachusetts School Act was passed with a quaint preamble:

It being one chief project of that old deluder, Satan, to keep men from the knowledge of the Scriptures, as in former times keeping them in an unknown tongue... and that Learning may not be buried in the graves of our fore-fathers in Church and Commonwealth, the Lord assisting our indeavours: it is therefore ordered by this Court and Authoritie thereof;

That everie Township in this Jurisdiction, after the Lord hath increased them to the number of fifty Housholders shall then forwith appoint one within their Town to teach all such children as shall resort to him to write and read, whose wages shall be paid either by the Parents or Masters of such children, — or by the Inhabitants in general...

And it is farther ordered, that where any Town shall increase to the number of one hundred Families or Housholders they shal set upon a Grammar-School, the Masters thereof being able to instruct youth so far as they may be fitted for the Universitie...

This is probably the earliest general education act of modern times which required local units to establish schools; and for two generations at least it was well observed. There are many instances of towns being fined for failure to keep the required school, the fine going to the nearest town that was obeying the law: a canny provision to bring the laggard promptly into line. The result was that Massachusetts Bay, with Connecticut and New Haven which promptly followed suit, had a remarkably comprehensive school system for newly settled states. Some rather elaborate and amusing attempts have been made by recent historians to turn this to the puritans' discredit. Charles and Mary Beard decry the Massachusetts school law as one flowing 'from a great desire to impose on all children the creed of the Puritan sect.' It is true that if you had asked a puritan schoolmaster that embarrassing question which makes even the modern peda- gogue squirm: 'What do you suppose you are educating these children *for?*' he would have replied, 'For godliness.' But it is probable that the 'three R's' and Latin grammar have values independent of the purpose for which they may be taught. James Truslow Adams accounts the common schooling of New England as naught, because there is no evidence that the graduates read contemporary authors such as Locke, Hobbes, Milton, Dryden, and Clarendon. One considers how large a proportion of high school graduates of to-day are familiar with the works of John Dewey, A. N. Whitehead, Edwin Arlington Robinson, Thomas S. Eliot, and Henry Adams? The common school system of early Massachusetts was intended to teach boys to write, cipher, and read the Bible, and that it did. Are we too sophisticated to admit that reading the Bible may be of some use to a people in forming their character, or instructing their taste?

'England makes me tremble,' says Olivier in Romain Rolland's *Jean-Christophe*, 'when I think that for centuries past she has nourished herself on the Bible. I'm glad the Channel is between us. I refuse to consider a people really civilized that feeds its mind on the Bible.'

'Then you'd better be afraid of me,' replies Jean-Chris- tophe, 'for I love the Bible. It's the marrow of lions. Those who feed on it have robust hearts. And I mean the whole Bible; the New Testament without the Old is stale and insipid. The Bible is the bone of people who have the will to survive!'

.   .   .   .

A school system such as this might well have satisfied the ambition of a new settlement in its first decade, or generation. It was not sufficient for the rulers of Massachusetts Bay. They must have not only schools but a university college, as the anonymous pamphlet of 1643, New England's First Fruits, explains:

After God had carried us safe to *New England*, and wee had builded our houses, provided necessaries for our liveli-hood, rear'd convenient places for Gods worship, and setled the Civill Government: One of the next things we longed for, and looked after was to advance *Learning*, and perpetuate it to Posterity; dreading to leave an illiterate Ministery to the Churches, when our present Ministers shall lie in the dust. And as wee were thinking and consulting how to effect this great Work; it pleased God to stir up the heart of one Mr. *Harvard* (a godly Gentleman and a lover of Learning, there living amongst us) to give the one halfe of his Estate (it being in all about 1700*l.*) towards the erecting of a Colledge, and all his Library: after him another gave 300*l.* others after them cast in more, and the publique hand of the State added the rest: the Colledge was, by common consent, appointed to be at *Cambridge*, (a place very pleasant and accommodate) and is called (according to the name of the first founder) *Harvard Colledge*.

This pamphlet, it must be said, reverses the order of events. The traditional date for the founding of Harvard, October 28, 1636, is taken from the vote of the General Court of the Massachusetts Bay on that date 'to give 400*l.* towards a schoale or colledge... the next Court to appoint wheare and what building.' Alarums and excursions followed: the Pequot war and the Hutchinson heresy; and over a year elapsed before the General Court appointed the first Board of Overseers, 'to take order for a colledge at Newetowne.' There was a good deal of competition among towns to get the college, and Hugh Peter, one of the first Board of Overseers, went so far as to purchase a site for it at Marblehead. Thomas Shepard informs us that Newtowne ('hencforward to be called Cambridge,' on May 3, 1638) won the competition because it was free from Antinomian taint. And in gratitude at securing the College, the town granted it a strip of land for a site.

The first Board of Overseers consisted largely of English university men: Governor Winthrop, John Humfry, John Cotton, Thomas Welde and Hugh Peter, all of Trinity College, Cambridge; Thomas Shepard of Emmanuel, John Wilson of King's, and John Davenport of Merton College, Oxford. The others were Roger Harlakenden, Deputy-Governor Dudley, Israel Stoughton, and Richard Bellingham, all well-read men of university families. These were the chief magistrates of the colony and the ministers of Boston, Cambridge, Salem, and Roxbury. With little change the Harvard Board of Overseers remained so constituted for over two hundred years. The College was child of the Colony.

The Board of Overseers, having secured the services of Nathaniel Eaton as Master, and purchased a house and lot in Cambridge, opened the College in the late summer of 1638. Shortly after John Harvard died at Charlestown; and it soon became known that he had left his entire library and half his estate, amounting to seven or eight hundred pounds, to the College. Wherefore, on March 13, 1639, it was ordered by the General Court 'that the colledge agreed upon formerly to bee built at Cambridge shalbee called Harvard College.'

Despite the vigorous researches of Harvard graduates, we know very, very little of John. He was born on the Surrey side of London, and baptized in St. Saviour's (now Southwark Cathedral) on November 29, 1607. His father was a prosperous butcher of Southwark; his mother, Katherine Rogers, the daughter of a cattle dealer and alderman of Stratford-on-Avon. Of John's life from his baptism to the year 1627, when he entered Emmanuel College at the unusually late age of twenty, we know nothing.

John Harvard seems to have made no mark at Emmanuel. He took his baccalaureate in 1632, and his master's degree three years later, as was customary. We find his name neither in the book of punishments, nor in the writings of his contemporaries — a remarkable intellectual group, including the astronomer Horrox; John Sadler, lawyer and orientalist; and the neo-Platonists Ralph Cudworth and Benjamin Whichcote. (I sometimes wish that New England had been founded by Cambridge neo-Platonists instead of by Cambridge puritans — but dukes and neo-Platonists do not emigrate.) Ann, sister to John Sadler, became the wife of John Harvard, and accompanied him to New England, where several college contemporaries were already settled. We do not know why John Harvard left England, for not a single letter of his has been discovered; we merely know that he sailed about the end of May, 1637, settled in Charlestown, Massachusetts, and became teaching elder of the Church. On September 14, 1638, he died of consumption, in his thirty-first year. He seems to have been a quiet young man of no great gifts or remarkable talents, who saw an opportunity to do good, and did not let it pass. As Thomas Shepard wrote: 'The Lord put it into the hart of one Mr. Harvard who died worth 1600*l* to give halfe his estate to the erecting of the schoole the man was a scholler and pious in his life and enlarged toward the cuntry and the good of it in life and death.'

Great things were expected of Nathaniel Eaton, the first head of the college. A contemporary of John Harvard at Cambridge, he had completed his education under William Ames at Leyden, the greatest of Dutch universities; and he was brother to the first governor of New Haven. With John Harvard's legacy, other gifts, and the funds granted by the General Court, Eaton began to erect a college building. In the meantime a small dwelling-house served well enough. Eaton set out thirty apple trees in the Yard, a narrow strip of land extending back from the house to the Charlestown road;

and fenced it with palings to keep out stray cattle, and per-haps wolves. Beyond that we know very little of the college during the year and a half that Eaton was master, and that little is not good. He took in scholars for £15 a year, all found, and found them little. Thomas Shepard was more than once asked to protect boys from excessive punishment; and finally an usher who had been belabored by Eaton with a stout club, had him into court, where the whole wretched story came out. Our only picture of this Dotheboys Hall is afforded by the following confession of Mistress Eaton, re-specting the sort of catering administered by herself, a corps of sluttish servants, and a 'moor.'

For their breakfast, that it was not so well ordered, the flower not so fine as it might, nor so well boiled, or stirred, at all times that it was so, it was my sin of neglect, and want of that care that ought to have been in one that the Lord had intrusted with such a work. Concerning their beef, that was allowed them, as they affirm, which, I confess, had been my duty to have seen they should have had it, and continued to have had it, because it was my husband's com-mand; but truly I must confess, to my shame, I cannot remember that ever they had it, nor that ever it was taken from them... And that they sent down for more, when they had not enough, and the maid should answer, if they had not, they should not, I must confess, that I have denied them cheese, when they have sent for it, and it have been in the house; for which I shall humbly beg pardon of them, and own the shame, and confess my sin. And for such pro-voking words, which my servants have given, I cannot own them, but am sorry any such should be given in my house. And for bad fish, that they had it brought to table, I am sorry there was that cause of offence given them. I acknowledge my sin in it. And for their mackerel, brought to them with their guts in them, and goat's dung in their hasty pudding, it's utterly unknown to me; but I am much ashamed it should be in the family, and not prevented by my-self or servants, and I humbly acknowledge my negligence in it. And that they made their beds at any time, were my straits never so great, I am sorry they were ever put to it. For the Moor his ly-ing in Sam. Hough's sheet and pillow-bier, it hath truth in it: he did so one time, and it gave Sam. Hough just cause of offence... And that they eat the Moor's crusts, and the swine and they had share and share alike, and the Moor to have beer, and they denied it, and if they had not enough, for my maid to answer, they should not, I am an utter stranger to these things... And for bread made of heated, sour meal, although I know of but once that it was so, since I kept house, yet John Wilson affirms it was twice; and I am truly sorry, that any of it was spent amongst them. For beer and bread, that it was denied them by me betwixt meals, truly I do not remember, that ever I did deny it unto them; and John Wilson will affirm, that, generally, the bread and beer was free for the boarders to go unto. And that money was demanded of them for washing the linen, it's true it was propounded to them, but never imposed upon them. And for their pudding being given the last day of the week without butter or suet, and that I said, it was miln of Manchester in Old England, it's true that I did say so, and am sorry, they had any cause of offence given them by having it so. And for their wanting beer, betwixt brewings, a week or half a week together, I am sorry that it was so at any time, and should tremble to have it so, were it in my hands to do again.

Whether it was the beatings, or the food, or the beer giving out that shocked the General Court most, we do not know; but the upshot was that they dismissed Eaton in September, 1639. He betook himself to Virginia, and finally to England, where, according to Cotton Mather, he turned Episcopalian and came to a bad end. As yet no one has come forward to claim that Eaton was the 'real founder' of Harvard College, a martyr to puritan bigotry and malice.

The College was closed during the academic year 1639–40. But some of the students must have been kept together somehow, since Dunster found a student body, though 'miserably distracted,' a year later.

Of Henry Dunster before he came to Massachusetts we know even less than of John Harvard. He was the fifth of nine children in a yeoman's family at Bury, Lancashire, where he was baptized November 26, 1609. At the time John Harvard was at Emmanuel, Henry Dunster was at Magdalene College, Cambridge. After taking his master's degree in

1634, he became schoolmaster and curate in his native place, a 'studious and painfull minister' according to one of his parishioners.

For what reason we know not, Henry emigrated to Boston with his brother Richard in the summer of 1640. Three weeks after his arrival, ten magistrates and sixteen elders waited upon him and elected him President of Harvard College. He was thirty years old, youngest in the long line of Harvard presidents. It would be interesting to know what evidence Dunster had given of the remarkable qualities he showed as a teacher, scholar and administrator. Cotton Mather says that a reputation for knowledge and piety preceded him; yet at the University, his scholarship was as undistinguished as John Harvard's. Peter Hobart, the pugnacious pastor of Hingham, had been at Magdalene with Dunster; and there were ten or twelve others in the Bay who had been his contemporaries at Cambridge, though at other colleges. Some of them must have known Dunster and convinced the Board that he was the man for the post.

Dunster, so he tells us, was told that the President's office would be only to instruct; but he soon found himself forced to become the college Pooh-Bah. He organized what was left of Eaton's distracted *discipuli* as Junior Sophisters, and put them hard at work so that they might graduate in 1642; and also undertook the complete instruction of two successive Freshman classes, before he had any assistant. Further, he was forced to 'bee their steward, and to direct their brewer, baker, butler, Cook, how to proportion their commons.' Mindful of Mistress Eaton's crime, he had to make certain that the beer would flow without stop; for until recent times, beer was considered as necessary an instrument of learning as books.

The completing of the college building had been committed by the Board of Overseers to the versatile but restless Hugh Peter, and to Samuel Shepard, Thomas's brother; but they, when they had got it merely framed, boarded and roofed, with the ground floor laid, returned to England. The President then 'took right a-holt,' as we say in New England, to such good purpose that in September, 1642, he was able to hold the first Commencement in the College hall, and bring all the students into residence and commons.

As you approached the college from the Charlestown road, along 'a spacious plain, more like a bowling green than a wilderness,' this new building loomed up quite imposingly from the young apple-trees in the Yard; against the background of village farmhouses it seemed enormous. It was 'thought by some to bee too gorgeous for a wilderness,' says Johnson, 'and yet too mean in other apprehensions for a Colledge.' The first Overseers had planned it on a generous scale, but simple plan. The old quadrangle at Eton College, where Master John Wilson had passed so many years that he could almost describe it in his sleep, served as a model; but the walls were clapboard instead of brick, and the windows plain square-headed casements. President Dunster and the master builder worked hard, with what means they had, to make it 'very faire and comely within and without.' As you viewed it from the Yard or northern side, Harvard College appeared E-shaped, two wings projecting from the main body to make a sort of open quadrangle, as was common at Cambridge; and the short bar of the E consisting of a square turret, containing the main staircase, and on the third floor, four small studies. Either here or astride the ridge-pole was a 'lanthorn' where the college bell was hung. A passage ran straight through the building, emerging through the ground floor of the turret. On the east side of this passage, as in all English colleges, was a carved 'screen,' through which a door led to 'a spacious Hall, where they daily meet at Commons, Lectures, Exercises.' The hall was provided with a dais for a high table at the east end, a large open fireplace, and forms and benches which would seat fifty at a pinch. Opposite the hall, on the west side of the passage, were doors leading to the kitchen (which occupied the west wing), the larder, corn room, and buttery. From the buttery hatch (a Dutch door opening upon the passage), was dispensed the college ale, and the 'bevers' or breakfasts and mid-afternoon lunches of bread and beer, over which the early college laws forbade the students to linger more than an hour. Nor might the pewter cans be removed out-doors 'without sight of the Buttery hatch'; so apparently in pleasant weather it was the custom of the students to take their morning and afternoon 'bevers' in the Yard, provided they remained under the butler's watchful eye.

The library which held John Harvard's legacy of books was on the second or 'middle' floor, which otherwise was taken up with spacious chambers, so planned that each had a fireplace, and room for two or three double beds. A tutor or resident bachelor was placed in each chamber to keep his three chamber-fellows or 'chums' in order. In addition to his share in a bed and a chamber, each student above the Freshman class was entitled to a study. A few of these were separate rooms provided with fireplaces; but for the most part they were partitioned off from the corners of the chambers, including at least half a window, and affording just room for a desk and chair. The first occupants paid for the lock and key and furnishings, and recouped themselves from their successors; much as Harvard students, in my time, used to sell gas fittings and mantelpieces to unwary freshmen. The Senior Fellow had the best study, renting at £5 annually, in the 'long chamber' over the hall, so placed that he could observe all in-comings and out-goings. The long chamber also contained two 'cabins,' sleeping-closets with bunks like the Breton *lits-clos*, a boon on cold winter nights. This English arrangement of chambers and studies was an excellent one to secure privacy and good companionship, each in their place; and all residential buildings were so arranged at Harvard until the nineteenth century. In Hollis Hall, some of the original study partitions are still in place. These *musaeolae*, as they were called in Latin, must have been dreadfully cold in winter, when we imagine that their occupants adjourned to the roaring fires in chamber or hall. However, we need waste little sympathy on the colonial students for cold. Until central heating was invented, people expected it to be cold in winter, and dressed accordingly.

Harvard College, or Old College, as this building we have just described was called, remained the only college building until 1652, when the dwelling-house of one Goffe was purchased, renamed Goffe College, and fitted with chambers and studies. At the expense of the Society for the Propagation of the Gospel in New England, a little brick 'Indian College' was put up in the Yard shortly after. It proved more useful for the English boys who needed space, than for the Indians who were expected and did not come. In front of the Old College was the President's lodging, built partly at Dunster's expense.

Within a year of his installation, Henry Dunster had the good fortune to marry a wealthy widow, relict of Master Josse Glover, who providentially died on the voyage out. But the marriage brought new responsibilities: a rather turbulent family of step-sons, and a printing press. Josse Glover had procured a small hand press and a few fonts of type for the use of the colony, and brought over a Cambridge locksmith named Stephen Day, with his son Matthew, to manage it. The press was moved to a lean-to on the presidential premises, and began an intermittent production of psalm books, commencement programmes, and almanacs; with occasionally a more ambitious work such as the Laws and Liberties and the Indian Bible, any copy of which is worth to-day as much as the entire equipment of Harvard College in 1640. Until 1675, when John Foster established a press in Boston, this Harvard University Press was the only one in the English colonies.

The first book to be printed was 'The Whole Book of Psalms,' the so-called Bay Psalm Book of 1640. As psalms-singing was the only church music for which the puritans found scriptural authority, it was important to have a metrical version of the psalms that was not only accurate but singable. The versions brought over from England were unsatisfactory. So three of the ministers conscientiously set to work to translate the Psalms of David from Hebrew into English verse. And what verse! As Tyler says, 'Sentences wrenched about end for end, clauses heaved up and abandoned in chaos, words disembowelled or split quite in two in the middle, and dissonant combinations of sound that are the despair of such poor vocal organs as are granted to human beings. The verses, indeed, seem to have been hammered out on an anvil, by blows from a blacksmith's sledge.' Even Cotton Mather, no stiff critic of his clerical brethren, records, 'It was thought that a little more art was to be employed.' Thomas Shepard even ventured to poke fun at the learned translators — Eliot and Welde of Roxbury and Mather of Dorchester — in the following stanza:

> You Roxb'ry poets, keep clear of the crime
> Of missing to give us very good rhyme.
> And you of Dorchester, your verses lengthen,
> But with the text's own words, you will them strengthen!

Indeed, the Bay Psalm Book proved so uncouth, that within ten years Henry Dunster, as the chief Hebrew scholar in the colony, was commissioned to do it over again; and the Harvard president, mistrusting his ability as a poet, called into collaboration Master Richard Lyon, the private tutor of Sir Henry Mildmay's son, who had been sent out to Harvard for his education. The result was 'The Psalms Hymns and Spiritual Songs of the Old and New Testament' printed at Cambridge in 1651.

A comparison of the first two verses of the first psalm in

these two versions of the Bay Psalm Book shows some improvement:

ELIOT, WELDE, AND MATHER, 1640

O Blessed man, that in th' advice
  of wicked doth not walk:
Nor stand in sinners way, nor sit
  in chayre of scornfull folk.

But in the law of Jehovah
  is his longing delight:
And in his law doth meditate,
  by day and eke by night.

DUNSTER AND LYON, 1651

O Blessed man that walks not in
  th' advice of wicked men,
Nor standeth in the sinners way,
  nor scorners seat sits in.

But he upon Jehovah's law
  doth set his whole delight,
And in his law doth meditate
  both in the day and night.

Most of us, however, will prefer the Sternhold and Hopkins version in the Book of Common Prayer:

1. Blessed is the man that hath not walked in the counsel of the ungodly, nor stood in the way of sinners, and hath not sat in the seat of the scornful.

2. But his delight is in the law of the Lord; and in his law will he exercise himself day and night.

One can hardly exaggerate the financial difficulties of conducting an American college in Dunster's time, or the resourcefulness and fortitude which he showed in coping with them. He found John Harvard's legacy and the colony grant largely dissipated by Eaton. His salary was paid for one year only by the General Court; thereafter he lived largely on his wife's property. The only free income he had to run the college with, were the tuition fees and the income from the Charlestown ferry, which was granted by the Colony. Thomas Welde and Hugh Peter obtained sundry small gifts for the college in England, and £100 from Lady Mowlson (Anne Radcliffe) for scholarships. But for want of a college treasury the Mowlson fund was deposited with the Colony treasurer, and only with difficulty could the Court be persuaded to disgorge even the interest on it. Moreover, Dunster had not been in office a year when the economic crisis of 1641–42 struck New England. The more active members of the Board of Overseers returned to England; debts were impossible to collect, and payments of any sort difficult to obtain. But for the energetic leadership of Dunster in this crisis, it is probable that Harvard College would have died before graduating a class, just as the plan for a college in Virginia was frustrated by the Indian massacre of 1622.

The General Court gave occasional relief by ordering one or two towns to turn over to the College their annual Colony tax, which was paid in kind, and which cost the President a good deal of horseback exercise to collect. Among the doubtful assets in the college steward's accounts is 'a goat of the Watertown rate, which died.' When the New England Confederation was formed, Dunster appealed to them for support, since Harvard was receiving students from all New England, and even one from New Netherland. The Confederation had no taxing power, but it recommended every family in New England to contribute to the College. Some towns taxed themselves for the purpose, others took up a contribution; and many were the little donations of pine-tree shillings, pecks of wheat and bushels of corn which the New England farmers sent in to 'maintain poor scholars at Cambridge,' and 'for the advancement of learning.'

The first steward's book shows vividly the difficulties of carrying on a college, or indeed of doing business, in the 1650's. Although tuition was the moderate price of 6s. 8d. per quarter in New England currency (about $4.75 a year);

and although no one managed to spend more than $60 a year for 'commons and sizings' (food and drink), and the average was half that; very little hard money was paid in by the students. Their credit accounts show all kinds of commodities, agricultural and otherwise. One boy whose father was a merchant brought in a barrel of sack for commencement, which was assessed all around on those who graduated. Another paid his bills largely with shoes, which President Dunster and lesser college officers took off the steward's hands. Sam Willard, '59, balanced his accounts with such varied commodities as pork, wheat, corn, meal, hens, eggs, boards, sheep, two calves, lambs, beef, veal, silver, and '17 quarts of hott watters at 2s. per quart.' Abijah Savage discharged his debts with cotton, lace, and wampum. The low cost of a college education in terms of these commodities, is striking. A quarter's tuition was almost covered by a bushel of wheat. Farnsworth, '55, came to college Freshman year with four bushels of malt, worth 22s., and he 'payd to Mr. Dunster in malte and silver, 15s.,' but had 8d. deducted for poor measure. For 'a lyttell browne Cowe' he was credited £4, less 3s. 6d. for bringing it to Cambridge. Cow and malt paid this student's commons and sizings, bedmaking by Goody Fox and study rent, for half a year. A hog, weighing 63 pounds, keeps Zachary Brigden in food and beer for a whole term; six bushels of barley malt, a bushel of parsnips, and 'waytinge in the hall,' pay his quarter's tuition, study rent, bedmaking, fire, and candle. Walter Hooke's father sends from New Haven a cask of butter and two barrels of salt beef, and is troubled with no further payments for nine months. 'A blacke Cow' and 'a fatt Cow' from George Babcock (who probably owed their father money), enabled the two Mather brothers, Increase and Eleazar, to increase in knowledge and godliness for the space of an entire year. And for those whose fathers could not spare an occasional cow or a few bushels of grain, there were scholarships. What a contrast to the burdens of the farming parent of a college student to-day! In three centuries grain has risen in price only twenty-five to fifty-five per cent; but the average board and lodging at Harvard has gone up three thousand per cent, and tuition is seventy times as costly as in Dunster's day!

Harvard College as an institution, was modelled on a Cambridge college as nearly as possible, save in one particular, where Scotland rather than England was followed. The early Harvard commencement programmes, with their effusive Latin dedications to presiding magistrates by the graduating class, and their superabundant list of Aristotelian *theses* and *quaestiones*, bear so close a resemblance to an Edinburgh commencement programme of 1641, that the latter must have been used as a model. As at Edinburgh, the names of Harvard graduates on the commencement sheets and in the early triennial catalogues were Latinized: *Josephus Cookaeus* for Joseph Cooke, *Crescentius Matherus* for Increase Mather, and *Marigena Cottonus* for Seaborn Cotton. As in the English and Scots universities, the names are arranged in order of academic seniority, an order of precedence which was followed for seating in hall, and on all formal occasions. The principles of determining this order have long proved an insoluble puzzle. It has often been said that the names of Harvard and Yale graduates, down to the Revolution, were arranged according to the social, official, or even occupational rank of their fathers. Descendants of early graduates have taken so much comfort from the position of their ancestors in class lists, that I regret to report that there is no foundation for this alleged principle of arrangement in the seventeenth-century Harvard classes. An analysis of the students' parents proves that it was not official or social, but roughly based on the impression that a freshman made at his entrance examination, on whether or not he showed promise of being a credit to his college; except that fellow-commoners always came first, no matter how 'dumb.'

If Dunster was consciously following the Cambridge *ordo senioritatis*, it was a part of a consistent policy to reproduce, so far as conditions would permit, the customs, standards, and amenities of the English universities. Dinner in the hall at eleven o'clock or noon; high table for the masters and the fellow-commoners (a superior rank of student who paid double fees and presented a piece of plate on graduation); 'sizars' or poor scholars ringing the bell, waiting on table, and doing odd jobs; ancient goodwives of unblemished reputation (still called 'goodies' at Harvard), serving as bedmakers; butlers drawing beer at the buttery and stewards presenting battels for commons and sizings; fellows' orchard where the masters might enjoy seclusion; sophisters going through the old Cambridge trial of *stare in quadragesima*, though not in the standing posture or at the Lenten season; bachelors in arts performing their acts and disputations with propositions of Aristotle *pro more Academiarum in Anglia*, voted their degrees with *placets* of the governing body, receiving them from the President with Book (though not with kiss and ring), and topping off with a prodigious Commencement feast. The fidelity with which Dunster reproduced these ancient customs, the imponderabilia of English college life, is touching; as their gradual dropping away in the eighteenth and nineteenth centuries is regrettable. Harvard to-day, with her many millions, is endeavoring to reproduce some of the amenities of college life which the puritan founders in their poverty and austerity cherished and enjoyed.

Of games and sports, we have no record in the early Harvard; unless one of Shepard's Sabbath-day similes, about the Devil appearing 'with the ball at his foot' threatening 'to carry all before him, and to kick and carry God's precious Sabbaths out of the world' may be taken as evidence that college students were already playing a primitive form of that manly sport. Bowling may well have been enjoyed on that plain 'like a bowling green,' which separated the College from the wilderness; there was certainly no college rule against it, and the puritans never denied a reasonable and wholesome recreation, however much they deplored the waste of precious time. Emmanuel, for instance, provided that 'the hours of recreation are one howre after dinner and after supper, viz. till one, and seven: also one houre before supper (unles some publique exercise of learning or religion doe require their presence).' The Charles River and its bordering marshes afforded excellent gunning, and a document in President Dunster's hand shows that he well approved that form of sport. His stepson, John Glover, inherited a 500 acre farm at Sudbury, on Lake Cochituate. In leasing it to Edmund Rice, at a time when the lad was in College, the President inserted the condition 'that the said Jno. Glover shall have liberty with any his friends to goe through all or any part of the said Lands at any time whatsoever in the prosecuccion of any Lawfull or honest Recreations, of fishing, fowling or hunting... Provided he shall be accountable for any Detriment he doth upon Cornefields.'

Another evidence of the President's humanity is that he welcomed a little competition for the college brewery. There is a letter of his extant, interceding with the selectmen of Cambridge in favor of one Sister Bradish, who sold penny beer on the site of Holyoke House:

Honored Gentlemen, as far as it may stand with the wholesome orders and prudential laws of the country for the publick weal, I can very freely speak with and write in the behalf of sister Bradish, that shee might bee encouraged and countenanced in her present calling for baking of bread and brewing and selling of penny bear, without which shee canot continue to bake: In both which callings such is her art way and skil that shee doth vend such comfortable penniworths for the reliefe of all that send unto her as elswhere they can seldom meet with. Shee was complained of unto me for harbouring students unseasonably spending there their time and parents estate but upon examination I found it a misinformation, and that shee was most desirous that I should limit or absolutely prohibit any. That in case of sickness or want of comfortable bread or beer in the Coll: only they should thither resort and then not to spend at any time above a penny a man nor above two shillings in a quarter of a year. Which order shee carefully observed in all ordinary cases. How far shee had publick allowance by the townsmen heretofore I leave to Brother Goff or any of the townsmen that are with you to shew: And how good Effects for the promoting of the weal publick And how Christian a thing in itself Godly Emulation is, as your historical knowledg informs you so your experience abundantly Demonstrates; as contrary wise the undoing pressures of monopolyes. The Lord to guide and prosper your administrations shall bee the prayer of

Yours ever in what hee can,

H. DUNSTER

In the Harvard college laws we find the familiar prohibitions of English college statutes for centuries, against gambling, profaneness, using the mother tongue, and wearing long hair. Benjamin Woodbridge who came to Harvard after a year or two at Magdalen Hall, probably introduced customs from Oxford; the initiation of Freshmen, one of the oldest of folkways for novitiates of every kind, would certainly have been one of these. At Oxford the newcomers were required to make a speech or sing a song in the college hall. If they showed wit or talent they were applauded and treated to beer. If neither, they were 'salted'— forced to drink beer with salt in it; and the surly or contumacious were 'tucked' by having their chins pinched with a thumb-nail until the blood came. By the early eighteenth century there was a recognized code of conduct for Harvard Freshmen designed to keep them in a proper frame of inferiority, and the beginnings of which probably date from Dunster's time.

Commencement was the gala day, not only for the College, but for the community. Leavings from the gargantuan commencement feast (costing every Bachelor about £3 and a Master even more) attracted outsiders, and before the century was over the Corporation had to take steps to quell extravagance and disorder at this joyous time. One institution of the English commencement the student must have missed: the *terrae filius* or university buffoon. The existence of a burlesque Harvard thesis sheet for 1663 suggests that the more intrepid spirits among the students staged a mock commencement, at which they argued such nonsensical *Theses* as the following:

Logicae.

Universalia sunt in se ἀειφανεῖs in re ἀφανεῖs Asterismi. (Universals are little Stars, in themselves ever shining but invisible in the concrete.)

Ethicae.

Ethica est vitiorum Emplastrum corrosivum. (Ethics is a corrosive plaster for vices.)

Grammaticae.

Ha Ha He vox est hilaris bene Nota. (Ha Ha He is a well-known sound of hilarity.)

Curriculum and standards at Harvard were very much what they had been for a century and more at Oxford and Cambridge. A boy was supposed to attend the university as soon as he knew his Latin grammar thoroughly. The full arts course occupied seven years, and was crowned by the master's degree. The early Harvard entrance requirement was to read Cicero at sight, to 'make and speake true Latine in Verse and Prose *suo ut aiunt Marte*' (by himself), and to know the Greek declensions and conjugations. In the first ten Harvard classes the average age of entering Freshmen was sixteen years and ten months.

During his first two years the undergraduate read Latin literature and studied logic, in order to give him the proper method and approach to philosophy. At the end of his second year he became a Junior Sophister and began to take part in disputations, or what we should call debates; and it was in this clash between mind and mind, teaching young men to think on their feet and to express themselves clearly, that the student of mediæval Europe and of seventeenth-century Oxford, Cambridge and Harvard got his best training. At all times he took notes on prescribed lectures, recited to his tutor, and read for himself. Having gone through certain public 'acts' or debates with credit, and certified by his tutor as having read certain books, the student received his first or bachelor's degree. That gave him the right to study alone, the privilege to be addressed as *Dominus* or Sir, and the duty to read lectures and assist the instruction of under-graduates. During the next three years he filled in gaps in the liberal arts, or, if he were to be a minister, specialized in Divinity. Residence at college was usual, but not required, during the period between the two degrees.

Such was the mediæval method which President Dunster introduced at Harvard; and an excellent system it was, one by which some of the greatest scholars and scientists in the world's history were trained. The list of Harvard studies given in 'New England's First Fruits,' if arranged in a tabular view, shows that President Dunster could have given the entire instruction of the three classes himself, as he must have done until the first tutors were appointed, in 1643. As in England the Freshman year was largely spent on logic and the classics. The Junior Sophisters took up Aristotle (probably read in a Latin translation, as at Cambridge), and Greek literature and composition. Only the Senior Sophisters had mathematics; they studied arithmetic and geometry the first three quarters, and in the last learned enough astronomy for purposes of surveying or navigation. A smattering of history, botany, and physics was also provided. No options or electives were allowed, at least in theory. This was in essence the mediæval arts course. It is erroneous to describe it as theological, except in the sense that theology was the leading intellectual interest of the day, the subject of the majority of books found in the college and university libraries of Europe, and an essential part of a gentleman's education. Undoubtedly the providing of learned ministry to the New England churches was a leading motive in the foundation of Harvard; but the College Charter of 1650 mentions 'all good literature, arts, and sciences' as an object of the foundation; and President Dunster begged the New England Confederation to provide suitable books, that his resident bachelors might study law and medicine.

In only two important features did the Harvard course differ from the Cambridge one. At first it was a three and not a four year course for the A.B.; but President Dunster added the sophomore year in 1653, greatly to the disgust of the students, seventeen of whom left without taking a degree. The other important innovation was the emphasis on Hebrew and other oriental languages, which were Dunster's specialty. Latin was the language of instruction throughout, and the college devotions were thriftily improved by having a student translate the Old Testament from Hebrew into Greek at morning prayers, and the New Testament from English into Greek at evening prayers. The College law forbidding students to use their mother tongue arouses scepticism. It is not to be supposed that the undergraduates constantly talked Latin with each other, but that they used it in the class-room is fairly certain. George Downing, who had all his education at Harvard, proved able to sustain a two-hour conversation in Latin with Cardinal Mazarin, when sent on an embassy by Cromwell a few years after his graduation.

Punishment of undergraduates as in England was by 'sconcing' (fining), admonition private and public, whipping, degradation in the class order, and rustication. Governor Winthrop, who liked to record the college gossip, writes that at the first Commencement 'complaint was made to the governors of two young men of good quality, lately come out of England, for foul misbehavior, in swearing and ribaldry speeches, etc., for which, though they were adulti, they were corrected in the college, and sequestered, etc., for a time.' In 1644, 'two of our ministers sons being students in the college, robbed two dwelling houses in the night of some 15 pounds. Being found out, they were ordered by the governors of the college to be there whipped, which was performed by the president himself — yet they were about 20 years of age.' On one of the President's absences to visit kinsfolk near Concord, word came to him that his charges had, literally, raised the Devil. Dunster saddled his horse and hastened back to Cambridge to find that the report was true. The students were thoroughly frightened at something: whether a practical joke or a bit of black magic, the reader can decide for himself. With great presence of mind the President emptied his horn of gunpowder, touched it off with a live coal, and 'blew the Devil out of Harvard College'!

Apart from these misdemeanors, we know almost nothing of the 'extra-curricular activities' of the early Harvard students, which perverse undergraduates persist in regarding as the main business of college life. One activity, however, was the reading, copying, and writing of verse — much of it very profane verse, from the puritan point of view. A commonplace book has been preserved of Elnathan Chauncy (A.B. 1661), son of the second President of Harvard. It starts off with a rather feeble acrostic on Henry Dunster, interesting only as showing the high esteem in which the first President was held at the college after his resignation. For the most part, however, the work is filled with copies of contemporary English poetry: Spenser in large measure, including a good part of his Shepherd's Calendar, Herrick's Hesperides, Sir John Harington's translation of Orlando Furioso, a little Beaumont, and poems of Quarles, Thomas Vaughan, Cleveland, Barclay, and Niccols. Works of these writers must have been floating about Cambridge, for internal evidence shows that Elnathan's book was compiled largely in his undergraduate days.

In the first twenty Harvard classes there were five graduates who wrote poetry that has at least been thought worth preserving — including Wigglesworth's 'Day of Doom,' the most popular piece of poetry New England has ever known. John Crowne of the class of '61 returned to England before taking his degree and became a Restoration dramatist. Samuel Danforth (A.B. 1643) got out the first American almanacs, wrote 'An Astronomical Description of the late Comet or Blazing Star, As it appeared in New-England in... 1664. Together with a brief Theological application thereof' (Cambridge, 1665); and was a poet withal. I will not say that he was the first graduate of an American college who ever wrote a poem, for it would be strange if in that day of ready verse no one of his eleven predecessors on the roll of Harvard alumni had not privily and secretly attempted somewhat in that way; but I venture to claim him as the first American college poet whose work has survived.

As poetry magazines did not then exist, Sam Danforth thriftily employed the vacant spaces of his own almanacs as a vehicle of the Muses. In the almanac for 1648, 'By Samuel Danforth of Harvard Colledge, Philomathemat.' is his topical poem from which we have already quoted the stanza on the 'fall of Cow.' Another on the Pequot War, in the almanac for 1649, shows some facility at working the barbarous Indian names into classic forms:

> But by & by, grave Monanattock rose
> Grim Sasacus with swarm of Pequottoes,
> Who smote our hindermost, whose arrows stung,
> Who vow'd with English blood their ground to dung.
> But Mystick flames & th' English sword soon damps
> This rampant crue; pursues them in their swamps,
> And makes them fly their land with fear & shame:
> That th' Indians dread is now the English name.

Samuel Danforth was a tutor in the College from his

graduation to 1654, when he became John Eliot's assistant in the ministry at Roxbury; and he was one of the first five fellows of Harvard College named in the charter. He was succeeded as tutor, fellow, and almanac compiler, by Thomas Shepard (A.B. 1653), son of the famous minister. Shepard, like Chauncy, would seem to have read considerable English poetry of the period, to judge from his stanza for April in the almanac for 1656:

> Now Sol hath scap't the Oxes horn,
> The Ram, the winds, the stormes, and harms;
> The loving Twins by Leda born,
> Will entertain him in their arms.
> And Flora smile's to feel those beams
> Which whilom were with-drawn so long,
> The pratling birds, the purling streams
> Do carroll forth her wedding song.

Thomas Shepard, after two years as a tutor, became minister of Charlestown, but retained his fellowship in the College until his death in 1677. His father's gift of inspiring affection seems to have descended upon him. At his death, 'the whole Country was fill'd with Lamentations,' writes Cotton Mather, but there was none who found 'a deeper wound at this Decease,' than his particular friend Urian Oakes (A.B. 1649), third minister of Cambridge, and fourth President of Harvard College. Oakes's elegy on the death of Thomas Shepard, printed at Cambridge in 1677, was the best New England elegiac poem of the century, written in the true classical tradition. Here are three of the many stanzas:

> Art, Nature, Grace, in Him were all combin'd
> To shew the World a matchless *Paragon*:
> In whom of Radiant Virtues no less shin'd,
> Than a whole Constellation: but hee's gone!
>   Hee's gone alas! Down in the Dust must ly
>   As much of this rare Person as could dy.

His Look commanded Reverence and Awe,
Though Mild and Amiable, not Austere:
Well Humourd was He (as I ever saw)
And rul'd by Love and Wisdome, more than Fear.
   The Muses, and the Graces too, conspir'd
   To set forth this Rare Piece, to be admir'd.

Learned he was beyond the common Size,
Befriended much by Nature in his Wit,
And Temper, (Sweet, Sedate, Ingenious, Wise)
And (which crown'd all) he was Heav'ens Favorite.
   On whom the God of all Grace did command,
   And show'r down Blessings with a lib'eral hand.

From the first, there seem to have been almost as many Harvard types as there were Harvard men, for the genius of the place was to bring out whatever qualities a boy had in him. Thus, Benjamin Woodbridge, Harvard's first graduate, became a famous non-conformist minister in England, 'accounted among his bretheren a learned and a mighty man' according to Anthony Wood; while his classmate 'Dog' Downing became one of the most successful scoundrels of the age. Increase Mather, '56, statesman and theologian, advised caution in the famous witchcraft trials, while William Stoughton, '50, helped to condemn some of the victims to death, and Joshua Moody, '53, helped others to escape. Elisha Cooke, '57, physician, merchant, and politician, was the democratic enemy to Joseph Dudley, '65, fighting chaplain, politician, royal governor, and aristocrat. George Stirk, who began his chemical studies in 1644, two years before his graduation, became one of the most eminent chemists of the century, and gave his life to cure victims of the great plague in London; while his classmate John Brock ministered to the fishermen on the Isles of Shoals. A majority of the alumni before 1660, returned to England for a career, probably because England after 1642 was the fighting front of puritanism and partly because the pulpits of New England were occupied by a long-lived race of Oxford and

Cambridge graduates. Conversely, so high a reputation for learning and discipline did the Harvard of Dunster win for itself, that several English puritan families sent their sons over there to be educated; among them two transfers from Emmanuel College. Some of these lads, it may be suspected, were sent to New England on account of its slender opportunities for dissipation; but they evidently managed to find some, for the General Court passed a law in 1647:

> Whereas sundry Gentlemen of qualitie, and others oft times send over their children into this country unto some freinds heer, hoping at the least therby to prevent their extravagant and riotous courses, who notwithstanding... are no lesse lavish & profuse heer to the great greif of their freinds, dishonour of God & reproach of the Countrie.
>
> It is therfore ordered... That if any person after publication heerof shall any way give credit to any such youth... without orders from such their freinds heer, or elswhere, under their hands in writing, they shall lose their debt whatever it be.

The best evidence of Harvard's reputation is the fact that the degrees granted by what Dunster modestly called 'our infant college, compared with the Academys in Europe, being like Mantua unto Rome,' were recognized by the universities of Oxford and Cambridge as equivalent to theirs. James Ward of the class of 1645, one of those publicly whipped by President Dunster for burglarizing the house of a Cambridge citizen, nevertheless took his bachelor's degree, and went to England bearing a Harvard diploma signed by President Dunster, attesting not only his proficiency *in artibus liberalibus*, but his *probitatem vitae*. On producing this diploma at Oxford, James was 'incorporated' to the same degree that he had taken at Harvard, and was able to proceed M.A. Oxon. without further delay. This privilege of incorporation, hitherto accorded only to graduates of such seats of learning as Paris, Padua, Leyden, Aberdeen, and Dublin, was extended to ten or twelve Harvard men between

1648 and 1660, at Oxford and Cambridge; but never to any later American university. It was a significant recognition that the ideals and standards of Harvard were equivalent to theirs. Of course the actual quality of education, in a place of such slender resources and so few students and teachers, was not comparable to that of a great university such as Cambridge, with almost three thousand members.

It was Dunster, too, who secured from the General Court the college charter of 1650, which is still in force. Therein was provided the English collegiate model of government: a governing body consisting of the President, the Treasurer and five fellows. It was doubtless intended that the fellows should be the teachers, and the teachers, fellows; with few exceptions that was the case for over a century. The Board of Overseers, to whom Dunster originally stood in relation of a hired teacher to a school board, now fell into the position of a board of visitors, representing the public. It was long, however, before the youthful fellows of the college dared exert their rights against the venerable magistrates and elders on the Board of Overseers.

It has always been a puzzle why no religious test was ever adopted at Harvard; the absence of one allowed the college to gain a reputation for liberalism. Every European university, even Franeker in tolerant Holland, had such tests. It is unlikely that the puritan founders merely forgot to insert one, for by 1650 they had had plenty of trouble with religious dissenters, and it would have been inconsistent with their way of thinking to have omitted a test from a liberal motive. Possibly Dunster and his fellows had uneasy twinges of conscience about their required subscription to canons of the Church in which they did not believe, when taking a degree at Oxford or Cambridge. The experience may well have shown them what a farce religious tests were in a university. In connection with this, the early form of college seal adopted in 1643, 'Veritas' on three books, is suggestive; as is the course that Dunster took when he saw new light and truth.

The story of Dunster's dismissal from the College has generally been related as an instance of puritan bigotry and intolerance. It seems to me that there was right on both sides. Dunster, since his arrival, had been an orthodox member of the Cambridge Church; but by careful study he reached the conclusion that the baptism of infants was unauthorized by scripture. Accordingly he refused to present for baptism his son who was born in the autumn of 1653. The news that President Dunster had become an 'Antipædobaptist' created about the same sensation in the Colony as would be aroused in the country to-day if a college president should announce his adherence to communism. For the Baptists were regarded at that time much as the Bolsheviks of our own era. Their wild orgies at Münster, and the attempt of John of Leyden to overturn the state, although in a previous century, had given them a bad name, and were mentioned in the preamble to the law forbidding them residence in the Colony. Just as to-day many good people see an obvious connection between criticism of the government and seeking to destroy it, so to the pious and orthodox of New England there seemed a necessary connection between denying infant baptism and destroying the basis of society. Of course the assumption that Henry Dunster would emulate John of Leyden was just as absurd as the apprehension, common among conservative American college graduates, that liberal professors are in league with Moscow. Yet, taking a reasonable view of the matter, a Baptist president of seventeenth-century Harvard was anomalous, as a Baptist president of Notre Dame or Holy Cross would be to-day.

Actually the authorities treated Dunster with a consideration that no other dissenter enjoyed, and the College let him go with great reluctance. Early in 1654 the magistrates of the Bay asked the ministers to confer with Dunster, and report 'how the matter stands in respect of his opinions.' The conference failed to move him, or to convert them. In May, the General Court voted that no man 'unsound in the faith' be allowed to instruct youth in school or college; but left enforcement to the Overseers. In June, the President handed in his resignation to the Board of Overseers, who submitted it to the Court. The Court referred it back to the Overseers, with instruction to procure a new President in case Dunster 'persisted in his resolution more than one month.'

The Overseers begged him to remain and keep his dangerous opinions to himself; Dunster, to his honor, refused to dissemble the faith that was in him. On July 30, 1654, he made open confession of his principles, by getting 'right up in meeting' at Cambridge to declare that only penitent believers should be baptized. Yet he was not prevented from presiding at Commencement, a week later. His final resignation was not made until October 24, 1654, about one year after he had publicly gone Baptist. It was then accepted, and his successor, President Chauncy, was inaugurated on November 27; but Dunster's request to reside in the President's house through the winter of 1654–55 was granted.

On April 4, 1655, either just before or just after leaving Cambridge, Dunster was found guilty by the county court for disturbing Cambridge meeting, and sentenced to a public admonition. A month later, Corporation and Overseers joined in a petition to the General Court to pay the ex-President £40 which the College owed him and could not pay; and, 'for the country's honorable discharge in the hearts of all,' to grant him £100 'in consideration of his extraordinary pains in raising up and carrying on the College for so many years past.' This petition was honored by the legislature two years later. Thus, the affair was concluded with equal honor to the three parties involved: the Colony, the College, and the President.

In the autumn of 1655 Dunster moved to Scituate in Plymouth Colony, a community of intelligent and liberal persons. He was never banished from Massachusetts Bay, nor expelled from the Cambridge Church; and when his Glover stepchildren sued him for alienation of their property, justice was done to the ex-President by the courts of Massachusetts. He died at Scituate 27 February 1659.

If Dunster cherished resentment for his treatment, it does not appear in his will, for he bequeathed books to the minister of Cambridge, 'Mathematicke books' and a 'great presse in the Hall Chamber' to President Chauncy. Further, he provided funds for bearing his body to Cambridge, there to be buried by the side of his 'lovinge wife,' within sight of the college he had loved and served. This action has been cited as a somewhat abject forgiveness for persecution. It appears to me rather as the fine gesture of a Christian gentleman, admitting that the motives of his opponents were pure, and that all were equal in the sight of God.

A Jesuit historian has recently called the early history of Harvard 'one of the brilliant pageants of American history,' a pageant of which the 'real theme is courage and devotion: courage under conditions which would seem to stifle all human effort save an avid grubbing for food and housing, devotion to the fine ideal of disciplining the human intellect and human will.' One may add that the courage was supremely Dunster's, and in devotion no one approached him. Harvard College might even have followed its founder to an early death and oblivion, but for the serene faith and the lively intelligence of Henry Dunster.

CHAPTER VII
NATHANIEL WARD, LAWMAKER AND WIT

IF we answer, as it should be answered, old Horace's question, 'What prevents us from laughing when we tell the truth?' we shall not fail to discover humor in the history of Massachusetts Bay; but we may not hope to find many humorists. Yankee humor, that rich and racy variety of the genial art, does not come to the surface much before the eighteenth century, although no doubt it was under the surface in the seventeenth century. I have no doubt that there was plenty of jest and laughter among men working in the fields and women at home, soldiers on the march and sailors on the sea; but the droll stories of our countryside did not get recorded. Laughter fled from literature in Massachusetts Bay at the fall of Merrymount, and returned only with Ben Franklin and his friends, to plague poor Cotton Mather. What humor we find in the puritan century is of a rather grim variety, such as the carpenter who overcharged the colony in making a pair of stocks, and who was punished by being made their first occupant.

I do not mean to imply that the New England puritans were not happy. Their religion and their business filled their minds and employed their energies: and that is the basis of all happiness. What President Eliot used to call 'the durable satisfactions of life' were theirs to a high degree. It meant something to people who had been tied down in England to rise out of their class or condition in New England and accomplish things: to hew a farm out of the forest, to build a fair house or ship, to be a deputy, a selectman, or even a hogreeve. As for the leaders, who had sacrificed material comfort to found this commonwealth, what men were ever unhappy with the enjoyment of power? Diversion was not wanting, of the simple kind that gives greater happiness than the elaborate and febrile pleasures of our own day: diversion such as shooting and fishing, horseback riding and sleigh-riding, social gatherings with vast amounts of food and plenty beside water to drink. The children, to be sure, had a rather thin time of it; but so did children in every civilized nation until Froebel and Pestalozzi taught parents not to thwart natural instincts. Even at that, reciting abstracts of two-hour sermons and learning the Westminster Shorter Catechism (forty-five thousand words short) was a small price to pay for growing up in a country where there were real Indians, and where every household had fascinating things going on, such as spinning, weaving and dyeing; carpentering, cobbling, and tinkering; husking corn and killing critters; raising colts and calves and lambs. But they left very few jokes for us to laugh over. Still, from the generation of puritan founders, I have managed to excavate one wit: Nathaniel Ward 'the Simple Cobler of Aggawam.' He was not a cobbler — that was only one of his jokes, but the parson of Ipswich, and the lawmaker who drafted the Body of Liberties, our first bill of rights. Of an older generation than Thomas Shepard, graduating from Emmanuel two years before Shepard was born, he got religion late in life, and in the mean time got so much of merry England into his system that he had plenty left to ooze out in Massachusetts Bay. Over the mantelpiece in his house at Ipswich was carved:

SOBRIE, JUSTE, PIE, LAETE
(Prudently, justly, reverently, and gladly)

It is just that note of gladness that we miss in early New England. They wanted a John Sebastian Bach, or some one, to teach them to praise the Lord with gladness. Nathaniel Ward, who did just that, flashes across our early history like a cock pheasant in the gray November woods; but, alas, we have only a feather or two from which to reconstruct the picture. Increase Mather tells us that he knew a hundred witty speeches of the celebrated Ward: but he tells us only one 'godly speech' instead: 'I have only two comforts to live upon; the one is in the perfections of Christ; the other is in the imperfections of Christians.' If this was a sample of Ward's godly speeches, what must his witty ones have been! For it is a true nugget from the genuine vein of Yankee humor, which in its essence is an appreciation of the humorous contrast between principles and practice, the ideal and the real, religion and business.

Beside the single godly speech, Ward has left us a humorous pamphlet — 'The Simple Cobler of Aggawam,' of which I promise you a few extracts later, if you will listen to what Ward did for law and liberty. He is the outstanding figure in a phase of our history that has received much less attention than it deserves: the legal phase. He shared, and in a sense led, minister as he was, the struggle of democracy against theocracy, the struggle to secure for the people of Massachusetts a government of laws and not of men.

Nathaniel Ward came to us a puritan minister deprived by Archbishop Laud. He was the son of a puritan minister, the brother of two, the father of a third, and of two more ministers who were not so puritan. He emigrated at the age of fifty-five: ten years senior to Winthrop, twenty-five years older than Shepard; and came from the same part of the country as they. John Ward, Nathaniel's father, was a 'painefull preacher' at Bury St. Edmunds, whose epitaph is not painful but witty:

> Quo si quis scivit scitius
> Aut si quis docuit doctius
> At rarus vixit sanctius
> Et nullus tonuit fortius

> Grant some of knowledge greater store,
>   More learned some in teaching;
> Yet few in life were holy more,
>   None thundered more in preaching!

Nathaniel's elder brother Sam was the puritan lecturer of Ipswich in Suffolk, and a wit. He had a talent for caricature. The Spanish ambassador took exception to one of his prints entitled 'Spayne and Rome Defeated'; and as King James was anxious to stand in well with Spain, Samuel Ward was haled before the Privy Council. He was released on making the witty explanation that he had drawn the caricature five years before, when the royal policy was different; and that a humble country parson like himself could not be expected to keep in touch with His Majesty's secret affairs! Wit, however, is a dangerous gift for a preacher, a politician or a professor — he is certain to offend the stupid persons who are always in a majority — and the reign of James I was a particularly dangerous time for a parson to have a sense of humor in. Sam Ward complained that, although he conformed to the discipline and ritual of the church, and John Cotton conformed in nothing, he was always in trouble and John Cotton never. The reason is clear: John Cotton had absolutely no sense of humor! Still, John Cotton got away to New England as soon as Laud became Archbishop, while Ward stayed and was imprisoned for two years — part of his offense being that he quoted George Herbert's famous lines:

> Religion stands on tiptoe in our land,
> Ready to pass to the American strand.

Nathaniel Ward, 'the simple cobler of Aggawam,' did not make the mistake of standing on tiptoe too long; by this time he had taken off for New England; and started life afresh at the age of fifty-five. Nathaniel was not bred up to the ministry. Taking his M.A. at Emmanuel in 1603, he studied and practised law in London for about ten years, and then traveled on the Continent. He must have gone well armed with letters of introduction, for his headquarters were at Heidelberg, at the court of the Elector Palatine and the Princess Elizabeth, daughter of James I. Their baby, the

Prince Rupert, was dandled on the knee of the future pastor of Ipswich, Massachusetts. At Heidelberg, too, he came under the influence of David Pareus, a learned Calvinist, and professor of theology in the University. Pareus persuaded him to enter the ministry; and under such auspices he entered it a puritan, whatever he may have been before. His first living was the chaplaincy of the factory or mercantile colony of the Eastland Company at Elbing, in Prussia — that same Eastland Company of which the deputy-governor was Theophilus Eaton, organizer of the Massachusetts Bay Company and first Governor of the New Haven Colony. At Elbing he remained until well after the outbreak of the Thirty Years' War, which gave him a first-hand knowledge of what the Counter-Reformation meant. One would have supposed that it might also have shown him the value of religious tolerance; but it only impressed him with the need of unity among Protestants.

Returning to England around 1624, Nathaniel Ward for a time served as curate at Saint James's, Piccadilly, and in 1628 was presented by Sir Nathaniel Rich with the rectorship of Stondon Massey, in Essex. Of his pastorate there, we know almost nothing, except one anecdote, which shows that his conversation was as brilliant as his wit was ready. The famous Irish prelate, Archbishop Ussher, while visiting Essex was taken with the shaking ague. Ward went to visit him just before the 'shakes' were due; but 'that fit they talked away' — the Bishop missed it altogether!

Ward's particular friends in Essex seem to have been puritans like Hooker and Welde, who emigrated, and Henry Jacie, who did not. A connection of the Winthrops by his daughter's marriage, Ward became a freeman of the Massachusetts Bay Company before the transfer of the charter, and in January, 1630, wrote the Governor, urging him to reserve room and passage on the fleet 'for two families, a carpenter and bricklayer, the most faithfull and dilligent workmen in all our parts; one of them hath put off a good farme this weeke, and sold all, and should be much dammaged and discouraged if he finds no place amongst you.'

For several years Nathaniel Ward was sheltered from the prelates by his patron, Nathaniel Rich. Bishop Laud seems to have dealt with him in a much more urbane manner than he did with Shepard, for Ward was a man of the world with powerful friends, twenty-five years Shepard's senior. A scrap of one of their dialogues is recorded. Ward pleaded the favorite text of the prohibitionists and vegetarians: Romans, xiv, 21, 'It is good neither to eat flesh, nor to drink wine, nor anything whereby thy brother stumbleth, or is offended, or is made weak.' To which Bishop Laud retorted, 'Yea, Paul said so when he was alone, but if he had been in a Convocation?' Good old Laud! And there is no evidence that Nathaniel Ward practised prohibition in New England.

There was, however, a limit to Laud's patience with nonconformity. He records in 1633, 'Having heretofore after long patience and often conference proceeded against Nathaniel Ward, parson of Stondon in Essex, to excommunication and deprivation for refusing to subscribe to the articles established by the canon of the church... I have now left him under sentence for excommunication.'

At this point it will occur to some staunch supporters of Church and State to say, 'The puritan preachers were never persecuted. They were simply punished for breaking the law.' Of course! So were victims of the Holy Inquisition; so are most of the political prisoners of to-day, from Russia around the world to China. Englishmen and Americans who break the law on principle will invariably justify themselves with a higher law, of God or of Nature, than the statute law which they cannot conscientiously observe. Nathaniel Ward would soon have an opportunity to codify that Law of God which he deemed a higher authority than the canons of the Church.

Nathaniel Ward decided to take refuge in Massachusetts Bay, toward the founding of which he had contributed. It must have been a hard decision for a genial and mellow minister of fifty-five. A letter that I read last summer in the stately library of Trinity College, Cambridge, opened for me a shaft of light on the pain that some New England puritans suffered in departing from their native land. The letter is from Roger Williams to Mistress Anne Sadleir, daughter of Lord Chief Justice Coke:

My much honored frend, that man of Honour and Wisdome and Piety your deare Father, was often pleased to call me his son, and truely it was as bitter as Death to me (when Bishop Laud pursued me out of this Land...) I say it was as bitter as Death to me when I rode Windsor way to take ship at Bristow, and saw Stoke-House where that blessed man [your father] was, and I durst not acquaint him with my Conscience and my Flight.

If flight was bitter as death to Roger Williams, a young man, a radical, and (as it proved) a lover of the wilderness; what must it have been to Nathaniel Ward, already an old man by the standards of the day, a conservative, a lover of good company and urbane conversation?

By the end of 1634 Nathaniel Ward was the minister of the town of Ipswich, as the plantation at Agawam had just been named. Ipswich was then the most remote and isolated settlement in Massachusetts Bay. Some people who attempted to settle there in 1630 had been ordered by the Court to remove, as their situation was supposed to be too dangerous. Salem was the nearest settlement, and there was no other along the coast until one reached the feeble hamlet on the site of Portsmouth, New Hampshire. Yet the place was settled in 1633 under the lead of persons of means and education, such as John Winthrop, Jr., and Richard Bellingham. There were others, too, described by Ward as 'ill and doubtfull persons... drinking and pilferinge,' whose goings-on caused the town to be more 'carefull on whome they bestowe lotts.' For, as he explains:

First, we conceive the lesse of Satan's kingdome we have in our towne, the more of God's presence and blessinge we may expect.

Secondly, we have respect to the creditt of our Church and towne....

Thirdly, we consider our towne as a by or port towne of the land, remote from neighbours, and had neede to be strong and of a homogeneous spirit and people...

Lastly, our thoughts and fears growe very sadd to see such multitudes of idle and profane young men, servants and others with whome we must leave our children for whose sake and safety we came over, and who came with us from the land of their nativity, their friends and many other comforts, which their birthright intitled them to.

Thus early did the frontier impinge upon social stability in Massachusetts Bay. Ward's letter shows what was in the minds of the elders when they declared 'that strict discipline ... was more needful in plantations than in a settled state.'

The strict discipline of the early laws and magistrates fell heavily on frontier individualists; but it gave to New England a law-abiding tradition. Massachusetts never passed through the lawless, gun-toting, frontier-bully stage of society; picturesque to read about, to be sure, but leaving a tradition of lawlessness to the cities and communities so unfortunate as to have been through it.

If Nathaniel Ward was a friend to strict discipline, he was equally a foe to arbitrary government. The deputies early in 1641 chose him to preach the annual election sermon at Boston, without consulting the magistrates: no doubt because they appreciated his racy wit; and knew that the magistrates would be annoyed by his indiscretion. The election sermon caused Governor Winthrop much pain. For the Simple Cobler propounded moral and political principles grounded 'upon the old Roman and Grecian government, which sure is an error; for if religion and the word of God makes men wiser than their neighbors... it is probable that by all these helps we may better frame rules of government to ourselves than to receive others... of those heathen commonwealths.' Further, Ward 'advised the people to keep all their magistrates in an equal rank, and not give more honor or power to one then to another'; in other words, to return to that rotation in the governorship which had been abandoned with the defeat of Vane.

Ward's most important service for the colony was his part in the struggle to secure a government of laws and not of men.

The political phase of that struggle we have already noted. Winthrop and the first board of Assistants set up an oligarchy, with all power, legislative, executive, and judicial, to themselves. The freemen first secured the right to elect the Governor, then the right to elect deputies to the General Court. They lost the fight against the negative voice, but defeated Cotton's plan for a life magistracy, and hamstrung his life council of three. But the Assistants still held the preponderance of political power, as long as the General Court merely passed occasional acts and resolves ('orders' they were generally called), applying mostly to special cases and local conditions, and left the Assistants (as magistrates and judges) to declare the law in all civil and criminal cases, and to fix the penalty. To the magistrates the right of the matter was that law, in a Bible Commonwealth, must be God's law as revealed in the Bible. The magistrate was God's own justice, appointed during good behavior, with complete discretion as to the particular law of God that he should apply and the punishments he should mete out. That was a logic the freemen could not deny. They shared the puritan idea that a fundamental law in any community should be the law of God, as found in the Bible. They shared the puritan theory of the identity of law and morality, sin and crime. But, it was a matter of common observation that the magistrates were so clever at finding exactly what they wanted in the Bible, that the magistrates' discretion, or maybe indigestion, was the real law.

In 1634, the year that Nathaniel Ward emigrated, the General Court began to function as a representative body, and as early as 1635 the deputies showed their conviction that liberty would not be secure until there were adopted and published a body of laws in which every man might read his rights and duties, and every magistrate learn 'where he got off.' Naturally the Assistants, considering themselves exclusive partners with God in the divine covenant to rule the Bay, resisted any limitation to their omnicompetence. They were able to postpone the evil day for several years by delay, evasion, and subterfuge. For the Deputies, mistrusting their own knowledge of divine law, committed the work of codification to magistrates and ministers. In modern America we have set up judges — or rather acquiesced in their setting themselves up — to check the mistakes, injustices, and progressive tendencies of elected bodies. The reverse process was the road to liberty in early Massachusetts: setting up a body of law to curb the whims and injustices of judges.

In 1635, records Winthrop, 'the deputies having conceived great danger to our state in regard that our magistrates, for want of positive laws, in many cases might proceed according to their discretions, it was agreed that some men should be appointed to frame a body of grounds of laws in resemblance to a Magna Charta, which... should be received for fundamental laws.' The committee appointed, consisting of Winthrop, Dudley, Haynes, and Bellingham, let the matter sleep. As magistrates, they were naturally not eager to proceed. It was not only that they were greedy of power. As Winthrop says, there were two great reasons which caused the magistrates and elders 'not to be very forward in this matter.' First, want of sufficient experience of the country and the people. It would be better to let customs be formed, and grow gradually into laws, like the common law of England. Second, the charter provided that the colony pass no laws repugnant to the laws of England. Any formal codification of the Law of God would certainly be repugnant to the laws of England. But if no laws were written or published, and merely allowed to grow like Topsy, the English government could find nothing 'repugnant' to put its finger on. For instance, marriage in Massachusetts was a purely civil ceremony. If any one had been bold enough to be married by a minister instead of a magistrate, the courts would have held it null and void. But any formal law to that effect would be obviously repugnant to the laws of England, and might provoke interference with the charter.

So the first committee appointed to frame a body of laws, simply stalled. And in 1636 it was replaced by another, of magistrates and ministers, 'to make a draught of lawes agreeable to the word of God, which may be the Fundamentalls of this commonwealth, and to present the same to the nexte Generall Court.' In the meantime, the magistrates were to 'determine all causes according to the lawes nowe established; and where there is noe law, then as neere the lawe of God as they can.'

John Cotton was the working member of this second committee. The Deputies had in effect committed their work to the greatest enemy to traditional English political ideas; for John Cotton's ideal was the theocracy of ancient Israel, where God was King, and the high priest ruled in his name by virtue of his laws. So it is not remarkable that the code presented to the General Court by John Cotton did not please the Deputies.

'Moses his Judicialls' was the name given to this Cotton code by Winthrop; an apt title, for the greater part of it was drawn directly from the Bible, and supported by marginal references to the Scriptures. There are ten chapters and seventy-five articles, with a snapper at the end:

The Lord is our Judge,
The Lord is our Law-giver,
The Lord is our King: He will save us.
                    (Isaiah, xxxiii, 22.)

The first chapter is a frame of government drawn largely from the Charter. Even provisions of that nature are supported by biblical references, in order to prove that the government of Massachusetts Bay is in harmony with God's law. For instance, section 6, providing that every court of justice shall have a secretary or recorder and a marshal, is supported by 'Judges and officers shalt thou make thee in all thy gates' (Deuteronomy, xvi, 18); 'Shaphan the scribe in the higher court... Elishama the scribe... and all the princes' (Jeremiah xxxvi, 10, 12); 'and Jehosaphat the son of Alihud was recorder: and Sheva was scribe' (2 Samuel xx, 24, 25). Chapter III provides for military training, taxation, and the encouragement of the fishing — but no reference to the Apostles' calling is inserted; Chapter IV, on the right of inheritance, and Chapter VI, on trespassers, are biblical in origin, and Chapters VII and VIII, on crimes, are drawn almost wholly from the Pentateuch.

The language throughout is archaic and smacks of the parson's study rather than the lawyer's office. But at least Cotton did not attempt to lift whole sections of the Bible into the fundamental law of Massachusetts. He might have found good precedent for so doing, since the Scots parliament in 1567 made the entire eighteenth chapter of Leviticus statute law, and as such it is interpreted by Scots courts to this day.

We have no record of the discussion on the Cotton code, or why the Deputies refused to adopt it; but one provision alone would have made it objectionable to them. In Chapter I, article 3, it is provided that the counselors (assistants) 'are to be chosen for life, unlesse they give just cause of removall, which if they doe, then they are to be removed by the Generall Court.' Here John Cotton attempts to 'put across' his favorite idea of life tenure for magistrates, which the freemen had clearly repudiated by beginning a rotation of office in the chief magistracy.

'Moses his Judicialls' were not adopted, but John Davenport, a friend of John Cotton, took a copy of the code with him to New Haven, where it served as the fundamental law and frame of government for that colony during the quarter-century of its existence. The famous if quasi-legendary 'Blue Laws' of New Haven are founded on this Cotton code.

During the year 1637 the General Court was so busy with the Pequot war and with Anne Hutchinson that the matter of a body of laws was allowed to rest. In the spring of 1638 it made a fresh start, with an original method. The freemen were asked to assemble in their several towns, and draw up a list of 'such necessary and fundamentall lawes as may bee sutable to the times and places whear God by his providence hath cast us.' Before June 5, 1638, they must deliver these lists in writing to the Governor to be acted upon further. Some of the towns acted upon the order; Charlestown, for instance, appointed John Harvard on a committee 'to consider of some things tending toward a body of laws.' These drafts, or heads of Laws were handed as they came in to a committee, with orders to 'make a compendious abrigment of the same... adding... or detracting therefrom what in their wisdomes shall seeme meete.'

This committee was a large one, and included Nathaniel Ward. We know nothing of its workings except that they were very slow, and in November, 1639, submitted to the General Court two codes for them to take their choice. One was Cotton's 'Moses his Judicialls'; the other, a body of laws drafted by Nathaniel Ward. Both these drafts were referred to a new committee, with orders to combine them in one. The resulting compendium was the Body of Liberties.

Manuscript copies of it were sent to the several towns,

which were requested to 'ripen their thoughts on the subject.' Nathaniel Ward did not approve this second referendum. He wrote to Governor Winthrop... 'I suspect both Commonwealth and Churches have discended too lowe already; I see the spirits of people runne high, and what they gett they hould. They may not be denyed their proper and lawfull liberties, but I question whether it be of God to interest the inferiour sort in that which should be reserved *inter optimates penes quos est sancire leges* [*tenure*].' That was just what Winthrop was always saying.

In the session of November, 1641, the Body of Liberties was formally adopted. The formal record of it is lacking, as the General Court records are wanting for that date; but Winthrop explicitly states in his journal:

This session continued three weeks, and established 100 laws, which were called the *Body of Liberties*. They had been composed by Mr. Nathaniel Ward (sometime pastor of the church of Ipswich; he had been a minister in England, and formerly a student and practiser in the course of the common law), and had been revised and altered by the court, and sent forth to every town to be further considered of. And now again in this court they were revised, amended, and presented, and so established for three years, by that experience to have them fully amended and established to be perpetual.

The Body of Liberties, then, is the work of Nathaniel Ward, in the same sense that the Constitution of 1780 is the work of John Adams. Let us see what sort of a code it was. Ward accepted the idea that all law was of God. 'Morall Lawes, Royall Prerogatives, Popular Liberties, are not of Mans making or giving, but Gods: Man is but to measure them out by Gods Rule: which if mans wisdome cannot reach, Mans experience must mend,' he wrote in the Simple Cobler. The Body of Liberties still contains a good deal of 'Moses his Judicialls,' but the selection was made carefully, with a view to local conditions and so-called universal morality; not with the idea of applying the sanctions and sanitary ordinances of the ancient Hebrews to Massachusetts Bay. Ward's point of departure is not the Bible, but the Common Law; and the preamble to the Body of Liberties places it in a class with the Petition of Right and the Instrument of Government, rather than with Cotton's Code:

The free fruition of such liberties Immunities and priveledges as humanitie, Civilitie, and Christianitie call for as due to every man in his place and proportion without impeachment and infringement hath ever bene and ever will be the tranquillitie and Stabilitie of Churches and Commonwealths. And the deniall or deprivall thereof, the disturbance if not the ruine of both.

We hould it therefore our dutie and safetie whilst we are about the further establishing of this Government to collect and expresse all such freedomes as for present we foresee may concerne us, and our posteritie after us, And to ratify them with our sollemne consent.

Wee doe therefore this day religiously and unanimously decree and confirme these following Rites, liberties and priveledges concerneing our Churches, and Civill State to be respectively impartiallie and inviolably enjoyed and observed throughout our Jurisdiction for ever.

1. No mans life shall be taken away, no mans honour or good name shall be stayned, no mans person shall be arested, restrayned, banished, dismembred, nor any wayes punished, no man shall be deprived of his wife or children, no mans goods or estaite shall be taken away from him, nor any way indammaged under colour of law or Countenance of Authoritie, unlesse it be by vertue or equitie of some expresse law of the Country waranting the same, established by a generall Court and sufficiently published, or in case of the defect of a law in any parteculer case by the word of God.

Naturally the Body of Liberties is not popular with those writers who enjoy picturing the founders of New England as a set of cruel and crack-brained religious fanatics. For the entire code shows the hand of a man familiar with the principles of English law and the securities of English liberty. Many of the provisions derived from the Mosaic law are more

humane than those of the contemporary common law. The
Liberties of Servants, derived from the Pentateuch, are
humanitarian in character; the number of lashes inflicted for
punishment is limited to forty; and the Capital Laws,
although taken over bodily from Cotton's code, are in some
respects more lenient than the contemporary practice in
England. Theft is not punishable by death, although in England robbery, burglary, and larceny above the value of one
shilling, were then capital felonies. On the other hand,
adultery, unnatural vice, blasphemy and perjury endanger-
ing life, were capital offenses in the Body of Liberties, though
not in England. Two adulterers were executed at Boston in
1644; but no instance of the death penalty being enforced
for the last two offenses is found in the court records. Cruel
and barbarous punishments were proscribed, and torture
was forbidden unless on a convict in a capital case to discover confederates, and then the torture must not be 'barbarous and inhumane.' Certain police methods of to-day, the
notorious 'third degree,' are no better.

Although animals then had no protection in common law,
'The Bruite Creature' has a section of his own in the Body of
Liberties. 'No man shall exercise any Tirranny or Crueltie
towards any bruite Creatures which are usuallie kept for
man's use,'[1] and cattle-drovers may rest or refresh their
cattle in any field not enclosed, without trespass. So much
for Macaulay's epigram, that the puritans objected to bear-
baiting not because it was cruel to the bear but because it
gave pleasure to the spectators. Macaulay could seldom resist the temptation to make a wise-crack.

Feudal dues are prohibited, complete testamentary liberty
is provided, and foreigners are assured the equal protection
of the laws. Juries, when unable to give a positive verdict,
are allowed to give a *non liquit*, leaving the judgment of the

---

[1] See an interesting case of condemnation for cruelty to an ox, in *Records of
Quarterly Courts of Essex County*, III, 305.

case to the Court — a practice somewhat analogous to the Scots verdict of 'not proven.' And in all cases it was the privilege of the defendant to 'put himself on the court' to avoid a jury verdict: a privilege only restored to the law of Massachusetts in 1925.

No definite penalty is affixed to any except the capital laws; and penalties were very rare in the early statutes of Massachusetts. This was in accordance with the magistrates' belief, well argued by Winthrop, that justice could best be secured by considering each case on its merits. The nineteenth century was shocked by so wide a judicial discretion, and endeavored by statute 'to make the punishment fit the crime.' Modern social jurisprudence reverts to the puritan practice, of making the punishment fit the criminal.

There are also certain features of the Body of Liberties that were original or peculiar to New England. No one was allowed to defend another for pay: hence the legal profession was practically outlawed. Corn or hay in the field, or perishable garden stuff, cannot be taken in distress. Taxes cannot be levied on a man for property that 'he hath in England, or in any forreine partes.' Fishermen and hunters, if householders, may not be excluded from the 'great ponds' and tidal waters of their home town. Monopolies, one of the things the puritans were striving against in England, may not be granted. And the right of the freemen to elect any of their body to the magistracy and to refuse to reëlect them without cause, is expressly asserted, in opposition to Cotton's code. A special chapter is devoted to the congregational way of church government, which is protected against the encroaching jurisdiction of church councils and synods.

Our modern laws are renowned for their 'jokers,' but we need not expect to find the sage of Ipswich intruding his wit into such a serious business as a codification of the law of God. Nevertheless, I think that at least one 'joker' may be found in the Body of Liberties. Nathaniel Ward had three chief antipathies: religious toleration, the Irish, and women. His 'Simple Cobler' is full of jokes on the fair sex.

> The World is full of care,
> Much like unto a bubble;
> Women and care, and care and women,
> And women and care and trouble.

Having been a solitary widower for almost twelve years, he says — an unprecedented length of time for a New England puritan — he intended to seek a new 'yoke-fellow' in his native country; but he cannot stand the new fashion, which 'transclouts them into gant bar geese, ill-shapen-shotten-shell-fish, Egyptian Hyeroglyphicks, or at the best into French flurts of the pastery, which a proper English woman should scorne with her heels: it is marvell they weare drailes on the hinder part of their heads, having nothing as it seems in the fore-part, but a few Squirrils brains to help them frisk from [one] ill-favor'd fashion to another.'

This may prepare us for the surprising article 80 of the Body of Liberties:

Everie marryed woeman shall be free from bodilie correction or stripes by her husband, unlesse it be in his own defense upon her assalt.

Yet, joking aside, this was an improvement on the English common law, authorizing a man to chastise his wife with a 'reasonable instrument,' which Mr. Justice Buller once defined as 'a stick no bigger than my thumb.'

The Body of Liberties is an enlightened body of laws and of principles that would have done credit to any commonwealth in the seventeenth century; but it did not wholly satisfy the Bay Colony. Its place is with the great constitutional documents of the Interregnum; and, like them, it was subject to improvement.

Postponing to the next chapter the steps that led from the Body of Liberties to the improved Body of Laws and Liberties of 1648, let us follow the career of the witty and learned author.

Nathaniel Ward had retired from his pastorate about 1636, on account of ill health.   For ten years he continued to reside at Ipswich, where there was a remarkably cultivated society for a frontier town.   Indeed, at one time, four of the eleven magistrates of the Bay — Bellingham, Saltonstall, Bradstreet, and Symonds — resided there.   After the foundation of Newbury and Rowley, Ipswich was less isolated.   Nathaniel Ward was active in promoting the settlement of Andover and Haverhill, where his son John was the first minister.

When the first shires were established in Massachusetts in 1643, all that part north of Boston and east of the Concord River became the shire of Essex.   One can discern a sort of Essex county consciousness developing very early.   It was a theory of the late Senator Lodge, who certainly ought to have known how the minds of Essex politicians work, that John Endecott and the Salem elders were sore at being superseded by Winthrop and Dudley, and bided their time to get even.   If so, the growth of Essex County gave them their opportunity, and a false step by Winthrop in 1643 offered the occasion.   The Governor, carrying a majority of the Assistants, had given unneutral aid to Charles de la Tour, who was contending with the Sieur d'Aulnay for the lordship of La Cadie (Nova Scotia).   It was a most imprudent decision, dictated it seems by La Tour's promise of trading privileges at a time when the colony was greatly in need of a market, and sanctioned by his claim to be a Protestant.   After Massachusetts had been already committed to La Tour, the Ipswich group sent a strong remonstrance to Governor Winthrop against his policy of intervention.   It was signed by Richard Saltonstall, Simon Bradstreet, Samuel Symonds, Nathaniel Ward; by John Norton and Nathaniel Rogers, Ward's two successors in the Ipswich ministry, and by Ezekiel Rogers,.

Ward's half-brother and the minister of Rowley. The remonstrance bears unmistakable traces of the pungent pen of
the Simple Cobler:

'The grounds of warre ought to be just and necessary,' and it is
highly doubtful whether La Tour or d'Aulnay have the right of it:
'We shall therefore runne into an unchristian premunire of pre-
sumption if we resolve upon such an enterprize with an irresolved
faith, *in causa dubia bellum non est suscipiendum*' — a typically
Wardian sentence. 2. 'Warres ought not to be undertaken without
the counsell and command of the supreme authority,' the Magistrates of Massachusetts-Bay are not King and Parliament. 3. 'The
ends of warre ought to be religious: what glory is intended hereby to
God we see not.' 4. 'Undertakings of warrs ought to be probably
feasable, but this seemes not soe to us'; D'Aulnay is the stronger of
the two. And they conclude as they began, 'we wash our hands
wholly of this designe...we are and desire to be cleare and innocent
of this undertaking.'

In other words, war may be declared, but Ipswich and
vicinity will remain neutral.

For petitions and remonstrances more respectful than this,
freemen of Massachusetts had been fined, imprisoned, and
banished; but the government dared do nothing to men of
such eminence as Saltonstall, Bradstreet, Norton, and Ward.
Governor Winthrop, though deeply offended at Ward's 'too
much bluntnesse and plumpnesse of speech,' wrote them a
long letter defending his policy. As it turned out, Ward and
his neighbors were right. Winthrop had bet on the wrong
horse. La Tour was completely beaten by d'Aulnay, and
Massachusetts was left holding an empty bag for the wonderful trade that La Tour had promised. In consequence, the
spring election of 1644 brought as complete a shakeup as the
firm structure of the body politic was capable of receiving.
Endecott was elected governor instead of Winthrop; Bradstreet and Hathorne of Salem (Nathaniel's ancestor), with
Saltonstall as alternate, were elected delegates to the New
England Confederacy in place of Winthrop and Dudley.

Further, the Essex men called a caucus of deputies before the General Court met, in order to prepare business; and from this caucus issued an interesting constitutional proposition.

It was proposed to appoint a standing committee consisting of seven magistrates, three deputies, *and* Nathaniel Ward, 'to order all affairs of the Commonwealth in the vacancy of the General Court.' Ward, as a cleric, was not eligible for the General Court, hence he had to be specially named. The object of this standing committee, of course, was to check the power of the Assistants, and to prevent them from committing more costly mistakes in foreign policy. It was a sort of democratic counter-proposal to John Cotton's life council of three. Naturally the Assistants resisted the proposal. Speaker Hathorne warned them that if they attempted to exercise their power as of old, they would not be obeyed. They contemplated appealing over the heads of the freemen to the unenfranchised, on the ground of supporting the government in war time; but wisely thought better of it. The negative voice enabled the Assistants to defeat the Essex proposition, and, despite Hathorne's prophecy, they were obeyed. For a time it seemed as if there would be fierce party strife; but Winthrop's admirable conduct in the Hingham militia case the following year seemed to appease the waves of faction, and to flatten out the Essex junto of Saltonstall, Ward, and Bellingham.[1] Ward's legal acumen and pungent pen had limited the Magistrates' judicial discretion by the Body of Liberties; and that was a great point won. But their executive and legislative power stood unimpaired.

As Ward had turned from preaching to lawmaking, and from lawmaking to politics, so now he took up literature. In 1645–46, he wrote the book that has given him a permanent place in American Literature. The Simple Cobler of

[1] See Chapter III above.

Aggawam is a serious but witty argument against religious toleration, arbitrary government, and extravagant fashions. It was written here but published in London, at the time when the Presbyterians were in power. The Army and the Independents were pressing their demands for religious liberty and republican government. Nathaniel Ward was opposed to both. He desired religious unity, legally established, with the ancient English constitution of King, Lords, and Commons. He was distressed to find so many Godly men's brains intellectually 'fly-blown' by the Devil's sting. 'Poly-piety,' as he calls toleration, 'is the greatest impiety in the world.' He knows what he is talking about, having lived in a Dutch city 'where a Papist preached in one Church, a Lutheran in another, a Calvinist in a third... the Religion of that place was but motly and meagre, their affections leopardlike.' Let colonies like Rhode Island provide free stable-room and litter for all kinds of consciences, be they never so dirty or jadish. He prefers a community like Massachusetts, where 'all Familists, Antinomians, Anabaptists, and other Enthusiasts,[1] shall have free Liberty to keep away from us, and such as will come, to be gone as fast as they can, the sooner the better.'

There is talke of an universall Toleration, I would talke as loud as I could against it, did I know what more apt and reasonable Sacrifice England could offer to God for his late performing all his heavenly Truths, then an universall Toleration of all hellish Errors, or how they shall make an universall Reformation, but by making Christs Academy the Devils University, where any man may commence Heretique *per saltum*; where he that is *filius Diabolicus*, or *simpliciter pessimus*, may have his grace to goe to hell *cum Publico Privilegio*; and carry as many after him as he can....

It is said, That Men ought to have Liberty of their Conscience, and that it is Persecution to debarre them of it: I can rather stand

---

[1] Enthusiast was used at that time in its original sense — one possessed by God — and was applied by the puritans to the self-illumined sort of sectary which they abhorred.

amazed then reply to this: it is an astonishment to think that the braines of men should be parboyl'd in such impious ignorance; Let all the wits under the Heavens lay their heads together and finde an Assertion worse than this (one excepted) I will Petition to be chosen the universal Ideot of the world.

As for the different sects,

Some are playing young Spaniels questing at every bird that rises; so others, held very good men, are at a dead stand, not knowing what to doe or say; and are therefore called Seekers...I cannot but feare, that those men never Moored their Anchors well in the firme soile of Heaven, that are weather-waft up and down with every eddy-wind of every new doctrine. The good Spirit of God doth not usually tie up the Helme, and suffer passengers to Heaven to ride a drift....

Next the Simple Cobler pays his respects to the women:

I shall therefore make bold for this once, to borrow a little of their loose tongued Liberty, and mispend a word or two upon their long-wasted, but short-skirted patience: a little use of my stirrup will doe no harme.

I am neither Nigard, nor Cinick. I honour the woman that can honour her selfe with her attire: a good Text alwayes deserves a fair Margent: I am not much offended if I see a trimme, far trimmer than she that wears it: in a word, whatever Christianity or Civility will allow, I can afford with *London* measure: but when I heare a nugiperous Gentledame inquire what dresse the Queen is in this week: what the nudiustertian [1] fashion of the Court; I meane the very newest: with egge to be in it in all haste, what ever it be; I look at her as the very gizzard of a trifle, the product of a quarter of a cypher, the epitome of nothing, fitter to be kickt, if shee were of a kickable substance, than either honour'd or humour'd.

Apparently the 'nudiustertian' fashion had already appeared in Boston, for, says Ward, 'we have about five or six' of these gentlewomen, 'surcingled' with 'gut-foundred goosdom,' in our colony; 'if I see any of them accidentally, I cannot cleanse my phansie of them for a moneth after.'

[1] Ward had a weakness for what he called 'new-quoddled words,' which to the academic minds of the day seemed the acme of wit.

'Most deare and unparallel'd Ladies,' he concludes, please set a sensible fashion, and then stick to it a while. I do not object to your changing it occasionally. 'I point my pen only against the light-heel'd beagles that lead the chase so fast, that they run all civility out of breath, against these Ape-headed pullets, which invent Antique foole-fangles, meerly for fashion and novelty sake.'

When he considers the state of the Church, Ward drops these euphuistic conceits for plain English and common sense. He cares less for the exact form the settlement takes in England, than for keeping up the authority of the ministry, by assuring to the clergy a regular and reasonable salary.

When Elders live upon peoples good wills, people care little for their ill wills, be they never so just: Voluntary contributions or non-tributions of Members, put Ministers upon many temptations in administrations of their Offices: two houres care does more dis-spirit an ingenuous man than two dayes study: nor can an Elder be given to hospitality, when he knowes not what will be given him to defray it: it is pity men of gifts should live upon men's gifts.

Ward proceeds to point out that reformed ritual or discipline is nothing, if the reformation does reach people's hearts; that evangelization is the main thing; and the easiest place for a hypocrite to lose his soul is through membership in a strict reformed church. Then follows a plea to both sides for political tolerance, for a settlement on the basis of the ancient constitution, King, Lords, and Commons, with an eloquent peroration. And then a collection of postscripts — or heel-pieces, as the Simple Cobler calls them, with 'half a dozen plaine honest Country Hobnailes' in the shape of verses such as

> There, lives cannot be good,
> There, Faith cannot be sure,
> Where Truth cannot be quiet,
> Nor Ordinances pure.

> No King can King it right,
>   Nor rightly sway his Rod;
> Who truely loves not Christ,
>   And truely fears not God.

Even this was not all; for as the Simple Cobler confesses:

Wee have a strong weaknesse in New England that when wee are speaking, we know not how to conclude: wee make many ends, before we make an end: the fault is in the Climate; we cannot helpe it though we can, which is the Arch infirmity in all morality: We are so near the West pole, that our Longitudes are as long, as any wise man would wish, and somewhat longer.

So that we have six pages more of humorous *Errata at non Corrigenda*, another postscript, and a farewell verse:

> So farewell England old
>   If evill times ensue,
> Let good men come to us,
>   Wee'l welcome them to New.

> And farewell Honor'd Friends,
>   If happy dayes ensue,
> You'l have some Guests from hence,
>   Pray welcome us to you.

One of the first 'guests from hence' was the Simple Cobler himself. He returned to England in the winter of 1646–47, arriving just about the time his book came out. The Civil War was drawing to a close, puritanism was in power, his friend John Winthrop, Jr., had left Ipswich for Connecticut, and his daughter, the wife of Giles Firmin, to whom he was very strongly attached, had returned to England. One son, John, was minister at Haverhill; the other, James, was one of the young burglars recently whipped by the President of Harvard College. 'We had yet no particular punishment for burglary,' records Winthrop with evident regret. Evidently there was not much of a career ahead of James in America.

Nathaniel Ward arrived in London to find himself famous. In a flood of pamphlets on the same questions of church and state, the Simple Cobler stood out conspicuous for wit without indecency. It went through four editions before the end of the year. In June, 1647, Ward was called upon to preach before the House of Commons. It was a time of peril and uncertainty, when everything was at loose ends once more, owing to the abduction of the King by the Army; and the Simple Cobler returned to his political last. The text was Ezekiel xix, 14: 'And fire is gone out of a rod of her branches, which hath devoured her fruit, so that she hath no strong rod to be a sceptre to rule.' He defended the King, censured the Army, flayed the Long Parliament, and urged them, if they could not keep the army under control, to give way to a new Parliament that could. The Commons were offended, refused him the usual vote of thanks, and did not offer to print the sermon; but it was printed by others, and in at least three editions. In 'A Religious Retreat Sounded to a Religious Army,' Ward appealed to the Army to lay down their arms, and leave to the people the liberty they had won. This started a pamphlet warfare between Ward and his old neighbor Hugh Peter, who replied to the 'Religious Retreat' in 'A word for the Armie and two words to the Kingdome.' Therein Peter called Ward a 'pedantick,' to which the Simple Cobler retorted with 'A Word to Mr. Peters and Two Words for the Parliament and Kingdom.' He played on the word pedantic, admitting he was a pedestrian, while Peter rode in pomp on horseback with the army. Having silenced Hugh Peter — no mean feat that! — Ward fell foul of the sectaries who disparaged learning in ministers, and proposed that their preachers should work like other men during the week, since all they really had to do was preach on the Sabbath. The title of this pamphlet was '*Mercurius Antimechanicus*, or the Simple Cobler's Boy with his lapful of Caveats or Take-heeds.'

By the middle of 1648 we find Nathaniel Ward happily installed as minister of the gospel over the parish of Shenfield, only four or five miles from his former home at Stondon Massey. He took no further part in politics, for which he had no heart now that the King was dead. Parish duties were enough to occupy a parson who had passed the age of three score and ten; and his only diversion was to visit the Giles Firmins and his grandchildren, at another Essex rectory not far away. Indeed the Simple Cobler lived so quietly and obscurely that we do not even know the exact date of his death; only that it was before November, 1652.

So he who had bequeathed to Massachusetts a government of laws and not of men, was spared the pains of living under the iron rule of the Major-Generals. I like to think that he passed with a jest on his lips and gladness in his heart; for in the fall of laws 'twas time a loyal man should die.

CHAPTER VIII
ROBERT CHILD, REMONSTRANT

THE man largely responsible for carrying on the work of Nathaniel Ward, was a person whom Governor Winthrop regarded as the greatest pest to Massachusetts Bay since Anne Hutchinson was banished. This was Dr. Robert Child, a man of scientific curiosity and wide attainments, and a lover of liberty withal, who found the body politic of the Bay much too cramped; who for his remonstrance to the General Court, asking an enlargement of the suffrage, was punished.

As a liberal, or, if you will, a rebel, the work of Robert Child seems to me so much more significant than that of Anne Hutchinson, that I have taken him rather than her as representative of the earnest men and women who dared to speak out in early Massachusetts, and suffered for it. Anne Hutchinson, brave and witty woman that she was, had little to offer for freedom or the future; at least I cannot see that the power of one woman, no matter how inspired and inspiring, to dictate high matters of religion and politics, had much in it for freedom or the future. Robert Child, however, was looking ahead. All that he demanded: a government of laws, an extension of the franchise, and religious toleration, eventually came; indeed they began to come before he had fairly turned his back on Massachusetts Bay. So often do governing classes stone the prophet, and then proceed to carry out his suggestions and claim the credit themselves.

Robert Child was the best educated man among the early settlers of New England. He was born in 1613, to a good county family in Kent. At the age of fifteen he entered Corpus Christi or Bene't College, Cambridge, and there remained for the usual course of seven years, taking his master's degree in 1635. Thence he proceeded to the University of Leyden in Holland, to study medicine, but probably did not stay long; for we find him passing his examinations for the degree of Doctor of Medicine at the University of Padua in 1638. It was then usual for young Englishmen to take their medical studies abroad. Oxford and Cambridge were not well organized for that branch of science, and the first Scots medical degree was granted in 1654 — to a Harvard graduate, curiously enough.

During his medical course Child had to travel far in Europe, and he was the sort of young man who kept his eyes open wherever he went. Scientific agriculture, chemistry, metallurgy, interested him much more than medicine. When Dr. Child got in wrong with the authorities of Massachusetts Bay they reproached him for not practising the healing art, and questioned his doctor's degree. But there were few inducements to practise medicine in the Bay. The people were too healthy, and for minor ailments they used household remedies or consulted some old-woman herbalist. 'The gaines of physick will not finde mee with bread,' complained Giles Firmin, when he was the only physician north of Boston. And Robert Child had more interesting things to do.

Not long after taking his M.D. at Padua, and at the age of twenty-six or seven, Robert Child made a perambulation of New England. He traveled on foot from one settlement to another, making a careful examination of the country and its resources: what would now be called a 'social and economic survey.' He brought letters of introduction, and met all the magnates. His particular friends appear to have been Samuel Maverick, the old planter of East Boston, and the Governor's gifted son, John Winthrop, Jr., who shared his scientific curiosity.

Dr. Child returned to England about 1640, convinced that New England was a good field for investment in agriculture and mining. He had half promised John Winthrop, Jr., to

return as partner in some scheme for exploiting the soil of the
New World. In 1641 Child writes the Governor's son about
some scientific and chemical treatises that Winthrop wished
to be sent to him at Boston; and alludes to a project for
starting vineyards in New England. He proposes to visit
Toulouse to salute Dr. Fabre, the celebrated French physician and chemist, and Bordeaux 'to procure vines and a
vigneron who can also manage silkewormes, if it be possible.'
Apparently it was not possible, but Child spent a vintage in
the wine-growing country of Charenton-sur-Marne, 'pur-
posely to see how wine was made in France.' Already in
imagination he saw the hills of New England lined with terraced vineyards, becoming the Beaune or the Chablis of the
New World. That this was no idle dream, is proved by the
later success of Huguenot settlers in Massachusetts at wine
production; and the recent facility of our Italian farmers in
escaping the rigors of the Volstead Act.

Winthrop himself returned to England in 1641, to obtain
capital for his projects of mining iron and blacklead, of which
I shall speak at more length in the next chapter. Child
invested in both enterprises, and in what was called the
Lake Company, as well. This Lake enterprise was a project
for capturing the fur-trade at its source in Lake Champlain,
or the Lake of the Iroquois, as it was then called. The utmost
confusion prevailed in New England as to where this lake
really was. An early colonizing company, the Laconia Company, had failed to find it. Darby Field, one of the earliest
Irish settlers in New England, and the first white man to
climb the White Mountains, reported in 1642 that he had
sighted the lake from their summits. Another theory was
that the Delaware River flowed out of Lake Champlain —
of course it might have, had it been as crooked as the Charles!
In 1644 the General Court, disregarding the prohibition of
monopolies in the Body of Liberties, granted a fur-trading
monopoly for twenty-one years to a Free Company of Ad-

venturers who proposed to discover the Lake. In the spring of 1644 they sent a vessel to the Delaware commanded by William Aspinwall, and provided with a Latin letter of introduction from Governor Winthrop to Governor Printz of New Sweden. Printz was not sufficiently impressed by Winthrop's plea (or by his Latin) to let a crew of Yankees sail up-river and cut off his colony's trade. He drove them seaward with a cannon shot. Whatever money Child invested in the Free Company of Adventurers was lost.

Dr. Child returned to New England in 1645, bringing with him various plants and seeds and fruit trees, and five or six sorts of wines, 'confident in three yeares wine may be made as good as any in France.' The intended site of the Château Child vineyards was probably the valley of the Nashua; for in his absence the General Court had made him grantee of the Plantation of Nashaway, a tract ten miles by eight in that pleasant, fertile valley. Child's associates in that grant were mostly men interested in the iron industry, and it is possible that the iron deposits in that region were the main motive of the enterprise. Be that as it may, the iron did not pan out, and the vines were not planted, and Child left to others the work of starting a settlement in the remote wilderness that was watered by the Nashua. He also purchased, shortly after his return to New England in 1645, a large tract of land on the Saco River in Maine. So, for a time, he had money invested in at least five enterprises: blacklead mine, iron works, fur trade, Nashaway plantation, and Maine land. In most, if not all, he lost every penny. One would have thought that so generous and hopeful an investor would have been given every encouragement by a colony that was just pulling out of a very severe economic crisis; but it was not so. When, the following year, Robert Child headed a movement to extend the suffrage and toleration in religion, he was treated as unceremoniously as if he had been some poor and friendless religious enthusiast.

Robert Child was unlucky in politics as in business. He played the market the wrong way in both cases. As we have seen, the years 1644–45 mark a sort of political tightening up in Massachusetts Bay. The Deputies got their Body of Liberties through in 1641, and in 1644 Winthrop was defeated for governor on the foreign policy issue. But in the same year the magistrates won the famous pig case, and got themselves established as an upper house of the Legislature; and in 1645 the attempted impeachment of Winthrop failed.

This was Civil War time in England. New England, very wisely, determined to keep out of it, although their sympathies were with the Roundheads. A considerable number of Massachusetts men, like Saltonstall, Leverett, Hugh Peter, and Nathaniel Ward, went back to England to take part in the struggle, but the colony remained officially neutral. When a parliamentary armed ship threatened a royalist ship in Boston harbor, the authorities ordered the captain to desist, and forced him to respect New England neutrality, as he was under the guns of the South Battery.

The attitude of Massachusetts Bay toward the English Civil War was like Abraham Lincoln's story of the frontier woman watching a combat between an exceedingly cruel husband and a prodigiously powerful bear. 'Go it, bear! Go it, husband!' A puritan colony could expect little mercy from the Cavaliers, and the Roundheads were divided into two religious camps, both of which were obnoxious to the New Englanders. On the one side were the Presbyterians, including most of the old non-conformists who had not followed the King. They proposed and Parliament promised, as the price of Scots aid, to maintain the Established Church, but make it Presbyterian in polity. On the other side were the Independents, including Cromwell, Vane, and Milton. They wished the church disestablished with each parish independent of every other — the New England Way as they called it — and for proof that this Congregational way was scriptural the Independents largely relied on New England intellectuals such as Cotton, Hooker, and Shepard. Their writings were constantly quoted; they themselves were urged to return to England and lead the struggle. But the Independents differed radically from the New England puritans in one important particular: toleration. They adopted religious toleration as a principle. They had to, for unlike the New England Congregationalists, the English Independents included not merely plain puritan non-conformists, but various Separatists — Brownists, Baptists, Seekers, and a score of other sects, upon which the Simple Cobler of Aggawam directed his satire. The only way these sects of divers doctrine could be kept in a single political party, was by agreeing upon toleration.

So whatever religious party won in England, the Massachusetts puritans stood to lose — unless the Colony could maintain itself as a free state. Otherwise, they feared lest a Presbyterian Church of England might force Presbyterianism upon them, or the Independents compel them to tolerate all and sundry. Although Nathaniel Ward went Presbyterian, most of the New Englanders who returned to England, supported the Independents. These were much chagrined that their old friends and associates in New England should be intolerant. Whenever the Independents pled for toleration in England, the Presbyterians retorted: 'Look at your New England friends!' Vane wrote to Winthrop, 'While the congregationall way amongst you is in its freedom, and is backed with power, it teach[es] its oppugners here to extirpate it and roote it out, from its owne principles and practice.' The same sentiment was expressed by a nephew of Governor Winthrop, who had no Independent axe to grind. George Downing, after a tour of the West Indies in 1645, wrote to his cousin John Winthrop, Jr., 'the law of banishing for conscience... makes us stinke every wheare.'

Events in England could not fail to have their influence

here. Edward Winslow of Plymouth informed Governor Winthrop in 1645 that a bill for toleration would have passed the General Court of Plymouth Colony, if Governor Prence had allowed it to come to a vote. William Vassall of Scituate, original member of the Massachusetts Bay Company, was responsible for the bill, which called for complete religious liberty of all peaceable persons and good subjects. 'You would have admired to have seen how sweet this carrion relished to the pallate of most of the Deputies!' wrote Winslow. His letter put the Bay authorities on their guard.

Robert Child was a puritan — of that there is no doubt, from his joy at the fall of the Bishops; but a Presbyterian. It must have annoyed him, as a man of means and a heavy investor in New England business enterprises, to be forced to attend a form of church service he did not like, and to be denied the vote. Still, I doubt whether he originated the protest. From various indications, it is evident that there were many political malcontents in the Bay Colony who remembered uneasily the fate of those who had petitioned in favor of Anne Hutchinson. Robert Child was a wealthy and well-connected bachelor of thirty-two. I infer that he generously offered to place himself at the head of the movement, and to suffer the consequences. At least that is the only way I can explain why this young man, whose interests were mainly scientific, and who had been in the country but six months, should have been first signer to the grand Remonstrance and Petition to the General Court, dated May 6, 1646.

Samuel Maverick was the best known of the remonstrants. An Anglican whom Winthrop found already established at Boston Harbor, and whose hospitality had filled many a hungry belly during the first winter of starvation, he had been admitted freeman in 1631 before the religious qualification had been imposed. He had never joined the Church, but naturally wished to open the franchise to others of his persuasion. None of the other signers were freemen, although the next, Thomas Fowle, was a tolerant church member who had petitioned for a repeal of the law against the Baptists. David Yale was a well-to-do merchant with an estate on Cotton Hill (now Pemberton Square) in Boston, where his son, the founder of Yale College, was born two or three years later. Thomas Burton was a respectable citizen of Hingham; John Dand was an aged and retired grocer of London, said to be of failing intellect; John Smith, of whom little is known, had already put himself on the safe side of the Rhode Island boundary.

The Remonstrance, it must be admitted, was a very truculent document. Beginning with the usual expressions of humility, the petitioners paint a sad picture of the lack of prosperity and failure of great designs, with a wholly unnecessary reference to a recent outbreak of venereal disease. They then declare outright that the Colony has no 'setled forme of government according to the lawes of England'; that no 'body of lawes' secures them enjoyment of their lives, liberties and estates, and no settled rules of judicature provide due process; for which reasons many are in fear of arbitrary government. That was an appeal to the deputies who were working to supersede the incomplete Body of Liberties by a Body of Laws. Thousands of Englishmen in the colony, righteous and peaceable men, taxpayers and soldiers, were not allowed the vote. 'We therefore desire that civill liberty and freedom be forthwith granted to all truely English,' without any religious qualifications. Next, they humbly intreat that all members of the Church of England (Presbyterian) be admitted to communion in the churches of the Bay. 'If not, we and they shall be necessitated to apply our humble desires to the honourable houses of parliament, who we hope will take our sad conditions into their serious considerations; to provide able ministers for us... or else... transport us to some other place, where we may live like

Christians and not be accounted burthens.' These things being granted, they expect to see piety quickened, discontents allayed, business improve, taxes lightened — in fact every good thing that is promised by contending candidates in our modern elections.

If the tone of Child's Remonstrance invited retaliation, there was nothing unreasonable in what he demanded. Massachusetts Bay, after all, was still a colony, although, as Child said, it acted like a free state. From the English point of view it was scandalous that an Englishman of puritan sympathies should come over to New England to invest money and develop the country, yet be denied the vote and the free exercise of his religion, which happened then to be the state religion of England. From the practical point of view, Child's demands were sensible. It is ridiculous to assert that if granted they would have overthrown the commonwealth. Massachusetts Bay was solidly established by 1646. It had recovered from the economic crisis of 1642, and its political arrangements had shaken down into a system. Whatever reasons there had been for caution in 1637, were now removed. An extension of the franchise to decent people who were non-church members, as had been done in Connecticut, would really have broadened and strengthened the commonwealth. An admission of English Presbyterian communicants to the 'seals of the covenant' would have been a gracious and harmless act of Christian comity. That Robert Child and his associates were prepared if they could not move heaven, to raise hell; or in other words appeal to Parliament for protection of their rights as Englishmen in Massachusetts Bay, is clear from the hints in their remonstrance, and from what followed. But they gave Massachusetts Bay the chance to do the right thing first.

The Remonstrance was presented to the General Court in May, 1646, near the end of the session, so formal consideration was postponed until the autumn. In the meantime manuscript copies of it were widely circulated, and a good deal of feeling stirred up. Samuel Symonds, a magistrate of Ipswich, wrote Governor Winthrop that the Remonstrance was making such headway among the younger generation in his home town that the Governor must send him some counter propaganda. But if the Remonstrants had all summer to circulate their paper, so the parsons had all summer to denounce them as sons of Levi, sons of Belial, and subverters of Church and State. In order to prejudice people against Child, he was declared to be a Jesuit in disguise. For had he not admitted a visit to Rome? Several replies to the Remonstrance were prepared, and when the General Court met in the autumn, these were committed to Winthrop, Dudley, and Bellingham, to prepare an official counterblast.

The resulting 'Declaration concerning a Remonstrance and Petitions exhibited at last Session of the Court by Doctor Child' and others, was an able controversial document. It was drafted by some one (Dudley, I suspect) who wielded a very sharp pen, with the aid of some one else (Bellingham or Winthrop), who possessed legal knowledge. Every flaw, weakness or inconsistency in the Remonstrance is exposed. There are masterly replies, intended of course for English ears, to many of Child's charges. Judicial procedure not limited by statute? How about equity jurisdiction in England? — Unjust taxes? How could the government be conducted more penuriously than with some of the magistrates accepting no salary, and not a penny spent on feastings, pensions, public gratuities, and the like? — Rights of Englishmen? Who ever claimed that it was the right of an Englishman to vote? — Church membership? If the petitioners are as sober and godly as they claim, why 'boggle at the covenants of these churches'; why not join up and become a freeman? And if they think religious toleration a practical policy, let them go to Rhode Island! Included in the Declaration is a very disingenuous and misleading parallel between

Magna Carta and the English Common Law on the one hand, and the 'Fundamentalls of the Massachusetts' on the other. There are some ironical references to the difference of condition and religious opinion among the remonstrants, who are compared to those who were called by Absalom to accompany him to Hebron. 'And with Absalom went two hundred men out of Jerusalem... and they went in their simplicity, and they knew not any thing.'

As this reply to the Remonstrance was intended for the ears of Parliament, it took no notice of the most interesting charge of Dr. Child: 'Our nativ Country and lawes [of England]... by some are stiled foreign, and this place termed rather a free state, than a colony or corporation of England.' A most significant statement which would be remembered one hundred and thirty years later. Massachusetts calling herself a free state in 1646! William Pynchon, writing confidentially to Winthrop, remarked on this: 'We are not a Free State, neather do I apprehend that magistrates, elders, or deputies doe think we are a Free State, neather do I think it our wisdome to be a Free state; though we had our liberty, we cannot as yet subsist without England.' So the idea of independence was already familiar, if not acceptable, to the leaders of the Bay.

Child's charge was substantially true; and it was repeated by Captain Thomas Breedon in 1661: 'They looke on themselves as a Free State.' There was no political connection between Massachusetts Bay and England, beyond a vague loyalty to the King whose name was not even used in the judicial warrants, or in the freeman's oath. By the economic test the Colony was a free state: for it applied against the world, including England, the mercantilist principles which were the very basis of nationalism.[1]

If the General Court tactfully ignored the Free State charge in its Declaration, it did not flinch from the issue. In its reply to the petitioners:

[1] See Chapter V.

WILLIAM PYNCHON

'Our allegiance binds us not to the laws of England any longer than while we live in England, for the laws of the parliament of England reach no further, nor do the king's writs under the great seal.'

In a petition to the parliamentary commission for plantations, the General Court assert their own complete jurisdiction over Massachusetts, without appeal to any English authority or court. If we conform to your orders and directions, they say, it is *salvo jure*, saving our right not so to conform, 'that when times may be changed (for all things here below are subject to vanity,) and other princes and parliaments may arise, the generations succeeding us may not have cause to lament and say "England sent our fathers forth with happy liberties, which they enjoyed many years, notwithstanding all the enmity and opposition of the prelacy, and other potent adversaries. How came we then to lose them,... when England itself recovered its own?" *In freto viximus, in portu morimur.*' [1]

So there you are — a beautiful example of the principle that both sides to a controversy may be right, and both wrong. The General Court's bold defense of autonomy under the Massachusetts Bay charter, strikes the note of American independence, and an answering chord in our hearts. On the other side, Robert Child and his fellow-signers stood for religious toleration, a wide franchise, and a government of laws and not of men: things no less dear to us, I trust, than independence. Yet their proposed appeal to Parliament, if successful, would have meant the loss of complete self-government, of the puritans' privilege to form their own institutions, and make their own mistakes. Now look upon the reverse of the official medal: the autonomy of Massachusetts meant the supremacy of the puritan régime, a rigid conformity to an officially established religion, a franchise narrow and growing narrower. It meant that no one could settle in the

[1] 'On the broad seas we have lived, in the closed port we die.'

country or bring in books without undergoing a test of
orthodoxy; and that any one within the colony who spoke or
wrote in a manner unpleasing to the authorities, would have
his book burnt, his estate diminished, himself perhaps banished. The only possible consequence of such a suppression
of ideas and of speech, would be a hard, narrow intellectual
poverty:

> Shrill, querulous women, sour and sullen men,
> Untidy, loveless, old before their time,
> With scarce a human interest save their own
> Monotonous round of small economies,
>
> .　.　.　.　.　.　.　.
>
> Church-goers, fearful of the unseen Powers,
> But grumbling over pulpit-tax and pew-rent,
> Saving, as shrewd economists, their souls
> And winter pork with the least possible outlay
> Of salt and sanctity.[1]

It is no accident that the puritan régime, which entered
Massachusetts as a model of Christian charity, went out in
a storm of witchcraft. It is surprising that so much of the
love and warmth kindled by the generation of founders, was
kept alive for later generations.

Dr. Child, having had his petition turned down, as doubtless he foresaw, prepared to go to England and see what
Parliament thought of the policy of Massachusetts Bay. But
he was not to get away easily. In accordance with current
English practice, which punished obnoxious petitions with
contempt proceedings (the right of petition was not secured
until the Bill of Rights of 1689), the Magistrates, with
Saltonstall, Bradstreet, and Bellingham dissenting, decided
to make an example of the remonstrants. Child was fined
£50, and the others, except Maverick, £30 or £40 apiece.
They were summoned before the General Court, informed
that they had transgressed the Apostle's rule 'that ye study
to be quiet, and to do your own business' (1 Thess. iv, 11),
and were compared with Korah, Dathan and Abiram, who

[1] Whittier, 'Among the Hills.'

'gathered themselves together against Moses and against Aaron, and said unto them, Ye take too much upon you, seeing all the congregation are holy, every one of them... wherefore then lift ye up yourselves above the congregation of the Lord?' The remonstrants were offered remission of their fines if they would repent and abjure; but they stood firm.

On the very day before Child was to sail for England, he and his trunks were brought off the vessel and searched, as was John Dand's study. There the authorities found John Smith, who rashly boasted that he would soon be back from England with a warrant to search the Governor's closet. They also found a petition to Parliament for Presbyterian churches and English laws and liberties to be established in Massachusetts Bay under a Governor-General appointed from England. This was high treason from the Massachusetts point of view; so Child, Dand, and Smith were arrested and prevented from sailing. One of the remonstrants, Thomas Fowle, did manage to get away, together with William Vassall, who as a resident of Plymouth Colony had not signed the Remonstrance, but was fully in sympathy with its objects.

When their ship, the *Supply*, was ready for sea, John Cotton preached a sermon on the favorite text applied to heretics: 'the foxes, the little foxes which destroy the vines.' Master Cotton could not hope that the earth would open and swallow up the remonstrants, as it had accommodated Moses and Aaron in the case of Korah; but he prophesied that if any of them crossed on the *Supply* they would have a rough passage, and perhaps worse — a safe prophecy for a winter voyage. And, added Master Cotton in an insinuating way, 'When the terrors of the Almightie shall beset the vessell wherein they are, the heavens shall frowne upon them,... and dangers shall threaten them (as I perswade myselfe they will),... I will not give the counsell [which] was taken concerning

Jonah, to take such a person and cast him into the sea: God Forbid; but I would advise such to come to a resolution... to desist from such enterprises,... and to cast such a petition into the sea.'

After this warning, at least one passenger changed to another ship, and those who did sail on the *Supply* were naturally somewhat nervous about it. She had to wait a long time in Nantasket roads for fair weather, and echoes of John Cotton's lecture must have rung somewhat unpleasantly in the ears of her passengers and crew. Doubtless sundry dark and meaning glances were directed at Fowle and Vassall, for it was a very rough passage. One storm, worse than the rest, caused most of the passengers to remember Master Cotton's words, if indeed they had ever forgotten them. A woman passenger became quite distracted with terror. Running up out of the between-decks into the after cabin at midnight, she rushed up to William Vassall who was looking out of the steerage companionway, and begged him to cast overboard any Jonah there might be on board at once. Vassall inquired why she should pick on him? 'Because I hear you have some Writings against the People of God' said she. Vassall said he had nothing but a petition to Parliament for the liberty of Englishmen, 'and that could be no Jonas.' But the poor woman would not be denied. She pulled Thomas Fowle out of his bunk and went on at such a rate that the kind gentleman got out a copy of the Remonstrance, read it to her, and said she was welcome to it if she thought that was the cause of the storm. So the woman took the petition below to the other passengers, and they decided it was the Jonah and threw it overboard.

This act seemed to appease the God of Massachusetts Bay for a short time only. There were other storms, and the *Supply* arrived in England only after a terrible buffeting. The godly passengers spread it about that they had been saved only by a miracle, which the jettisoning of the petition had produced; to which Robert Child's brother John replied in 'New-Englands Jonas Cast Up at London; or, A Relation of the Proceedings of the Court at Boston . . . against divers honest and godly persons, for Petitioning for Government in the Commonwealth, according to the Lawes of England... Together with a Confutation of some Reports of a fained Miracle upon the foresaid Petition being thrown overboard at Sea.'

Realizing that they must have an important person to defend their side in London, the Massachusetts authorities talked of sending over Governor Winthrop. He was averse from the voyage — and so many important people, like Nathaniel Ward, had been returning to England of late that it was feared his absence would create 'hard thoughts and apprehensions.' So Edward Winslow was appointed agent, 'to manifest and declare the naked truth of things,' according to Captain Johnson. He was armed with the stout instructions from which I have quoted, denying Parliamentary jurisdiction in terms that carry one forward to 1774; and he was provided with £100, which probably proved more useful than the Massachusetts declaration of rights. Winslow answered 'New Englands Jonas Cast Up' in a pamphlet called 'New Englands Salamander, discovered by an irreligious and scornfull Pamphlet, called New-Englands Jonas Cast up at London, &c owned by Major John Childe, but not probable to be written by him.' This contained anything but 'naked truth'; it was an able diplomatic document. And as a result of Winslow's efforts the Lords Commissioners for Plantations gave Massachusetts Bay a clean bill of health, and disclaimed any intention to encourage appeals to themselves.

Among Child's papers seized just as he was about to embark was a petition from twenty-five non-freemen to Parliament, asking for the rights and privileges of Englishmen, for Presbyterian churches and a governor-general, and request-

ing a general investigation of the Massachusetts government.
The Magistrates certainly had caught Child with the goods!
A recent law imposed the death penalty on any one who
'shall treacherously or perfidiously attempt the alteration
of our frame of Polity or Government fundamentally.'
Robert Child had now placed himself in the uncomfortable
position of Absalom, the story of whose fate (2 Samuel, xviii)
was cited as the scriptural sanction for the above-mentioned
law. But the authorities had sense enough not to overreach
themselves by encompassing the death of a man of property
and good connections in England. On being summoned before the Assistants to answer for this seized document, Child
'fell into a great passion and gave big words,' says Winthrop,
who replied that the intention was to treat him as 'a gentleman and a scholar, but if he would behave himself no better,
he should be committed to the common prison and clapped
in irons, upon this he grew more calm.' He was confined in
the Boston jailer's house for three months.

The second trial of Child and four fellow remonstrants, for
sedition, was held by the General Court in May, 1647. They
were found guilty, and fined from £100 to £200 apiece, Child
being assessed the maximum. There was much apprehension
on the part of the authorities that he would be rescued, for a
goodly section of public opinion was with the remonstrants;
but nothing happened. And in September, having paid his
heavy fine, equal in purchasing power to fifteen or twenty
thousand dollars to-day, Child departed from our shores
forever.

Yet, as with so many forlorn hopes and lost causes, the
depth of defeat is really the beginning of victory. Not, in
this case, for religious toleration. The effect of Child's
Remonstrance was to pull the strings a little tighter; and the
period 1647–70 was the most intolerant in the history of
Massachusetts. In government and law, however, the very
people who punished the remonstrants took up their suggestions.

At the spring election of 1647, the freemen of Massachusetts returned to the Board of Assistants a new member, Colonel Robert Bridges of Lynn, who sympathized more or less with the remonstrants. Supported by the liberal Ipswich group, he persuaded the Assistants that something must be done to placate the non-freemen. Accordingly the General Court passed an act making non-freemen aged twenty-one, who would take an oath of fidelity to Massachusetts Bay, eligible to serve on juries, and to be elected selectmen of towns. Non-freemen were given the right to vote in town-meeting on assessments of rates, distribution of lands, laying out highways, ordering of schools, and herding of cattle: in a word on all strictly local matters, including the three important subjects of taxes, cattle, and land, which were of vital interest to every man. This township act of 1647 was the entering wedge for democracy in Massachusetts Bay; it gave manhood suffrage in the towns, and opened to non-church members the town-meeting, the most important school of self-government in New England if not in the United States. For this, may Robert Child be thanked.

The effect of the Remonstrance on an intelligent magistrate may be seen in a letter of William Pynchon to Governor Winthrop. He deplores the 'malignant spirit that breathes out in their endeavors because... it seemes to me they would destroy both Church and Commonwealth in laboring for a generall governor.' Nevertheless the General Court 'should not turne off all the particulars wherein they desyre a reformation, without making a right use of so much of their position as doth iustly call for reformation.' In particular, Child's reproach of the vagueness of law, the carelessness in judicial procedure, the loose wording of warrants, and the like, appealed to Pynchon, who had been a justice of the peace in the old country.

Indirectly we owe to the remonstrants The Book of the General Lawes and Libertyes of 1648. Consider this quotation from the Epistle to that book: 'For a Common-wealth without lawes is like a Ship without rigging and steeradge. Nor is it sufficient to have principles or fundamentalls, but these are to be drawn out into so many of their deductions as the time and condition of that people may have use of.' Just what Robert Child had recommended in his Remonstrance! The Deputies never had been satisfied with Nathaniel Ward's Body of Liberties. It was all very well so far as it went, but it did not go far enough. Although guaranteeing the subject's liberty and rights, the Body of Liberties did not contain all the general laws that the General Court had enacted. There was nothing in it on the body of economic regulations and restrictions that the General Court had gradually worked out; nothing on education, highways, local government, and a score of subjects that closely touched the average man in Massachusetts Bay. What the freemen of Massachusetts wanted was a 'body of laws,' a code which would contain as near as might be all the law, common, statute, or biblical, that was applicable to them; and not merely some of the law. And they insisted that the Body of Liberties were not 'fundamentalls,' but subject to alteration by the same body which enacted them.

Consequently, the Body of Liberties had no sooner been adopted when the committees were appointed to supplement them by a selection and revision of the important statute laws of the colony. These committees, however, were going through the same process of elaborate stalling which had characterized their early work on the Body of Liberties, and it is quite possible that the whole matter would have been allowed to go quietly to sleep, or have been given a little dose of chloroform by the Magistrates, if Robert Child had not waked them up with the Remonstrance. In that seditious document, the remonstrants say: 'Neither do we so understand and perceyve our owne lawes or libertyes, or any body of lawes here so established, as that thereby there may be a sure and comfortable enjoyment of our lives, libertyes, and estates, according to our due and naturall rights, as freeborne subjects of the English nation.' Just what the deputies and freemen had been saying time and again! On November 4, 1646, the very day that the General Court issued an official reply to the Remonstrance, it declared itself 'deeply sensible of the earnest expectation of the country in general for this Court's completing of a Body of Laws... whereby we may manifest our utter disaffection to arbitrary government and so all relations be safely and sweetly directed and protected in all their just rights and privileges.' A new committee was appointed, with Richard Bellingham the important member. There was further delay, until the Court could procure for the Committee suitable books such as Coke on Littleton and on Magna Carta, Dalton's Justice of the Peace, and some term and entry books; but finally Bellingham's committee made things move. Having suitably persecuted prophet Child, and driven him out of the country, the General Court prepared a fine sepulchre for him in the shape of the printed 'Book of the General Lawes and Libertyes concerning the Inhabitants of the Massachusetts,' which went to press in June, 1648.

Curiously enough, it is not until 1929 that those interested in our colonial history have been able to consult this law book of 1648. It was superseded by a revised Book of Laws in 1660; and when historians began to get interested in early Americana, about fifty years ago, not a copy of the 1648 Lawes and Libertyes could be found. Sabin, in 1879, wrote 'its discovery would be a bibliographical wonder.' William H. Whitmore in 1890 predicted that a copy remained in some library in England, 'to appear at some unexpected moment.' So it did a few years later, in a private library at Rye, in England. It was sold in 1906, and after passing through a number of dealers' hands was purchased by one of that despicable class of bibliomaniacs who put their treasures to no use themselves and refuse to let any one else see them. The only person who did succeed in getting a glimpse of it was the late Nathan Matthews, who wished to look up a point in colonial law for an important case, and threatened, if the permission were not granted, to impound the book by judicial process. At the death of the owner, and dispersal of his collection, this unique copy was sold to Henry E. Huntington, a very different sort of collector, who has built a great library in California to house his collections, opens them to the use of students, and at his own expense has had a perfect reproduction of the Laws and Liberties printed by the Harvard University Press.

The Laws and Liberties of 1648 is a printed quarto of fifty-nine pages, incorporating not only such parts of the Body of Liberties of 1641 as had not been repealed, but all general laws (those not of a special, private, or local nature) which were then in force. They are arranged under alphabetical headings, such as Abilitie, Actions, Age, Ana-Baptists, etc. This practical form had been in use in England for centuries, in the alphabetical 'Abridgments of the Statutes' which had long been current in manuscript form and had been printed in twenty or more editions, since 1485. The Massachusetts book, however, was an official compilation, guaranteed to be complete, and all general laws not found in it were deemed null and void; so it accomplished the purpose of binding down the judges to known laws, and limiting their law-finding function to such cases as had not been foreseen by the legislature.

The book is a compilation and arrangement of statutes, not a code; and comparisons to the work of Justinian and Napoleon are extravagant. But it is a highly creditable compilation for a little colony like Massachusetts Bay; and, except for the capital laws, is lay in character. 'Moses his Judicialls' had been pretty well squeezed out. It reproduces many of the mediæval economic and military regulations of

England, as we have seen in the chapter on John Hull; as well as the Elizabethan Poor Law, requiring each parish or township to care for its own poor; and the Elizabethan Statute of Laborers, allowing the courts to fix maximum wages for workers. The last, however, has some humanitarian modifications taken over from the Body of Liberties.

Robert Child was not in any sense the author of this compilation, which represents the work of many hands and minds. Richard Bellingham, one of the Assistants who protested against the punishment of Child, probably was the principal compiler; for Bellingham had been a lawyer and a judge in the old country. But for Child's work in arousing the non-freemen to political consciousness, it is doubtful whether the General Court could have addressed this pithy part of its Epistle to them:

You have called us from amongst the rest of our Bretheren and given us power to make these lawes: we must now call upon you to see them executed: remembring that old & true proverb, *The execution of the law is the life of the law.* If one sort of you *viz*: non-Freemen should object that you had no hand in calling us to this worke, and therfore think yourselvs not bound to obedience &c. Wee answer that a subsequent, or implicit consent is of like force in this case, as an expresse precedent power: for in putting your persons and estates into the protection and way of subsistance held forth and exercised within this Jurisdiction, you doe tacitly submit to this Government and to all the wholesome lawes thereof, and so is the common repute in all nations and that upon this Maxim. *Qui sentit commodum sentire debet et onus.*

And what of Robert Child? In spite of the treatment he had received and the money he had lost, the young man continued to be interested in New England. To John Winthrop, Jr., he wrote letters such as these:

If I had not quarrelld in the country, I should have bin willing to have ventured an 100*l.* or two upon your mine of lead, but shall not have any thing to doe with that country hereafter in this kind, unles my fines be restored, which I had destined to this end, and yet will adventure them with you, if they be returned. I am not so offended with the country but I may be reconciled and pass by such iniuryes as I have there received, knowing to doe good for evil is Christian-like. I, for my part, am more than halfe weaned from New-England, by their discourtesye, yet if they would return me my fine, I would adventure it with you and perhaps might see you. Otherwise either I shalbe for Ireland where at Kilkenny a new Acadamy is to be erected or I shall retreate to a more solitary life, where I can commaund myself, with 6 or 7 gentlemen and scollars, who have resolved to live retyredly and follow their studyes and experiences.

John Winthrop, Jr., paid Child's first fine of £50 out of some money that he owed the doctor; but if he made any efforts to get the £200 fine remitted, they did not succeed. From his father's journal we find that there was a deficit of £1000 in the colony treasury just before the remonstrants' case; hence their fines, amounting to £750, came in very handy to fill up most of this very bad hole.

Child's plans for an academy at Kilkenny or elsewhere came to nothing; but on returning to England he became associated with the learned and scientific circle at London, which a few years later founded the Royal Society: with Robert Boyle, the father of modern chemistry; with George Stirk, the Harvard graduate who was interested in alchemy; John French, physician in the new model army and translator, who dedicated to Robert Child his translation of Agrippa's Three Books of Occult Philosophy; Elias Ashmole, from whom the Ashmolean Museum is named; and others whose common bond was experimental science, and particularly alchemy. Child has been often identified by writers on the Hermetic art with the mysterious Eirenaeus Philalethes, an adept who wrote several treatises on Alchemy, and to whom are attributed several well-attested instances of transmutation. For instance, Johann Conrad Creiling states in his *Die Edelgeborne Jungfer Alchymia* (Tübingen, 1730), that the writings of Philalethes are familiar to alchemists as their daily bread, and are by some attributed to a 'Dr. Zcheil, residing in America' — who is of course Dr. Child, and by others to 'Georgius Sterkey, an apothecary in London.' Professor Kittredge believes that Eirenaeus Philalethes 'was the creation of George Stirk's teeming brain and not too scrupulous conscience.'

The interest in alchemy of certain New England settlers such as Winthrop, Jonathan Brewster, Child and Stirk is not evidence of their credulity and superstition: quite the contrary. Alchemy, usually associated by a too-confident nineteenth century with witchcraft and black magic, is now dropping into its proper place as a branch of chemistry. Through the study of alchemy the science of chemistry was greatly advanced; and chemistry has now proved that the basic idea of the alchemists, that all elements were fundamentally of the same substance, was essentially sound.

Robert Child does not appear to have been as active in alchemy as others of his circle. His leading interest was scientific agriculture. He became a warm friend and associate of Samuel Hartlib, the leading English writer on agriculture in the seventeenth century, an educational reformer as well, and a friend of John Milton. In 1651, at Hartlib's request, Child wrote an essay on the Defects and Remedies of English Husbandry which ran through three editions. In it he makes good use of his observations on the Continent and in New England. There is a detailed description, for instance, of the colonial practice of manuring cornfields with herring or cods' heads, which Child thinks might be done in England when fish is cheap, only he warns the English that 'dogs will scrape them up, unless one of their legs be tyed up.' He proposes that some of the wild berries and native timber of New England be introduced into the old country. He tells about John Winthrop's graphite mine at Tantiusque, of pine trees four feet in diameter, of sassafras and rattlesnake weed, and beer brewed from cornstalks, 'pompions,' and squashes. And other useful information was in the essay.

We next hear of Robert Child in 1651, as agricultural expert for Colonel Arthur Hill of Hillsborough Castle near Belfast, the owner of vast estates, and a parliamentary commissioner for handling the sequestered and forfeited lands. Robert Boyle, who was also a great Irish landowner, went over about the same time, as did William Petty, who afterwards became a distinguished economist. Hartlib wrote to Boyle in February, 1654, 'Sir, you complain of that barbarous (for the present) country, wherein you live; but if you would but make a right use of yourself,' and look up Dr. Child, Dr. Petty, and others, 'they would abundantly cherish in you many philosophical thoughts, and encourage you... to venture even upon divers choice chemical experiments, for the advancement both of health and wealth.'

Not long after this — in March or April, 1654, Robert Child died. He was still in the service of Colonel Hill, but we know nothing of the cause or circumstances of his death.

In the forty-one years of his life, Robert Child had seen a good deal of the world; but there was no part that he liked so well as New England. Of that considerable number of men and women who have served Massachusetts disinterestedly and well, and in return have been persecuted, imprisoned and banished by her, or simply ridiculed and neglected; not the least is Robert Child, 'a gentleman and a scholar,' a man of wealth, a scientist and an investor, who though 'a mere sojourner among us,' risked his life and fortune to obtain liberty and justice for those to whom both were denied.

CHAPTER IX

JOHN WINTHROP, JR., INDUSTRIAL PIONEER

JOHN WINTHROP, JR., has the same relation to science and industry in New England as his father to the institutions of the Commonwealth. He had the energy, optimism and resourcefulness of the American business pioneer, and with other qualities that are rare in business men. Born at Groton Manor on February 12, 1606, a month after his father's eighteenth birthday, he was a very different man from the future Governor. His portrait [1] shows parental traits: brown, heavy-lidded eyes, delicate arched eye-brows, long Roman nose, dark coloring, and full lips; but the total impression is altogether different. John Winthrop the elder is severe, dignified, stern, introspective, mediæval; John Winthrop the younger is eager, outgoing, genial, responsive, modern. The younger man was broad-minded, but never sounded the depths of religious experience as his father had done; the elder had seen much of life, but only from the angle of a puritan magistrate.

John attended the grammar school at Bury St. Edmunds, and then went to Trinity College, Dublin, a recent offshoot of the University of Cambridge; an Irish Harvard as it were. After Dublin he studied law in London and was admitted a barrister of the Inner Temple in 1624; but the law was not for him. Through a family connection in the naval office, he obtained a post in the fleet that failed to relieve the Huguenots of La Rochelle. That over, he was ready to emigrate to 'London's Plantation in the Massachusetts Bay,' but John senior advised seeing the world first; and as supercargo on a ship of the Levant Company John junior made a voyage to Italy and Constantinople. Returning, he wrote his father

[1] See frontispiece.

that different countries were to him no more than so many inns for the weary traveller, 'I shall call that my country where I may most glorify God and enjoy the presence of my dearest friends' — and that country, after his father's emigration, could only be New England. To New England he went as soon as Groton Manor was sold, accompanied by his young wife and escorting his stepmother, the Governor's lady.

It speaks well for the popular esteem of the Winthrop family that when the *Lion* dropped anchor in Boston Harbor on November 4, 1631, after two days' detention in Nantasket Roads, the people came flocking to welcome the young couple, and to start off their housekeeping with presents of fat hogs, poultry, and game. 'The like joy and manifestation of love had never been seen in New England,' wrote the Governor. 'It was a great marvel that so much people and such store of provision could be gathered together at so few hours' warning.' During the forty-five years that he served New England, the younger Winthrop frequently received these New England equivalents of bay-leaves and roses, and from all sorts of people. There was something in his personality that made every company welcome him, and feel a void when he left.

At the next election John Winthrop, Jr., was elected to the Board of Assistants. For eighteen successive years, even when temporarily absent, he was a Magistrate of the Bay. Possibly he agreed with the family point of view, tersely expressed by the old Governor's graceless nephew George Downing, that the Massachusetts government was too popular, and 'thers not the meanest of those three or foure men they so tosse and tumble' at annual elections, 'but if chosen for life would be able to manage the affayres of the country far otherwise than now.' But I rather think that it was filial piety which made him vote his father's way in the Board of Assistants. For as Governor of Connecticut, the younger

Winthrop's policy was mild and tolerant. Robert Child and Roger Williams were his warm admirers; and the liberal Ipswich group, Bellingham, Bradstreet, Richard Saltonstall, Jr., and Nathaniel Ward, were his friends and neighbors.

John Winthrop, Jr., was one of the founders of Ipswich in 1633, and continued a landowner and absentee planter for years after he had transferred residence to Connecticut. Ipswich was a lonely, isolated frontier settlement at first, and John was doubtless glad of the 'three wolf doggs and a bitch, with an Irish boy to tend them' which an English friend sent him to protect his cattle. When the Governor visited his son at Ipswich, he had to walk the thirty miles by Indian trail.

Mistress Winthrop and their little daughter died at Ipswich in the autumn of 1634. This caused a sudden change in John's plans. Back he went to England, by way of Ireland and Scotland; always welcome, and always enjoying himself. A man of his talents could not long be unemployed. Lord Say and Sele and Lord Brook, having been repulsed in their desire to become hereditary magistrates of Massachusetts Bay, obtained a grant of the land about the mouth of the Connecticut River, and engaged John Winthrop, Jr., to go out and begin a settlement there for them. Returning to Boston with a second wife (the stepdaughter of Hugh Peter) in 1635, Winthrop sent an advance party to build a fort at the mouth of the river: the place that was soon named Saybrook, after the two lords proprietors. After a visit to the fort, he put it in charge of Lyon Gardiner of Gardiner's Island and returned to his home in Ipswich, resumed his magistracy, and became lieutenant-colonel of the Essex militia. A rumor that he was to be appointed commander of the castle in Boston Harbor, in 1637, occasioned a fervid protest against his removal by the principal inhabitants of Ipswich, who declared 'it would be too great a grief to us and breach upon us' to lose 'not a magistrate only but our Lieutenant Colonell so beloved of our Soldiours and military men,

that this remote Corner would be left destitute and desolate.'
The rumored appointment was not made, but Ipswich was
indeed too remote a corner to retain a man of Winthrop's
energy and wide interests.

The library of one thousand volumes that John Winthrop,
Jr., brought to Massachusetts in 1631, shows that he was already a man of scientific tastes and attainments. Increased
by purchase and gift during his lifetime, it remained for a
century the best scientific library in the English colonies, of
which we have any knowledge; and it was long kept intact by
his descendants. The nucleus of it, two hundred and seventy
volumes, is now in the New York Society Library. An analysis of this fragment shows that one hundred and thirty-
five volumes are scientific (fifty-two devoted to chemistry),
sixty-one are religious, thirty-six relate to history and belles
lettres, twenty-four to languages, law, and philosophy, and
twelve to the occult arts. One half of the total are in Latin,
seventy-one in English, twenty-three in German, and the
rest in French, Dutch, Italian, Greek, and Spanish.

The library is no less remarkable for its choice than for its
range. All the famous chemical authors of the time, such as
Paracelsus, Dorn, Dee, and Glauber are represented; indeed
one volume of Paracelsus contains the manuscript annotations of Dr. John Dee, whose monadic emblem Winthrop
used to employ as a private book mark. Another volume, by
Basil Valentine, the occult philosopher and alchemist, formerly belonged to Cornelius Drebbel, the reputed inventor of
the thermometer, and was given to Winthrop by his son-in-
law, Abraham Keffler. Others belonged to Winthrop's friend,
Dr. Robert Child the Remonstrant. George Stirk, also a
friend and correspondent of Winthrop, is represented by his
'Nature's Explication and Helmont's Vindication.' There
are thirty-three volumes in medical science, of which John
Winthrop was a practitioner, and eight of mathematics. One
of those, Richard Norwood's 'Trigonometrie,' contains on

the fly-leaf the signature of Winthrop's neighbor Richard Saltonstall, with a Latin epigram referring to Norwood's obscure style:

> Non quia difficilia, non aggressimur
> Sed quia non aggressimur, difficilia

(We don't catch on, not because they [Norwood's propositions] are difficult, but because we don't catch on, they are difficult.)

Under this Winthrop retorts:

> Non quia difficilia sunt pulchra
> Sed quia pulchra difficilia

(They are beautiful, not because they are difficult, but they are difficult, because they are beautiful.)

Winthrop's excellent reputation as a man of science was recognized by his being asked to become one of the first Fellows of the Royal Society. There are two scientific contributions of his in the early volumes of their Transactions. During his visits to England and Holland he met and while he lived in America he corresponded with such men as Robert Boyle, Sir Isaac Newton, Prince Rupert, Sir Christopher Wren, Sir Kenelm Digby, the universal genius of his age (who at Winthrop's request, though a Catholic, gave books to the Harvard College Library), the Moravian bishop Komensky or Comenius, a pioneer in modern educational methods whom Winthrop probably tried to secure for the Harvard presidency. Like many wide-awake scientists of the day, John Winthrop was keenly interested in alchemy. His commonplace book, containing copies of alchemical diagrams and poems of Thomas Norton and Sir George Ripley, perhaps also notes of his own experiments in the Hermetic art, is still preserved. At his death, Winthrop enjoyed the reputation of having discovered the philosopher's stone. Benjamin Tompson in his 'Funeral Tribute to the Honourable Dust of that most Charitable Christian, Unbiassed Politician and Unimitable Pyrotechnist John Winthrop Esq.,' alludes to this tradition:

Some thought the tincture Philosophick lay
Hatcht by the Mineral Sun in Winthrops way,
And clear it shines to me he had a Stone
Grav'd with his Name which he could read alone.

A century later, Governor Trumbull of Connecticut told the President of Yale that a mountain in East Haddam, Connecticut, was called the Governor's Ring, because John Winthrop, Jr., 'used to resort [thither] with his servant, and after spending three weeks in the woods of this mountain in roasting ores and assaying metals and casting gold rings, he used to return home to New London with plenty of gold.'

Astronomy was another science that interested Winthrop. He owned a three and one half foot telescope which he presented to Harvard College in 1672, and with which (so he reported to Sir Robert Moray, President of the Royal Society) he observed a fifth satellite of Jupiter at Hartford, in 1664. Whether he really saw it may be doubted, as the existence of a fifth satellite was not definitely and finally ascertained until 1892.

It must not be supposed, however, that Winthrop's scientific activities were purely speculative. He was continually bringing his knowledge to bear on the natural resources of New England, in the hope of founding an industry that would benefit the community. Perhaps his first experiment in that way was in salt making. Absence of natural deposits of salt was a great handicap to the colonists, not only in their fishing, but also in household industry as well; since salting was the only known method of preserving flesh and fish for export or winter use. Repeated and unsuccessful attempts had been made, both in Plymouth and the Bay Colony, to evaporate salt from sea water. In the summer of 1638 John Winthrop, Jr., received authority from the Court to set up salt works at Ryall Side in Beverly, across Bass River from Roger Conant and the old planters. He lived there for a year and a half, and the salt works apparently were not a success. Winthrop continued to work at the subject, and in 1656 obtained from the General Court a patent for a new process. The secret was imparted to his friend Richard Leader, who raised capital at Barbados to try it there. The system was to pump sea water by a windmill into a series of terraced ponds or pans, where the water was evaporated by the sun. The rainy season set in just as Leader was on the point of success, and his backers deserted him. In any case, the system could hardly have worked in a country so rainy as New England; and it was not until the American Revolution that a practical method of obtaining salt by evaporation was invented on Cape Cod.

More important were Winthrop's prospectings for minerals, and his organization of the iron industry. Valuable minerals were among the principal inducements that led the puritans to New England. We need not ridicule them for their persistent search of this form of wealth, or argue a superior virtue on their part over Virginians and Mexicans because they failed to find it. Rocky, hilly country generally abounds in minerals, and small quantities even of gold and silver and lead have been found in New England.

John Winthrop, Jr., not only prospected in person a large part of southern New England, but he was constantly assaying samples of ore which were brought to him, such as a reputed gold nugget of Rhode Island, sent by Roger Williams. For this purpose he had a considerable chemical apparatus, and incidentally accumulated a mineralogical cabinet. It was he who first saw the possibilities of a deposit of graphite or blacklead — the substance that gave lead pencils their name — at a place known to the Indians as Tantiusque, in the present town of Sturbridge, Massachusetts. Winthrop purchased the land from the Indians, who used the graphite for painting their faces, obtained confirmation from the General Court, and organized an informal company to exploit the mine. Robert Child, a prominent and enthusiastic investor, wrote Winthrop that graphite was used by mathematicians, painters, and limners; and if it were of the right sort, and in big enough pieces, the stuff could be made into combs, which were in great demand by the ladies of Italy and Spain to color gray hair a glittering raven-like blackness. There was also hope of finding silver with the graphite. Several attempts were made by Winthrop to 'dig lustily,' as Dr. Child advised; but the mine was so remote from a settlement that the workmen would not stay, and transportation ate up the profits. When the region was settled, long after his death, the mine was reopened and operated at a profit; it has even been worked in the present century.

Iron was the most common and useful mineral in New England. Limonite bog iron ore of the sort that the English exploited for centuries in the weald of Sussex, existed in large quantities in the ponds and swamps of Massachusetts. There was plenty of oak wood for burning charcoal, a necessity for smelting; and the colonies offered a wide market for iron and ironmongery, expensive to import from England. John Winthrop, Jr., travelled far and wide looking for iron deposits and 'fitt places for the erecting of ironworks.' By 1641 he had decided that they were feasible at Saugus and Braintree, and returned to England to find the capital. With the aid of his uncle Emmanuel Downing and his father-in-law Hugh Peter, he finally effected his object, and formed a company of 'Undertakers' headed by an Englishman with the curious name of Becx or Beex.

Ill fortune attended Winthrop's iron enterprise from the start. He embarked on the *Ann Cleve* at Gravesend in May, 1643, with a company of skilled ironworkers, and £1000 worth of supplies and materials. A grafting custom-house officer detained him until the favorable wind was lost, the voyage took fourteen weeks, ship fever broke out among the workingmen, and they arrived in New England too late to do anything before frost sealed the ponds and bogs. Winthrop then boarded out some of the workmen, and took the more skilled ones on a prospecting tour. He preferred Braintree for the first works, as in a settled region where labor and draft cattle could be hired from the farmers; but the desired land there was already privately owned, so as a second choice he set up the first furnace in that part of Lynn which is now Saugus. The iron workers called it Hammersmith, either as a joke, or because some of them came from the like-named suburb of London. The old Ironworks House built for the managers, and the 'Scotch-Boardman House' built to shelter the workers, still stand, and in recent years the former has been carefully restored. The imported workers were not puritans, and proved refractory to puritan discipline, frequently getting into the courts for fighting, swearing, drinking, and Sabbath-breaking.

Before anything but preliminaries had been accomplished, the Undertakers sent out Richard Leader in the summer of 1645 to take charge of the works, at a salary of £100. Leader was a cultivated puritan gentleman who had had experience with ironworks of the same sort in Ireland. He and Winthrop became warm friends, and under his management things began to move. Shells instead of limestone had to be used for the flux, but the farmers dug the ore and provided the necessary charcoal, and a forge was set up as well as a bloomery or furnace. A capacity of eight to ten tons a week — large compared with most of the contemporary English ironworks — was soon attained; a large quantity of bar and wrought iron was produced for local blacksmiths; kettles, anchors, and other simple articles were cast. Within a few years the Hammersmith plant was producing enough iron for the colony's needs, and even a surplus for export: a hundred pounds' worth of ironmongery was adventured to New Amsterdam and the Delaware in 1651.

The Colony seems to have appreciated this very creditable enterprise. A twenty-one year monopoly, and ten years' tax

exemption, were granted by the General Court before production began; later the period of tax exemption was extended, and the ironworkers were exempted from watchings
and wardings and military training. Smelting even received
the blessing of the clergy: Thomas Shepard conceded that it
was not a profanation of the Sabbath, to keep the fires going
in the furnaces! Neighboring farmers fairly lived off the ironworks, what with digging ore, cutting wood, burning charcoal, and hauling with ox teams. Samuel Danforth celebrated
the ironworks and the blacklead mine in his almanac verse:

> Of late from this tree's root within the ground
> Rich Mines branch out, Iron and Lead are found,
> Better than Peru's gold or Mexico's
> Which cannot weapon us against our foes,
> Nor make us howes, nor siths, nor plough-shares mend.
> Without which tools mens honest lives would end.
> Some silver-mines, if any here doe wish,
> They it may finde i' th' bellyes of our fish.

About three years after the works were started, we find
evidence of serious trouble. The Undertakers were not getting the dividends they expected, the labor cost was too high,
and various unavoidable accidents consumed the profits.
Lynn obtained permission from the General Court to rate
the works for local purposes, and abused the power, as industrial towns will. There began a long and costly series of
law suits against the company for alleged damages, unre-
quited services, and unpaid rates. Richard Leader got into
a row with the authorities, threw up his position, and went to
Barbados to try salt works. From there he wrote to John
Winthrop that he could do anything with a coffle of negro
slaves. 'Plantations are worth nothing in themselves, were it
not for the vast number of slaves they have on them' — a
sage observation. Smelting iron was heavy work, and labor
was one of the constant troubles of the company. John Gifford, Leader's successor, was less successful than he at managing labor. A parcel of white slaves, Scots prisoners taken

at Dunbar, was sent out by the Undertakers in 1654, but they proved as troublesome as the hired men.

From that time on the story of the Lynn ironworks is largely one of lawsuits against the company, of American partners against English partners, of mortgageors against mortgagees, and so forth. Gifford was put in jail for selling over eighty-five tons of products for his personal account. Managers were changed, and there were several reorganizations of the company. At this distance it is impossible to determine the rights and wrongs; but it is clear that unwilling labor, a nagging absentee ownership, and local jealousy of big business, were all at fault.

Nevertheless, this ambitious project of John Winthrop, Jr., was not a failure or a blind alley. When Hammersmith broke up, the more highly skilled workers established local bloomeries and forges at various parts of New England. The Leonard brothers, who were imported from Wales in 1643, became a distinguished family in New England economic history. In 1653 they set up a bloomery and a forge at Taunton and Raynham respectively. Another iron enterprise of this family grew into the town of Norton; the Taunton Iron Works and the very considerable metal industry in that section of Massachusetts are derived in direct line from them. These works were locally capitalized, and paid dividends in iron bars, which passed as currency in the Taunton valley. Small furnaces at Groton, Concord, Ipswich, Rowley and North Saugus were offshoots from Hammersmith. Joseph Jencks, another imported ironworker, became the first of a long line of Yankee inventors. He received a patent from the General Court for the modern type of scythe, long and slender with a bar along the back of the blade; he built a fire engine for Boston, and tried experiments in wire drawing. If the history of all the local ironworks and tool factories established in New England before 1800 were followed up, it would probably be found that most of them could be traced through

Jencks and the Leonards to the old Hammersmith plant in Saugus.

The difficulties of doing business with inelastic currency and cumbrous exchange, became so apparent to Winthrop during his connection with the ironworks undertakers, that he turned his thoughts to matters of currency and credit. Potter's 'Key to Wealth' (1661) inspired him to outline a 'way of trade and banke without money' to his friend Samuel Hartlib. It was a scheme of notes or bills based on land or mortgages, not redeemable in specie. The basic idea was sound, as the recent German *Reichsmark* has proved; but America was destined to suffer much from ill-conceived land banks and banks based on nothing, before the germinal idea of Potter and Winthrop could be made profitable to the community.

The Pequot country, including all Eastern Connecticut between the river towns and the Narragansetts, was conquered by the joint efforts of Massachusetts and Connecticut in 1637, and claimed by both. John Winthrop, Jr., from his first visit to the Saybrook fort, was much attracted by the possibilities of this region for industry; and any one who visits to-day the valleys of the Thames, the Quinebaug and the Shetucket, with their chain of manufacturing cities such as Norwich, Putnam, and Willimantic, must agree that Winthrop was far-sighted. In 1640 he obtained a grant to Fisher's Island, which commands the Pequot coast and the entrance to Long Island Sound; and in 1644 the General Court gave him authority to make a plantation in the Pequot country.

Winthrop wisely selected the river-mouth site of New London, with its excellent harbor, for the settlement, and began to plant settlers there in the spring of 1646. The family spent the winter of 1646–47 on Fisher's Island, where they long maintained a stud and herd of cattle. John retained his interests in Ipswich, Lynn, and Boston. Until his father's death in 1649, he was not certain of settling down permanently at New London. In the meantime the Pequot country had been awarded by the New England Confederation to Connecticut, so if Winthrop decided to take root there, he would have to give up the Massachusetts magistracy which he had held so long.

Every one wanted the younger Winthrop to live with them. He was the most sought-after person in New England. Connecticut had already made him a magistrate, and was ready to elect him Governor. Peter Stuyvesant, Governor of New Netherland, urged him to settle on the site of Brooklyn, promising him 'accomodation... soe large and ample as hee hath power to give.' Roger Williams, with whom Winthrop always stayed on his journeys between Boston and Pequot, assured him of an even warmer welcome if he would choose the Providence Plantations. A little later we find the strait-laced New Haven Colony, church and state, elders and magistrates, offering Winthrop a free house with well cleared and pump fixed, winter wood laid in, wheat and candles found, and the promise of a maid servant 'reported to be cleanly and saving, her mother is of the Church,' if he would only reside at New Haven a part of the year, and put the local ironworks on their feet. Sir Kenelm Digby wrote to him from London, early in 1655:

I hope it will not be long before this Iland, your native country, do enjoy your much desired presence. I pray for it hartily, and I am confident that your great judgement, and noble desire of doing the most good to mankinde that you may, will prompt you to make as much hast hither as you can. Where you are, is too scanty a stage for you to remaine too long upon. It was a well chosen one when there were inconveniences for your fixing upon this. But now that all is here as you could wish, all that do know you do expect of you that you should exercise your vertues where they may be of most advantage to the world, and where you may do most good to most men.

Digby's warm invitation to London might have been irresistible if Winthrop had had the means; but he wished to retrieve the family fortunes, sadly wasted by the old Governor's lavish hospitality and too great devotion to the public weal. The best opportunity seemed to be in the rocky, rugged Pequot country with its mineral prospects; and Connecticut Colony gave him a grant in perpetuity of any minerals he might discover and any mines he might work.

Winthrop's removal to New London was a very severe loss to Massachusetts. Had he remained a resident of the Bay, there is every reason to suppose that a man of his universal popularity would have been elected governor, and that once freed from the parental influence on the Board of Assistants, he and his old Ipswich friends would have liberalized the government. Certainly there would have been no execution of Quakers in Massachusetts under a Governor of whom Roger Williams wrote, 'You have been noted for tendernes toward mens soules, especially for conscience sake to God.' Instead, John Endecott, a man of strength and integrity, but harsh, bigoted and narrow-minded, was elected governor for thirteen of the fifteen years following the elder Winthrop's death; and under him the tightening-up policy of the last few years became more intense.

Sadly the First Church of Boston dismissed John and Elizabeth Winthrop to 'the Church of Christ at Seabrooke Fort,' beseeching the brethren there 'to receive them in the Lord as becometh Saints,' pending the institution of 'the good ordinances of Christ' in 'the new plantation at Pekott.' For the rest of his life 'the sachem of Pequot' as Dr. Child playfully called Winthrop, made New London his principal home, although he retained landed property in the Bay, and paid frequent visits there. Three of his daughters, visiting Ipswich, report themselves 'all in health, and as merry as very good cheere and Ipswich friends can make them.' The invitation to spend a part of the year at New Haven was accepted. When one of the last visits became unduly prolonged,

Jonathan Brewster wrote to Winthrop from New London, 'Wee and the whole Towne and Church wantes you. We are as naked without you, yea indeed, we are as a body without a head, and would that we might injoye your presence.' The town will 'grant you what encouragement they can afford you to sett up a Forge here, which may be one means to bringe you backe againe.' Brewster also wrote Mistress Winthrop to use her influence in that direction, for 'you know weomen are very strong and powerfull to act this way, and overcome the strongest and wisest men that ever were or are in the world, by perswations and swete alurements.' This Jonathan Brewster, the son of Elder Brewster of Plymouth, was probably Winthrop's most congenial neighbor; for he too was a scientist and experimenter, who had what to-day would be called a private laboratory at his Indian trading post on the site of Norwich. Perhaps it was his influence which secured for Mistress Winthrop an Indian servant, subject of a contract between the Governor and a local sagamore.

John Winthrop could not escape public service, if he would, by emigrating to the Pequot wilderness. In 1651 he became Assistant, and in 1657 Governor of Connecticut Colony, which granted him the housing and lands belonging to the late Governor Haynes, and sent a mounted escort to convoy him from New London to Hartford. In 1658, according to the Connecticut practice, the former Deputy-Governor succeeded to his position, and he to the Deputy's; but Winthrop proved so able and popular a chief magistrate that the rule was changed, and from 1659 to his death in 1676, he was annually elected governor.

As Governor of Connecticut, Winthrop gave that colony a distinguished administration. Although the General Court passed laws as stringent as those of the Bay against Quakers and other heretics, Winthrop's enforcement of them was such that Roger Williams thanked him for his 'prudent and moderate hand in the late Quakers trials amongst us.' Historians have wondered why Connecticut dealt so diplomatically with Charles II, while Massachusetts rudely defied him. The cause was the character and worldly experience of John Winthrop, who knew how to speak to a Stuart in his own language; while Massachusetts told him to go to hell, and hoped for a miracle. As a result, in the same reign that the Bay lost her charter, John Winthrop gained one for Connecticut, giving her self-government on the Massachusetts model, gobbling up New Haven, and extending her boundaries west to Lake Erie and the Mississippi. Probably the £500 that Connecticut appropriated for the 'expenses' of the Winthrop mission were also of some assistance.

These two years that he spent in England, enjoying the society of statesmen and scientists, taking an active part in the affairs of the Royal Society, must have been one of the happiest periods in Winthrop's life. If he felt depressed at returning to New England and the society of men uncivil and uncouth, he did not show it. For John Winthrop, Jr., loved all sorts of people, ignorant or educated, red men or white; and as a proof of this love he employed his gifts not only for science and public welfare, but in the art of healing. There is still preserved a notebook of his medical practice which shows that he handled every sort of case, from treating the stricken wife of a governor, to relieving a sick Indian after an orgy of gluttony.

Oliver Wendell Holmes used this notebook in his Lowell lecture on the Medical Profession in Massachusetts delivered sixty years ago, and I cannot better the genial Doctor's witty description of his predecessor in the healing art:

The Governor employed a number of the simples dear to ancient women, — elecampane and elder and wormwood and anise and the rest; but he also employed certain mineral remedies, which he almost always indicates by their ancient symbols, or by a name which should leave them a mystery to the vulgar. I am now prepared to reveal the mystic secrets of the Governor's beneficent art, which rendered so many good and great as well as so many poor and dependent people his debtors — at least, in their simple belief — for their health and their lives.

His great remedy, which he gave oftener than any other, was nitre; which he ordered in doses of twenty or thirty grains to adults, and of three grains to infants. Measles, colics, sciatica, headache, giddiness, and many other ailments, all found themselves treated, and I trust bettered, by nitre; a pretty safe medicine in moderate doses, and one not likely to keep the good Governor awake at night, thinking whether it might not kill, if it did not cure. We may say as much for spermaceti, which he seems to have considered 'the sovereign'st thing on the earth' for inward bruises, and often prescribes after falls and similar injuries.

One of the next remedies, in point of frequency, which he was in the habit of giving, was (probably diaphoretic) antimony; a mild form of that very active metal, and which, mild as it was, left his patients very commonly with a pretty strong conviction that they had been taking *something* that did not exactly agree with them. Now and then he gave a little iron or sulphur or calomel, but very rarely; occasionally, a good, honest dose of rhubarb or jalap; a taste of stinging horseradish, oftener of warming guiacum; sometimes an anodyne, in the shape of mithridate,—the famous old farrago, which owed its virtue to poppy juice; very often, a harmless powder of coral; less frequently, an inert prescription of pleasing amber; and (let me say it softly within possible hearing of his honored descendant), twice or oftener, — let us hope as a last resort, — an electuary of *millipedes* — sowbugs, if we must give them their homely English name. One or two other prescriptions, of the many unmentionable ones which disgraced the pharmacopoeia of the seventeenth century, are to be found, but only in very rare instances, in the faded characters of the manuscript.

The excellent Governor's accounts of diseases are so brief, that we get only a very general notion of the complaints for which he prescribed. Measles and their consequences are at first more prominent than any other one affection, but the common infirmities of both sexes and of all ages seem to have come under his healing hand. Fever and ague appears to have been of frequent occurrence

His published correspondence shows that many noted people were in communication with him as his patients. Roger Williams wants a little of his medicine for Mrs. Weekes's daughter; worshipful John Haynes is in receipt of his powders; troublesome Captain

Underhill wants 'a little white vitterall' for his wife, and something to cure his wife's friend's neuralgia (I think his wife's friend's husband had a little rather have had it sent by the hands of Mrs. Underhill, than by those of the gallant and discursive captain); and pious John Davenport says, *his* wife 'tooke but one halfe of one of the papers' (which probably contained the medicine he called *rubila*), 'but could not beare the taste of it, and is discouraged from taking any more;' and honored William Leete asks for more powders for his 'poore little daughter' Graciana, though he found it 'hard to make her take it,' delicate, and of course sensitive, child as she was, languishing and dying before her time, in spite of all the bitter things she swallowed, — God help all little children in the hands of dosing doctors and howling dervishes! Restless Samuel Gorton, now tamed by the burden of fourscore and two years, writes so touching an account of his infirmities, and expresses such overflowing gratitude for the relief he has obtained from the Governor's prescriptions, wondering how 'a thing so little in quantity, so little in scent, so little in taste, and so little to sence in operation, should beget and bring forth such efects,' that we repent our hasty exclamation, and bless the memory of the good Governor, who gave relief to the worn-out frame of our long-departed brother, the sturdy old heretic of Rhode Island.

What was that medicine which so frequently occurs in the printed letters under the name of 'rubila'? It is evidently a secret remedy, and, so far as I know, has not yet been made out. I had almost given it up in despair, when I found what appears to be a key to the mystery. In the vast multitude of prescriptions contained in the manuscripts, most of them written in symbols, I find one which I thus interpret:

'Four grains of (diaphoretic) antimony, with twenty grains of nitre, with a little salt of tin, *making rubila*.' Perhaps something was added to redden the powder, as he constantly speaks of 'rubifying' or 'viridating' his prescriptions; a very common practice of prescribers, when their powders look a little too much like plain salt or sugar.

Dr. Holmes' conjecture concerning *rubila* has since been confirmed by the microanalysis of a red stain and powder found on one of Winthrop's papers, yielding nitre and antimony sulphide.

The governor-physician also possessed a so-called unicorn's horn, which he lent to ailing friends; and an anti-monial cup, which was supposed to impart the virtue of antimony to any liquid contained in it. He extracted or compounded his own medicines in his private laboratory, and as Tompson wrote:

> His fruits of toyl Hermetically done
> Stream to the poor as light doth from the Sun.

No wonder that the diseased of both races, English and Indian, flocked about him wherever he went, as Cotton Mather records.

Winthrop asked to be relieved of the governorship in 1667 and in 1670, in order to pay more attention to his private affairs; but the assembly refused to hear of it, and by tax exemption and grants somewhat eased the burden on his estate. Again at the age of seventy, and at the approach of King Philip's War, Winthrop asked to be let off, but such a chorus of remonstrance arose that he resigned himself to die in harness; nor had he long to wait. On a visit to Boston to attend a meeting of the Commissioners of the United Colonies, he took cold, and died on April 5, 1676. To the sound of drum and trumpet, and minute guns from the Artillery Company, his body was laid to rest beside that of his father in New England's *campo santo*, the King's Chapel burying-ground.

One of the last letters that he received was from his old friend Roger Williams, together with a 'little volume of poetry':

I have heard that you have bene in late consultacions *semper idem, semper pacificus*, and I hope therein *beatus*. You have always bene noted for tendernes toward mens soules, especially for conscience sake to God. You have bene noted for tendernes toward the bodies and infirmities of poor mortalls. You have bene tender too toward the estates of men in your civill steerage of government, and toward the peace of the land, yea, of these wild savages. I presume you are satisfied in the necessitie of these present hostilities, and that it is not possible at present to keepe peace with these barbarous men of bloud.... But... I fear the event of the justest war....

Dear Sir, if we cannot save our patients, nor relations, nor Indians, nor English, oh let us make sure to save the bird in our bozome, and to enter into that straight dore and narrow way, which the Lord Jesus himselfe tells us, few there be that find it.

And so, with the blessing of New England's prophet of democracy, there passed away the finest flower of her aristocracy. In John Winthrop were combined as in few Americans of any age the power to think and the power to do, a creative genius and a quality of leadership, the zest of a scientist and the faith of a puritan, a pioneer's energy and the tenderness of a saint. New England honored herself in honoring such a man; and to humble folk throughout the length and breadth of the land, the desolation wrought by King Philip's warriors bore less heavily than the loss of their just magistrate and beloved physician.

CHAPTER X

JOHN ELIOT, APOSTLE TO THE INDIANS

CONVERSION of the natives to Christianity had been one of the first objects of colonization alleged by promoters such as Raleigh, Hakluyt, and Captain John Smith. Whether this showed a genuine aspiration or an argument to empty the purses of the pious, may well be debated; but there is no doubt that it won clerical and charitable support for the Virginia, the Dorchester, and the Massachusetts Bay Companies. John White had the missionary motive very close to heart. In 'The Planters Plea' he showed some embarrassment because the slate of conversion was still a complete blank. Not a few Indians had been brought to England by the early voyagers, and some few returned; but none were sufficiently impressed by the Englishman's virtues to adopt his faith until Squanto, the Pilgrim Fathers' volunteer guide, 'fell sick of an Indean feavor... and within a few days dyed ther; desiring the Governor to pray for him, that he might goe to the Englishmens God in heaven.' Morton of Merrymount thought the Indians were splendid fellows, and recorded an instance of their humanity to a crack-brained preacher benighted in the woods; but Morton was a fur-trader, and history has not yet recorded a fur-trader converting the natives.

The charter of the Governor and Company of the Massachusetts Bay declares the main object of the colony 'to wynn and incite the natives of the country, to the knowledg and obedience of the onlie true God and Saviour of mankinde; and this Christian faith, which is our royall intentions, and the adventurers' free profession, is the principall ende of this plantation.' As a reminder of this promise, the Macedonian cry 'Come over and help us,' was placed in an Indian's mouth on the Colony seal; and the Indian still holds his place on the great seal of the Commonwealth of Massachusetts.

Nevertheless, years elapsed after the settlement of New England before any attempt was made to convert the natives. As John White said, the great stumbling-block was the language. It proved no obstacle to trading, but that could be done largely by the sign language. A more extensive vocabulary is required for conversion than for commerce. The author of 'New England's First Fruits' (1643) evidently raked the annals of the colony for instances of Indian conversion, but could only furnish his readers with such poor gleanings as the pious death of Sagamore John, who rebuked an Englishman for felling a tree on the Sabbath. An occasional gesture was made, as when Kutshamakin the sagamore of the Massachusetts, the squaw sachem of Nashobah, Masconomo, the sagamore of Agawam, and Sholan and Wasamegin 'two sachems near the great hill to the west called Wachuset,' drifted into the General Court and tendered their allegiance to the Colony. Secretary Rawson, who must have had a sense of humor, records this dialogue between the visitors and the 'Solons' of the Bay:

> Member of the General Court: Will you worship the only true God?
> Indians: We do desire to reverence the God of the English,... because we see he doth better to the English than other gods do to others.
> Member: You are not to swear falsely.
> Indians: We know not what swearing is.
> Member: You are not to do unnecessary work on the Sabbath.
> Indians: That will be easy: we haven't much to do any day, and can well take our ease on the Sabbath.

The authorities were becoming a bit ashamed of their deafness to the Macedonian cry. In 1644, the General Court ordered the county courts to take care that the Indians residing in their several shires should be 'civillized,' and 'instructed in the knowledge and worship of God.' Before anything was done to fulfil this pious wish, the work had been taken in hand by a man of simplicity, directness, and strength: John Eliot, 'Apostle to the Indians.'

Like so many of his colleagues in the New England ministry, John Eliot was the scholar of a family in humble circumstances. Born at Widford, Herts., in 1604, at fourteen he entered the University of Cambridge, taking his B.A. in 1622 from Jesus College. In the ancient library of that college, there is proof that John Eliot did not forget Jerusalem: a copy of the first edition of his Indian Bible, with this inscription:

Pro Collegio Jesu

Accipias mater quod alumnus humillimus offert

filius, oro preces semper habens tuas[1]

Johannes Eliot

John did not remain to take the master's degree, but left with a good equipment in the ancient languages to take a junior mastership in a school near Chelmsford, of which Thomas Hooker was the head. Eliot must have been well known and beloved in the community, for when he decided to emigrate to New England in 1631, he promised 'a select number of his pious and Christian friends' to be their pastor, if they would follow him. John Wilson of the Boston church had to leave for a visit to England shortly after John Eliot arrived in Boston, and Eliot was chosen his substitute. The Boston church liked him so much that he had difficulty in getting away when his English neighbors and friends arrived, and settled in Roxbury. Boston offered him the teaching eldership which afterwards went to John Cotton; but John Eliot kept his promise, and in 1632 became the first settled minister of Roxbury. As there is no reason to suppose that Eliot took holy orders in England, he was probably the first New England minister who was never 'bishoped,' whose sole ordination was in the Congregational way.

[1] For Jesus College. Accept, mother, I pray, what a most humble alumnus offers, a son ever having thy prayers.

The town to whose church Eliot ministered for nigh three score years, was named after natural features, and generally spelled by him 'Rocksborough.' Its center was an outcrop of conglomerate rock which stood guard over the narrow neck leading into Boston. The fields and woods were well strewn with 'Roxbury pudding-stone,' attributed by Indian legend to the bad table manners of an angry giant on the Great Blue Hill. It was not a rich town, though not one of the poorer communities of the Bay. About 1640, John Eliot owned only 39 acres of land, valued at £13; yet of the 68 real estate holders, 51 held less than he. There was only one prominent citizen, Thomas Dudley, who moved thither from Ipswich to be under Eliot's ministrations.

Of Eliot the country parson, we have a most engaging picture in Mather's 'Magnalia.' He was not an 'intellectual.' None of his sermons were thought worth printing, for unlike Cotton he cared little for doctrinal points, and he lacked the evangelical fervor of Shepard. His idiom was that of East Anglia, which became the idiom of New England. 'I been't afraid, thank God I been't afraid to die!' is a scrap of it recorded by Mather. His manner was gentle and winning, unless there were sin to be rebuked or corruption fought. Simple were his sermons, but often deep: — 'the very lambs might wade in the shallows, but there were depths in which elephants might swim.' Simplicity was Eliot's strength. Others might spin logical webs about the five points of Calvinism. Faith to him meant three things: love, duty, and prayer.

Cotton Mather, who knew Eliot well in his old age, wrote:

He was indeed a man of prayer... Especially, when there was any remarkable Difficulty before him, he took this way to encounter and overcome it; being of Dr. Preston's Mind, *That when we would have any great things to be accomplished, the best Policy is to work by an Engine which the World sees nothing of*... He kept his heart in a frame for Prayer with a marvellous constancy; and was continually provoking all that were about him thereunto. When he heard any considerable news, his usual and speedy reflection thereupon would be 'Brethren, let us turn all this into prayer!' And he was perpetually jogging the wheel of prayer, both more privately in the meetings, and more publickly in the churches of his neighbourhood. When he came to an house that he was intimately acquainted with, he would often say, 'Come, let us not have a visit without a prayer; let us pray down the Blessing of Heaven on your Family before we go.' Especially when he came into a society of ministers, before he had sat long with them, they would look to hear him urging, 'Brethren, the Lord Jesus takes much notice of what is done and said among his Ministers when they are together; come, let us pray before we part!' And hence also, his whole breath seemed in a sort made up of ejaculatory prayers, many scores of which winged messengers he dispatched away to Heaven upon pious errands, every Day. By them he bespoke blessings upon almost every person or Affair that he was concerned with; and he carried every thing to God with some pertinent *Hosannah's* or *Hallelujah's* over it. He was a mighty and an happy man, that had his quiver full of these heavenly arrows... He was indeed sufficiently pleasant and witty in company, and he was affable and facetious rather than morose in conversation; but he had a remarkable gravity mixed with it, and a singular skill of raising some holy observation out of whatever matter of discourse lay before him; nor would he ordinarily dismiss any theme without some gracious, divine, pithy sentence thereupon.

A schoolmaster seldom works the teaching urge out of his system, and Eliot did not attempt to. The youth of the congregation were weekly catechized and examined on the Sabbath's sermons, and Roxbury did not wait for the statutory one hundred families to establish a grammar school. That, Eliot 'would always have upon the place, whatever it cost him,' says Mather; and in consequence, 'Roxbury has afforded more scholars, first for the College and then for the Publick, of any town of its Bigness... in all New England... I persuade myself that the good people of Roxbury will forever scorn to be grutch the cost or to permit the death of a school which God has made such an honor to them; and this rather, because their deceased Eliot has left them a fair portion of his own estate for the maintaining of the school in Roxbury.' Nor have they; for the Roxbury Latin School, successor to the old grammar school that Eliot founded, still flourishes, and still produces scholars.

Anne Mumford, to whom John Eliot became engaged in England, came over with his friends in 1632, and married him that year. Mistress Eliot was a careful and efficient housewife, fortunately for her unworldly husband. She 'attained unto a considerable skill in Physick and Chirurgery, which enabled her to dispense many safe, good, and useful medicines unto the poor'; and she had the rare distinction among the Pilgrim mothers of New England to live to the ripe old age of eighty-six. They had one daughter and five sons; three of them ministers, and one a Fellow of Harvard College, destined for the ministry. It was a happy, affectionate family of simple piety and plain living, with none of that tense straining for perfect righteousness which made many a New England parsonage an unpleasant home for healthy children.

A new turn came in the Indian relations of Massachusetts with the Pequot War of 1637. The power of that warlike tribe was completely broken, its survivors sold into bondage or slavery or distributed among the friendly tribes, 'and from savage warfare the land had peace forty years.' The Indians of southern New England were impressed by the powers of the white man, and became more interested in the God to whom he attributed his success. From the captives John Eliot obtained a bond servant from whom he began to learn the Indian language. This teacher was succeeded by a youth named Job Nesutan, who remained many years as his master's servant, teacher, and assistant missionary. Eliot's college training in linguistics, and his early-rising industry, enabled him to master the Algonkian dialect of the locality, and get a clue to the intricacies of its grammar; for like all primitive languages, this Indian tongue was highly inflected and exceedingly complicated.

At the age of forty-two, Eliot was ready for his first missionary experiment. 'Master Eliot engaged in this great work of preaching unto the Indians upon a very pure and sincere account,' wrote his friend and colleague Gookin. 'I being his neighbor and intimate friend, at the time when he first attempted the enterprise he was pleased to communicate unto me his design, and the motives that induced him thereunto.' These motives were simple and strong, as we might expect: the glory of God, compassion for the Indians, and a puritan's duty to heed the Macedonian cry.

In 1646 he visited the nearest Indian village, Nonantum, on the Newton bank of the Charles, opposite Watertown. It was a beautiful October day before the trees had been stripped of their gorgeous foliage by the autumn rains. Waban, the local sagamore, bade Eliot welcome. He preached a sermon of an hour and a quarter in the Indian language which his audience declared that they understood. Then came a distribution of apples and biscuits to the children and tobacco to the men, an excellent method of holding audiences which Eliot always followed, but which proved a heavy item in the cost of conversion. Other visits and talks followed shortly; and before the end of the year Eliot had blocked out a policy. Civilization and Christianity must go hand-in-hand. The Indians must be induced to 'sit down orderly' in self-governing villages of their own, apart from the whites; to accept Christian ethics, to take up a more productive agriculture than the wasteful and intermittent efforts of their squaws; to learn carpentry, blacksmithing, and other useful trades; and to be taught their letters that they might read the Bible — if only the Bible could be translated into their tongue!

That same autumn of 1646, the General Court appointed Eliot one of a committee to select and purchase land from the

Indians, at the colony's expense, 'for the encouragement of the Indians to live in a more orderly way amongst us.' Yet from the start he encountered suspicion and hostility among his own people, whose attitude was always a heavy obstacle to his work. Frenchmen and Spaniards mingled easily with the American Indians; but the English pride of race forbade. Your New England settler quickly acquired what has become the traditional attitude of the English-speaking pioneer: 'A good Indian is a dead Indian.' To him the native was a dirty, lazy, treacherous beast: 'the arrow that flieth by day,' and 'the terror that flieth by night.'

A good beginning in coöperation was made by enlisting the services of Wilson and Shepard, and of President Dunster, who wished Harvard to become the Indian Oxford as well as the New English Cambridge. And, fortunately, Eliot had something of that showman's instinct which gains support for missionary efforts. When the church council met at Cambridge in 1647, he arranged a great demonstration: a vast concourse of Indians to whom he delivered a lecture in the open air, followed by a catechism, to which they fairly roared out the replies. This demonstrative piety 'did marvellously affect all the wise and godly ministers, magistrates, and people.' New trophies of the assault on Indian godlessness were shortly gathered by the conversion of sachems and sagamores, who had held back from a natural jealousy of the remarkable influence that Eliot obtained over his converts. Kutshamakin, the contumacious sagamore of Neponset, was brought to some knowledge of God; Nashobah demanded preaching; a visit was paid to the Nauset tribe on Cape Cod; the Apostle was escorted by a guard of twenty sannups to the sachem of distant Quabaug, 'hungry after instruction'; even the mighty Passaconaway of Pennacook was visibly affected.

England was not long in hearing of these great doings, for Eliot and his friends knew perfectly well that money for missionary work must come from England. So Master Wilson, probably with Shepard's aid, prepared a lively tract: 'The Day-Breaking, if not the Sun-Rising of the Gospell with the Indians in New England' (London, 1647), vouched for by twelve eminent puritan pastors of the old country, and by them commended to the pious. This went off so briskly that it was followed by a whole series, the next being Thomas Shepard's 'The Clear Sun-Shine of the Gospel Breaking Forth upon the Indians in New England' (London, 1648). Both tracts are still interesting to read; especially the sample dialogues between missionary and Indian, whose 'untutored mind' seems to have been remarkably acute in finding some of the logical flaws in the puritan doctrine:

Qu. How comes it to passe that the Sea water was salt, and the land water fresh?

Ans. Tis so from the wonderfull worke of God, as why are Strawberries sweet and Cranberries sowre?

Qu. If God could not be seene with their eies, how could hee bee seene with their soule within?

Ans. If they saw a great wigwam, would they think that Racoones or Foxes built it that had no wisedome? No, but they would beleeve some wise workman made it though they did not see him; so should they beleeve concerning God, when they looked up to heaven, Sunne, Moone, and Stars, and saw this great house he hath made, though they do not see him with their eyes.

One wonders if the actual answers were quite as apt as they read in the printed book.

To some of the questions no answer is printed, says Shepard, 'lest I could clog your time with reading'; but we could well spare the time to learn what learned graduates of the University of Cambridge had to say to questions like these:

How may one know wicked men, who are good and who are bad?

If a man should be inclosed in Iron a foot thick and thrown into the fire, what would become of his soule, whether could the soule come forth thence or not?

Why did not God give all men good hearts that they might bee good?

Why did not God kill the Devill that made all men so bad, God having all power?

On one occasion a somewhat inebriate Indian named George, a scapegrace who stole a cow and skinned it and sold it to President Dunster for moose, disturbed the meeting by crying out, 'Master Eliot, who made sack? did God make sack?' George was put out.

For some years there had been talk of establishing in England a missionary society for propagating the Gospel among the Indians. Dr. John Stoughton, friend of John White and brother to Israel Stoughton, planned a New England college for training missionaries, both native and English. The disillusioned White urged that if the natives were ever to be converted, no further dependence be placed on the Virginians, who were becoming themselves 'exceedingly rude, more likely to turn Heathen than to turne others to the Christian faith.' In that same year, 1641, the Bay authorities, disheartened by the sudden stoppage of the puritan emigration and the consequent economic crisis, sent over Hugh Peter and Thomas Welde on a begging mission for the Colony, the College, and the heathen. Hugh Peter obtained a chaplaincy in the New Model Army, which for a time absorbed his restless energy; thereafter he did little for New England charitable enterprises, except to interfere and criticize. Thomas Welde collected some £1625, of which about £75 were earmarked for conversion. Most of this came from a well-born lady, celebrated for her piety, learning and benevolence: the Lady Mary Armine. This wealthy and childless widow of a noted parliamentarian founded two hospitals, and was a very fountain of good works dear to puritans. Her annual contributions of £20 were deposited in the Bay treasury, but paid over to John Eliot as soon as he began to convert; and for twenty-five years she was a mainstay of his work. Except for this timely 'touch,' Thomas Welde proved of slight use. He obtained a comfortable parish in the north of England and remained there; his accounts were inaccurate and long delayed; and both the colony and its friends saw that if the good work were to continue, it must be put on a sound business basis.

Edward Winslow, who at this juncture became the English agent of Massachusetts Bay, proved the ideal organizer. Gathering a group of sixteen charitably disposed men, he obtained from the Rump Parliament in 1649 a charter, as 'The Society for the Promoting and Propagating the Gospel of Jesus Christ in New England.' It was a corporation resident in London, and the act provided that the Commissioners of the United Colonies of New England — the Confederation — should have the disbursal of such funds as the Society might send over. Every parish minister in England and Wales was required to read the act of incorporation from his pulpit, and to make a house-to-house canvass for the heathen in New England. The proceeds from this drive showed that the Wilson-Shepard-Eliot advertising campaign had completely broken down English sales-resistance. Propagating the Gospel in New England went over big. Although the country was just recovering from civil war, the Corporation in four years raked in £511 from the Army, £961 from the London parishes, as high as £436 from individual counties, and £861 from individuals. In 1654, £7625 more flowed in. At that point receipts began to fall off, and the Corporation wisely invested the larger part of its receipts in landed property, to provide for the future. In ten years £4673 were transmitted to New England.

It was upon this English corporation that Eliot in the Bay, Mayhew at the Vineyard, and James Fitch in Connecticut, depended for the support of their work of conversion. If collections ever were taken up for the Indians in the New England churches, they yielded only pence for the English pounds. Eliot's policy of introducing civility and Christianity hand in hand, was an expensive one; it required, as he wrote to Hugh Peter, 'a Magazine of all sorts of edge tools, and instruments of husbandry, for cloathing, etc.,' salaries for native teachers and missionaries; in a word, the apparatus of civilization, as well as the means of conversion.

It did not do, from the puritan point of view, to catch your Indian and baptize him and then turn him loose, with an occasional round-up for exhortation and prayer. From the way the ancient Hebrews used to break out into idolatry, the puritans were convinced that a nomadic state was incompatible with good morals. Eliot wished to have his converts prosperous and self-respecting. Cleanliness he did not unduly insist upon, but one-family lodges he did require; and his converts were not only deprived of the pleasure of scalping their enemies, but were urged to give up their mutual and friendly offices on that part of their anatomy. Nor did Eliot seek to cover the bronzed, athletic bodies of the red men with the cast-off clothing of his parish, indeed he is said to have adopted the Indian undress himself in his wilderness visitations; but a settled life for the Indians meant a loss both of aptitude and opportunity to procure fur garments. Eliot tried without much success to teach the squaws to spin and weave, and he had to call on his English supporters for blankets, cloth, and clothing. Those who have laughed at the picture of Mrs. Jellyby, making red flannel undies for the natives of Borrioboola-Gha, may smile if they will at Lady Armine and her kind, providing the integumentary emblems of civilization for the worthy red men of Hassanamisco, Wabsquasset, and Titicut.

The General Court in 1651 set off for the first praying Indian town the plantation of Natick; a 'place of God's providing' Eliot called it, 'as a fruit of prayer.' It was about eighteen miles by bridle path from Roxbury, and five or six miles from the nearest settlement. Eliot took full charge of the foundation. A village was laid out on both sides of the Charles, connected by a footbridge which withstood the spring floods when others built by white men were carried away. In the center was a palisaded square containing the meeting-house, fifty foot by twenty-five, as neatly framed and boarded as if built by English carpenters, and containing a prophet's chamber for the Apostle when he came to preach, as he did fortnightly. In the village each family had a house-lot and a share in the common cornfield and meadows. The praying Indians did not, however, take to frame houses. Their lodges or 'long houses' of poles and withes, roofed with bark or rush mats, were sufficiently warm and neat.

Having settled Natick, John Eliot found an opportunity to carry out a little experiment in pure theocracy which he had in mind. 'The only Magna Carta in the world is in the holy Scriptures,' he wrote Hugh Peter. 'Oh! what an opportunity the Parliament hath now to bring in Christ to rule in England.' If Parliament let the opportunity slip, Natick would not be denied the holy experiment. So at Eliot's suggestion, the Indians adopted a theocratic compact for their town, to the effect that the Lord was their judge, lawgiver and king; and his work would be their only guide.

For a frame of government, the eighteenth chapter of Exodus pointed the way; and under Eliot's direction the Indians elected rulers of tens and of fifties, each choosing the tithing man whom he would obey. This done, the Apostle advised a day of fasting and prayer, as atonement for their sins, which had been visibly rebuked by the shipwreck of a supply ship at Cohasset. Kutshamakin, who had been drunk again, took this to heart; and on the fast day, to the apostle's intense gratification, made a humble confession. One Indian brother expounded Luke VII, another read Matthew VII with suitable comments, and Eliot delivered a sermon. Then came a much-needed pause for refreshment, at which some bold convert inquired whether it were lawful to take a pipe of tobacco, to which Eliot gave his consent; for although he deemed tobacco-taking a sin, he was too tactful to try prohibition on the Indians. Fortified by nicotine the company returned to their devotions, and as the sun went down Eliot concluded the second sermon of what he always referred to as 'that blessed Day.' A full account of it, together with the personal religious experiences of the Indians who joined the church, was written up for the edification of the charitable in England.

Whether the Indians became imbued with the true theocratic spirit may well be doubted. A new tithing man is said to have asked the aged Waban for advice what to do when Indians got drunk and quarrelled, to which that noted convert replied: 'Hah! tie um all up, and whip um plaintiff, whip um 'fendant, whip um witness!' But Eliot was so well pleased with the results that he proposed to extend the benefits to the whole world. His little contribution to political theory, 'The Christian Commonwealth,' presents a logical, uncompromising theocracy. As there is only one Faith, one Word and one Truth, so there is only one Government authorized by Scripture, and one lawful sovereign, Christ. All principles of political science were laid down by God long ago, and recorded in the Bible. There is no need for legislature, judiciary, or temporal king. Starting with the scheme of Exodus xviii, let rulers be chosen of tens, fifties, hundreds and thousands; and these rulers send delegates to an ascending series of decimal councils, culminating in the supreme council of the nation. A scheme at once so simple and so scriptural would have made its mark on New England in the 1630's, although even Cotton would have gagged at so raw a theocracy; but theocracy had been routed by representative government and the Body of Lawes. The Christian Commonwealth was obsolete in 1649, when Eliot wrote it, and somewhat scandalous in 1660, when it appeared in print.

A pamphlet so 'justly offencive... to kingly government in England' could not be ignored by the General Court of a colony under suspicion of republicanism. So The Christian Commonwealth was officially censured, and all copies ordered to be handed in to the magistrates and destroyed. John Eliot, with becoming humility, signed a recantation. He could not allow pride of authorship to interfere with the success of his main work.

Eliot had originally intended to gather all the converts at Natick, but as their numbers increased, he saw that Natick would be too small to hold them all, and decided on a series of Indian towns. Punkapog in the present town of Canton, settled by the Cohannet Indians from the Taunton River, was the second praying Indian town. Natick, however, always remained the Apostle's favorite. For several years he conducted a sort of summer school there, 'setting up a lecture among them in logick and theology once every fortnight.' No doubt by this time Eliot had sufficiently grasped the limitations of the savage mind, and was able to convey to his pupils all that they could assimilate of Aristotle, Burgerdicius, and the *Medulla Theologiae*. It was certainly a much more successful school than the Indian College at Harvard, erected at great expense by the Society with the long name as a residential college for such Indian youth as were fitted to take the higher degrees. Few of them proved so fitted. Some became discouraged and ran away; others, including Eleazar (class of 1679), who stayed long enough to write Latin and Greek poetry, did not graduate; Joel Hiacoomes (class of 1665), on his last college vacation was murdered by his pagan fellows at Nantucket; his classmate Caleb Cheeshateaumuck *Indus*, as he is called in the Latin catalogues, took his bachelor's degree, but died of tuberculosis shortly after. Natick, however, proved a true seminary for native teachers and pastors.

Although several ministers of the Bay Colony learned the

Massachusetts dialect and preached to the Indians near their respective towns, Eliot's principal colleague in the work of civilizing and converting was a layman named Daniel Gookin, first fruit of a New England puritan mission to Virginia. When the puritans were driven out of Virginia, Gookin came to Massachusetts Bay. He settled in Cambridge, and became prominent in the affairs both military and political of town and colony. On the Apostle's recommendation he was appointed in 1656 the first Superintendent of the Praying Indians, with magisterial powers. It fell to him to appoint petty magistrates from among the Indians, to watch over their local government, to protect them and the whites from each other, and to help youths of promise to become teachers or preachers to their people. Gookin was a man of great energy and keen intelligence. His 'Historical Collections of the Indians in New England,' written in 1674, is a good, straightforward description of the Eliot system, devoid of that evangelistic whine which becomes so tedious in missionary literature.

In 1674, according to Gookin, there were seven 'old praying Indian towns' in the Bay jurisdiction. The most interesting after Natick was Wamesit, 'where Concord river falleth into Merrimack,' the site of Lowell. Only fifteen families lived there permanently with a native teacher Samuel; but the fishing was so good as to attract a great concourse of Indians every spring, including divers 'vicious and wicked men and women: which Satan makes use of to obstruct the prosperity of religion.' As the Wamesit Indians owned horses, Gookin tried to persuade them to establish a pony fish-express to Boston in the salmon season; but when the fishing was good, they could not be bothered; and when the fishing was poor, it was not worth their while to go. Gookin and Eliot visited them at the height of the salmon run every May, the former to hold court and the latter to fish for souls. For many years the Apostle had been casting for Wannalancet, a fine upstanding Indian chief and eldest son of Passaconaway; and in 1674 he had the satisfaction of landing him. Wannalancet, so he said, left the old canoe in which he had been content to pass the river all his days, and entered a new canoe, which he hoped would carry him across the river of life.

Another prosperous praying Indian town was Nashobah, a plantation four miles square near Nagog pond, between Acton and Littleton. The Indians there planted orchards and made cider 'which some of them have not the wisdom and grace to use for their comfort, but are prone to abuse unto drunkenness,' says Gookin. The Superintendent confesses that he cannot reach that vice common to red men and white. 'For if it were possible, as it is not, to prevent the English selling them strong drink; yet they having a native liberty to plant orchards and sow grain, as barley and the like, of which they may and do make strong drink that doth inebriate them: so that nothing can overcome and conquer this exorbitancy, but the sovereign grace of God in Christ.' Poor benighted Gookin! Prohibition never occurred to him.

Beside the seven 'old praying Indian towns' of Massachusetts Bay, Gookin and Eliot organized in 1673–75 seven new praying Indian towns in the Nipmuc country, in what is now Worcester County. Superintendent and Apostle made the circuit of these villages in 1674, holding court and preaching; they had the great satisfaction of confirming as teacher at Wabsquasset one Sampson, 'an active and ingenious person,' but a notorious bad actor hitherto. There was much rejoicing over the washing of this black sheep whiter than snow. Gookin estimated that in the Massachusetts Colony, in 1674, there were eleven hundred 'souls yielding obedience to the Gospel,' not counting the praying Indians of Plymouth Colony [1] who amounted to several

---

[1] One of these Indian churches may be said to be still in existence: that of Mashpee on Cape Cod, where the descendants of the Mashpee Indians still live, and maintain their Congregational church. This church was formed in 1670, Richard Bourne of Sandwich being ordained pastor by John Eliot and John Cotton of Plymouth.

hundred more, or the Christian Indians on Martha's Vineyard and Nantucket, who were converted and cared for by Thomas Mayhew.

Weighed as to quantity, the number of converts was not large, and apparently it cost the Society in London an average of £10 per soul. The Catholic missionaries in Canada saved souls much more cheaply, and on a larger scale. If communicants alone were counted, Eliot's achievement would seem almost negligible, for the puritan standards were too rigorous for the Indians; and the attitude of Eliot's colleagues, who were apt to regard the Indian churches as comic or blasphemous parodies of their own, prevented him from tempering the wind to the shorn lamb.

One cannot read of these sincere and long-continued efforts without wondering how much of the puritan's faith the Indians received, and what good came of it all. The answer will depend less on ascertainable facts, than upon one's personal attitude toward religion. From a cynical point of view, perhaps Eliot did nothing more than to ease the passing of a doomed race. Indian converts could have grasped none of the intellectual subtleties of puritanism; but those were but frills of a doctrine which went back to the fount and origin of Christianity, which taught repentance, prayer and fellowship with Christ as the first duty and privilege of the Christian. If the mental attitude of prayer is worth anything, Eliot performed a great and a noble work; for he was of all things a man of prayer, and prayer was the beginning and the ending of all that he taught and did.

Eliot had one opportunity to compare notes with a Catholic missionary. This was none other than that Jesuit father Gabriel Druillette who scored what Parkman calls 'the most remarkable success in the whole body of Jesuit Relations': a prayer from his Indian converts to forgive their enemies, the Iroquois. It was in order to obtain an alliance against these same Iroquois that the good father came to

New England in 1650. He has left an account of his experiences, most valuable as one of the few outsiders' views we have of seventeenth century New England. He found the puritans an ordinary kindly sort of people, courteous and hospitable, serving him a fish dinner on Friday and giving him privacy for his devotions. Father Druillette, too, was of the seventeenth century; and despite the fact that he was a Catholic and a Frenchman, and his hosts were puritan Protestants and Englishmen, he and they had much more in common as contemporaries and fellow Americans, than they and we.

It was on December 28, 1650, Druillette tells us, that on his way back from Plymouth to Boston, 'J'arrivay à Rosqbray ou le ministre nommé Maistre Heliot, qui enseignoit quelcques sauvages me reçust chez lui à cause que la nuict me surprenoit, et me traita avec respect et affection; me pria de passer l'iver avec luy.' But he only passed a night. What would we not give to know more of that meeting and that conversation! They must have conversed in Latin, since Druillette knew only a word or two of English, and Eliot's only modern language was Indian. And why did Eliot invite his Catholic guest to spend the winter? Did he want a papist whetstone on which to sharpen his puritan axe? Or to pick up hints on missionary methods? Or did he simply recognize in the Jesuit a Christian and a cultured gentleman, whom he would spare the discomfort of a winter journey to Canada? From what we know of Eliot, the latter reason is the more probable. And I like to think that those two saints, as they looked into each other's eyes and fumbled for college Latin in which to express their thoughts, felt their brotherhood more than their differences; that each recognized in the other a true disciple of his Master.

The puritan missionary, like the Catholic, was financially supported almost entirely from his mother country. Gookin and Eliot both had an annual salary from the Society, paid through the Commissioners of the Confederation, who also supported Thomas Mayhew on the Vineyard, and paid small sums to the native preachers and teachers. A few other New England ministers learned the Indian tongue and preached to near-by natives; they too obtained an occasional honorarium. Eliot never knew where his salary went, and he was always asking for more — a constant source of irritation to the solid burghers of London who conducted the affairs of the Society with the long name. For Eliot did not preach a 'cautious statistical Christ.' Of all men he was the most impulsively charitable and unbusinesslike. Money burned in his pocket, and so much of his salary used to vanish between date of payment and the time his good wife could lay hands on it, that on one occasion the Roxbury deacons handed it to him in a handkerchief, tied up in several hard knots. On the way home, Eliot stopped to call upon a family who were poor and sick. He comforted them with the news that the Lord had sent them relief by him. He pulled at the knots of the handkerchief, but they would not come undone; so he gave the whole to the mother saying, 'Here, my dear, take it! I believe the Lord designs it all for you.' Indeed Eliot used up so much money in his work, continually doling out a bit here to Indian converts and a bit there to native teachers, buying on the spur of the moment tools and implements and anything they happened to need — things impossible for him to remember when the moment was past — that the Society and its contributors began to ask awkward questions. Was Eliot setting up a luxurious establishment at Roxbury? Were his sons going through Harvard College on what should have gone to the Indians?

They did not know how abstemiously the Apostle lived. As Cotton Mather describes it:

Rich varieties, costly viands, and poinant sauces, came not upon his own table, and when he found them on other mens, he rarely tasted of them. One dish, and a plain one, was his dinner; and when invited unto a feast, I have seen him sit magnifying of God, for the plenty which his people in this wilderness were within a few years arisen to; but not more than a bit or two of all the dainties taken into his own mouth all the while. The drink which he still used was very *small*; he cared not for wines or drams,... good, clear water was more precious, as well as more usual with him... When at a stranger's house in the summer time, he has been entertained with a glass which they told him was of water and wine, he has with a complaisant gravity reply'd unto this purpose: 'Wine, 'tis a noble generous Liquor, and we should be humbly thankful for it; but as I remember, Water was made before it!'... When he thought the countenance of a minister look'd as if he had made much of himself, he has gone to him with this speech: 'Study Mortification, brother; study Mortification!'

After all, the relations between Eliot and the Corporation were much more sympathetic than those between Eliot and the Commissioners of the United Colonies of New England. For many years his correspondence with them is studded with his demands for a raise of salary, their requests for an accounting, and his evasion of that unwelcome and impossible task. Practical men and magistrates as the Commissioners were — men like Haynes and Hopkins and Hathorne and Bradstreet — they felt that the reputation of New England with the old-country puritans depended on the fidelity with which they administered the Corporation's funds. Still they knew that there was only one Eliot. In the strongest of their many letters, the Commissioners informed the Apostle that if he chose 'to rest satisfied with a smaller allowance from us out of the Corporation stocke,' rather than give an account of what he received from private donors, he might; and they conceived that his Roxbury salary of £60, plus £20 from Mr. Rawson and the same from Lady Armine, 'might prove comfortable and satisfying.' They fear lest his 'carriage herein may be thought not only irregular but turbulent and clamorous which crosseth the meekness of wisdom wherein we believe you desire to follow our lord and master.'

Eliot knew only that he was worse off at the end of every year. If the Corporation would not support the work, his friends might, and they might also stir up the Corporation to greater efforts. To Richard Baxter, author of 'The Everlasting Saints' Rest,' he writes: 'My request to you is, that you would please stir up the honorable Corporation to it. Here is means sufficient, as I suppose.' Ample means there were indeed; but the Corporation preferred to invest them rather than spend them. What Nipmuc was denied in 1650 will be reaped by Chinook in 1950, if any there be. To another friend Eliot writes to collect all the money and materials he can and send it along — but for goodness' sake don't tell the Honorable Corporation! A touch of slyness in this simple character, if you will; but it was the slyness of the child who asks his grandmother for what his parents deny.

This indirect pressure had its effect. In 1656 the salaries of Eliot and Mayhew were raised to £50 per annum. Eliot now became a trifle more accommodating, and acknowledged having received a parcel of goods valued at £11 from private sources.

This acknowledgment made such a favorable impression on the Corporation that when Eliot proposed a great and expensive work, the printing of the Bible in the Indian language, they did not demur. But before the Bible was well under way, Charles II had come into his own again. By his theory that all proceedings of the Long Parliament were null and void, the Corporation with the long name died an unnatural death. It was a critical moment for Eliot's work; but Richard Baxter was equal to the emergency. Calling the members of the ex-corporation together, he persuaded the more prominent Republicans to retire, and induced Robert Boyle, the noted chemist and son of the Great Earl of Cork, to step in as President. Then, using his influence with the Earl of Clarendon, Baxter had the Corporation rechartered under an even longer name. This second 'Society or Company for the Propagation of the Gospel in New England and the parts adjacent' still exists. The last four words enabled it after the War of Independence to divert its funds from the disloyal and well gospelized province of New England, to New Brunswick; and finally, when all Indians in parts adjacent had been converted, to parts exjacent, such as British Columbia.

By the time the Corporation was collecting comfortable rents from its restored real estate, John Eliot was so involved in establishing new praying Indian towns, in sending out native missionaries, and in publishing Indian books, that his salary of £50 was no longer sufficient, and he was £80 in debt.

'My humble request is,' he writes the treasurer of the Corporation, 'that it shall be paid, and then I shall be out of debt; but if it should be refused, then my hands are tied, I can do little; yet I am resolved through the grace of Christ, I will never give over the work so long as I have legs to go.... And when these debts are paid it will not be long ere I shall run into debt again; but God knowth what shall be, and not man.'

John Eliot never had to complain of the support given to him by the Corporation in his literary labors, which were many and prolonged. The number of things that he did, and did well, is astonishing. During many years he had no assistant in the ministry at Roxbury, yet no one complained that he slighted his pastoral duties. He was a member of the Honorable and Reverend the Board of Overseers of Harvard College, and attended their meetings regularly. Every fortnight in midweek he visited Natick, riding the eighteen miles on horseback — and a stout horse it must have been to carry the donations as well as himself. Alternate weeks he visited some other Indian village, and in between he translated the Bible and wrote his other works in the Indian language.

No Protestant missionary could feel that his labors were successful until his converts could read the Bible, and had copies of it placed in their hands. Yet no Christian missionary since Ulfilas, had translated the sacred scriptures into a barbarous unwritten language, and taught the people to read it. One would suppose that it would have been easier to teach the Massachusetts Indians to read the English Bible than to translate it into their tongue; but Eliot had begun his labors with the doctrine that God spoke Indian as well as English, and on that line he continued.

Eliot appears to have begun his translation of the Bible as early as 1650, and it was a labor of years. For the Algonkian language had never before been written. It was a simple tongue, unfit to express abstract ideas. Many of the consonants and vowel sounds were strange to English ears, and needed definition. Eliot, for instance, uses *aukooks* and *ohkukes* for the same word, meaning a kettle; just as the early missionaries to the South Seas found it difficult to decide between k and t, r and l. He had no assistance in the work of translation. Eliot's method appears to have been to try out words and phrases on Job Nesutan and other converts until he had hit upon something which appeared to convey to the Indians something akin to what Eliot thought to be the meaning of the original Hebrew or Greek. Of course the work had to be done on the Cambridge press — the only press in the English colonies until 1674 — so that Eliot could superintend the typesetting and read the proofs.

At the same time he had to teach the Indians to read. So the first work that he composed and printed was a primer (1654) now known only by a unique copy of the third edition of 1669. It is a tiny book of 64 pages, called 'The Indian Primer, or The way of training up of our Indian Youth in the good knowledge of God, in the knowledge of the Scriptures, and in an ability to Reade. Composed by J. E.' The first reading lesson gives us a clue to the Eliot method of in-

struction.   It states, in Indian, 'Wise doing to read Catechism.   First Read Primer.   Next read "Repentance Calling."   Then read Bible.'

Not a single copy is known of the next four imprints of the
Indian library.   Eliot states that Genesis was put through
the press in 1655, as a sort of trial balloon; but all copies of
that have disappeared.

In 1658, Eliot writes to the Corporation that his translation of the entire Bible is complete.   They had not yet committed themselves to the expense of printing it; but as puritans they could not resist the logic that without the Bible,
propagation of the Gospel would be a mere fraud.   Eliot
wrote hopefully, asking them to send out 'some honest young
man who hath skill to compose' to help the college printer
put the Bible through the press, and 'a convenient stock of
paper to begin withall.'   Governor Endecott and the Commissioners added their entreaties to his; and the Governor
added to his letter: 'Mr. Eliot will be ready at all times to
correct the sheets as fast as they are Printed, and desireth
nothing for his paines.'   By the summer of 1660 an honest
young man named Marmaduke Johnson had been secured,
apparently because a voyage to New England was his only
means of escaping from an intolerable wife.   The stock of
paper came withal, but it proved to be a job lot, and had to
be replaced by another.   Enough brevier type was imported
to set up at the same time four pages of the Old Testament
and four of the New; and in 1660 the actual printing began
on the little hand press, housed in the Indian College at
Cambridge, somewhere in the Harvard Yard.   One thousand
copies of eight pages of St. Matthew were printed by Samuel Green, the college printer, with the aid of James Printer,
an Indian pupil from the praying town of Hassanamisco.
Then Marmaduke Johnson arrived with the news that the
Corporation wanted an edition of fifteen hundred copies; so
these pages had to be set up over again.   The work proceeded

at the rate of one sheet of eight pages a week. Delay was threatened at one time, because Marmaduke Johnson, having just asked one of his partner's daughters to marry him, was discovered to have a wife in London. Samuel Green had Marmaduke haled before the court, but the authorities decided that Marmaduke's morals should not be allowed to interfere with the great work, and it went on.

First, and within a year, the New Testament was done. Forty presentation copies were sent over to England, and two hundred were at once bound up for distribution to the Indians. There was no separate edition of the Old Testament; but the entire Bible of twelve hundred printed pages was ready in 1663. It was dedicated to Charles II, to whom a copy was presented by Robert Boyle. Unfortunately, diplomatic business interrupted the interview, so we shall never know what the Merry Monarch thought of the first Bible printed in his overseas dominions, or in the New World.

Typographically, the Indian Bible is a credit to the Cambridge press. The workmanship is good; there is none of the cheap and hasty appearance of much missionary literature. The title pages show an artistic appreciation of the use of type, and of simple ornament. As to the quality of the translation, doubt has been expressed ever since Eliot's day as to whether his language could be understood by those for whom it was intended. One even meets with the absurd statement that by the time the Bible was printed, all the Indians who understood the Massachusetts dialect were dead. J. Hammond Trumbull, a great scholar in the Indian languages, declared that Eliot's translation 'was probably as good as any *first* version that has been made, from his time to ours, in a previously unwritten and so-called barbarous language. It is certainly much better than some modern specimens of mission-translation.' Professor Frank G. Speck of Pennsylvania, the leading authority on Algonkian, assures me that the dialect used by Eliot was understood by the Indians throughout central and eastern Massachusetts, in the Plymouth Colony, and on Nantucket and Martha's Vineyard. Naturally errors were made in translating words or ideas for which there was no near Indian equivalent. Throughout the Bible, wherever the word 'virgin' occurs, Eliot uses an Indian word that means 'a chaste young man.' That was because chastity was accounted by the Indians a masculine virtue. They had a word for virgin, but seldom any occasion to use it. No doubt it seemed much more suitable to the Indians to have the bridegroom met by ten 'chaste young men.'

The second edition was carefully revised by Master John Cotton of Plymouth, who knew the language even better than Eliot. Cotton Mather, who never got the hang of the Massachusetts language himself, reported that 'many words of Mr. Eliot's forming' were unintelligible to the natives; but there are in existence several copies of this second edition which actually belonged to Indians, and bear witness by marginal notes in their language, and the worn edges and the soiled pages, of the use to which they were put. This edition appears to have been used largely in the Old Colony and on Martha's Vineyard, where the Gay Head Indians held services in their own language until the close of the eighteenth century, and where some of the ancients were still reading their Eliot Bibles a hundred years ago. So it may be said that 'Mamusse wanneetupanatamme up-biblum God' was in practical daily use for over a century.

The decade after the Bible appeared was Eliot's harvest. One Indian book followed another off the Cambridge press. Robert Boyle and the Corporation with the long name were proud of his work, and no longer troublesome about what he did with their money. The number of converts increased. The public was reconciled to his policy. And then came the tragedy that swept away almost everything he had accomplished.

King Philip's War, most devastating for Massachusetts of

all the many wars she has survived, was started and pro-
secuted by pagan Indians who had absolutely refused to
allow missionaries into their dominions. Although a number
of the recent converts in the Nipmuc country fell away, those
of the 'old praying Indian towns' were loyal almost to a
man. These seven towns, situated in an arc from the Merrimac to the Connecticut line, formed a natural first line of defense for the English. Daniel Gookin wished to use them as
such. He begged the Court to send a small file of soldiers to
each praying town to keep up its morale and organize the
men for scouting. But the Court would not listen. A war-
time frenzy broke out against the 'enemy in our midst,' of
the same sort that prevailed here a few years ago. Nothing
would satisfy the people but to intern the praying Indians in
Boston Harbor. Even Eliot's ewe-lambs of Natick were deported, 'patiently, humbly and piously without murmuring
or complaining against the English.' Three forlorn winters
they spent on Deer Island, living largely on shellfish, and more
than once threatened with extermination by the meaner sort
of Bostonians, patriots too cowardly to fight at the front, but
ready to fall on the helpless within their power. Daniel
Gookin, as a 'pro-Indian,' had his life threatened more than
once; and when he and Eliot were sailing down harbor on a
mission of mercy, their boat was deliberately run down, and
with difficulty they were saved by their companions. 'Some
thanked God, and some wished that we had been drowned,'
wrote Eliot. 'Soon after, one that wished we had been
drowned, was himself drowned about the same place.' That
incident, one gathers, afforded Eliot the only pleasure he got
out of the war, although he lost 'a good castor hat worth ten
shillings.'

There is on record a noble protest of the Apostle against
the selling of war captives into slavery:

The terror of selling away such Indians unto the Islands for perpetual slaves, who shall yield up themselves to your mercy, is like

to be an efectual prolongation of the warre... This useage of them is worse than death. The designe of Christ in these last dayes, is not to extirpate nations, but to gospelize them. When we came, we declared to the world, and it is recorded, yea we are ingaged by our letters Patent from the King's Majesty, that the indeavor of the Indians conversion, not their exstirpation, was one great end of our enterprize in coming to these ends of the earth... To sell soules for money seemeth to me a dangerous merchandize.

His protest was in vain. Ten years later we find him writing Robert Boyle, begging him to look up some Indian captives who had been dumped at Tangier by a slave-trader, and to procure their return to America.

A considerable number of the praying Indians were employed as scouts and auxiliaries, especially toward the end of the war, when they had proved their loyalty. King Philip was killed by such an one. Gookin believed that these allies turned 'the balance to the English side, so that the enemy went down the wind amain.' It is very probable that but for the previous work of Eliot, Mayhew, and Gookin, Massachusetts Bay as an English colony would have been exterminated.

By the end of the war, the numbers of praying Indians had been greatly reduced. Many died of sickness at Deer Island, others were lost to the church by service in the army. Most of the Indian Bibles had been lost. At the age of seventy-four, Eliot had to begin all over again. At his earnest request, the New England Confederation authorized him to print a second edition of the Indian Bible, and the Corporation provided the funds. The second edition of the New Testament came out in 1680, and the whole Bible in 1685.

In the summer of 1680, while the printing was under way, we have a pleasant picture of Eliot from the pen of two Dutchmen, Dankaerts and Sluyter, who passed through Boston on their way home to Holland. Desiring an Indian Bible, and finding it unobtainable at the Boston booksellers, they visited Roxbury to see if one could be had of Master Eliot, the translator.

On arriving at his house, he was not there, and we, therefore, went to look around the village, and the vicinity. We found it justly called *Rocksbury*, for it was very rocky, and had hills entirely of rocks. Returning to his house we spoke to him, and he received us politely. Although he could speak neither Dutch nor French, and we spoke but little English, and were unable to express ourselves in it always, we managed, by means of Latin and English, to understand each other. He was seventy-seven years old, and had been forty-eight years in these parts. He had learned very well the language of the Indians, who lived about there. We asked him for an Indian Bible. He said in the late Indian war, all the Bibles and Testaments were carried away, and burnt or destroyed, so that he had not been able to save any for himself; but a new edition was in press, which he hoped would be much better than the first one, though that was not to be despised. We inquired whether any part of the old or new edition could be obtained by purchase, and whether there was any grammar of that language in English. Thereupon he went and brought us the Old Testament, and also the New Testament, made up with some sheets of the new edition, so that we had the Old and New Testaments complete. He also brought us two or three small specimens of the grammar. We asked him what we should pay him for them; but he desired nothing.

The rather hybrid copy that they thus obtained, reposes in the library of the Zealand Academy of Sciences, at Middleburg in the Netherlands. It contains an inscription by Dankaerts, describing as above his meeting with the 'good old man, Mr. Hailot,' who 'out of special zeal and love gave me this copy.'

'Our Indian work yet liveth, praised be God,' Eliot writes to Robert Boyle in 1686. 'The Bible is come forth, many hundreds bound up, and dispersed to the Indians, whose thankfulness I intimate and testify to your honour.' Two thousand copies were printed of this edition, at a cost of £460. It became better known than the first, Pope Clement XI even taking the wholly unnecessary precaution to order the Archbishop of Saragossa to prevent its introduction among the Indians of Spanish America.

Two years after the second edition appeared, good Mistress Eliot died at the ripe age of eighty-six. Four of their sons had died, and John Eliot prayed that he might join them soon. He used to remark whimsically that good Master Mather and Master Cotton would suspect him to have gone the wrong way, he stayed so long behind them. During the long drawn out difficulties between the Colony and the later Stuart kings, men said to one another that Massachusetts Bay would not perish while Eliot lived; but he survived the charter government, living into the rule of Governor Andros and the Dominion of New England; living even to see the Dominion fall, and Governor Bradstreet, his only fellow survivor of the first generation, once more seated in the governor's place.

To the last, Eliot was a worker. When he became too feeble to preach to the Indians, or even to perform his pastoral duties, he induced people to send him their Negroes for religious instruction. Finally in 1690 came the illness that promised release. Neighbors and friends crowded into the little low-studded parsonage to catch their pastor's last words and final blessing. A young minister officiously prayed that the Apostle might yet be spared. Eliot gently rebuked him: 'Pray return to thy study for me, and give me leave to be gone.' Silence, and then a final confession:

'There is a dark cloud upon the work of the Gospel among the poor Indians. The Lord revive and prosper that work, and grant it may live when I am dead. It is a work which I have been doing much and long about... Alas, they have been poor and small and lean doings, and I'll be the man that shall throw the first stone at them all.'

'Welcome, Joy!'

'Pray... pray... pray...'

CHAPTER XI
MISTRESS ANNE BRADSTREET

JUST as their rejection of religious symbolism closed for the puritans many opportunities for pictorial, plastic, and musical art, so their dismissal of the drama as 'the Devil's chappell' cut them off from one great branch of literature. But they could not have been hostile to literature as such, or they would not have made so many efforts to write poetry. Had they regarded art as a 'waste of precious time,' New England puritan divines like Danforth, John Wilson, Benjamin Tompson, Urian Oakes, and Michael Wigglesworth, would not have spent so much of that precious commodity in sweating out verse, when less ambitious prose would have expressed their thoughts fully as adequately, and with more economy. It is true that their verse seldom attains the dignity of poetry, and much of what we have already quoted was little more than patter, interesting only for historical reasons. Nor did they write poetry for poetry's sake. Their very definite motive was to edify or instruct. They regarded poetry as a handmaid to divinity; and under such conditions of servitude it takes the genius of a Milton, a Herbert, or a Donne, to attain beauty and enduring dignity in verse.

Yet there was one person in early Massachusetts who wrote poetry for poetry's sake, or merely to express her own thoughts and aspirations, with no hope or expectation of an audience beyond her family and friends. This 'Tenth Muse lately sprung up in America,' 'a Gentlewoman in those parts,' as she is called on the title-page of her first book of poems, was Mistress Anne Bradstreet, wife to a magistrate of the Bay, and daughter to Governor Dudley.

Born in England in 1612, Anne Dudley was brought up in

comparative luxury at Tattershall Castle, where her father was the Earl of Lincoln's steward, or what we should now call business manager. Anne Dudley had the usual religious experiences of the more sensitive children in puritan families. At fourteen or fifteen 'I found the follyes of youth take hold of me,' she writes; but at the age of sixteen she married Simon Bradstreet, 'in whose loving and grave companionship she passed the remainder of her life.' He was the son of a non-conformist minister, a recent student of Emmanuel College, and successor to Dudley's stewardship. In 1630, two years a wife, she accompanied her husband and father to Massachusetts Bay in the *Arbella*.

In an autobiographic fragment Anne declares, 'I changed my condition and was marryed, and came into this country, where I found a new world and new manners, at which my heart rose. But after I was convinced it was the way of God, I submitted to it and joined to the church at Boston.'

A new world and new manners, at which her heart rose.

That little sentence throws a shaft of light into the dark, yet unwritten history of the American pioneer woman. The story of the settling of America has been told largely in the terms of men — of Giants in the Earth for whom the old world was too cramped, who found release and creative joy in building houses, stocking farms, erecting towns and com-monwealths, and running church and state, taking a man's place in a man's world. But it was a brutal life for the things that women love, the tender heirlooms of the soul. Rölvaag has revealed to us the tragedy of a Norwegian peasant woman in the West loathing the crude frontier life where nothing was settled, nothing in its proper place; distraught by the breach with ancient ways and standards of ordered living. How much more hard it must have been in the New England wilderness for puritan women of gentle nurture, accustomed to a settled town or a well-groomed countryside, to the impalpable ameni-ties of life which reach through even to the poor in a country settled and civilized six hundred years! Anne Bradstreet was not the only woman, we may feel sure, who felt her heart sink when first she looked on the shores of Massachusetts Bay, and made her home in a raw village, where everything must be provided by hard labor, and where the forest full of wild beasts and skulking Indians, impinged like a threatening dagger. It unsettled everything: made men stern and silent, children unruly, servants insolent. Governor Bradford in his great ninth chapter has recorded in stately prose the feelings of the stout-hearted Pilgrims when they found the mighty ocean behind them, and the wilderness before. Anne Hutchinson, a stouter-hearted woman than Anne Bradstreet, 'when she came within sight of Boston and looking on the meanness of the place... uttered these words, if she had not a sure word that England would be destroyed, her heart would shake.' The man who reported those words said it seemed to him 'very strange that she should say so' — of course a man would! Hawthorne inferred that the horror of wilderness life brought the Lady Arbella Johnson to an early grave; and I suspect some such thing behind the silence of Governor Bradford on the death of his young wife Dorothy, drowned from the *Mayflower* in Provincetown Harbor, after gazing for weeks on the desolate sand dunes of Cape Cod.

Anne Bradstreet did not enjoy the physique proper to a pioneer woman. Delicate as a child, she 'fell into a lingering sicknes like a consumption, together with a lamenesse' not long after arriving in Massachusetts. She was eight times in peril of childbirth, and often laid low by fits of weakness, pain, and fainting, for which the physicians of that time were unable to do anything. Nor did she have a continual and absolutely trusting faith in the God of the puritans to keep her up. There were times when she doubted whether there were such a Triune God as she worshipped, or such a Saviour as she relied upon. And when she had 'gott over this block,' other doubts flew up to vex her: 'Admitt this bee the true

SIMON BRADSTREET

God whom wee worship, and that bee his word, yet why may not the Popish Religion bee the right? They have the same God, the same Christ the same word: they only enterprett it one way, wee another.' As I turn the pages of Anne Bradstreet's poems, and try to project myself into her life and time, I catch the merest hint of that elfin, almost *gamin* attitude of Emily Dickinson to God. Even Emily in the nineteenth century would so express herself only to her dearest friends. Anne, in the seventeenth century, would hardly have dared admit as much even to herself. Her mature poem on 'The Flesh and the Spirit' is one of the best expressions in English literature of the conflict described by St. Paul in the eighth chapter of his Epistle to the Romans. It has a dramatic quality which can only have come of personal experience:

> In secret place where once I stood,
> Close by the Banks of *Lacrim* flood,
> I heard two sisters reason on
> Things that are past and things to come.
> One Flesh was called, who had her eye
> On worldly wealth and vanity;
> The other Spirit, who did rear
> Her thoughts unto a higher sphere.
> Sister, quoth Flesh, what livest thou on —
> Nothing but Meditation?
> Doth Contemplation feed thee, so
> Regardlessly to let earth go?
> Can Speculation satisfy
> Notion without Reality?
> Dost dream of things beyond the Moon,
> And dost thou hope to dwell there soon?
> Hast treasures there laid up in store
> That all in the world thou countest poor?
> Art fancy sick, or turned a Sot,
> To catch at shadows which are not?
> Come, come, I'll show unto thy sense
> Industry hath its recompense.
> What canst desire but thou mayst see
> True substance in variety?
> Dost honor like? acquire the same,
> As some to their immortal fame,

And trophies to thy name erect
Which wearing time shall ne'er deject.
For riches dost thou long full sore?
Behold enough of precious store;
Earth hath more silver, pearls, and gold
Than eyes can see or hands can hold.
Affect'st thou pleasure? take thy fill,
Earth hath enough of what you will.
Then let not go what thou mayst find
For things unknown, only in mind.

Spirit. Be still, thou unregenerate part,
Disturb no more my settled heart,
For I have vow'd, (and so will do)
Thee as a foe still to pursue,
And combat with thee will and must
Until I see thee laid in th' dust.
Sisters we are, yea twins we be,
Yet deadly feud 'twixt thee and me;
For from one father are we not,
Thou by old Adam was begot,
But my arise is from above,
Whence my dear father I do love.
Thou speak'st me fair, but hat'st me sore;
Thy flatt'ring shows I'll trust no more.
How oft thy slave hast thou me made
When I believ'd what thou hast said,
And never had more cause of woe
Than when I did what thou bad'st do.
I'll stop mine ears at these thy charms,
And count them for my deadly harms.
Thy sinful pleasures I do hate,
Thy riches are to me no bait,
Thine honors do nor will I love,
For my ambition lies above.
My greatest honor it shall be
When I am victor over thee,
And triumph shall, with laurel head,
When thou my Captive shalt be led.
How I do live thou need'st not scoff,
For I have meat thou know'st not of:
The hidden Manna I do eat,
The word of life it is my meat.
My thoughts do yield me more content
Than can thy hours in pleasure spent.

Nor are they shadows which I catch,
Nor fancies vain at which I snatch,
But reach at things that are so high,
Beyond thy dull Capacity.
Eternal substance I do see,
With which enriched I would be;
Mine Eye doth pierce the heavens, and see
What is Invisible to thee...

Anne Bradstreet was fortunate in having a wise and tender husband, who was able to give her every convenience that New England could afford. This was not the only poem she wrote to him, but the best, which begins:

If ever two were one, then surely we.
If ever man were loved by wife, then thee;
If ever wife was happy in a man,
Compare with me, ye women, if you can.
I prize thy love more than whole Mines of gold,
Or all the riches that the East doth hold.
My love is such that Rivers cannot quench,
Nor aught but love from thee, give recompense.

Anne was fortunate, too, in her father Thomas Dudley, first Deputy-Governor of the Colony, one of those 'stern men with empires in their brains' who founded the commonwealth. Thomas Dudley was a loving and indulgent father to Anne, as stern men often are to their daughters; she calls him 'a magazine of history' (but doubtless meant well) and attributes to him her love of books. As a statesman, he seemed to her almost perfect. The lines carved on the Dudley gate at Harvard College are hers:

One of thy founders, him New-England know,
Who stayed thy feeble sides when thou wast low,
Who spent his state, his strength, and years with care
That after-comers in them might have share.
True Patriot of this little Commonweal,
Who is't can tax thee ought, but for thy zeal?

His rôle as *malleus haereticorum* seemed to her perfectly consistent and proper:

> Within this Tomb a Patriot lies
> That was both pious, just, and wise,
> To truth a Shield, to right a Wall,
> To Sectaries a whip and maul.

The Bradstreets on their arrival camped at Charlestown a few months, and in December removed to Newtowne. Their house faced that part of the common which later became the Harvard Yard; and near by was the 'great house' of Thomas Dudley, which Governor Winthrop thought too luxurious. There was not much luxury there that first winter, when Deputy-Governor Dudley had to write to the Countess of Lincoln on his knee by the fireside, for want of table, surrounded by his family who 'break good manners, and make me many times forget what I would say, and say what I would not.' We may suppose that Anne often 'ran over' from her own house to join this circle.

It was a humiliation to this eighteen-year-old wife that she did not at once become a mother. 'It pleased God to keep me a long time without a child, which was a great grief to me,' she writes. Samuel, the first born

> The Son of Prayers of vowes, of teares,
> The child I stay'd for many years

was probably born at Newtowne in 1633–34, just before his parents joined John Winthrop, Jr., in the founding of Ipswich. He proved to be first of a large family, of whom she wrote pleasantly in her forty-sixth year, when all but three were grown:

> I had eight birds hatcht in one nest;
> Four Cocks there were, and Hens the rest,
> I nursed them up with pain and care,
> Nor cost nor labor did I spare,
> Till at the last they felt their wing,
> Mounted the trees, and learn'd to sing.

The neighbors, it appears, did not wholly agree with Anne's view of the Bradstreet family:

> I am obnoxious to each carping tongue,
> Who say my hand a needle better fits.
> A Poet's pen all scorn I should thus wrong,
> For such despite they cast on Female wits;
> If what I do prove well, it won't advance,
> They'l say it's stol'n, or else it was by chance.

But the good lady had the last laugh on the village gossips. All eight of her children grew to a useful manhood and womanhood. Samuel, who studied medicine in England after leaving Harvard, and then practised in Jamaica:

> Chief of the Brood then took his flight
> To regions far, and left me quite;
> My mournful chirps I after send
> Till he return or I do end.

Then Dorothy, who married the sea-born son of John Cotton, spent two years in Connecticut, after which he became the minister at Hampton, New Hampshire:

> My second bird did take her flight,
> And with her mate flew out of sight;
> Southward they both their course did bend,
> And Seasons twain they there did spend,
> Till after, blown by Southern gales,
> They Norward steered with fillèd sails.

Sarah, who married her brother's classmate Richard Hubbard, was apparently living Down East:

> I have a third, of color white,
> On whom I plac'd no small delight;
> Coupled with mate loving and true,
> Hath also bid her Dam adieu,
> And where Aurora first appears
> She now hath perched to spend her years.

Simon, Jr., who was at Harvard when she wrote, was her favorite son:

> One to the Academy flew
> To chat among that learned crew;
> Ambition moves still in his breast
> That he might chant above the rest.

It is to Simon's piety that we owe the second edition of Anne Bradstreet's poems with her 'Contemplations.' He was then settled over the church in New London.

> My fifth, whose down is yet scarce gone

was Dudley, later a valiant defender of Andover against enemies of the visible and the invisible world, Indians and witch-hunters.

> My other three still with me nest
> Until they're grown, then as the rest,
> Or here or there they'll take their flight;
> As is ordain'd, so shall they light.

These were Hannah, John, and Mercy, and all but Mercy had married and taken their flight before their mother died.

All the poetry we have quoted so far, is of Anne's maturer years. At what period she began to write, we do not know, but all that has come down to us was done in America. We may suppose that the more pretentious and imitative part of her very considerable output belongs to the three or four childless years at Newtowne, between the ages of eighteen and twenty-one, rather than the first busy years of pioneering and frequent childbearing at Ipswich. Her efforts were appreciated by the several cultivated people in that remarkable frontier town: by the Saltonstalls, Bellinghams, Symondses, and Nathaniel Ward, who prefaced a congratulatory poem to her volume of poems.

This volume, 'The Tenth Muse,' was published without Anne's knowledge and consent by the admiring husband of her sister Mercy, Master John Woodbridge. Returning to England in 1647, he brought with him one of the manuscript copies of her verses which were being circulated among her friends; and, doubtless on the advice of friends in England, decided to publish them. According to the advertising methods of the time, of which Captain John Smith was so fond, he collected a flock of poetical prefaces to be printed with it by way of commendation. Nathaniel Ward was then in England. The Simple Cobler as we know, was something of a woman-hater; but the Tenth Muse sprung up in Ipswich tickled his fancy. His dedicatory verses describe Mercury and Minerva submitting the book to Apollo for judgment as to which were the better poet, Guillaume du Bartas or the unknown American.' Apollo put on his spectacles and 'peer'd and por'd and glar'd' over both texts, but gave it up, when 'both 'gan laugh and said... The Auth'ress was a right du Bartas girle.'

> 'Good sooth' quoth the old Don, 'tell ye me so?
> I muse whither at length these Girls will go;
> It half revives my chil frost-bitten blood,
> To see a woman once, do ought that's good!'

Guillaume du Bartas was one of those poets who enjoyed tremendous vogue in their day, only to fall into complete neglect. His scriptural epics, translated into English by Joshua Sylvester not long before Anne was born, were all the rage in England, especially among puritans. 'Who is there that now can endure to read the Creation of Du Bartas?' wrote Wordsworth. 'Yet all Europe once resounded in his praise; he was caressed by kings; and when his poem was translated into our language, the Faery Queen faded before it.' Dryden wrote that as a boy he thought Spenser a mean poet in comparison with Sylvester's Du Bartas, and was rapt into an ecstasy when he read these lines:

> Now when the winter's keener breath began
> To crystallize the Baltic ocean,
> To glaze the lakes, to bridle up the floods,
> And perriwig with wool the baldpate woods.

This euphuistic style, with its strained metaphors and pedantic conceits, was a baneful example for Anne Bradstreet.

> Mongst hundred Hecatombs of roaring verse
> Mine bleating stands before thy royal Herse

she writes in honor of Queen Elizabeth. In her poem on the

Four Seasons, obviously inspired by Du Bartas' Creation, Anne draws upon the worn-out literary stock of the old world, instead of working up the fresh material before her very eyes. In summer:

> Now go those frolic Swains, the Shepherd Lads
> To wash their thick cloth'd flocks with pipes full glad
> .   .   .   .
> Blest rustic Swains, your pleasant quiet life
> Hath envy bred in Kings that were at strife.

And if we get an occasional verse that might refer to New England:

> Now go the mowers to their slashing toil,
> The meadows of their riches to dispoil,

we naturally suspect that she is thinking of the Fens, and not the salt meads of Massachusetts. 'The Tenth Muse' is not attractive. No one of its long poems, The Four Elements, The Four Humours of Man, The Four Ages of Man, The Four Seasons, The Four Monarchies, and A Dialogue between Old New England and New, would be read by any one save a literary historian.

Anne would have been less than human if she had not been pleased at seeing 'The Tenth Muse' in print; but she quickly made the discovery that words look very differently in print from what they do in writing, and that the kindest friends cannot be depended upon to correct printers' proofs. Her verses to the book ('Thou ill-form'd offspring of my feeble brain') are among the most playful that came from her pen:

> At thy return my blushing was not small,
> My rambling brat (in print) should mother call.
> I cast thee by as one unfit for light,
> Thy visage was so irksome in my sight;
> Yet being mine own, at length affection would
> Thy blemishes amend, if so I could:
> I wash'd thy face, but more defects I saw,
> And rubbing off a spot, still made a flaw.

I stretcht thy joynts to make thee even feet,
Yet still thou run'st more hobbling then is meet.
In better dress to trim thee was my mind,
But naught save home-spun cloth i' th' house I find.
In this array, 'mongst vulgars mayst thou roam,
In critics' hands, beware thou dost not come!

She did not have the pleasure of seeing a revised edition
in print; but six years after her death, in 1678, the second
edition was printed in Boston; a substantial book of 255
pages. In this the author's corrections were inserted, together with sundry 'improvements' that were not of the
author's hand; and some hitherto unpublished poems were
included. But much of her less formal and best work remained in manuscript long after her death.

'The Tenth Muse' did this for Anne Bradstreet: it completely cured her of the Du Bartas disease, and of writing
imitative poetry. She was thirty-eight when the book came
out in 1650. For the remaining twenty-two years of her life,
she wrote lyrical poetry.

It is a curious fact that the historians of American literature, most of them New-Englanders, have treated Anne
Bradstreet with almost offensive condescension as a worthy
puritan housewife who merely imitated the worst English
style of the period, and served up warmed-over English
scenery to her benighted if admiring neighbors. It would
seem impossible that these pontiffs of criticism could have
read anything but 'The Tenth Muse.' Conrad Aiken, however,
has done the memory of Anne Bradstreet the great service of
printing a few later poems at the beginning of his anthology
of American poetry, without a word of comment, footnote, or
other lumber. Thus presented, it is clear that Anne was a
poet *sub specie aeternitatis*. In music, technique, and above all
in the admirable qualities of reticence and economy, she was
superior to some of the favorite poets of the 'Augustan age'
of New England literature. And it was New England that
furnished her material. The primeval forest beside her later

home in North Andover, and the yet untamed Merrimac near by, inspired these stanzas of her 'Contemplations':

> Some time now past in the autumnal tide,
> When Phœbus wanted but one hour to bed,
> The trees all richly clad, yet void of pride,
> Were gilded o'er by his rich golden head.
> Their leaves and fruits seem'd painted, but was true
> Of green, of red, of yellow, mixed hue;
> Rapt were my senses at this delectable view.
>
> . . . .
>
> When I behold the heavens as in their prime,
> And then the earth (though old) still clad in green,
> The stones and trees insensible of time,
> Nor age nor wrinkle on their front are seen;
> If winter come, and greenness then do fade,
> A spring returns and they more youthful made,
> But Man grows old, lies down, remains where once he's laid.[1]
>
> . . . .
>
> Under the cooling shadow of a stately Elm,
> Close sat I by a goodly river's side,
> Where gliding streams the rocks did overwhelm;
> A lonely place, with pleasures dignified.
> I once that lov'd the shady woods so well
> Now thought the rivers did the trees excell,
> And if the sun would ever shine, there would I dwell.
>
> While on the stealing stream I fix'd mine eye,
> Which to the long'd for ocean held its course,
> I mark'd nor crooks nor rubs that there did lie
> Could hinder aught, but still augment its force:
> O happy Flood, quoth I, that holds thy race
> Till thou arrive at thy beloved place,
> Nor is it rocks or shoals that can obstruct thy pace.

Simon Bradstreet was one of the pioneers in opening up the new settlement at Cochichawick, incorporated as the town of Andover in 1646. He owned a mill site on the Cochichawick brook, but how early he built a house, and when he settled there permanently, is not certain. As Andover was not far

---

[1] Compare Shelley's 'Ode to the West Wind':

> The Trumpet of a prophecy! O, wind,
> If Winter comes, can Spring be far behind?

from Ipswich by forest trail, it is likely that the Bradstreets spent a part of the year in each place for some time. Probably it was about 1650, when 'The Tenth Muse' came out, that Anne made what she hoped would be her final move on earth.

Happy years passed in the new settlement, while the children were growing up. The round of household tasks may have been varied by visits to old friends at Ipswich, and to her many relatives in Roxbury, Boston, Charlestown, and Salem. Her father, marrying again at the age of sixty-eight, produced a second family; and what with brothers and sisters, and half-brothers and half-sisters, and nephews and nieces and cousins, Mistress Bradstreet could probably have found a relation in half the towns of New England. But very likely she had not the strength to make journeys by horseback, the most luxurious mode of transport available.

Physically weak she was, but morally robust. Imagine a gentlewoman in her position in the eighteenth or nineteenth century, living under pioneer conditions without the slightest hope of returning to the stately home of her youth, bearing eight children with little or no medical aid, suffering frequent illness, fainting fits, and finally a wasting consumption. Such a woman in a later century, if given the gift of poesy, would have employed it to weave fantastic romances of the old world, or spent it in self pity and romantic introspection. Yet the poetry of Anne Bradstreet is without a trace of romanticism or sentimentalism. Her art was not an escape from life, but an expression of life. It was shot through and through with her religious faith; a faith that made weak women strong, taught them to face life and take what came without flinching, as the inscrutable decree of a just God.

Anne Bradstreet could express a tender sentiment without being sentimental. This appears best in her poem on the burning of her home at Andover, in 1666, and her feelings as she passed the blackened ruins of the house.

When by the ruins oft I passed
My sorrowing eyes aside did cast,
And here and there the places spy
Where oft I sat, and long did lie.

Here stood that trunk, and there that chest;
There lay that store I counted best;
My pleasant things in ashes lie,
And them behold no more shall I.
Under thy roof no guest shall sit,
Nor at thy table eat a bit.

No pleasant tale shall e'er be told,
Nor things recounted done of old.
No candle e'er shall shine in thee,
Nor bridegroom's voice e'er heard shall be.
In silence ever shalt thou lie;
Adieu, Adieu, all's vanity.

This, I maintain, is good poetry, minor if you will but not *minima*, superior to most of the English minor poetry of that day, or of ours. Note the economy of the language, and the suggestiveness of it. To those of the time, and to us who know the background, this little poem lights up Anne's home in early Andover: the 'pleasant things' and chest of keepsakes which reminded her of old times in old England, the candle-lighted hall where she dined and received guests; telling tales before the great open fire; shy maids and bashful swains dropping in to be married by her magistrate husband. In the poem on her family, Anne Bradstreet had promised:

Meanwhile my days in tunes I'll spend
Till my weak lays with me shall end;
In shady woods I'll sit and sing,
And things that past to mind I'll bring —
Once young and pleasant, as are you.
But former toys, — not joys, — adieu!

But her periods of illness became more frequent, and in the last poem dated by her hand, of the summer of 1669, she represents herself as a weary pilgrim, who longs to be at rest. A wasting consumption set in, and on September 16, 1672, her son Simon records in his diary, 'My ever honoured and most dear Mother was translated to Heaven.'

Anne left to her children many unpublished poems, and a little manuscript book of seventy-seven 'Meditations Divine and morall,' witness to her ripe wisdom and to her robust soul:

Youth is the time of getting, middle age of improving, and old age of spending; a negligent youth is usually attended by an ignorant middle age, and both by an empty old age. He that hath nothing to feed on but vanity and lyes must needs lye down on the Bed of sorrow.

A ship that beares much saile, and little or no ballast, is easily overset; and that man whose head hath great abilities, and his heart little or no grace, is in danger of foundering.

Fire hath its force abated by water, not by wind; and anger must be alayed by cold words, and not by blustering threats.

A sharp appetite and a thorough concoction is a signe of a healthfull body; so a quick reception and a deliberate cogitation, argues a sound mind.

There is no object that we see; no action that we doe; no good that we injoy; no evill that we feele or fear, but we may make some spirituall advantage of all.

This was the strength of the puritan woman, that she could employ every adversity to some spiritual advantage, and make good come out of evil. Anne Bradstreet was a true daughter of the puritan breed, whose soul was made strong by faith. From the day her heart fell at beholding New England, to her last wasting illness, she had many, very many days of pain; but uttered no complaint. She was unusual, and so far as we know unique, among the men and women of the first generation, in that her character, her thoughts, and her religion were expressed in poetry that has endured, and will endure. Her life was proof, if it were needed, that creative art may be furthered by religion; and that even the duties of a housewife and mother in a new country cannot quench the sacred flame. It was another question whether that flame could be passed on to others in an isolated frontier commonwealth, where material life clutched greedily at all that spiritual life relinquished. This question was not answered for two centuries, when the genius of Anne Bradstreet was reincarnated in Emily Dickinson.

CHAPTER XII

WILLIAM PYNCHON, FRONTIER MAGISTRATE AND FUR TRADER

I N THE ENGLISH county of Essex, about thirty miles northeast of London, lies the shire town of Chelmsford where Thomas Hooker, founder of Connecticut, acquired his great reputation as a preacher. Writtle, the ancestral home of the Pynchon family, and the village of Springfield are near by. Springfield's ancient Norman church is crowned with a low square tower, on which is inscribed "Prayse God for all the good Benefactors."

During the ten years that Master Hooker lived at Chelmsford, the squire of Springfield was a quiet country gentleman named William Pynchon. The Pynchons were a Norman family, who after long eclipse had risen in the world during the prosperous reign of Queen Bess. William's grandfather John increased the family property and prestige by marrying a wealthy heiress, daughter of Sir Richard Empson, who lost his head for "constructive treason" in the early part of Henry VIII's reign. They left a son, who inherited the family property at Springfield, resided there after he had taken his bachelor's degree at New College, Oxford, married Frances Brett, and brought up two sons and six daughters. The eldest of this moderately large family, William Pynchon, the founder of Springfield, Massachusetts, was born about 1590.

Of William's early life and education we know next to nothing, but he was "well connected" indeed; his first cousin Elizabeth, daughter of an uncle who inherited the Writtle property, married Sir Richard Weston, later Chancellor of the Exchecquer and Earl of Portland. Her brother Edward married Weston's sister and was later knighted by Charles I. Sir Edward remembered cousin William in his will, even though an ocean then separated them.

Not long after his father's death in 1610, William Pynchon came of age, inherited the Springfield property, and married Anna Andrews, daughter of a squire in a neighboring county. He was now a large landowner, with a social position in Essex very similar to that of John Winthrop in Suffolk. Like other country gentlemen of the day, he took part in public affairs by serving as churchwarden of the parish, and as justice of the peace. In preparation for that magisterial function, he must have read a certain amount of law, as his later letters and judicial records prove. If it were then no longer true that gentlemen learned the rules of law "as they learned the rules of sword play,"[1] the law was not yet an organized profession, and every man with property to protect had to be moderately well versed in it. How or where Pynchon obtained that training or aptitude for business which marks his American career, we are ignorant.

Pynchon for many years was a neighbor, though never a parishioner, of Master Thomas Hooker, a famous Puritan divine who induced many persons to emigrate to New England. We would not be justified in assuming that the unpleasant relations which developed in Connecticut between Hooker and Pynchon went back to the period when they both resided in or near Chelmsford, but it is certain that no desire to live under Hooker's teaching formed any part of Pynchon's emigrating motives, for he never settled in the same town with that "Son of Thunder."

John White, if anyone, was responsible for bringing Pynchon into the great Puritan migration. White's great-uncle, a Warden of New College, Oxford, was a friend and legatee of William Pynchon's grandfather, and William's father obtained his education at New College. Our William

[1] Holdsworth, *History of English Law* (ed. 1923), II. 416; cf. 556.

did not enter the University, but it seems reasonable to assume that friendship between the White and Pynchon families continued, so that when Master John White, also a New College alumnus, was seeking support for his project of a colony in New England, William Pynchon was the natural person for him to seek out in East Anglia. After the emigration it was our William to whom John White wrote on matters of New England business; and he chose a former member of John White's Dorchester congregation as his second wife.

Whatever the cause, William Pynchon became one of the founders of the Massachusetts Bay Company. Together with Cradock, Johnson, Bellingham, and Saltonstall, he obtained the royal charter dated March 4, 1629, creating the Governor and Company of the Massachusetts Bay in New England. He is one of the assistants named in the charter; and the receipt for his subscription of £25 to the joint stock has been preserved. With Winthrop, Saltonstall, and others, Pynchon signed the Cambridge Agreement binding himself to emigrate to Massachusetts Bay if the charter and government could be transferred; and he was present at the discussion of that question at Thomas Goffe's house in London on August 28–29, when it was decided. We may fairly assume that a regular attendant at company meetings, such as he was, would have played an active part in the preparations for the voyage. It is probable that he sold his Springfield estate to meet the expense of removal, since he lived elsewhere after returning to England, and in his will mentioned no property near his old home.

With his wife, five-year-old son, and three young daughters, William Pynchon sailed on the ship *Ambrose* with the Winthrop fleet. Departing Cowes with the *Arbella*, the *Talbot*, and the *Jewell* on March 29, 1630, she managed to keep within sight of the "admirall" or flagship during most of the voyage. Winthrop's Journal tells that one day when the fleet was about halfway across, and the wind was blowing a small gale, Captain Milborne of the *Arbella* "putt forthe his Auncient [ensign] in the poope, and heaved out his skiffe, and lowred his topsayles to give sign to his Consortes that they should come a board us to dinner," and how at six bells the Captain "sent his skiffe, and fetched aboard us the masters of the other 2 shippes, and mr. Pincheon, and they dined with us, in the rounde house, for the Lady [Arbella] and gentle women dyned in the great Cabbin."

William Pynchon first settled in Dorchester with the West-Countrymen who came over in the *Mary and John*, but shortly after moved to the adjoining settlement at Roxbury. During the great sickness which carried off Isaac Johnson and the Lady Arbella, Mistress Pynchon died, leaving four young children for her husband to bring up. He did not remarry immediately, possibly because suitable unmarried women were scarce in this frontier community; but "after some years," says the Reverend John Eliot, "he married Mistress Francis Samford, a grave matron of the church at Dorchester," who had already buried two husbands. William Pynchon's name stands first on the roll of members of the First Church of Roxbury, which was gathered in 1631 when John Eliot arrived to be their minister. Most of the Roxbury people were from the neighborhood of Chelmsford, where John Eliot had taught school and made many friends.

Pynchon was present at the first Court of Assistants held on Massachusetts soil, was annually reëlected until after he had settled on the Connecticut, and for two years also served as treasurer of the colony. He must have brought over considerable capital, because he promptly began fur-trading. Governor Winthrop records in his Journal for October 30, 1631: "Mr. Pynchon's boat, coming from Sagadahock, was cast away at Cape Ann, but the men and chief goods saved, and the boat recovered."

Although the peltry trade did not have the same relative importance in New England as in New France or New Netherland, it was a much heavier factor in the economy of our region than has generally been admitted. The Pilgrim Fathers, after some initial errors due to their inexperience, and after the Dutch had taught them the use of wampum, became expert fur traders. In the years 1631–36 they collected and shipped to England 12,530 pound weight of beaver which enabled them to get clear of debt; and it was doubtless their trading post on the Sagadahoc (Kennebec) River that attracted Pynchon's boat. In the original area of the Bay Colony there was relatively little peltry to be had, since the rivers were short and the Indians few, but Thomas Morton of Merrymount records that beaver skins, bringing 10s. a pound in London, were an immensely profitable export, one servant of his having cleared £1000 from that commodity in five years. The Massachusetts Bay Company, when transformed into a political rather than a trading organization, had no time to handle the trade itself, and so gave individuals a monopoly over definite areas for so much a year, or at the rate of one shilling in every pound weight of beaver collected. Thus William Pynchon in 1632 was granted the fur trading privilege at Roxbury for one year for the sum of £25. In rendering his accounts as treasurer, however, he credited the colony with £20 only, on the ground that they had broken the agreement by admitting others to trade at Roxbury. The General Court accepted this composition, but at the same time got the full amount out of Pynchon by dint of fining him £5 "for refuseing to pay his part of the last rate of Rocksbury ... because, as hee alleadged, that towne was not equally rated with others." Pynchon and Thomas Mayhew, the future founder of Martha's Vineyard, were also fined £5 each for the dangerous practice of "employing Indians to shoot with pieces."

As treasurer of the colony, Pynchon had to be at once storekeeper, wholesale merchant, and private banker, for the colony fines and taxes were mostly paid in commodities which had to be sold in order to provide funds for public expenses. These were of the most various nature: salaries to the two military captains, Underhill and Patrick; bounties for killing wolves, messenger service, lumber for a public wharf; work on the fort; witness fees; £2 to Samuel Maverick, ship's husband of the pinnace sent to capture Dixie Bull the pirate; £13 2s. 6d. for provisions and £7 for two fat hogs "for to victual the pinnace for the taking of Dixie Bull." In addition Pynchon had to distribute an arsenal of assorted cannon, powder, match, shot, priming irons, sponges, muskets with rests and bandoliers, carbines, swords, and "wolfhooks," which arrived in the *Griffin*. These, the gift of Dr. Edmund Wilson, brother of the Reverend John Wilson, were wanted to protect the colony from wolves, Indians, and Sir Ferdinando Gorges.

As a fur trader Pynchon must have been one of the first in the Bay to hear of the Connecticut River and its wonderful resources in peltry. If he remained at Roxbury, he must content himself to be a middleman, but by locating nearer the source of supply he could obtain furs directly from the Indians. Competition for the Connecticut River fur had begun in 1633. John Oldham went exploring by the Indian trail; the Dutch established their "House of Hope" at the site of Hartford; the Pilgrims located a trading post on the site of Windsor; the Governor's bark, *Blessing of the Bay*, bearing a committee of discontented Newtowners, tried the river and found it good. How hazy were the current views of geography is shown by an entry in Winthrop's Journal the same year. Following a tradition which came from imperfect accounts of the Great Lakes which explorers had obtained from Indians in the previous century, the Governor imagined that there existed somewhere in the interior a vast lake surrounded by swamps, from which issued the Connecticut, the Potomac, and the St. Lawrence, source of all peltry that the Indians brought to Quebec, Virginia, and the lower Connecticut. He supposed that the upper Merrimac lay within a day's journey from the upper Connecticut, hence the game for Massachusetts was to tap the Great Lake by the Merrimac–Connecticut route, and cut off the Pigrims' as well as the Dutchmen's source of supply.

If this uncharitable design was called to the attention of Pynchon, he wisely rejected it, for in 1630 the Laconia Company, an English organization formed to exploit the mythical great lake, had sought it in vain. Pynchon's plan was a much more practical one: to found a settlement at Agawam, an Indian village on the further bank of the Connecticut, only a few miles above the head of navigation for sea-going vessels, and at the exact point where the principal trail from Massachusetts Bay to Albany crossed the river. We may suppose Pynchon's plan to have been formed as early as May, 1634, when he gave up his treasurership of the colony at the same General Court in which the Newtowne people were pressing for permission to remove. But as magistrate of the colony, Pynchon could hardly leave until his colleagues on the Board of Assistants decided no longer to oppose what they could not prevent — the migration to the Great River.

During September, 1635, Pynchon and a few of his followers visited the site of his proposed settlement, made an oral agreement with the Indians to sell the land, and erected a house on the west bank of the Connecticut where it is joined by the Agawam or Westfield River. Whether or not any white man passed the winter there is not known, and the first certain trace of a permanent settlement by Pynchon is in May, 1636. Romance has been industrious with the Pynchon migration; purple paragraphs will be found in the local histories about Pynchon and the men of Roxbury pushing through the "trackless forest" guided by a friendly Indian, or only by the compass needle. But Mrs. Pynchon certainly came by sea, in Governor Winthrop's *Blessing of the Bay*, which sailed from Boston on April 26, 1636, and there is every reason to suppose that the rest of the party chose the same conveyance. Presumably the *Blessing* landed them at the foot of the Enfield Falls, whence there was already a well-beaten path to the site of Springfield.

Pynchon soon decided that Agawam side, the west bank, where he had erected a house, was so "incombred with Indians" that he would "loose halfe the benifit." He decided, therefore, to plant on the opposite side to avoid trespassing on the Indians' cornfields. Hence, unlike the other early Connecticut River settlements, Pynchon's was founded on the east bank. Until 1641, when the name was changed to Springfield, it was known as the "plantation at and over agaynst Agaam," or simply the "plantation of Agawam."

The first settlers included only seven men besides William Pynchon. Even so, it was a corporate enterprise. The agreement, dated May 14, 1636, that the eight men drew up on the spot, suggests that Pynchon did not aim to establish a mere trading post for his personal benefit, that his purpose was to plant a regular New England town with a sufficient population of independent farmers to support a church and a local government. The leading spirits of the enterprise, who "have constantly continued to prosecute this plantation when others fell off for feare of the difficultys, . . . at greate charges and at greate personall adventures," as states the agreement, were Pynchon, Henry Smith, his son-in-law, and Goodman Jehu Burr, an illiterate member of the Roxbury church whose chief title to fame is through his descendant Aaron. The agreement declares that the eight men "intend by Gods grace" to procure a minister and form a church, that their town shall be composed of not less than forty nor more than fifty families, and that every inhabitant shall have a ten-acre house lot, a portion of cow pasture, a share of both the "hasokey Marish" and the meadow or planting ground of Agawam on the opposite side of the river, and, if needed, of the "long meddowe lyinge in the way to Dorchester." The Nayas meadow is to go to those who will undertake to improve it for tillage and pasture, and so relieve the other pasture grounds. All rates shall be in proportion to the amount of land. Pynchon was granted a twenty-acre house lot and half the meadow which is now Hampden Park, the other half being divided between Smith and Burr, in consideration of their special pains and expenses. All agreed to divide the meadow and planting ground on the principle of giving a man as much as he could use: two acres of mowing for every head of neat cattle and double for every horse, "because estate is like to be improved in cattell, and such ground is aptest for theyr use"; but no man, even if without cattle, should have less than three acres besides his house lot. These house lots were laid out between the river and a road (the present Main Street) running parallel to it. Across the river, opposite his house lot, each man had a strip of the planting ground.

The next step was to extinguish the title of the Indian proprietors. This was done in a deed dated July 15, 1636, by which certain meadows which the Indians did not value, and planting grounds which they did not use, on both sides of the river, were sold by the local sachems for eighteen fathoms of wampum, eighteen blanket-coats, eighteen hatchets, eighteen hoes, and eighteen knives. It was agreed that the Indians should continue to enjoy hunting and fishing privileges on this land, to gather groundnuts, walnuts, acorns, and wild pease, and that no hogs be placed on Agawam side until acorn time. This was to guard against the well-known skill of hogs in getting through fences and at the Indian corn. Pynchon, in the meantime, started his trading operations, and built a warehouse at the lower end of the Enfield Falls,[1] to which he hauled or boated his peltry for

---

[1] This place at Winsor Locks is still called Warehouse Point.

transfer to sea-going vessels. As early as June, 1636, we find him exchanging pointers on the Indian trade with John Winthrop, Junior, who was in charge of the colony and fort at Saybrook, established by Lord Say and Sele and Lord Brook. The Saybrook people were long on wampum, which was made from sea-shell, but short of peltry and goods, which Pynchon had in abundance, hence a profitable exchange was effected.

By the end of 1637 some of the eight men had left, but others had come in, with wives and children; probably there were no more than ten families in all. True to the agreement of 1636 they now took measures to procure a settled minister. As Harvard College had not yet begun to produce parsons, their choice was restricted to graduates of the English universities. Fortunately there was living in Dorchester, with his wife and children, George Moxon, a young Cambridge B.A. in holy orders, who was looking for a pastorate. Pynchon persuaded him to take a sporting chance with this little frontier community, and as long as Pynchon remained there he served it well.

In January, 1638, the plantation taxed itself £40 for building the minister's house, and the same amount "For Mr. Moxons maintenance till next michaellmas." The £40 house seems to have been ample: two stories and a cellar, with two rooms to a floor, a double clayed chimney with oven, and a projecting square turret with the front door below and the minister's study above. Jehu Burr charged £18 for thatching the house; the rest of the expense was for labor. Henry Smith did the chimney and the "daubing" or plastering, the lumber seems to have been given. For several years services were held in Pynchon's house, but in 1645 a meeting-house was built by each inhabitant's contributing twenty-eight days' work, while Thomas Cooper received £80 from the plantation for overseeing the work and providing the materials — lumber, iron, nails, stone sills, and glazed windows. Agawam was evidently eager to establish its reputation as a proper godly plantation, the same as Hartford or Roxbury, and no mere trucking post. John Matthews received 6d in wampum or a peck of corn from every family in town for beating the drum for meeting: at 9 A.M. on the Lord's Day and 10 A.M. on weekly lecture days.

We are fortunate to have unusually complete town and plantation records of Agawam and Springfield. These records relate mainly to the allotments of land and the regulation of its use. In accordance with the strong community spirit of early New England towns, the land titles to the allotments were not finally confirmed to the grantees for a number of years. A quick abandonment of the plantation meant return of the grantee's land to the town; or if after a few years' trial he wished to sell out, his "chapman" or purchaser had to be acceptable to the community; and "no man that is posessed of a lott by the dispose of the Plantation, shall after sell it to another, of the plantation." Like other early settlers of New England, the Springfield people were not land grabbers. They took every precaution to prevent a few people from monopolizing the land, and to reserve enough of it for later comers, and for their descendants. Land was a socialized commodity.

The use of the land was also regulated. Cattle could be pastured in the tilth and mowing only between the first of November and the fourteenth of April — in Old England the usual dates had been from Michaelmas to Lady Day. There was trouble about plowing teams breaking into the green corn in spring, so it was agreed that plowing oxen must "be kept in some house or yeard." John Leonard was appointed to see that the highways be kept in repair and cleared "of all stubs sawpitts or timbyr." William Pynchon erected a grist mill on the Mill River, and a bridge was built leading to it, at town expense. Maximum wages and hours of labor were fixed — that of "husbandmen or ordinary laborers" at 18d. for an eight-hour day in winter and 20d. for a ten-hour day in summer "besides eatinge and sleepinge"; carpenters to have 20d. and 2s., mowers to have 2s. a day, but tailors to receive only 10d. for a twelve-hour day. These rates were lowered as the plantation became more populous. All Massachusetts towns had been delegated this power to regulate wages and prices by the General Court, which had failed in trying to enforce a uniform wage scale for the entire colony. But as William Pynchon was the only inhabitant of Springfield in a position to hire labor, the regulation by town meeting was essentially a wage agreement between him and his fellow townsmen.

Canoes were very important to a river town, especially to Springfield where the planting lots were across the river. Any inhabitant could fell a "canoe tree" — a great white birch — on common land, and make canoes for his own use or that of his fellow townsmen; but no one might sell or give a canoe out of the plantation until it was five years old — a wise measure for the conservation of birch. Three men who "sold or pawned away theyer cannoes" in the winter of 1640 were ordered to redeem them by spring or forfeit 20s. each.

Undeniably, all this has a democratic flavor. The town was the New England institution where democracy seeped in and leavened the rest, and although until 1647 only free-men of the colony were supposed to take part in town meet-ings, Springfield paid no attention to the requirement. All admitted inhabitants voted in town meeting and were fined one bushel of corn for failing to attend. Yet even at the earliest date Springfield was not a social democracy. William Pynchon paid about half the town taxes, and had the most land. He was the only trader. His son John, his sons-in-law Henry Smith and Elizur Holyoke, and his friend the minister, formed with him a local aristocracy, commanding a weight of moral and material influence which would have made short shrift of a local opposition. And, most important, William Pynchon was the local magistrate and judge, invested with power to probate wills, hold petty sessions, and try all causes not involving loss of life or limb. In other words, the squire of Springfield in Essex had become the squire of Springfield in Massachusetts.

In the early years of the plantation it formed part of the same government as the River Towns, and might well have become permanently attached to the Colony of Connecticut, but for the failure of William Pynchon to get along with Thomas Hooker. The circumstances form an interesting little chapter in New England politics, diplomacy, and economic thought.

Agawam was first included with Windsor, Hartford, and Wethersfield under the governing commission of eight appointed by the General Court of Massachusetts on March 3, 1636, and William Pynchon was one of the commissioners. During the ensuing year the commissioners held several courts, or meetings, in the three River Towns, but only one of these was attended by the founder of Springfield. After the term of the commissioners expired on March 3, 1637, the people of the River Towns set up what amounted to an independent government by electing a new set of magistrates, including Pynchon, and sending three deputies from each town to join with the magistrates in a General Court.

It was the first court so composed which declared "offensive war against the Pequoitt." There was no one from Springfield at this court, and apparently the Connecticut authorities agreed that if the ten or twelve men at Springfield would take care of themselves, nothing more would be expected of them. Pynchon nevertheless was taxed for his Agawam property by Massachusetts Bay. His friend and fellow-magistrate Roger Ludlow wrote to him from Windsor on May 17, 1637, to be careful and watchful of the friendly Indians, to keep his powder dry, and trust in God, for however pressing the danger, it would be impossible for the River Towns to come to his assistance. Accordingly Pynchon and his little band kept strict watch against surprise. Some unpleasantness was caused by the River authorities impressing one of Pynchon's boats with her crew into the public service without asking by-your-leave; and relations were not bettered when, despite the agreement to let Agawam alone, they levied a war tax of £86 16s. on the little plantation, and summoned Pynchon to Hartford to answer for non-payment. He wrote to Ludlow in January, 1638, that it was impossible to go down-river — snow was up to a man's middle at Agawam and his people could not even get out to cut paling. At the next court, on March 8, 1638, Pynchon appeared, and, from absence of any record to the contrary, it is likely that he paid the tax out of his own pocket.

At this same General Court the River colony conferred upon Pynchon a benefit that he did not ask, and a responsibility that he did not seek. It adopted the Massachusetts system of granting exclusive rights in the beaver trade to one or two men in each town in return for a tax of one shilling per skin, and Pynchon was given the monopoly for Agawam. Having already experienced this system in the Bay and found that it could not be enforced, Pynchon protested to Ludlow:

I cannot see how it can well stand with the public good and the liberty of free men to make a monopole of trade. I have often heerd this very thing in agitation in the Bay and yet it could not be brought to passe: I hope the Lord in his mercy will keep me from coveting any unlawful gaine: or [consenting to] any man's hindrance where God doth not hinder them.

Although the tone of this letter is certainly generous, it should be remembered that a man with Pynchon's capital and shrewdness was likely to monopolize the beaver trade at Agawam in any case, and would not care to be taxed a shilling a skin for the legal privilege. Business men in the seventeenth century were moving away from monopoly and finding free competition more profitable, but the new little colony on the River preferred old, tried methods.

More serious trouble developed out of Pynchon's contract for supplying corn. The corn crop of the war summer, 1637, proved insufficient, and, by the middle of the severe winter that followed, it was clear that if a supply were not imported there would be a famine next spring in the River Towns. Here was a case when a monopoly was wise, as our recent war experience has proved. Free trade in corn with the Indians would have resulted in the natives being robbed and cheated, and the people being charged famine prices by speculators. Hence the General Court on March 8, 1638, "ordered with the consent of Mr. Pincheon" that he should purchase from the Indians and deliver to the three River Towns 500 bushels of corn at 5s. per bushel — or a penny or two more if he had to pay as much as "sixe sixes of Wampom a pecke."[1] Private persons were forbidden to trade, unless in case of necessity and upon order of three magistrates. On returning a few days later to Agawam and finding the Indians determined either to get more than the contract price or to hold their corn for a rise, Pynchon wrote back to Hartford that he feared he could not carry out the contract at the price fixed. The Connecticut authorities, fearful at the approach of famine, lost no time in sending Captain John Mason upriver to procure the necessary corn. It was but a few months since Mason had earned the name of a mighty warrior by leading the devastating slaughter of Pequots at Mystic fort. Obviously, sending him on such an errand was disturbing, to say the least. The Indians at first refused to trade with Mason. A conference was held between him, Pynchon, Moxon the minister, and a Nonotuck Indian, in

---

[1] As wampum passed at three beads a penny, this expression meant 12d. for a peck or 4s. for a bushel of corn.

Pynchon's house at Agawam. Here it appeared that Mason wished to pay the Indian in advance to go up to Woronoco and bring down corn. Pynchon advised him that it was fatal to pay Indians in advance, they always skipped off to the woods with the wampum and never delivered the goods, and Moxon chimed in with a homely simile: "An Indian promise is noe more than to have a pigg by the taile." Mason finally agreed to pay no money until he saw the corn, but little or none was forthcoming for the price he offered, and the hot-tempered Captain returned downriver, convinced that Pynchon was thinking only of his own profit and prestige, and trying to hold up Connecticut for higher prices.

Within a month the Connecticut General Court summoned Pynchon to Hartford and placed him on trial for "unfaithfull dealing in the trade of corne" and for breach of his oath as a magistrate. The particular charges were that he had obstructed the Mason mission, both by forbidding the Indians to trade with the Captain, and by refusing to procure a canoe that they needed for transportation. In defense he alleged that he acted as Mason's interpreter and "took off the fears" of an Indian reluctant to do business with the warrior, and that, when his own plantation was in dire necessity, when the beer had given out and he himself had less than half a bushel of corn on hand for his family, when the neighbors were begging him to raise the price so that Indians would sell, he refused to exceed the maximum limit allowed by his instructions. In the matter of the canoe, it appears that there was only one in Agawam which the Indians would use, and the owner refused to lend it because he needed it for the planting season.

The court, before coming to a decision, sent for Masters Thomas Hooker and Samuel Stone, respectively pastor and teacher of the Hartford Church, to express an expert opinion on the ethical question involved. As usual it was Hooker who did all the talking. He accused Pynchon of holding off buying "that he should have all the trade to himselfe, and have all the corne in his owne hands, . . . and so rack the country at his pleasure." "He then delivered his judgment peremptorily that I had broken my oath," says Pynchon. "To this I was silent, being grieved at so hard an answer." Upon Hooker's opinion the Court fined Pynchon forty bushels of corn for "unfaithfulness." Two months later Captain Mason was sent north again, with a squad of soldiers and a threatening message to the Indians to deliver corn, or they would regret it. Even at that, Mason had to pay 12s. a bushel, more than double the price allowed Pynchon by the Court. This fact alone seems a complete justification of Pynchon's policy.

Naturally a gentlemen like Pynchon would not tamely submit to imputations on his good name and faith. He prepared and circulated in manuscript an "Apology" or defense of his conduct throughout the transactions. To the General Court he protested:

> I conceive . . . that either you will see mr Hooker mak it good or acquit me of the guilt: for if mr Hooker do not mak it good many wronges will follow. 1. his credit is wronged by undertaking to mak that good which yet he hath not don in a long distance of tyme. 2ly. I am wronged in my Cause and made a grieved magistrate unjustly. and 3ly the general Court are wronged to ground their censure uppon his judgment. But I must expect to see this Charge demonstrated by positive proofe such as may stand with the just censure of a Court of equity, for certaine punishment must be grounded uppon certaine proofe, and not uppon surmises or prejudice. . . .

In the matter of the canoe, Pynchon's words are even stronger.

> I was charged with neglect of my duty and breach of my oath because I did not presse the cano for the Indians use: A strange reason to prove the breach of my oath: If magistrates in N. E. should *ex officio* practise such a power over mens proprieties, how long would Tyrany be kept out of our habitations: Truly the king might as legaly exact a loan *Ex officio* of his subjects by a distresse on mens proprieties (because he pleades as greate necessity) as to

presse a Cano without a legall order. The lawes of England count it a tender thing to touch another mans propriety and therefore many have rather chosen to suffer as in a good cause then to yeeld their goods to the king *ex officio:* and to lose the liberty of an English subject in N. E. would bring woefull slaviry to our posterity: But while governments are ordered by the lawlesse law of discretion, that [which] is transient in particular mens heades may be of dangerous consequence.

Thus was turned against Master Hooker, and in a concrete case, the protest he had made to Governor Winthrop against the discretionary power of magistrates. Pynchon was defending not only his personal honor but the traditional liberties of an Englishman against the arbitrary judgment of an irritated and possibly hungry clergyman.

There was more to this case than a personal dispute; it was the clash of paternalism with *laissez faire.* Hooker doubtless believed in the same economic principles as did Cotton, Winthrop — and, for that matter, St. Thomas Aquinas.[1] That is to say, he believed in the medieval figment of a "just price," of the unlawfulness of usury, or of raising prices to meet a brisk demand. Corn was scarce and Connecticut in danger of starving; *ergo*, argued Hooker and the General Court, the Indians should charge them even less for corn than in normal years. If Pynchon did not see eye-to-eye with them, he must be a usurer, a profiteer, an evil person. Pynchon, on the contrary, represented the instinctive theory of the seventeenth-century business man, impatient of ecclesiastical and political trammels. Observe the conclusion of his letter to Ludlow: ". . . I cannot see how it can well stand with the public good and the liberty of free men to make a monopole of trade." Nor will he consent to "any man's hindrance when God doth not hinder them." Even the Indians had a more exact appreciation of economic laws

[1] See Winthrop, *History of New England* (1908), i. 315–18, on Cotton's principles in the dispute between the Boston Church and Keayne; and E. A. J. Johnson, "The Economic Principles of John Winthrop," *New England Quarterly* (April, 1930), iii. 235–50.

than did Thomas Hooker and the General Court, for they observed that having obtained "eight sixes" of wampum for a peck of corn the year before, when corn was plenty, they would certainly not sell it for "six sixes," when corn was in brisk demand.

Moreover, the Connecticut authorities followed up the case in a petty and persecuting manner, writing to the Church at Roxbury that Master Hooker regarded their distinguished brother Pynchon to be a profiteer and an oath-breaker, and that they ought to proceed against him "in a church way" — i.e., to censure or excommunicate him. Although the Roxbury church eventually gave Pynchon a clean bill of health, his defense cost him much trouble, journeying, and anxiety, and was not concluded for three years.

After this it is not surprising to find that Pynchon preferred to live under some other government than the one at Hartford. Six weeks after he had been condemned and fined, he was appointed one of a Connecticut commission of three to treat with the Bay authorities about a confederation. During the conference Massachusetts claimed that Springfield came within her line. Pynchon readily accepted this claim as an excuse for seceding from Connecticut, "and that motion by Mr. Pincheon," declared Connecticut at a later date, "arose (as is verily conceived) from a present pange of discontent upon a sensure hee then lay under by the Government of Conectacutt."

Massachusetts refused to confederate unless Agawam were admitted to be hers. It is rather difficult to see why, if it were moral for Thomas Hooker and his congregation to secede from Massachusetts, it should be immoral for Springfield to secede back, but Master Hooker thought otherwise. In an angry letter to Governor Winthrop he passed this pungent sentence on William Pynchon:

If Mr. Pyncheon can devise ways to make his oath bind him when he will and loosen him when he list: if he can tell how, in faithfulness to engage himself in a civil covenant ... yet can cast it away at his pleasure before he give in sufficient warrant, more than his own word and will, he must find a law in Agaam for it; for it is written in no law nor gospel that ever I read. The want of his help troubles not me, nor any man else I can hear of. I do assure you we know him from the bottom to the brim and follow him in all his proceedings, and trace him in his privy footsteps; only we would have him and all the world to understand, he doth not walk in the dark to us.

There is no record of Pynchon or of Agawam taking part in the government of Connecticut after April 5, 1638. Early next year the Fundamental Orders were put into effect without any reference to Springfield, and Pynchon's court record[1] opens as follows:

February the 14th 1638 [-39]   We the Inhabitantess of Agaam uppon Quinnettecot takinge into consideration the manifould inconveniences that may fale uppon us for want of some fit magistracy among us: Beinge now by Godes prouidence fallen into the line of the Massachusets Jurisdiction: and it beinge farr of[f] to repayer thither in such cases of justice as may often fall out amonge us doe therefore thinke it meete by a general consent and vote to ordaine (till we receive further directions from the generall court in the Massachuset Bay) mr William Pynchon to execute the office of a magistrate in this our plantation of Agaam.

Massachusetts Bay was apparently willing to leave the question open pending a final agreement on the subject with Connecticut. It was not until 1642 that Pynchon was elected to his former chair in the Court of Assistants, and until 1649 Springfield was not represented in the General Court. Rival surveys of the boundary line were made by the two colonies, appeals to the King were threatened on both sides, and Connecticut attempted to prejudge the case by authorizing her then Governor, Edward Hopkins, to purchase Woronoco (Westfield) and erect a trading-house there. Connecticut

[1] Joseph H. Smith ed. (Cambridge, 1961).

attempted to tax exports downriver from Springfield, and Massachusetts proposed to retaliate on imports from Connecticut. In 1650 the Commissioners of the United Colonies washed their hands of the question, declaring their "desire to bee spared in all further agitations concerning Sprinkfield." And from that time the incorporation of Springfield in Massachusetts was never seriously challenged.

Undeniably, with three days' marches of wilderness between him and the capital, it was much easier for Pynchon to do business under the Bay jurisdiction than under Connecticut. It was not that the Bay was any less paternalistic than the River, but that Boston was far away and Hartford only a short distance downstream. Pynchon's palisaded storehouse "over agaynst Agaam" was the business center of the Upper Valley. Indians came down the Great River and its tributaries, bringing packs of beaver and other furs to exchange for wampum, blanket-coats, bright-colored cottons, axes, knives, and trinkets. These furs were bundled up into hogsheads, which were teamed to Pynchon's warehouse at the site of Windsor Locks, together with pickled beef and pork, Indian corn and wheat, and other agricultural products of the Valley. At Warehouse Point the hogsheads were transferred to a coasting vessel which took them to Boston, whence they were forwarded by sailing packet to London, the great fur market of Europe. The provisions were more apt to be transshipped at Hartford to a West India trader. Back from London came all manner of textiles and manufactured goods, and from the West Indies, sugar, molasses, and rum, which were sold both at wholesale and retail to the growing white population of the Valley, in return for more furs, meat, grain, and wampum. Governor Stuyvesant of New Netherland complained to the New England Confederation in 1650 that Pynchon had monopolized the fur trade of the Connecticut, leaving nothing for the Dutch trading post in Hartford, and the Mohawks called New Englanders "Pynchon's men."

For several years before 1660, William's son and partner, John Pynchon, consigned a hogshead of peltry annually to Thomas Mainwaring, merchant of London, and another to Henry Ashurst and Nicholas Griggson. Most of these were on his own or his father's account, but Mainwaring and other London merchants sent "adventures" of their own in the shape of cloth and hardware, the proceeds of which were laid out in fur. A sample hogshead, sent in 1658, contained 184 beaver skins weighing 279 pounds, eighteen otter and twelve fox skins, four "nottamags" (mink) and forty-three "musquash" (muskrat) skins; wildcat, marten, and "woodshaws" (fishers) are occasionally mentioned. Pynchon also did a considerable trade in moose skins, which were in demand in London for making stout leather. The testicles of the beaver were valued for making musk, and these were packed separately. John Pynchon paid from 9s. 6d. to 11s. a pound for good winter beaver — less for "summer bever." Some of it was procured directly from Indians, who are named, some was "Mohock bever," procured from a Dutch trader, but a great deal of it came from English middlemen. Of these the principal was Joseph Parsons of "Nalwotogg" (Northampton), who kept store there and took beaver in trade. An astonishing variety of goods was sent to this small frontier town in the year 1657. For textiles there were red shag cotton, pink penistone, blue duffield, Devonshire kersey, coronation tammy, "sad-colored" and black serge, holland linen. With these were "notions" such as tape, binding, thread, points (garters), pins, needles, children's hats, "silk flagon coat buttons." The hardware included knives, scissors, awls, axes, "mackhooks," and burning-glasses for lighting fires. The presence of inkhorns shows that the Upper Valley was not illiterate; while the large variety of articles such as looking-glasses, ivory and bone combs, rings, and gilt boxes in nests, shows that even primitive Northampton was no stranger to the feminine graces. Altogether £615 worth of goods was sent to Joseph Parsons in 1657, and nearly the entire amount was paid in peltry.

Besides these wholesale accounts, John Pynchon carried retail book accounts with almost every family in Springfield. Seldom was any part of these accounts discharged in money. A domestic servant, for instance, was credited with £6 for a year's wages; she spent more than this on clothing and fur-belows. Other citizens were furnished with everything from a Bible and a pair of spectacles to read it with, to wine, rum, and tobacco. They paid mostly in grain and provision — a bushel of wheat paid for three quarts of rum — or by hauling goods from Warehouse Point, trimming the Pynchon or-chard, and doing odd jobs about the Pynchon house. There could have been very few people within thirty miles of Springfield whose labors, wants, and appetites did not con-tribute to swell the fortunes of the Pynchon family.

There is no reason to suppose that this great power wielded by the Pynchons was abused. New Englanders with a sense of grievance were not slow to make their grievances vocal, and after the corn case of 1638 I have discovered no charges against the dealings of Pynchon in the records of River or Bay. The records of Pynchon's own court of petty sessions at Springfield, kept in his own hand, are still extant, and give the impression of a conscientious magistrate who respected the English traditions of justice, and who denied it not to the poorest and most pestiferous man under his jurisdiction.

We are fortunate in having a contemporary portrait of William Pynchon, painted in England a few years after his return from America. It represents him a little older than he appeared when holding court at Springfield, and in the same plain dress of a Puritan gentleman: dark cloak with rows of metal clasps or buttons, a plain "band" or white collar, and a close-fitting skull cap, such as ministers and magistrates wore in the house. His face is distinguished by an unusually large and heavy Roman nose, very full lips set off by moustache and goatee, and an unusually long chin. It is a strong face, marked by poise, dignity, and sincerity. There is a glint of Yankee shrewdness in the eyes, but not a trace of humor, and such humor as we shall find in Pynchon's record of his court will be entirely unconscious. We may imagine Pynchon wearing this same costume, and the same grave expression was doubtless on his face, when he presided over the local court in the hall of his own house, perhaps seated in the massive wing chair which is still preserved at Springfield and attributed to him. He has to act as his own clerk and recorder. There is no other court official except the town constable. In front of him sit the six jurors — for the population of Agawam was insufficient to provide a full panel — and the body of the hall is filled with friends and neighbors of the litigant, eager to enjoy one of their rare recreations.

Most of the cases before the court were petty: leaving timber on the road, not paying for a hog, slander such as "false imputations of wrong dealinge in taking of those pompions" — the regular grist that passed through all the early New England courts. In the thirteen years covered by the record there is hardly a case which would come before a court of justice today. So much has been written of late about the sexual irregularities of the Puritans that it is perhaps worth recording that only two cases in Pynchon's magistracy were of that nature. In the one, a case of fornication attempted but not achieved, both parties were whipped. In the other, of masturbation in public, Pynchon tried the accused in private, swore the accusing witnesses to secrecy, and administered his own sentence himself, by whipping the man's back with a rod (July 28, 1650).

There were few actions concerning Indians. The widow Horton, accused of having sold her husband's gun to the Indians, declared that she had merely lent it, because

it lay spoilinge in her seller, but she saith that the Indian is suddenly to bring it againe and he hath lost about six fatham of wampam in pawne for it: . . . . I tould her if [records Pynchon] she would speedily get it home againe or else it would cost her dere for no commonwealth would allow of such a misdemenor.

Francis Ball's cattle were frightened by Indian boys on Agawam side; he could not catch the boys but struck their mother with a stick, and their father complained. Squire Pynchon in this case dispensed the oriental variety of justice:

Francis Ball saith it was but two blowes with a litle shorte stick about two foote long and not so big as his litle finger and he strock her only on her beare skin coat. I ordered him to pay her 2 hands of wampam but I also ordered that the boys that skared his cattell and hindered his cattell to pay 3 hands and when they paid the said 3 hands then Francis Ball should pay the two hands. . . .

The chief trouble maker in Springfield, whose name came most frequently before the court, was one John Woodcock. Master Moxon summoned him in December, 1639, to answer for a slander, in having declared that the reverend gentleman had taken a false oath against him somewhere downriver.

The said John desyred that this difference might be tried by a priuate hearinge below in the River: Mr Moxon referred himselfe to the Judgment of the plantation present present whether it were fitter to be heard by a private refference below in the River, or tryed here publikly by a Jury. The generall voa[t] of the plantation is that seeing the matter is publike it should be publikly herd and tryed her[e] by a Jury: Liberty is granted to John Woodcoke to produce his witnesses against this day fortnight being the 26 of Dec[e]mber. Also at the said tyme Jo Woodcoke is warned to answer for his laughinge in Sermon tyme: this day at the Lecture. Also he is then to answer his misdemenor [of] idlenese.

The jury found for the plaintiff, with the heavy damage of £6 13s. 4d., but this was not the end of the case.

When Mr Moxon gaue the Constable the warrant to distraine for the said damages the said Jo Woodcoke answered that he ought Mr Moxon no mony nor none he would pay him.
Also Jo Woodcoke said that he had showed Mr Moxon more

respect and reverence than ever he would againe — witnesse Henry Smyth Samuell Hubbard and Thomas Horton. (January 2, 1639–40.)

Before the end of the year our village cut-up was in court again, sued by Henry Gregory for accusing him of cheating about some pigs. The record here is mutilated. It seems that the jury found £4 7s. 3d. damage for the plaintiff, but that Squire Pynchon allowed him a writ of error and a new trial. On that occasion, "The Jury find for the plaintiffe [in error] about the pigg and give to Jo Woodcoke in damages Twenty shillings and costs 4s." Pynchon's record continues:

Henry Gregory after the verdict was much moved and said: I marvill with what consi[ence] the Jury can give such damages: Seeinge in the case of John Searles I had of him but Twenty shillinges for three slanders: and he added: But such Juries: he was about to speake more But Mr Moxon bid him take heed take heed, and so gave him a grave admonition: presently after the admonition Henry Gregory acknowleged his fault and earnestly craved pardon and promisd more care and watchfulnesse for tyme to come: and so all the Jury acknowledged satisffaction in hope of reformation. (September 10, 1640.)

John Woodcock's triumph was short-lived, for he had never paid the fine levied upon him for slandering the minister the year before, or made the retraction with which Mr. Moxon declared that he would rest content. Pynchon records (Oct. 1, 1640):

John Woodcoke not appearinge to give satisfaction to Mr Moxon accordinge to the liberty tendered to him: Therefore I ordaine the execution as followeth.

To John Searles Constable of Springfeild   Thes are in his Ma[jes]ties name to require you presently uppon the receite hereof That you attach the body of John Woodcoke uppon an execution granted to Mr George Moxon by the Jury against the said John Woodcoke for an action of slander: and that you kepe his body in prison or irons untill he shall take some course to satisfie the said George Moxon: or else if he neclect or refuse to take a speedy course to satisfie the said execution of 6li 13s 4d granted by the

Jury January 2d 1639. That then you use what meanes you can to put him out to service and labor till he make satisfaction to the said Mr George Moxon for the said 6*li* 13*s* 4*d* and also to satisfie yourselfe for such charges as you shall be at for the keeping of his person: And when Mr Moxon and yourselfe are satisfied, Then you are to discharge his person out of prison: faile not at your peruill Springfield this 5 October 1640

WILLIAM PYNCHON

By what means Woodcock satisfied Master Moxon and the Constable we do not know; but he was out of jail by January of the following year and in court again, sued by Robert Ashley for not delivering a gun for which Ashley had paid twenty shillings. The jury found for the plaintiff. Again to quote Pynchon's record:

After the Jury had given in their verdict John Woodcock denied that Robert had paid for the said gunn notwithstanding the action was tried before him and he never denied it: but I offered him a new tryall by a writ of error if he would present it (February 15, 1640–41).

In the course of this trial one Goody Gregory testified against Woodcock and called him a "prating fellow." John got his revenge on the goodwife promptly by accusing her of swearing, "Before God I could break thy head."

She did acknowledge it was her great sin and fault and saith she hath bin much humbled for it: She is fined 12*d* to the pore to be paid to Henry Smyth within a month: or if she doe not she is to sit 3 houers in the stocks.

After this final fling at the Agawam aristocrats, John Woodcock shook the dust of Springfield from his shoes, and migrated downriver.

That the procedure in this court was irregular, every lawyer will admit. On one occasion the "sense of the meeting" was taken as to whether a certain case should be tried there or elsewhere. Culprits were neither indicted nor regularly presented, and at the conclusion of one case the losing party haled a hostile witness into court for some irrelevant offense. On the other hand, so far as one can judge from the records, substantial justice appears to have been done, and even such a public nuisance as John Woodcock was instructed by the presiding justice as to his rights of appeal.

On May 29, 1649, Squire Pynchon asked the entire town to assemble at the opening of court, for he had an important function to perform. He read to them the lately printed Laws and Liberties of the Massachusetts Bay, in order that they might know their rights and duties. We may be sure that a thrill passed through the audience when he reached the section on "Capital lawes" and read: "If any man or woman be a WITCH, that is, hath or consulteth with a familiar spirit, they shall be put to death. *Exod.* 22. 18. *Levit.* 20. 27. *Deut.* 18. 10. 11."

There had long been talk that forces of the invisible world were active in Springfield, and the Squire, as soon as he had finished reading the laws, promptly took up a case involving witchcraft — the case of Hugh Parsons.

In the amusingly malicious romance, *The History of Connecticut*, by the Reverend Samuel Peters, it is stated that Hugh Parsons was the handsomest man in Springfield, so admired by the women that the men of Springfield in self-defense cried out upon him for a witch. Unfortunately the records do not bear out this genial explanation. Most of Hugh Parsons's accusers were women, and the principal one, his wife. Hugh was a farmer who did odd jobs at sawing and bricklaying, a good workman, apparently, but a very disagreeable person with whom to deal. A sullen, morose fellow who quickly took a grudge and nursed it long, Parsons was always imagining he was being wronged, when he would exclaim: "I'll get even with you," or, if he were forced to pay a debt or to deliver a paid-for pig: "It will do you no good." In fact, Hugh Parsons was just the unsocial, unpopular sort of person who in a New England town was apt to get denounced as a witch in the seventeenth century, a tory in the eighteenth century, an atheist in the nineteenth century, and a communist in the twentieth.

It was Hugh's wife, Mary, who started the trouble by telling the neighbors that the widow Marshfield, who had recently come to town from Windsor, was a witch. Goody Marshfield entered an action for slander against Mary Parsons before Squire Pynchon who wrote down just what was said, or alleged to have been said, in his court records. John Matthews testified that Goody Parsons said that the widow Marshfield

was suspected to be a witch when she lived in Windsor and that it was publikely knowen that the divill followed her howse in Windsor "and for aught I know," said she, "followes her here."

Goodwife Mathewes saith uppon oath that when Goody Parsons came to her howse she said to her "I wonder what is become of the half pound of your woll?" Goody Parsons said that she could not tell except the witch had witched it away. "I wonder" said I "that you talke so much of a witch doe you think there is any witch in Towne": "yes" said shee, "and she came into my howse while the wool was a cardinge." "Who is it?" said I: she said that An Stebbinge had told her in Mr Smiths Chamber that she [Goody Marshfield] was suspected to be a witch in Windsor, and that there were divers strong lights seene of late in the meddow that were never seene before the widdow Marshfeild came to Towne and that she did grudge at other weomen that had children before her daughter had none and about that tyme (namely of her grudging) the child died and the cow died.

Goody Parsons did stiffly denie the truth of this Testimonye: but because the said witnesses had delivered their testimony uppon oath and finding that she had defamed the good name of the widdow Marshfield I sentenced her to be well whipped on the morrow after lecture with 20 lashes by the Conestable unlesse she could procure the payment of 3*li* to the widdow Marshfeild for and towarde the reparation of her good name.

Hugh Parsons elected to pay the fine with Indian corn. He

asked the widow Marshfield to abate one-third, which she refused; whereupon he said: "Well, if you will not it had bin as good you had — it will be but as wild Fier in this Howse, and as a Moth in your Garment, and it will doe you no Good, Ile warnt it."

Soon after this, Goody Marshfield's daughter was taken with strange "Fitts of witchcraft," and the Moxon girls, the minister's daughters, with still stranger fits, which caused someone to remember that when the minister had held Parsons to a bargain about some bricks for the parsonage chimney, Hugh said: "I will be even with him, he shall get Nothinge by it." Master Moxon, with evident reluctance, admitted that Hugh had threatened him thus — but said he always talked like that.

And now everyone in town began to recollect hard words and ugly looks from Hugh Parsons, and there were more strange happenings which the people were convinced were due to the powers of darkness. Mary Parsons, wife of Hugh, had a baby. It was an ill-favored, puling brat — a regular witch-child, who wasted away in a mysterious manner and died. Poor Mary then went completely off her head, and accused her own husband of having bewitched the babe. Squire Pynchon, finding it impossible to ignore the hue and cry any longer, held an inquest. Here all the pent-up fear, malice, and superstition of the little settlement boiled up.

The Langdons told how twice in succession their pudding had been cut in its bag, how after the second time they threw a bit of it in the fire, and how shortly after there came Hugh Parsons a-muttering and a-mumbling at the door, summoned by the spirit who had bewitched the pudding — though Hugh Parsons said he came to get some hay. Three men who went woodchopping with Hugh testified how one of them, who told the pudding story when they "were at Dinner, and merry together," got black looks from Hugh, and within fifteen minutes his axe slipped and cut his leg. Squire Pynchon's storekeeper, when he refused to sell Parsons a piece of leather because he was busy with his team, promptly had the team run away with him, and was almost killed. When Blanche Bedortha intruded on a men's discussion, Hugh Parsons turned to her and said: "I spake not to you; but I shall remember you when you little think on it." Since then Blanche had had a painful confinement, with pinchings and prickings, she had seen strange lights, and her two-year-old child was repeatedly frightened by a great dog in the house that no one else could see — Hugh Parsons's dog, the child said it was. Goody Myrick in company with Hugh Parsons had pulled out with a mere touch a beer tap which no one else could move, even with a hammer; and a man who exclaimed at this: "What, are you a Witch?" that night after the beer party was over, had seen snakes in his room. There were two "great ones" and one "little one with blackish and yellow streaks," which climbed on his bed and struck him in the forehead, and at that moment he heard a voice like Hugh Parsons's, saying: "Death!" Mary Parsons said she knew all about that visit of the snakes, and the one that bit him was Hugh. She wouldn't tell who the other two were, but she could. A woman refused to sell milk to Hugh. Then her cow's milk turned yellow, and then "to some od Cullor or other and also it grew lesse and lesse," and there were many more trivial coincidences of that sort with which in one way or another Hugh could be connected. To all these charges "that dumb Dogg," Hugh, as his wife called him, remained sullenly silent.

It was from Mary Parsons that the weightiest testimony came. If mad, there was method in her madness, for she deposed very coolly that she had four reasons to believe him to be a witch.

1. Because when I say Anything to any Body, never so secretly, to such Freinde as I am sure would not speak of it, yet he would come to know it; by what Meanes I cannot tell: I have spoken

some Thinges to Mrs. Smith, that goes litle Abroad, and I am sure would not speak of it, yet he hath knowen it, and would speak of it to me as soone as I came Home.

2ly. Because he useth to be out a Nights till Midnight (till of Late), and about half an Hower before he comes Home, I shall here some Noyse or other about the Dore, or about the Howse.

3ly. Because he useth to come Home in a distempered Frame, so that I could not tell how to please him; sometymes he hath puld of the Bed Clothes and left me naked a Bed, and hath quenched the Fier; sometymes he hat thrown Pease about the Howse and made me pick them up.

4. Because oftentymes in his Sleepe he makes a gablinge Noyse, but I cannot understand one Word that he says, and when I did aske what it was that he talked in his Sleepe, he would say that he had strange Dreames; and one Tyme he said that the Divell and he were fighting, and that the Divell had almost overcome him, but at last he got the Mastery of the Divill.

Worse than that, she was certain that he had bewitched their baby and caused its death, and the neighbors were the more ready to believe that, since Hugh had been harsh and cruel both to mother and child, and had shown no grief when he was told of the babe's death. But Mary too was involved, for a neighbor who was told off to watch her reported that she admitted having talked with the Devil,

and that Night [said she] I was with my Husband and Goodwife Mericke and Besse Sewell, in Goodman Stebinges his Lott: and we were sometymes like Catts and sometymes in our owne shape, and we were a plodding for some good Cheere; and they made me to go barefoote and mak the Fiers, because I had declared so much at Mr. Pynchons.

The upshot of this all was that Squire Pynchon, not empowered to try a crime involving loss of life, indicted both Mary and Hugh Parsons for witchcraft, and sent them for trial to Boston, where several of the witnesses attended court. Hugh Parsons was convicted by the trial jury of having bewitched his child to death, but the magistrates refused to accept the verdict, since poor mad Mary, perhaps out of remorse for her horrible accusation, had in the meantime confessed that she herself had killed the child. Hugh's case was appealed to the Great and General Court, which decided he was "not legally guilty of witchcrafte and so not to dye by lawe." But Mary Parsons was condemned to die for infanticide, and sentenced to be hanged. Upon the morning set for her execution she was too weak to be moved, and was respited; on the second day she was found dead in her cell. Hugh, saved by her confession of murder, never returned to Springfield, but settled in Watertown, and disappears from the ken of history.

Perhaps Hugh Parsons, when indicted by Squire Pynchon, remarked: "It will doe you no good." Possibly he even added, in his resentful way: "I'll get even with you." For it is a curious coincidence that at the very same General Court in Boston where Hugh Parsons was tried for witchcraft, and Mary for murder, William Pynchon was called upon to answer for heresy. When the people of Springfield heard that their squire had been censured by the government, and humiliated to a point which compelled him out of self-respect to return to England, I have no doubt that they believed Hugh Parsons and his friend the devil to be the cause of it all.

William Pynchon, it appears, had always thought deeply on theological subjects, especially on the mysterious doctrine of Christ's atonement for the sins of man. Orthodox Calvinists agreed with the medieval church in believing that Christ literally, in the words of the Apostles' creed, "descended into hell," there to suffer the torments of the damned as a part of His price for our salvation. Himself a father, Pynchon could not conceive of God the Father exacting for our sins such a terrible price of His only begotten Son as to doom Him not only to die in agony on the Cross, but to suffer the torments of hell-fire. Pondering the question during long winter evenings at Springfield, and on his lonely horseback journeys over the Bay Path, discussing and searching the Bible with Master Moxon, he reached the conclusion that there was no authority in Scripture for the orthodox view. Christ never actually bore Adam's sin, or suffered God's curse for Adam's fall; His descent into hell, if indeed He ever visited the place, was a mere sightseeing expedition like those of Aeneas and Dante. Christ made a full and sufficient sacrifice for the sins of the world by perfect obedience to His Father's will and by His death and passion. In the course of years, after how many painful rewritings and redraftings we know not, Pynchon completed a book to prove his point, written in the form of a dialogue between a tradesman and a divine. It was sent over to London to be printed, and printed there it was by one James Moxon — probably a kinsman of the minister at Springfield — in 1650. *The Meritorious Price of Our Redemption, Justification,* etc., was the title of this book of 170 pages, "By *William Pinchin*, Gentleman, in New-England."[1]

It is hard for us to imagine a state of society in which a mere difference of opinion as to the amount and kind of suffering that Christ had to undergo before He could induce His Father to save a selected few of mankind from hell should be regarded as a matter of great pith and moment, akin to sedition and treason, undermining the basis of the state, and corrupting the consciences of the people. But so it was. Massachusetts Bay had just entered the narrowest, most bigoted period in her history, the half-century which came in with the persecution of Quakers, and went out in a storm of witchcraft. Robert Child and the Remonstrants had been

---

[1] Frank H. Foster, *Genetic History of the New England Theology* (1907), 16–20, regards Pynchon's work as "the protest of plain common sense against the current representations of the atonement," and in the same line of thought as the teachings of Anselm; but he finds no trace of Pynchon's influence on later writers. "The book seems to have exhaled its life in the flames in which it was burned upon Boston market place."

heavily fined and practically banished for proposing toleration to Presbyterians. The New England synod of 1647–48 had adopted an official confession of faith and platform of church discipline, revoking the great promise of freedom that lay in the Congregational polity by inviting the civil authorities to punish heresy as well as "corrupt and pernicious opinions that destroy the foundation." This was, of course, a logical consequence of the puritanic purpose to found a medieval church-state; but logic sometimes defeats its own ends. Even before the synod had sat, the General Court had passed a law condemning to banishment anyone who broached certain "damnable heresies," among which was specified the denial of the orthodox doctrine of the atonement. Pynchon belonged to the governing class. A member of the Board of Assistants, he had taken part in the repressive legislation, and must have been well acquainted with the intolerant temper of his fellows. He can hardly have been surprised at the reception of his book.

A copy of *The Meritorious Price of Our Redemption* arrived in Boston during the autumn of 1650. It was passed around among the members of the General Court of Massachusetts which then, as now, undertook to set up the standards of truth and the bounds of permissible opinion. The Court "judged it meete and necessary" for the vindication of the truth, and the preservation of the interests of true religion in Massachusetts, and for clearing themselves to their Christian brethren in England, to disclaim any part or share in "writing, composing, printing, or divulging" the book, but, on the contrary, to protest that they detested and abhorred it as "false, erronious, and hæretticall."

Just why the Court should have considered it necessary to clear itself does not appear, for Pynchon did not describe himself in the book as a member of their body, but as a gentleman — a very nice distinction. So far as English opinion was concerned, Pynchon's tract was but a grain in a heap of sand — one of thousands of religious and theological pamphlets with which the English public was being smothered; and far from imputing any blame to Massachusetts for the book, the only expression of English opinion on the subject was a letter from Sir Harry Vane and others to the General Court urging them to let Pynchon and the book alone. But we shall better understand the frame of mind of the General Court if we compare it, not with a legislature, but with a college board of trustees. They conceived themselves trustees of orthodox Christianity, just as many American college boards consider themselves trustees of orthodox Americanism, capitalism, or whatnot; and they condemned Pynchon and his book in just the same spirit that many alumni have demanded, and some colleges have conceded, the dismissal of professors who write books which are considered unpatriotic or socialistic.

And for proofe of our sincere and plaine meaning therein [continued the Court in 1650] wee doe heereby condemne the said bookes to be burned in the markett place at Boston by the marshall, . . . and doe purpose, with all convenient speede, to convent the said Mr William Pinchon before authoritie, to finde out whether the said William Pinchon will oune the said booke as his or not, which if he doth, wee purpose, God assisting, to proceede with him according to his demerritts, unlesse he retract the same . . .

This Resolve passed. Governor Dudley, Deputy-Governor Endecott, and Nowell, Bradstreet, and Bellingham of the Assistants, who had been Pynchon's associates for almost twenty years on the Board of Assistants, voted for it. But the Resolve was not passed unanimously, and the six deputies who voted against it ought to be remembered as pioneers of freedom of speech and of the press: William Hathorne (the ancestor of Nathaniel), Henry Bartholomew, Joseph Hills, Richard Walker, Stephen Kingsley, and Edward Holyoke, the deputy of Springfield.

Having condemned Pynchon's book to the flames, the Gen-

eral Court piously proclaimed a day of fasting and humiliation, "taking into consideration how farr Sathan prevailes
amongst us in respect of witchcrafts, as also by drawing
away some . . . to the profession and practize of straunge
opinnions." At the same time John Norton and two other
clergymen were commissioned to reason with Pynchon, and
to answer his book if he did not recant. So Squire Pynchon
appeared, under a cloud, at the Court of Elections in Boston
on May 7, 1651. For the first time since Springfield seceded
from Connecticut, he was not chosen an Assistant. For a few
days he was concerned with the trial of Mary Parsons, and
on the thirteenth, the Court sentenced Mary to death. Immediately after comes the entry: "Mr. Wm Pinchon . . .
made his appearance before the Court," and "ouned it [the
Meritorious Price] to be his." He was allowed to confer with
the three clergymen. He acknowledged that the book was
not quite as explicit as he would have wished about the
"prize and merrit of Christs sufferings" — they were not
merely trials of obedience but a punishment for our sins as
well. This fell short of the complete recantation that the
Court required, but they believed him in a "hopefull way
to give good satisfaction," hence "out of their tender respect
to him" he was not imprisoned for his opinions but, having
already lost his magistracy, he was allowed to go home to
Springfield and decide whether he would not recant the
whole. The Reverend John Norton received from the government the large sum of £20 — about three months' salary —
for writing an answer to the Pynchon tract, a singular tribute
to the force of Pynchon's arguments.

So William Pynchon returned to pass his last summer by
the river that he loved, in the community which he had seen
grow from a band of eight men to a prosperous trading and
farming town. He was due to reappear at the next General
Court, which met on October 14, 1651, to retract the rest of
his errors, or suffer the consequences. Instead, he decided

to return to England, where he might enjoy that liberty of opinion which was denied him in the colony he had helped to found. On September 28, 1651, he conveyed all his lands and buildings in Springfield and along the River to his son John. The General Court never saw him again. On October 24, 1651, with an air of gracious concession, the Court gave Pynchon another six months to consider, retract, and renounce his horrid heresies. But before that time elapsed, Pynchon and his wife quietly left the colony for England. With them went the Reverend George Moxon, who, as Pynchon's sympathizer and spiritual adviser, must have known that his turn to be questioned, censured, and ejected would come next.

A return to England was doubtless the wisest course for Pynchon. The General Court of Massachusetts was no respecter of persons; he could expect only trouble if he stayed to fight for the truth that was in him. It is, however, probable that he would have returned to England in a short time even if there had been no question of persecution, as did contemporaries like Nathaniel Ward. England under the Protectorate was a desirable place or residence for an elderly, scholarly, and well-to-do Puritan. William Pynchon was over sixty years old, and had fairly earned a rest after twenty years' labor in the public service, and seating civilization securely on the upper Connecticut Valley. An ample fortune to provide for his old age had been accumulated in the fur trade, and he left a capable son and son-in-law at Springfield to carry on the business.

Upon reaching England, Pynchon retired to a modest estate at Wraysbury, about three miles from Windsor. Nearby was the Thames, a tame and placid miniature of the Connecticut, to be sure, but where the plash of oars or the cry of wildfowl might serve to remind him of the Great River, majestically flowing between Agawam and the "long meddowe."

In this quiet retreat, ten years of life remained to William Pynchon — he died on October 29, 1662.

Of the occupations of his old age we know little. Doubtless he journeyed to London occasionally to see to the selling of furs that John Pynchon consigned to him, to straighten out accounts with London merchants, and to give them some good advice on matters connected with peltry. But much of his time must have been spent in his study, searching the Bible and the Church Fathers for the light of truth. In answer to Norton's printed denunciation of *The Meritorious Price of Our Redemption*, Pynchon published a book of 440 pages, *The Meritorious Price of Man's Redemption*, which ran into a second edition with a new title.[1] Three other pamphlets by him have been found: one on the Jewish Synagogue, another on the Jewish Sabbath, and a third on the Covenant with Adam.[2] These pamphlets made no stir in their day. The sea of opinion in England was too much roiled for another stone or two to add even a ripple. Today they are of value only as rare Americana, and as proof that things of the spirit were no strangers to this founder of Massachusetts Bay, the sometime autocrat of the frontier outpost on the Connecticut River.

[1] *A Farther Discussion of that Great Point in Divinity the Sufferings of Christ* (London, 1655).

[2] *The Jewes Synagogue* (London, 1652), which, from its date, was probably written in America; *The Time When the First Sabbath was Ordained* (London, 1654), and *The Covenant of Nature made with Adam* (London, 1662).

APPENDIX

BIBLIOGRAPHY

INDEX

APPENDIX

WERE THE SETTLERS OF MASSACHUSETTS BAY PURITANS?

THE traditional view — a tradition created by the settlers themselves — that the great emigration to New England from 1630 to 1640 was a puritan migration, composed of persons who left England primarily for religious purposes; and that the population of the colonies of Plymouth, Massachusetts Bay, Connecticut, Rhode Island, and New Haven was predominantly, overwhelmingly puritan in character, was challenged by Mr. J. Truslow Adams in chapter VI of his *Founding of New England* (1921). He believes that the people of Massachusetts as a whole were not really puritans; that 'four out of five' had no sympathy with the puritan church, and merely passively acquiesced in the rule of a high-handed minority, in order to enjoy the benefits of the New England soil, climate, and water.

The reason why the mystic number 'four out of five' has been selected, is because John G. Palfrey, many years ago, computing the relation of freemen (voters) to population in Massachusetts (a computation obviously based largely on guesswork, since we have no accurate census), concluded that in 1670 only one in four or one in five of the adult males had the vote.[1] Mr. Adams founds upon this estimate the bold inference: 'not more than one in five of the adult males who went even to Massachusetts was sufficiently in sympathy with the religious ideas there prevalent to become a church member, though disfranchised for not doing so.' In 1640 (thirty years earlier than Palfrey's estimate) the puritan element 'in New England amounted to only about four thousand persons' out of a population of sixteen thousand! He points out that in the 1630's more English were emigrating to Virginia, Maryland, and Barbados, than to New England; and concludes that the 'four out of five' who were called but not chosen, came to New England because 'the Puritan colonies were the only ones in which land could be owned in fee simple, without quit-rent or lord, and in which it was freely given to settlers.'[2]

[1] *History of New England*, III, 41, note 3.
[2] *Founding of New England*, pp. 121–22.

Mr. Adams' ability to balance inferences upon one another to make a convincing theory for those who are ready to believe it, compels admiration. His theory fits in so neatly with the economic interpretation of history, with the fashionable dislike of what to-day is called puritanism, and with the American love for statistics, that the 'four out of five' unpuritan New Englanders are even getting into the school textbooks, where historical theories seldom penetrate until they are obsolete.

The first fallacy of Mr. Adams is to ignore, for purposes of this theory, the technical New England meaning of church membership. A church member, as we have seen, did not mean a mere believer, churchgoer, or member of the parish. It meant a 'visible saint,' admitted to the church (the body of communicants) only after rigorous examination by himself and by them, as to his 'conversion' and ability to walk with God. Thomas Shepard, for instance, held up the organization of a neighboring church, because the charter members did not succeed in convincing him that they were really 'converted.' Church membership was not conferred automatically by baptism and confirmation in childhood, as in the greater part of Christendom. It was an ordeal, the successful passing of which involved new obligations of mutual watchfulness, helpfulness, and rigorous conduct.

Further, it was the voters, not the church members, whom Palfrey computed to be only one in four or five. The church members were more numerous. An Act of the General Court of 1647 declares: 'Whereas there are within this Jurisdiction many members of Churches who to exempt themselves from all publick service in the Common-wealth will not come in, to be made Freemen,' such persons must serve, if chosen, as town officers.

There are other reasons, beside this act, to believe that church members were more numerous than one in four or five, before 1660. Edward Johnson, writing in 1652, estimated that the town of Roxbury then had 120 houses, and the same number of church members.[1] The actual roll of church membership shows that he was nearly right in that particular; in 1652 it included about 130 people, of whom 57 were men and 54 were voters.[2] Assuming that his count of houses was correct, and that each household would contain on the average one grown man, almost half the adult male population were church members. Ten or twelve years earlier the proportion

[1] *Wonder-Working Providence* (Jameson ed.), p. 72.
[2] W. E. Thwing, *Hist. of Church of Roxbury*, pp. 47–59.

was even greater. A list of Roxbury householders of 1638–40 contains 69 men, of whom 58 were both church members and voters. Allowing for a dozen or so grown-up sons or servants who were neither householders nor church members, the proportion of adult males who were voters was sixty-five to seventy-five per cent.[1] There is no reason to suppose that Roxbury was an unusually pious community. But there is much evidence that the proportion of church members to population fell off rapidly after 1652, and that Palfrey's estimate of twenty to twenty-five per cent, may be substantially correct for 1670. This falling off was not, however, caused by immigration, but by the decline of religious interest in the new native-born generation. By that time, however, the church member restriction had ceased to operate; it had been repealed in 1664. It has been said that public opinion enforced the restriction, nevertheless. But John Hull, in his diary for 1665, says, 'The first day of the Court there was about seventy freemen admitted, sundry whereof were not members of any particular church, which had been the general rule of admission hitherto.'[2]

It is really too bad that no one had the bright idea to circulate the following questionnaire among the inhabitants of New England in 1640:

1. Why did you come to New England? Check correct answer: (a) persecution; (b) attracted by 'come to New England' literature; (c) wages; (d) health; (e) free land.
2. Are you a church member? If not, check reason why: (a) not called; (b) too busy; (c) waiting for new clothes; (d) not a believer.
3. Check preferred denomination: (a) Anglican; (b) New England way; (c) Antinomian; (d) Anabaptist; (e) Familist; (f) if other, write name in this space:
   Answers will be held strictly confidential, and will not be inspected by magistrates or elders. A reply is earnestly requested to help our historians 300 years hence.

Common sense tells us that the population could not have been one hundred per cent puritan; and the testimony of such men as Shepard and Winthrop shows that economic motives weighed even with the more religiously minded, although on the same side of the scale as religion. Indented servants were not asked about their religion before they were hired, and puritanism was not a way of life that appealed to base or ignorant persons. Even on board the *Ar-*

---

[1] C. M. Ellis, *History of Roxbury Town*, I, 17–19.
[2] *Archaeologia Americana*, III, 217.

bella there were 'notorious lewd persons' who got at the liquor while the holy ones were fasting and praying.[1] And John Winthrop called some of the early settlers 'the very scum of the earth.'[2] If, as William Stoughton declared in his election sermon of 1670, 'God sifted a whole Nation that he might send choice Grain over into this Wilderness,'[3] it is clear from our records that a fair number of horse-thieves, cheats, drunkards, and libertines managed to elude the all-seeing eye. But apart from these, the way the 'great emigration' to New England was conducted precludes any possibility of a large section of the English public being deceived, and suddenly finding themselves in a puritan colony against their will. An analysis of the passenger lists that survive — mostly for the year 1635 — shows that emigration was heaviest from East Anglia, London, and the Home Counties, notoriously the most puritan sections, and from the West Country, where puritanism was strong.[4] Further analysis shows that emigrants came mostly from the middle classes in town and country, among whom were the backbone of the puritan and parliamentary movement: 'men of substance, will-making families.' As suggested in the 'come alonge' ballad I have quoted in Chapter II, they came in small family and neighborhood groups, often following some popular non-conformist preacher such as Cotton or Shepard; or Ezekiel Rogers, who brought a colony of Yorkshire clothworkers to Rowley, or Richard Mather, who brought a Lancashire group to join the West Countrymen at Dorchester. Hingham was settled by the followers of Peter Hobart of Hingham in England; Gloucester by men of that county, under Richard Blynman; and so one might go on.[5] Old Joshua Scottow, who came over with his parents during the great emigration, wrote 'A letter then from New England . . . was Venerated as a Sacred Script, or as the Writing of some Holy Prophet, 'twas carried many Miles, where divers came to hear it.'[6] If a group of liberty-loving people to-day, desirous of enjoying certain creatures of God which the laws of the land now deny to them, should for that purpose found a colony in the Philippines, or some other part of the American Empire — if

[1] *Life and Letters of John Winthrop*, I, 390.

[2] *Calendar of State Papers Colonial, 1574–1600*, p. 155.

[3] Sibley, *Harvard Graduates*, I, 207.

[4] Colonel Banks, in *Proceedings Mass. Hist. Soc.*, LX, 372.

[5] G. Andrews Moriarty, in A. B. Hart, *Commonwealth History of Massachusetts*, I, 49–90.

[6] 4 *Coll. Mass. Hist. Soc.*, IV, 293.

any there be — to which the Eighteenth Amendment does not extend; is it to be supposed that prohibitionists would follow them there, unless to annoy them? Similarly, there was no reason except religion, to make Englishmen prefer New England to Barbados or Virginia. Free land was more easily obtained in the Southern colonies than in New England, and far more productive when you got it.[1]

Indeed the founders of the Bay Colony were at pains to discourage people to emigrate in hope of gain. Thomas Dudley says in his letter to the Countess of Lincoln, 'If any come hither to plant for worldly ends, that can live well at home, he commits an error, of which he will soon repent him; but if for spiritual... he may find here what may well content him.' He admits that previous accounts of New England were too highly colored. 'If any godly men, out of religious ends, will come over to help us in the good work we are about, I think they cannot dispose of themselves nor of their estates more to God's glory and the furtherance of their own reckoning. But they must not be of the poorer sort yet for divers years, for we have found by experience that they have hindered, not furthered the work.'[2] In 1633, Governor Winthrop invites Sir Simonds D'Ewes to 'drive a trade with the Lord heere... by sending over some poore godly [puritanical] familyes with a yeares provision,' but dissuades him from any other investment.[3] And the same gentlewoman who complained of the strawberry-time boosters, thus concludes her pungent letter: 'Look upon it, as it hath the means of grace, and, if you please, you may call it a Canaan. — I perceive some among you have imagined they might enlarge their estates by coming here, but I am taught that great men must look to be losers, unless they reckon that gain which, by the glorious means of life, comes down from heaven.'[4]

That the settlers of New England were predominantly puritan was admitted even by their enemies. I will quote a raspingly satirical ballad on the New England emigration, highly amusing since

[1] Newcomers in Virginia and Maryland obtained fifty acres of land gratis for every member of their family or servants they brought over. The quit-rent on such land amounted to very little. In Massachusetts, to obtain any land you had to be admitted to a town, and then obtain house-lot, planting lots, meadows, etc., according to your number of cattle. So far as profitable agriculture was concerned, the Southern colonies had it all over New England.

[2] Young, *Chronicles of Massachusetts*, p. 324.

[3] *Publications Colonial Society of Massachusetts*, VII, 70.

[4] Hutchinson, *History of Massachusetts Bay*, second edition, I, 484.

it accuses the puritans not only of fanaticism and radicalism, but of free love — the favorite method at all times of discrediting new liberal and religious movements:

A PROPER NEWE BALLETT CALLED THE SUMMONS TO NEWE ENGLAND

to the tune of The Townesmens cappe[1]
Lett all that putrifidean secte,
I meane the counterfeite electe,
All zealous banckrupps, puncks devout,
Preachers suspended, rable rout,
Lett them sell all, and out of hand
Prepare to goe for Newe England,
    To build newe Babel strong and sure
    Now calld a 'Church unspotted, pure.'

There milke from springs like rivers flowe
And honie upon hawthornes growe;
Hempe, woll, and flaxe there growes on trees —
The mowlde is fatt and cuttes like cheese;
All fruites, all hearbes growes in the fields,
Tobacco in great plentie yeelds —
    And there shal be a Church most pure
    Where you shall finde salvacion sure!

There's venison of all sortes great store,
Both stag and buck, wilde goat and bore;
And yet soe tame as you with ease
Maie eate your fill, take what you please;
Ther's Beavers plentie, — yea, soe many
That you may buy two skinnes a pennie;
    Above all these, a Churche so pure
    That to be sav'd you may be sure.

There flightes of fowle doe cloude the light,
Greate Turkies sixty pound in weight,
As bigge as Oistreges; their geese
Are sould with thankes for pence a peese;
Of Ducke and mallard, wiggion, teale,
Twentie for twopence mak a meale:
    Yea! and a 'Church unspotted, pure'
    Within whose bosom all are sure!

---

[1] Bodleian Library, Tanner MSS., cccvi, 286–87. Another copy in the Public Record Office, with variations, is printed in *Proceedings Mass. Hist. Soc.*, v, 101–03.

Loe! there in shoales all sorts of fishe
Of the salt sea and waters freshe:
Linge, codde, poore John, and haberdins
Are taken with the hooks and lins:
A painfull fisher on the shore
May take of each twentie an hower.
   But, above all, a Church most pure,
   Where you may live and die secure.

There twice a yeere all sortes of graine
Doe downe like hayle from th' heavens rayne;
You never need to sowe, nor plowe,
Ther's plentie of all thinges enowe:
Wine sweet and holesome drops from trees,
As cleere as christall without lees.
   Yea! and a 'Church unspotted, pure'
   From dreggs of Papistrie secure.

No feastes or festivall set Daies
Are heere observed — the Lord we praise!
Thoughe not in churches riche and strong,
Yet where no Mass was ever sunge
The Bulls of Basan roare not heere;
Surplice or cap durst not appeare,
   Old orders all they will abjure;
   This church hath all thinges new and pure.

No discipline shall there be us'd —
The lawe of nature they have chus'd;
All that the spiritt seemes to move
Each man maie take and that approve.
Ther's governement without commande,
Ther's unitie without a bande;
   A sinagogue unspotted, pure,
   Where lustes and pleasures dwell secure.

Loe! in this Church all shal be free
T'enjoye all Christian libertie:
All thinges made comon; t'avoide strife
Each man may take anothers wife,
And keepe a handmaid to if neede
To multiplie, encrease and breede.
   And is not this foundacion sure
   To raise a Church unspotted, pure?

The native people, though yet wilde,
And all by Nature kinde, and milde —
And apt already by report
To live in *this* religous sorte —
Soone to conversion they'le be brought
When Warchams [1] miracles are wrought,
 Who being sanctified and pure
 May by the spiritt them allure.

L'ENVOY

Let Amsterdam send forth her bratts,
Her fugitives and renegates;
Let Bedlam, Newgate and the Clinke
Disgorge themselves into this sincke;
Let Bridewelle and the stewes be swept
And sent all thither to be kepte
 Soe may the Churche, cleans'd and made pure
 Keepe both itself and State secure!

It is quite natural that the religious motives of the founders of New England should be questioned, and replaced by the economic. Material success is a motive which the present age can understand, while the mind of a man willing to sacrifice comfort and security in order to worship in a particular way, is to most people incomprehensible. Similarly, nineteenth-century historians often ascribe the puritan emigration to democracy, republicanism, or political discontent. My own opinion, one arrived at by considerable reading of what the puritans wrote, is that religion, not economics nor politics, was the center and focus of the puritan dissatisfaction with England, and the puritan migration to New England. When you find a puritan writing about the fine material prospects of the new world, he is usually trying to counteract the argument that liberty of conscience is not worth the loss of friends, comforts and civilization.

[1] Reading doubtful. Probably 'Marcham's miracles,' as a synonym for the 'Greek kalends' — as the canonization of Bishop William de Marcham, a reputed miracle worker of the thirteenth century, was indefinitely postponed. The other version reads 'Warham's' — possibly a reference to the Reverend John Warham of Dorchester, Massachusetts.

BIBLIOGRAPHY

GENERAL

James Truslow Adams' *Founding of New England* (1921) is mainly political history, and fundamentally unsympathetic to the puritans. With these limitations, it is still the best general survey of seventeenth-century Massachusetts that we have, and a salutary one for New-Englanders to read. John Fiske's *Beginnings of New England* (edition of 1929, Houghton Mifflin Co.) was written a generation earlier, with more sympathy but less knowledge. Palfrey's *History of New England* (5 vols., 1858–90) is still a valuable work of reference. I have a higher opinion than most historians of Cotton Mather's *Magnalia Christi Americana* (1702). Although Mather is inaccurate, pedantic, and not above *suppressio veri*, he does succeed in giving a living picture of the persons he writes about; and he was near enough to the first generation to catch the spirit and flavor of the times.

The standard source collection is the 'Colony Records' (*Records of the Governor and Company of the Massachusetts Bay*, 5 vols., 1854), published by the Commonwealth, but this contains little more than the journal of the General Court. Massachusetts is the only one of the original thirteen States, except South Carolina, which has not printed its archives for the colonial period *in extenso*. Of the contemporary authorities, besides Winthrop (see below), there is Bradford's *History of Plimmoth Plantation* (the best edition, with copious notes, is that of the Massachusetts Historical Society, 1912), and Edward Johnson's *Wonder-Working Providence* (1654), republished in Scribners' *Original Narratives* in 1910. Alexander Young, *Chronicles of the First Planters of Massachusetts Bay* (1846), is a useful collection of contemporary works such as Roger Clap's *Memoirs*, Higginson's *New England Plantation*, and parts of Hubbard's *History*.

The best general survey of the literature of seventeenth-century New England is Moses Coit Tyler's *History of American Literature*, vol. 1 (1879). Vernon L. Parrington's *The Colonial Mind* (New York, 1927) is a brilliant synthesis of history and literature, but the writer shows little evidence of having read carefully the works of the authors he writes about, and his preconceived notion that puritanism was primarily an economic movement causes him to miss the point of much that he did read. Kenneth B. Murdock's introduction to *Handkerchiefs from Paul* (Cambridge, 1927, including poetry of Samuel Danforth and John Wilson) contains some thoughtful remarks on the relation of puritanism to literature, as does Howard J. Hall in his introduction to the *Works of Benjamin Tompson* (Houghton Mifflin Co., 1924). The other verses that I have quoted will be found in various reprints by the Club of Odd Volumes; excepting Thomas Shepard's almanac verse, which I think has not been reprinted before.

I. HAKLUYT, SMITH, AND MORTON

The best general account of the voyages to the New England coast before 1620 is in Justin Winsor's *Narrative and Critical History of America*, vol. III; the most convenient collection of narratives is in H. S. Burrage (ed.), *Early English and French Voyages* (*Original Narratives* series, New York, 1906). This volume also contains extracts from Hakluyt's *Voyages*, of which there are several recent editions. The best Life of him is George B. Parks, *Richard Hakluyt and the English Voyages* (American Geographical Society, 1928). A beautifully printed and illustrated edition of the *Travels and Works of Captain John Smith*, edited by Edward Arber and A. G. Bradley, came out in 1884, and has since frequently been reprinted. It provoked the devastating examination of Smith's earlier travels by Lewis L. Kropf in the *American Historical Review*, III, 737. Henry Adams won his historical spurs by an examination of the Pocahontas episode in the *North American Review* for January, 1867. The various biographies of Smith are uncritical, and say little of his work for New England. Thomas Morton's *New English Canaan* is found in Force's *American Tracts*, and in the *Publications* of the Prince Society (1883) with critical notes and an introduction by Charles Francis Adams. A few more details about him are in *Proceedings of the Massachusetts Historical Society*, LVIII, 147, LIX, 92. The account of his capture is from Bradford's *Plimmoth Plantation*. John Smith's and other early maps of the New England coast are well reproduced in Fite and Freeman, *A Book of Old Maps* (Cambridge, 1926).

II. JOHN WHITE

In addition to the monumental *John White, the Patriarch of Dorchester (Dorset) and the Founder of Massachusetts, 1575–1648* (New York, 1930) by Mrs. Frances Rose-Troup, we have her

Massachusetts Bay Company and its Predecessors (Grafton Press, 1930) and her pamphlet on *Roger Conant and the Early Settlements on the North Shore of Massachusetts* (Roger Conant Family Association, 1926). Mrs. Rose-Troup has kindly furnished me with several details of White's life, and with the complete list of the members of the Dorchester Adventurers. The article on White in the *Dictionary of National Biography* gives references to material on him in the *Calendars of State Papers*, etc. White's *Planters Plea* (London, 1630), the principal source for his colonizing activities, was reprinted in Force's *Tracts*, vol. II (1838), and, more accurately, in the *Proceedings of the Massachusetts Historical Society* for 1930. A part of it is in the *Old South Leaflets*, no. 154, which series, published at the Old South Meeting House, Boston, contains also the *Humble Request* (no. 207). Hubbard's *General History of New England* (printed in 2 *Collections Mass. Hist. Soc.*, v) is an important source for the Cape Ann settlement. There is much information on early Salem in Sidney Perley, *History of Salem*, vol. I (Salem, 1924), and Daniel A. White, *New England Congregationalism* (Salem, 1861). There is no authentic portrait of John White; the engraving of the Westminster Assembly, including his alleged portrait, being a fancy production of a much later date.

III. JOHN WINTHROP

The only complete edition of Winthrop's *Journal* for the years 1630–49 is James Savage's (his title being *The History of New England*), 2 vols., Boston, 1853. Hosmer's edition of 1908 in the *Original Narratives* series, will suffice most readers. The Massachusetts Historical Society has begun the systematic publication of *The Winthrop Papers* (5 volumes are now out), the most important family collection in our colonial history. Much of John Winthrop's correspondence has already been printed in various volumes of the *Collections* and *Proceedings* of that Society, and in Robert C. Winthrop's *Life and Letters of John Winthrop* (2d ed., 2 vols., Boston, 1869), a useful but rather uncritical biography. Israel Stoughton's letter is printed in the *Proceedings of the Massachusetts Historical Society*, LVIII, 450–57. Where my quotations from Winthrop's writings differ from the printed version, it will be understood that mine have been collated with the original manuscripts. Winthrop's *Modell of Christian Charity* and John Cotton's sermon are in the *Old South Leaflets*, nos. 207 and 53. The different portraits of Winthrop are reproduced and discussed in Bolton's *The Founders* (see v).

I can recommend to my readers no good history of the puritans and puritanism, later than old Neal. One has to get it from the writings of the puritans themselves. My own paragraphs on puritanism were inspired by, and are in part quoted from, Phillips Brooks' sermon 'The Seriousness of Life,' in his *Light of the World and other Sermons*.

IV. THOMAS SHEPARD

The collected edition of Shepard's Works was published at Boston in three volumes, in 1853. I have used the original editions of his sermons, in the Harvard College Library. The extracts quoted in the text are from *The Parable of the Ten Virgins* (London, 1660), pp. 34, 96, 61. Shepard's letter to Peter is in the *American Historical Review*, IV, 105. His *Autobiography* and meditations, edited by Nehemiah Adams, were printed separately in 1832, and again in Young's *Chronicles of Massachusetts*. My quotations from it have been collated with the original manuscript by kind permission of its owners, the First Church of Cambridge, Congregational. Shepard's account of his interview with Laud was copied from another manuscript of his about a century ago into the back of the manuscript autobiography. Alexander Whyte's *Thomas Shepard, Pilgrim Father and Founder of Harvard* (1909), is rather a series of sermons on Shepard's works than a proper biography. The church accounts are in Paige's *History of Cambridge* (1877). On the New England church as a whole, see Henry M. Dexter, *Congregationalism* (1880), Williston Walker, *Creeds and Platforms of Congregationalism* (1893), and George M. Ellis, *The Puritan Age* (1888). On the Antinomian controversy, see Charles Francis Adams' monograph in the *Publications* of the Prince Society (1894), and his brilliant account in *Three Episodes in Massachusetts History* (Houghton Mifflin Co., 1892). No portrait of Shepard exists.

V. JOHN HULL

John Hull's two diaries and a few of his letters are printed in modernized spelling, and with a good memoir by Samuel F. Haven, in *Archaeologia Americana*, III (1857) — the first series of publications of the American Antiquarian Society, which owns both the diaries and the letter-book for 1671–83. My quotations from both have been collated with the originals. Hull's accounts as Treasurer of the Colony are in the New England Historical and Genealogical

Society's Library; and there are numerous petitions, etc., from him in the Massachusetts Archives. Samuel Sewall's Diary (5 *Coll. Mass. Hist. Soc.*, IV–VII) is an important source for his later life. Fiske Kimball, *The Architecture of the Colonies and the Early Republic* (1923), is the best work on that subject; and *Old Time New England*, the organ of the Society for the Preservation of New England Antiquities, is full of good articles and photographs. I am indebted to this Society for the loan of photographs, and other civilities; and to Mr. Wallace Nutting of Framingham for access to his remarkable collection of negatives of seventeenth-century houses. Mr. Julius H. Tuttle, Librarian of the Massachusetts Historical Society, has helped me to determine the site of Hull's house, and in countless other ways.

The best works on New England silver and silversmiths of the seventeenth century are E. Alfred Jones, *The Old Silver of American Churches* (Letchworth, 1913); Francis H. Bigelow, *Historic Silver of the Colonies and Its Makers* (New York, 1917); *American Silver... Exhibited at the Museum of Fine Arts* (Boston, 1906), with excellent introduction by R. T. H. Halsey; and *American Church Silver in the Seventeenth and Eighteenth Centuries, Exhibited at the Museum of Fine Arts* (Boston, 1911); and Hollis French, *A List of Early American Silversmiths and their Marks* (The Walpole Society, 1917), a valuable work of reference. My illustrations were made especially for this book at the Museum of Fine Arts, Boston, through the kindness of Mr. Edwin J. Hipkiss, Curator of that department; they represent pieces in the Museum's own collection, and those owned by the First Church, First Baptist Church, and Hollis Street Church of Boston; the First and the Second Church of Dorchester, the First Church of Rehoboth, the Chelmsford Congregational Church; Dwight Blaney, Esq., Miss Susan H. Pickering, Dudley L. Pickman, Esq., Philip L. Spalding, Esq., and another who does not wish his name mentioned. Sylvester Crosby, *Early Coins of America* (Boston, 1875), is the best book on Hull's work as mint master; and there is an excellent article on the subject by Dr. Malcolm Storer in *Old Time New England*, XX, 65–86 (1929).

Charles K. Bolton, *The Founders, Portraits of Persons born abroad who came to the Colonies before 1701* (3 vols., Boston Athenæum, 1919–26), is most valuable for the early portraits and painters; and Mr. Bolton himself has been most generous of suggestions. Harriette M. Forbes, *Gravestones of Early New England* (Houghton Mifflin Co., 1927), is the only work on that subject, and a good one, well illustrated; compare Odell Shepard's review of it in *The New England Quarterly*, III, 165. Hermann F. Clarke, *John Hull, a Builder of the Bay Colony* (Portland, Me., 1940).

William B. Weeden, *Economic and Society History of New England, 1620–1789* (2 vols., Houghton Mifflin Co., 1890) is still the standard work on that subject, though valuable largely for its quotations, including many from the Hull manuscripts. *Records and Files of the Quarterly Courts of Essex County, 1636–1683* (8 vols., Salem, the Essex Institute, 1911–21), edited by George F. Dow, are a mine of information on all matters connected with the life of the people. Mr. Dow has also written a too-brief book on *Domestic Life in New England in the Seventeenth Century* (Topsfield, 1925). John Dickinson, *Economic Regulations and Restrictions on Personal Liberty in Massachusetts*, published by the Pocumtuck Valley Historical Association in 1929, is a useful digest of the legislation.

VI. HENRY DUNSTER

For most of the information in this chapter I refer the reader to my *Founding of Harvard College* and *Harvard in the Seventeenth Century* (1936). Jeremiah Chaplin, *Life of Henry Dunster* (1872); Albert Matthews' introduction to the Harvard College Records, in *Publications of the Colonial Society of Massachusetts*, XV and XVI, an important letter of Dunster in the same series, III, 419–23; and *New England's First Fruits* (1643), reprinted in *Old South Leaflets*, no. 51. The quotation on the last page of my chapter is from the review by the Reverend S. K. Wilson, S.J., in *The New England Quarterly*, I, 571. No portrait of Dunster or of John Harvard is known to exist, and it is unlikely that any was ever painted.

For the schools, I have depended largely on the articles by Marcus W. Jernegan in the *School Review* for 1915–18. Cotton Mather's sermon and verses on Cheever are in his *Corderius Americanus* (Boston, 1708, reprinted 1828); Cheever having died too late to get into the *Magnalia*.

VII. NATHANIEL WARD

The Simple Cobler of Aggawam has several times been reprinted, most recently in 1843, edited by David Pulsifer. John Ward Dean, *Memoir of Nathaniel Ward* (1868), is the only proper biography of Ward. John Cotton's code was printed in London in 1641 as *An*

Abstract of the Lawes of New England, and reprinted in Thomas Hutchinson, *Collection of Papers* (1769), pp. 161–79; also, with many of the Biblical references omitted, in 1 *Collections Mass. Hist. Soc.*, v, 171–92, and Force's *Tracts*, III. See the valuable article by Isabel M. Calder, 'John Cotton and the New Haven Colony,' in *The New England Quarterly*, III, 82–94 (January, 1930). No portrait of Ward is known to exist.

Of the Body of Liberties, the most convenient text is *Old South Leaflets*, no. 164. The best account of it is by Francis C. Gray in 3 *Collections Mass. Hist. Soc.*, VII (1843). The Essex Remonstrance of 1643 and Winthrop's reply are in Hutchinson's *Collection*, pp. 115–19, 121–34.

VIII. ROBERT CHILD

George Lyman Kittredge's exhaustive and scholarly paper on Robert Child in the *Publications of the Colonial Society of Massachusetts*, XXI, 1–146 (1920), has been my principal reliance for this chapter, although I have ventured to differ from the learned and witty author in my interpretation of his Remonstrance. The arguments of Professor Kittredge to prove that Child *et al.* did *not* stand for toleration, but rather wished to force Massachusetts into the Presbyterian mould, are plausible but entirely inferential. He assumes (1) that because Child was a Presbyterian he was intolerant, which is not a fair assumption; and several of his associates were not Presbyterians. (2) That if Parliament interfered at all in New England it would enforce Presbyterianism and suppress every other -ism. Since Parliament was forced tacitly to tolerate the sects in England, it seems unlikely that it would have attempted the impossible task of putting them down abroad; and in Anglican Virginia and Barbados, where Parliament did interfere, it left wide religious liberty. The Remonstrance and Declaration are found only in Hutchinson's *Collection of Papers* (1769), pp. 188–96. The petition to Parliament no longer exists, but there is a good summary of it in Hutchinson's *History of Massachusetts Bay* (1760), 1, 148. W. T. R. Marvin's edition of *New England's Jonas* (1869) contains a useful introduction. Richard B. Morris, 'Massachusetts and the Common Law,' *American Historical Review*, XXXI, 443–53 (1926), is a capital article, with an effective criticism of the Declaration. *The Book of the General Lawes and Libertyes* of 1648 was reprinted in 1929 by the Harvard University Press, with an introduction by Max Farrand. See also T. F. T. Plucknett's review of it in

The New England Quarterly, III, 156–59 (1930). On the Lake Company and other fur-trading projects, see A. H. Buffinton's article in *Publications Colonial Soc. Mass.*, XVIII, 160–92 (1916). On the Free State issue, see letter of Pynchon in 4 *Collections Mass. Hist. Soc.*, VI, 381–85, and Edgar A. J. Johnson, 'Mercantilism in the Massachusetts-Bay,' *New England Quarterly*, I, 371–95 (1928). No portrait of Child is known to exist.

IX. JOHN WINTHROP, JUNIOR

The best biography is Thomas F. Waters, *A Sketch of the Life of John Winthrop the Younger* (*Publications* of the Ipswich Historical Society, VII), 1899. It gives extracts from Winthrop's correspondence which is printed among the Winthrop Papers in the *Collections of the Massachusetts Historical Society*, and will be reprinted in the new series of *Winthrop Papers* (above, III). C. A. Browne, 'Scientific notes from the books and letters of John Winthrop, Jr.,' is in *Isis*, IX, 325–42; and Mr. Browne's account of the manuscript volume on Alchemy is in *Journal of Chemical Education*, V (December, 1928). Of Winthrop's experiments in salt-making, ironworks, and paper money, there is much material in Weeden's *Economic History* and the *Quarterly Courts of Essex County* (see V). Dr. Holmes' lecture will be found in *Massachusetts and its Early History* (Mass. Hist. Soc., 1869). The portrait of John Winthrop, Jr., used as frontispiece in this work by the kind permission of the Mass. Historical Society, is a copy of the original, painted in England, and now owned by Harvard University.

X. JOHN ELIOT

Cotton Mather's *Life of John Eliot* (1694), reprinted in the *Magnalia*, I have found more useful than any other biography of the Apostle. J. Hammond Trumbull's chapter in *The Memorial History of Boston*, IV, and Francis S. Drake, *History of the Town of Roxbury* (1878), are useful. Eliot's letters and the Indian tracts are very scattered. Gookin's *Historical Collections of the Indians in New England*, the best contemporary account of his work, is printed in I *Collections Mass. Hist. Soc.*, I, 141–224; the *Day-Breaking* and other tracts are reprinted in the third series, volume IV. G. P. Winship's introduction to *The New England Company of 1649 and John Eliot* (Prince Society, 1920) is most informing, especially on the printing of the Bible. Diary and letters of John Eliot are in the *N.E. Historical and Genealogical Register*, v and xxxiii; *Proceedings Mass. Hist. Soc.*, xvii; Ebenezer Hazard, *Historical Collections, Consisting of State Papers* (Philadelphia, 1792), ii; Thomas Birch, *Life of Robert Boyle*, v, appendix (1744). The so-called portrait of John Eliot which has often been reproduced, showing a rather fleshy and humorous person with St. Paul's Cathedral in the background, is a palpable fake, the inscription stating that it is Eliot, having been placed on an unknown portrait of the correct period. Fr. Druillette's narrative is in the *Jesuit Relations* (Thwaites ed.), xxxvi.

Eliot's Bible has long been one of the most sought after *Americana*, although far from being one of the rarest curiosity. About fifty copies of the first edition are known, a few even in the original binding, which was done by John Ratcliff, the first bookbinder in New England whose work can be identified. The top price reached so far for a complete copy is $3500. But this is not the highest price for an Eliot Indian item. The only known copy of his translation of Richard Baxter's 'Call to the Unconverted,' a present from John Winthrop, Jr., to the Royal Society, was sold by the august body in 1925 for £6800. If a copy of the first or second edition of the Indian Primer should turn up, it would be worth much more — provided that bibliomania, var. *Americana*, continues to be a favorite malady of the wealthy. Wilberforce Eames' bibliography of Eliot's Indian books and translations, in James C. Pilling, *Bibliography of the Algonquian Language* (United States Bureau of Ethnology, Washington, 1891), is exhaustive, describes individual copies of the Bible, and contains a translation of Dankaerts and Sluyter's narrative.

XI. ANNE BRADSTREET

Anne Bradstreet's *Tenth Muse* (207 pp.) appeared in London in 1650; her *Several Poems* (255 pp.), including the above with additions, were printed at Boston in 1678; and there was a second and enlarged edition of the *Several Poems*, Boston, 1758. There are two editions of her complete works: John Harvard Ellis' (434 + lxxvi pp., Charlestown, 1867), and Charles Eliot Norton's (New York, the Duodecimo Series, 1897). Ellis has the best introduction, and Norton the most accurate text. Both are hard to come by. The best selection of her poems is in Conrad Aiken's *American Poetry 1671–1928* (The Modern Library, 1929). No portrait of Anne Bradstreet is known to exist. The fancy drawing of her in the 1897 edition of her poems is ridiculously incorrect as to costume and accessories.

XII. WILLIAM PYNCHON

Henry M. Burt, *The First Century of the History of Springfield* (1898); Mason A. Green, *Springfield, 1636–1886* (Springfield, 1888); Simeon E. Baldwin, "The Secession of Springfield from Connecticut," *Publications of the Colonial Society of Massachusetts*, XII, 55–82; Letters of Pynchon in *Proceedings of the Massachusetts Historical Society*, XLVIII, 35–36; Joseph H. Smith ed., *Colonial Justice in Western Massachusetts; the Pynchon Court Record* (Cambridge: Harvard University Press, 1961); Samuel G. Drake, *Annals of Witchcraft in New England* (1869).

INDEX